CASE CLOSED™

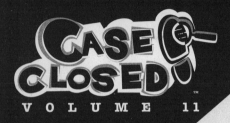

VOLUME 11

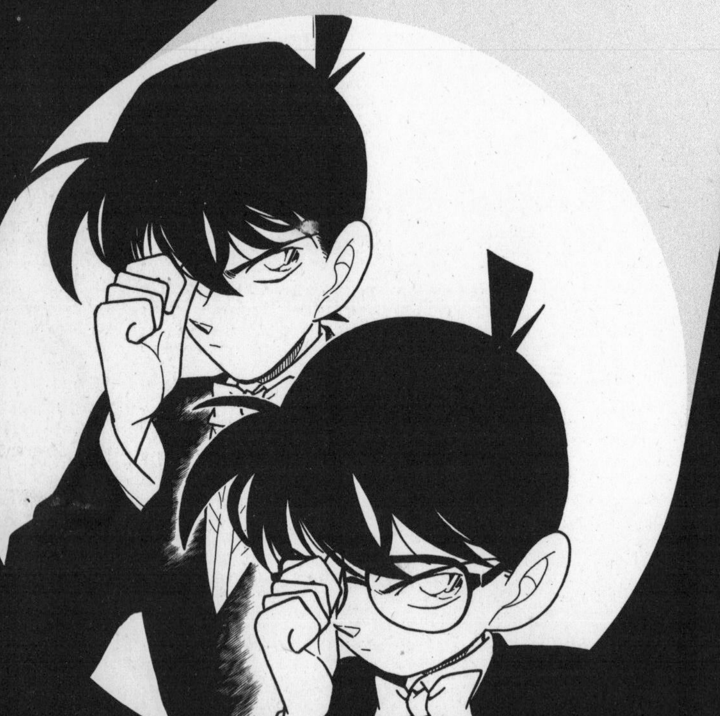

Gosho Aoyama

Case Briefing:

Subject:
Occupation:
Special Skills:
Equipment:

Jimmy Kudo, a.k.a. Conan Edogawa
High School Student/Detective
Analytical thinking and deductive reasoning, Soccer
Bow Tie Voice Transmitter, Super Sneakers,
Homing Glasses, Stretchy Suspenders

The subject is hot on the trail of a pair of suspicious men in black when he is attacked from behind and administered a strange substance which physically transforms him into a first grader. When the subject confides in the eccentric inventor Dr. Agasa, they decide to keep the subject's true identity a secret for the safety of everyone around him. Assuming the new identity of first-grader Conan Edogawa, the subject continues to assist the police force on their most baffling cases. The only problem is that most crime-solving professionals won't take a little kid's advice!

Table of Contents

CASE CLOSED

CONFIDEN

CASE CLOSED
Volume 11
Shonen Sunday Edition

Story and Art by GOSHO AOYAMA

© 1994 Gosho AOYAMA/Shogakukan
All rights reserved.
Original Japanese edition "MEITANTEI CONAN" published by SHOGAKUKAN Inc.

English Adaptation
Naoko Amemiya

Translation
Joe Yamazaki

Touch-up & Lettering
Walden Wong

Cover & Interior Design
Andrea Rice

Editor
Urian Brown

Printed in the U.S.A.

Published by VIZ Media, LLC
P.O. Box 77010
San Francisco, CA 94107

10 9 8 7 6 5 4 3 2
First printing, May 2006
Second printing, May 2011

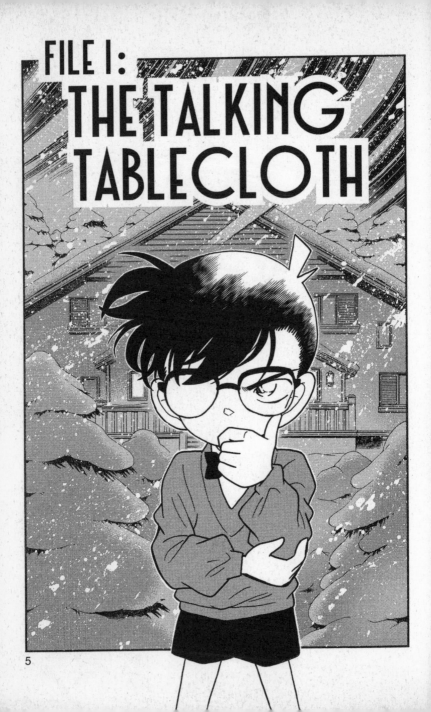

FILE 1:
THE TALKING TABLECLOTH

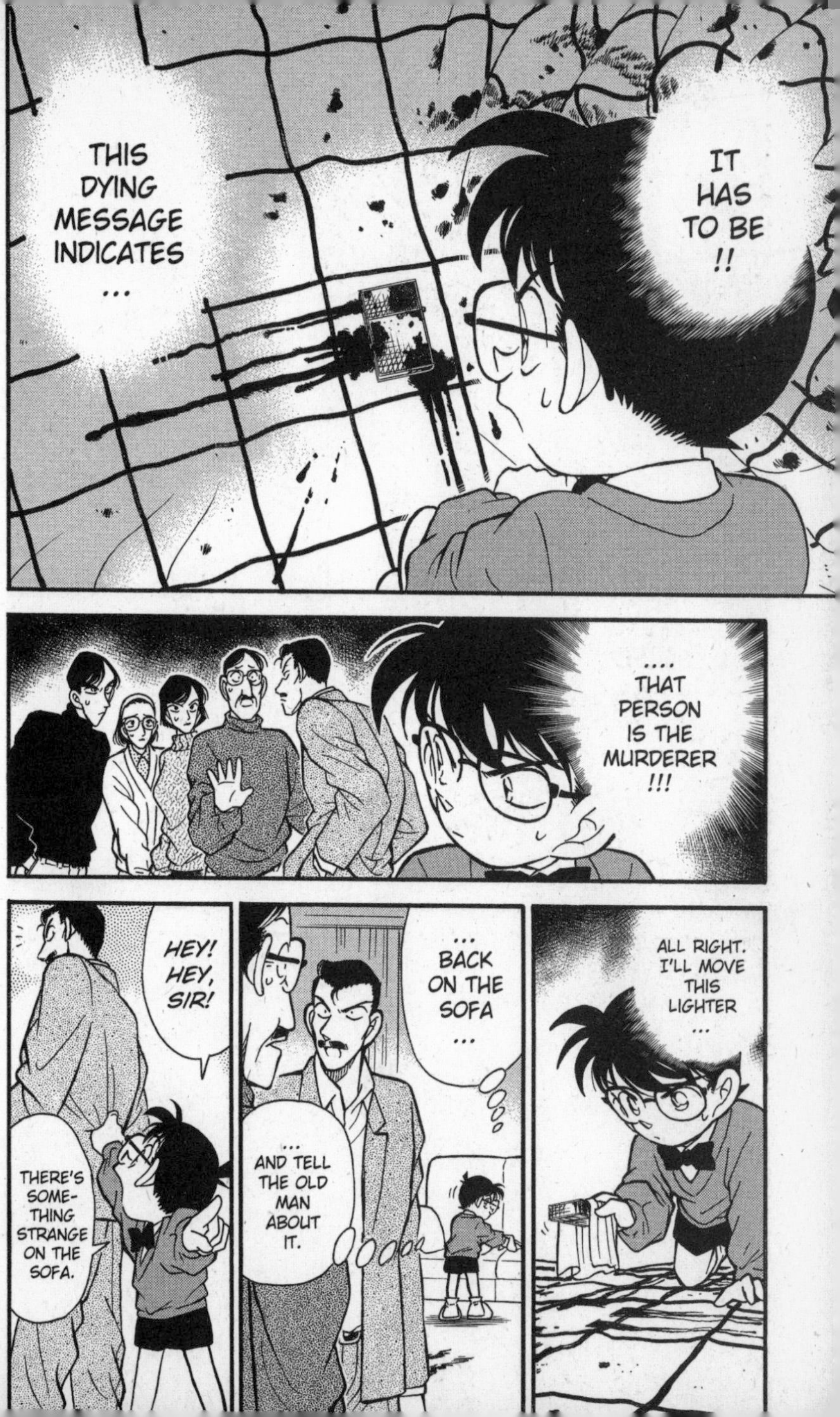
IT HAS TO BE !!
THIS DYING MESSAGE INDICATES ...
.... THAT PERSON IS THE MURDERER !!!
ALL RIGHT. I'LL MOVE THIS LIGHTER ...
... BACK ON THE SOFA ...
... AND TELL THE OLD MAN ABOUT IT.
HEY! HEY, SIR!
THERE'S SOME-THING STRANGE ON THE SOFA.

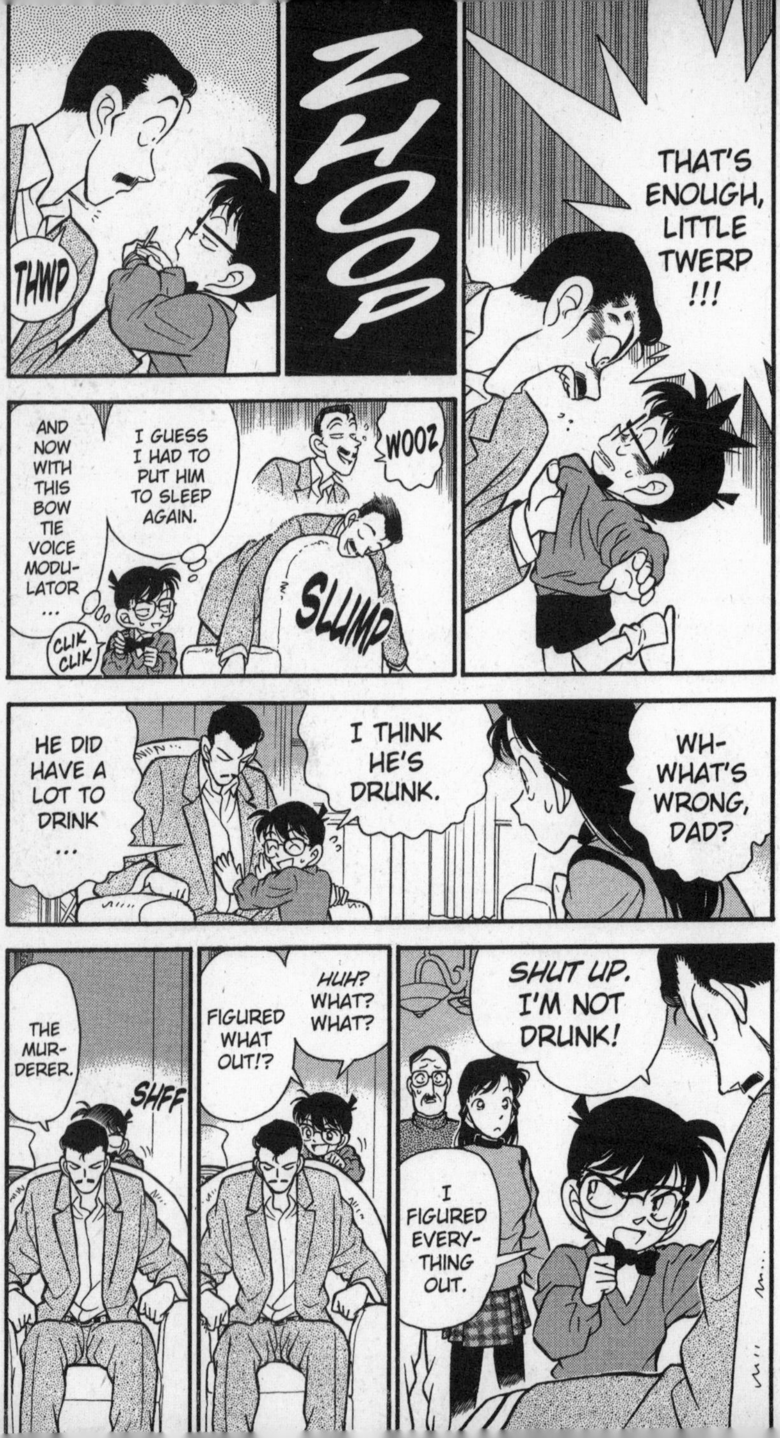
THAT'S ENOUGH, LITTLE TWERP !!!
ZHOOP
THWP
WOOZ
SLUMP
I GUESS I HAD TO PUT HIM TO SLEEP AGAIN.
AND NOW WITH THIS BOW TIE VOICE MODULATOR ...
CLIK CLIK
WH-WHAT'S WRONG, DAD?
I THINK HE'S DRUNK.
HE DID HAVE A LOT TO DRINK ...
SHUT UP. I'M NOT DRUNK!
I FIGURED EVERYTHING OUT.
HUH? WHAT? WHAT?
FIGURED WHAT OUT!?
SHFF
THE MURDERER.

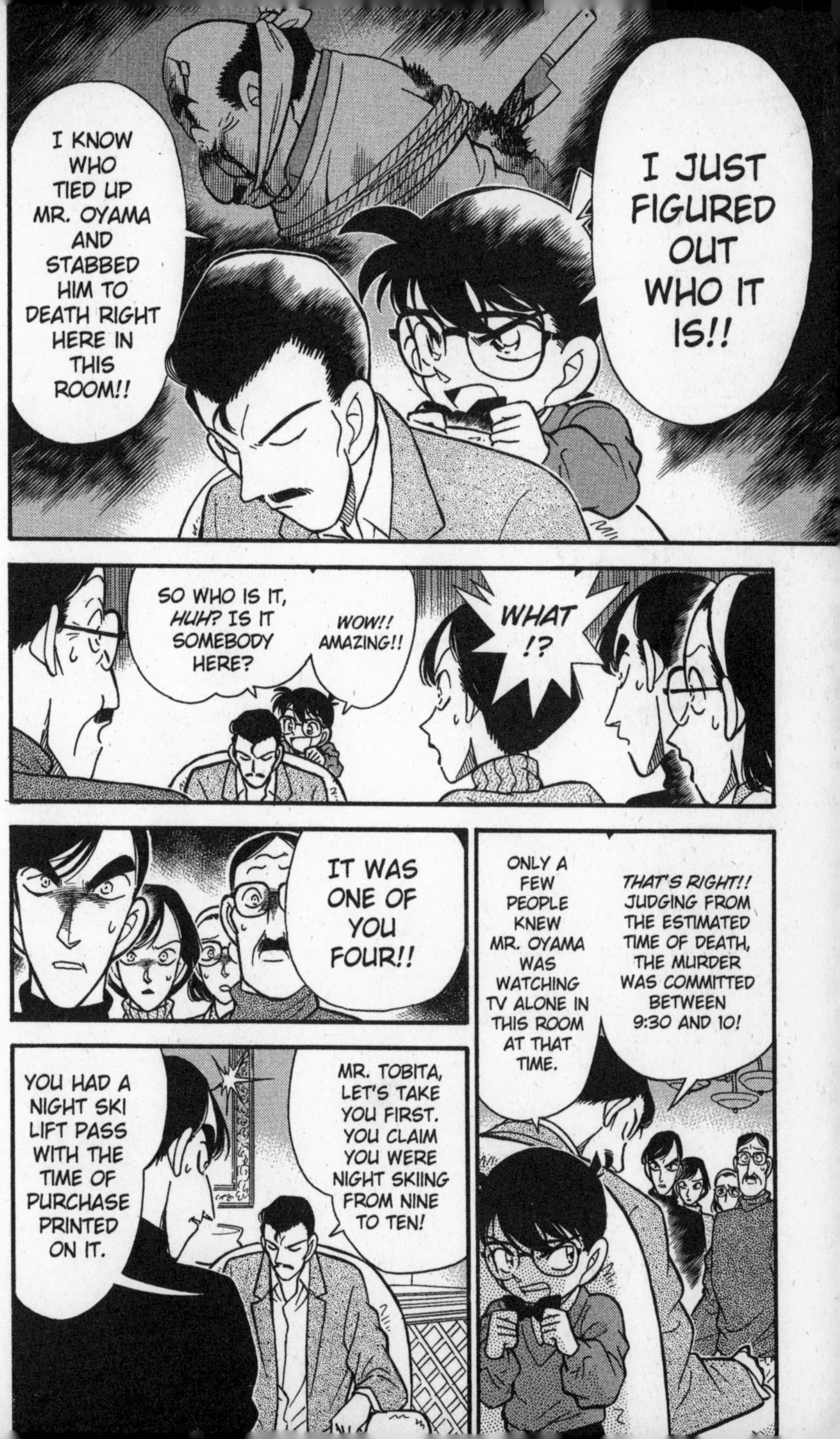
I JUST FIGURED OUT WHO IT IS!!
I KNOW WHO TIED UP MR. OYAMA AND STABBED HIM TO DEATH RIGHT HERE IN THIS ROOM!!
WHAT!?
WOW!! AMAZING!!
SO WHO IS IT, *HUH?* IS IT SOMEBODY HERE?
THAT'S RIGHT!! JUDGING FROM THE ESTIMATED TIME OF DEATH, THE MURDER WAS COMMITTED BETWEEN 9:30 AND 10!
ONLY A FEW PEOPLE KNEW MR. OYAMA WAS WATCHING TV ALONE IN THIS ROOM AT THAT TIME.
IT WAS ONE OF YOU FOUR!!
MR. TOBITA, LET'S TAKE YOU FIRST. YOU CLAIM YOU WERE NIGHT SKIING FROM NINE TO TEN!
YOU HAD A NIGHT SKI LIFT PASS WITH THE TIME OF PURCHASE PRINTED ON IT.

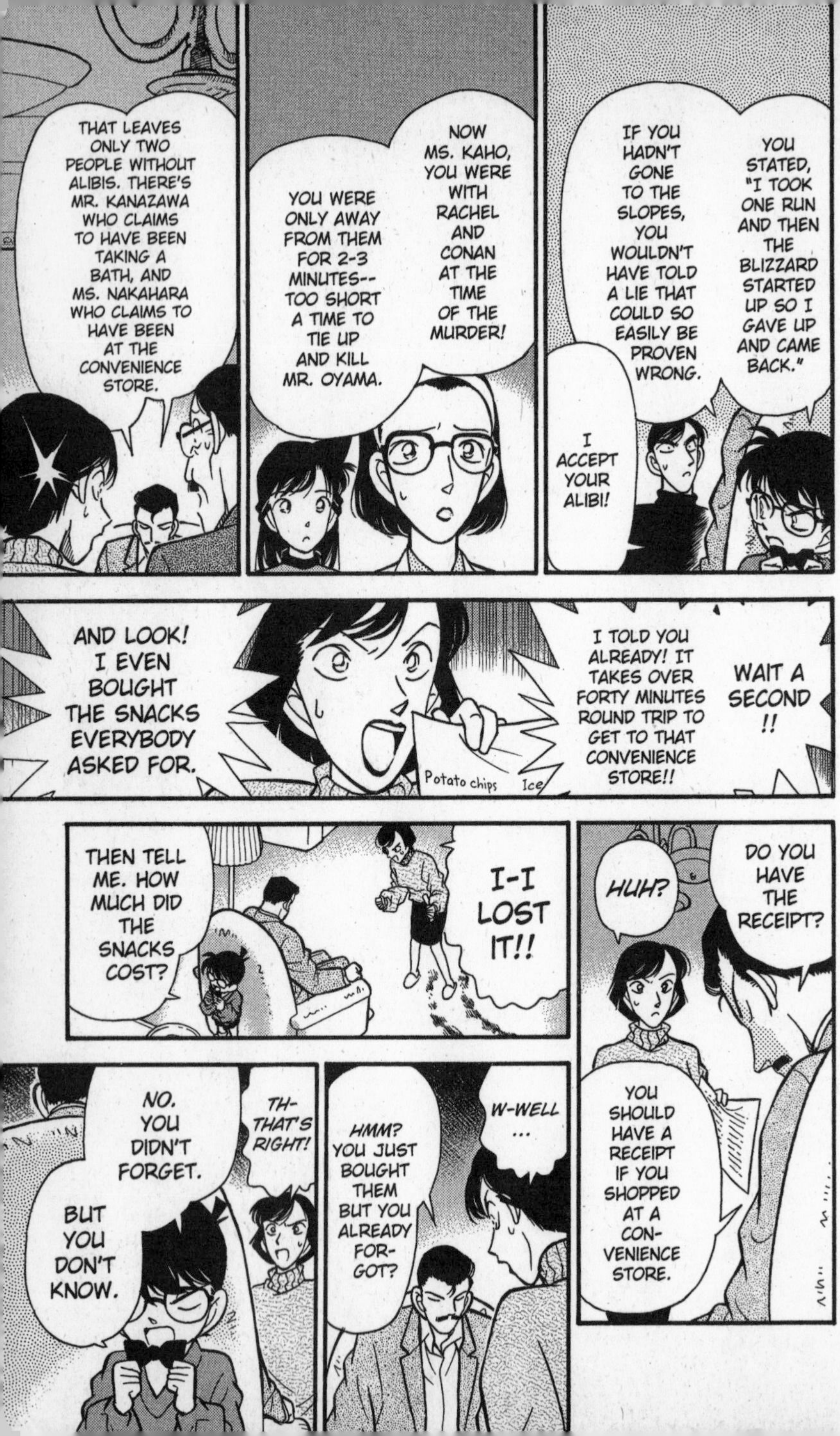
YOU STATED, "I TOOK ONE RUN AND THEN THE BLIZZARD STARTED UP SO I GAVE UP AND CAME BACK."
IF YOU HADN'T GONE TO THE SLOPES, YOU WOULDN'T HAVE TOLD A LIE THAT COULD SO EASILY BE PROVEN WRONG.
I ACCEPT YOUR ALIBI!
NOW MS. KAHO, YOU WERE WITH RACHEL AND CONAN AT THE TIME OF THE MURDER!
YOU WERE ONLY AWAY FROM THEM FOR 2-3 MINUTES-- TOO SHORT A TIME TO TIE UP AND KILL MR. OYAMA.
THAT LEAVES ONLY TWO PEOPLE WITHOUT ALIBIS. THERE'S MR. KANAZAWA WHO CLAIMS TO HAVE BEEN TAKING A BATH, AND MS. NAKAHARA WHO CLAIMS TO HAVE BEEN AT THE CONVENIENCE STORE.
WAIT A SECOND !!
I TOLD YOU ALREADY! IT TAKES OVER FORTY MINUTES ROUND TRIP TO GET TO THAT CONVENIENCE STORE!!
AND LOOK! I EVEN BOUGHT THE SNACKS EVERYBODY ASKED FOR.
Potato chips
Ice
DO YOU HAVE THE RECEIPT?
HUH?
YOU SHOULD HAVE A RECEIPT IF YOU SHOPPED AT A CON-VENIENCE STORE.
I-I LOST IT!!
THEN TELL ME. HOW MUCH DID THE SNACKS COST?
W-WELL ...
HMM? YOU JUST BOUGHT THEM BUT YOU ALREADY FOR-GOT?
TH-THAT'S RIGHT!
NO. YOU DIDN'T FORGET.
BUT YOU DON'T KNOW.

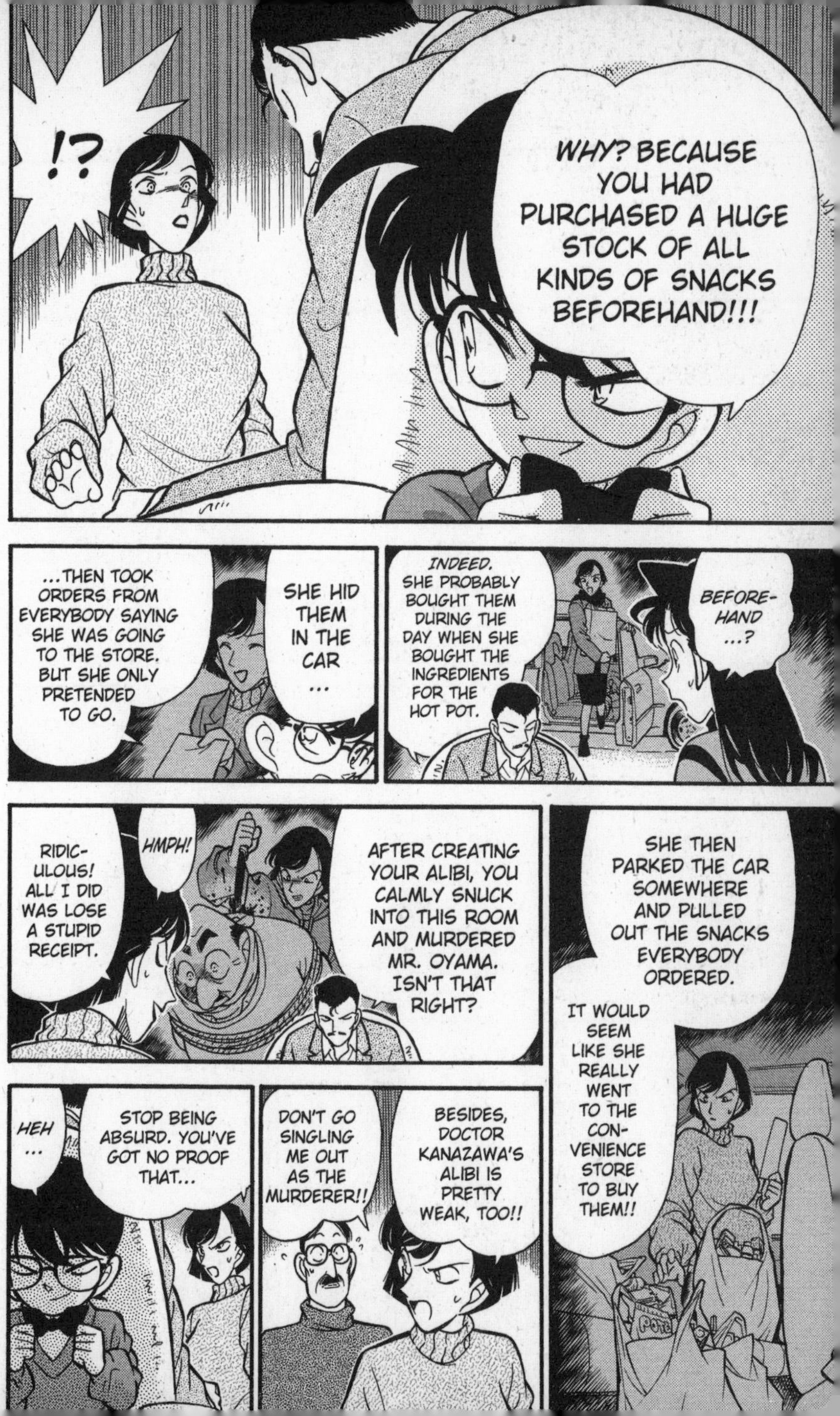
WHY? BECAUSE YOU HAD PURCHASED A HUGE STOCK OF ALL KINDS OF SNACKS BEFOREHAND!!!
!?
BEFORE-HAND ...?
INDEED. SHE PROBABLY BOUGHT THEM DURING THE DAY WHEN SHE BOUGHT THE INGREDIENTS FOR THE HOT POT.
SHE HID THEM IN THE CAR ...
...THEN TOOK ORDERS FROM EVERYBODY SAYING SHE WAS GOING TO THE STORE. BUT SHE ONLY PRETENDED TO GO.
SHE THEN PARKED THE CAR SOMEWHERE AND PULLED OUT THE SNACKS EVERYBODY ORDERED.
IT WOULD SEEM LIKE SHE REALLY WENT TO THE CON-VENIENCE STORE TO BUY THEM!!
AFTER CREATING YOUR ALIBI, YOU CALMLY SNUCK INTO THIS ROOM AND MURDERED MR. OYAMA. ISN'T THAT RIGHT?
HMPH!
RIDIC-ULOUS! ALL I DID WAS LOSE A STUPID RECEIPT.
BESIDES, DOCTOR KANAZAWA'S ALIBI IS PRETTY WEAK, TOO!!
DON'T GO SINGLING ME OUT AS THE MURDERER!!
STOP BEING ABSURD. YOU'VE GOT NO PROOF THAT...
HEH ...

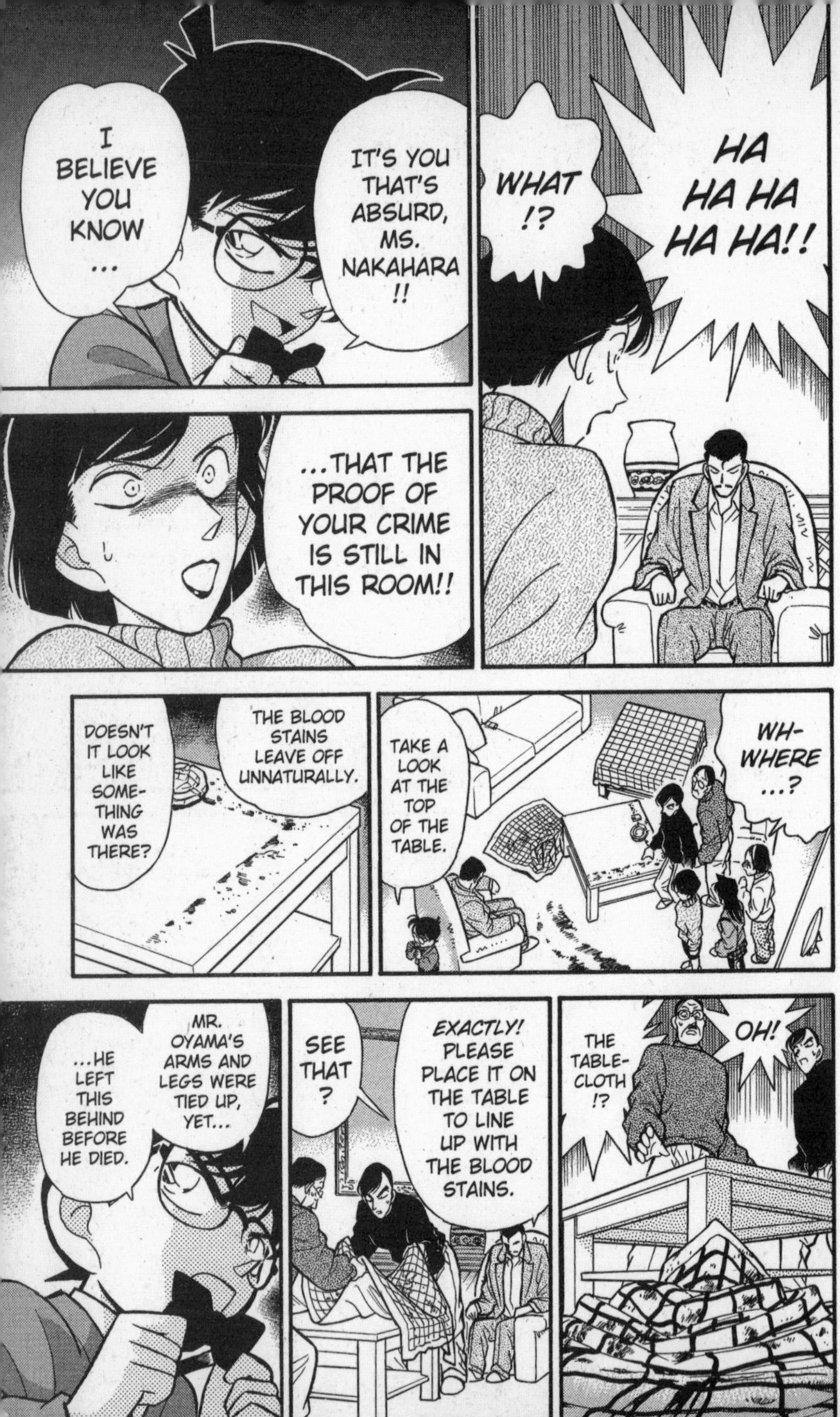
HA HA HA HA HA!!
WHAT!?
IT'S YOU THAT'S ABSURD, MS. NAKAHARA!!
I BELIEVE YOU KNOW...
...THAT THE PROOF OF YOUR CRIME IS STILL IN THIS ROOM!!
WH-WHERE...?
TAKE A LOOK AT THE TOP OF THE TABLE.
THE BLOOD STAINS LEAVE OFF UNNATURALLY.
DOESN'T IT LOOK LIKE SOMETHING WAS THERE?
OH!
THE TABLECLOTH!?
EXACTLY! PLEASE PLACE IT ON THE TABLE TO LINE UP WITH THE BLOOD STAINS.
SEE THAT?
MR. OYAMA'S ARMS AND LEGS WERE TIED UP, YET...
...HE LEFT THIS BEHIND BEFORE HE DIED.

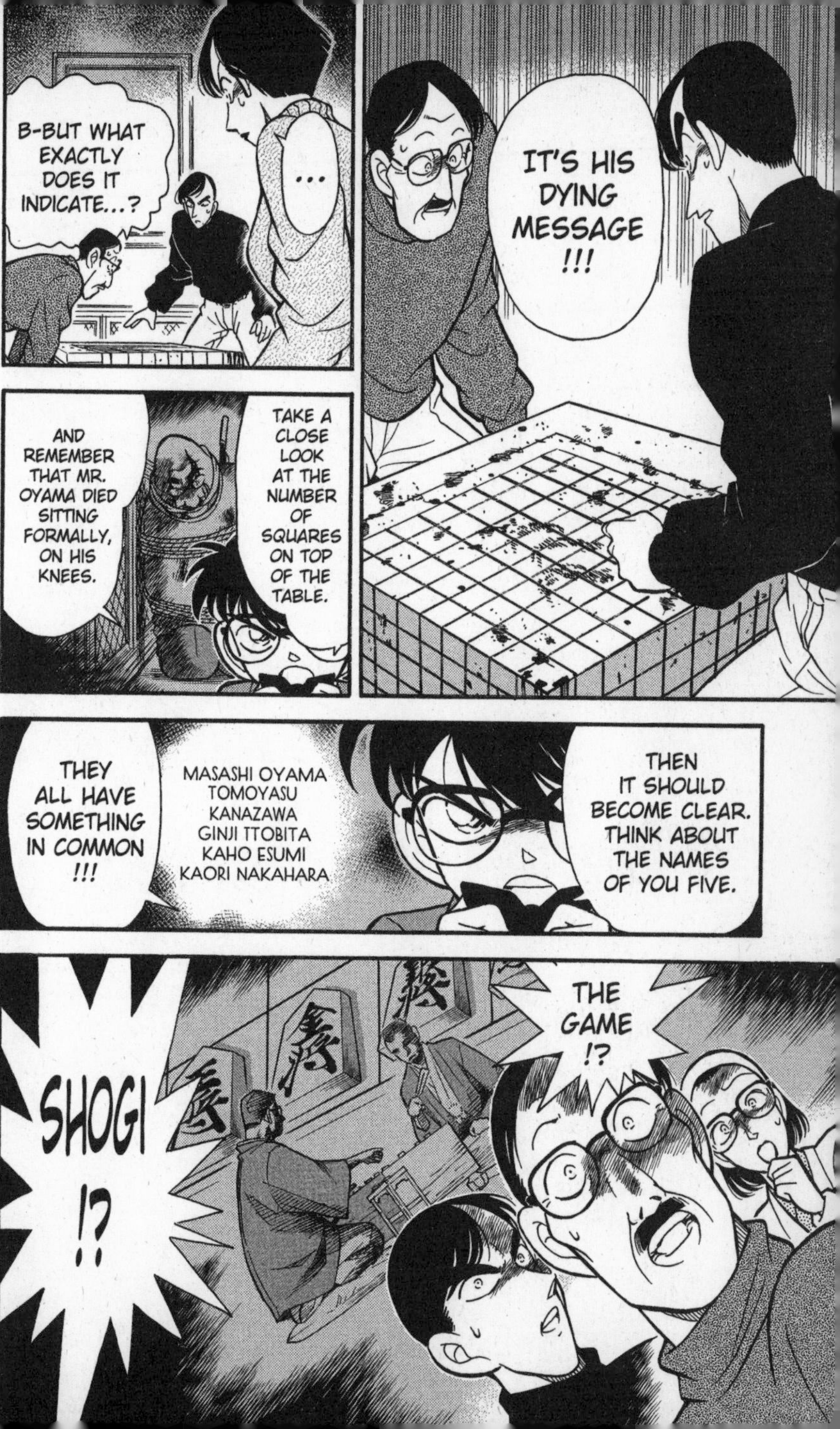
IT'S HIS DYING MESSAGE !!!
...
B-BUT WHAT EXACTLY DOES IT INDICATE...?
TAKE A CLOSE LOOK AT THE NUMBER OF SQUARES ON TOP OF THE TABLE.
AND REMEMBER THAT MR. OYAMA DIED SITTING FORMALLY, ON HIS KNEES.
THEN IT SHOULD BECOME CLEAR. THINK ABOUT THE NAMES OF YOU FIVE.
MASASHI OYAMA
TOMOYASU KANAZAWA
GINJI TTOBITA
KAHO ESUMI
KAORI NAKAHARA
THEY ALL HAVE SOMETHING IN COMMON !!!
THE GAME !?
SHOGI !?

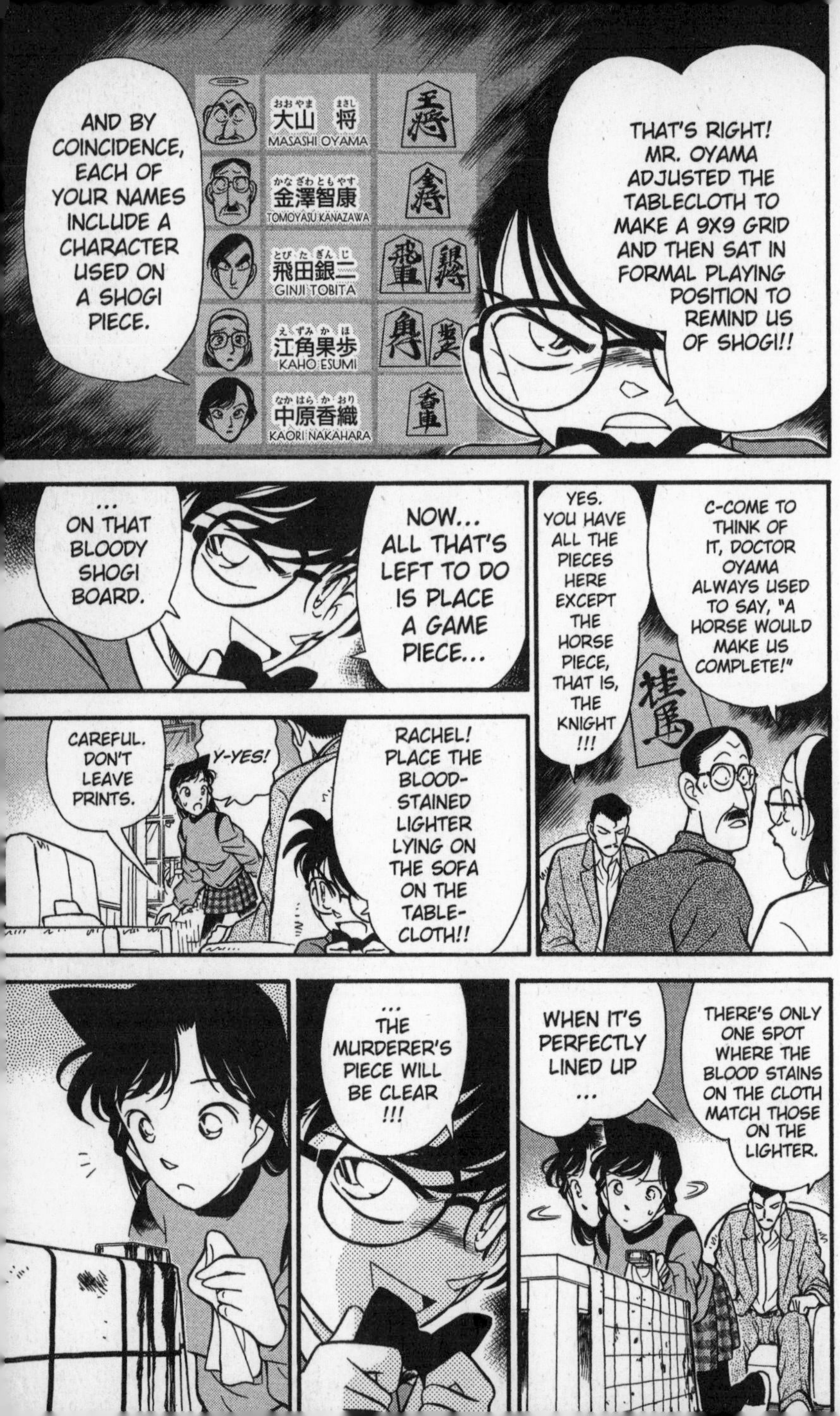
THAT'S RIGHT! MR. OYAMA ADJUSTED THE TABLECLOTH TO MAKE A 9X9 GRID AND THEN SAT IN FORMAL PLAYING POSITION TO REMIND US OF SHOGI!!
大山 将
MASASHI OYAMA
金澤智康
TOMOYASU KANAZAWA
飛田銀二
GINJI TOBITA
江角果歩
KAHO ESUMI
中原香織
KAORI NAKAHARA
AND BY COINCIDENCE, EACH OF YOUR NAMES INCLUDE A CHARACTER USED ON A SHOGI PIECE.
C-COME TO THINK OF IT, DOCTOR OYAMA ALWAYS USED TO SAY, "A HORSE WOULD MAKE US COMPLETE!"
YES. YOU HAVE ALL THE PIECES HERE EXCEPT THE HORSE PIECE, THAT IS, THE KNIGHT !!!
NOW... ALL THAT'S LEFT TO DO IS PLACE A GAME PIECE...
... ON THAT BLOODY SHOGI BOARD.
RACHEL! PLACE THE BLOOD-STAINED LIGHTER LYING ON THE SOFA ON THE TABLE-CLOTH!!
Y-YES!
CAREFUL. DON'T LEAVE PRINTS.
THERE'S ONLY ONE SPOT WHERE THE BLOOD STAINS ON THE CLOTH MATCH THOSE ON THE LIGHTER.
WHEN IT'S PERFECTLY LINED UP ...
... THE MURDERER'S PIECE WILL BE CLEAR !!!

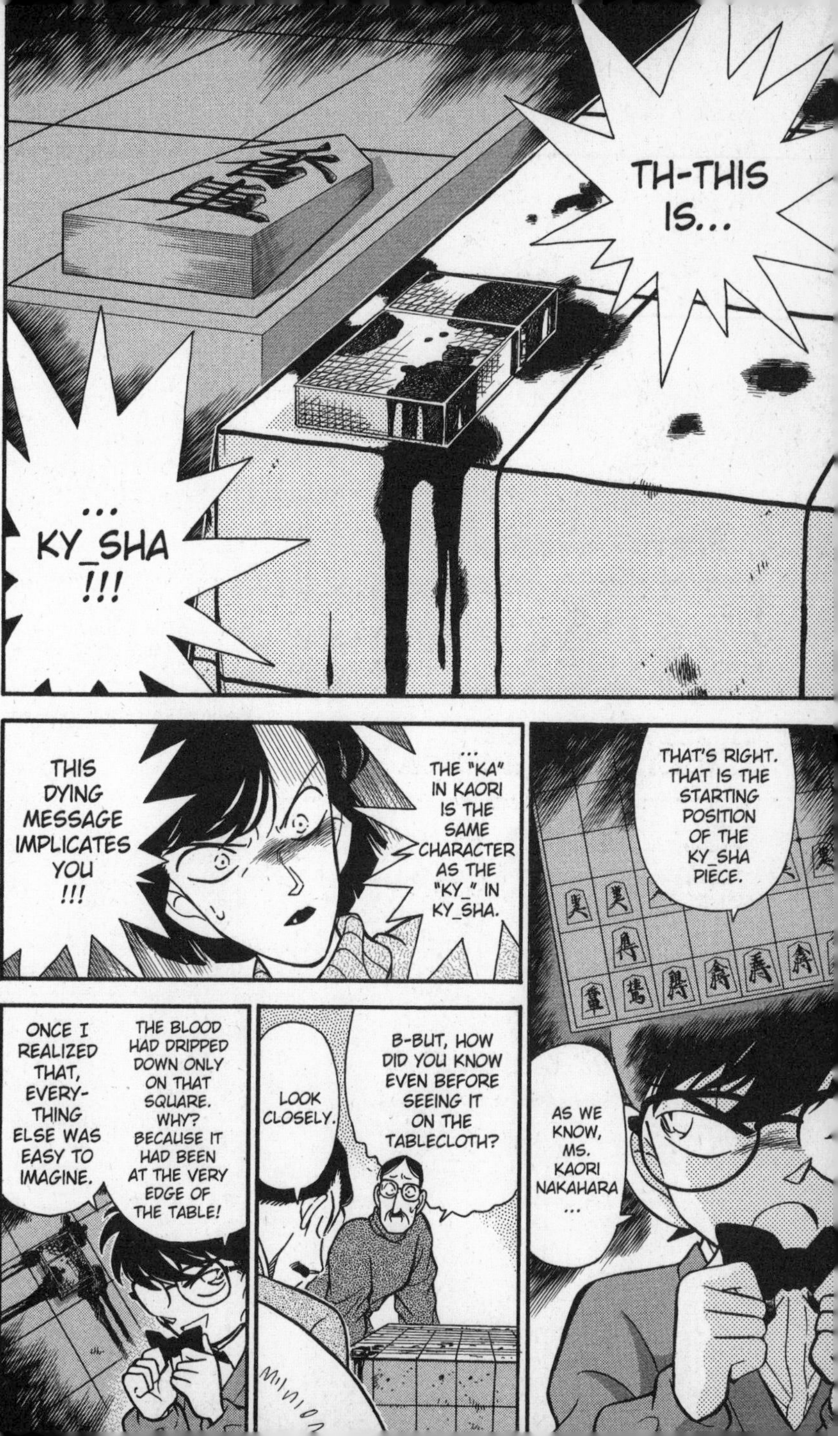
TH-THIS IS...
... KY_SHA !!!
THAT'S RIGHT. THAT IS THE STARTING POSITION OF THE KY_SHA PIECE.
AS WE KNOW, MS. KAORI NAKAHARA ...
... THE "KA" IN KAORI IS THE SAME CHARACTER AS THE "KY_" IN KY_SHA.
THIS DYING MESSAGE IMPLICATES YOU !!!
B-BUT, HOW DID YOU KNOW EVEN BEFORE SEEING IT ON THE TABLECLOTH?
LOOK CLOSELY.
THE BLOOD HAD DRIPPED DOWN ONLY ON THAT SQUARE. WHY? BECAUSE IT HAD BEEN AT THE VERY EDGE OF THE TABLE!
ONCE I REALIZED THAT, EVERY-THING ELSE WAS EASY TO IMAGINE.

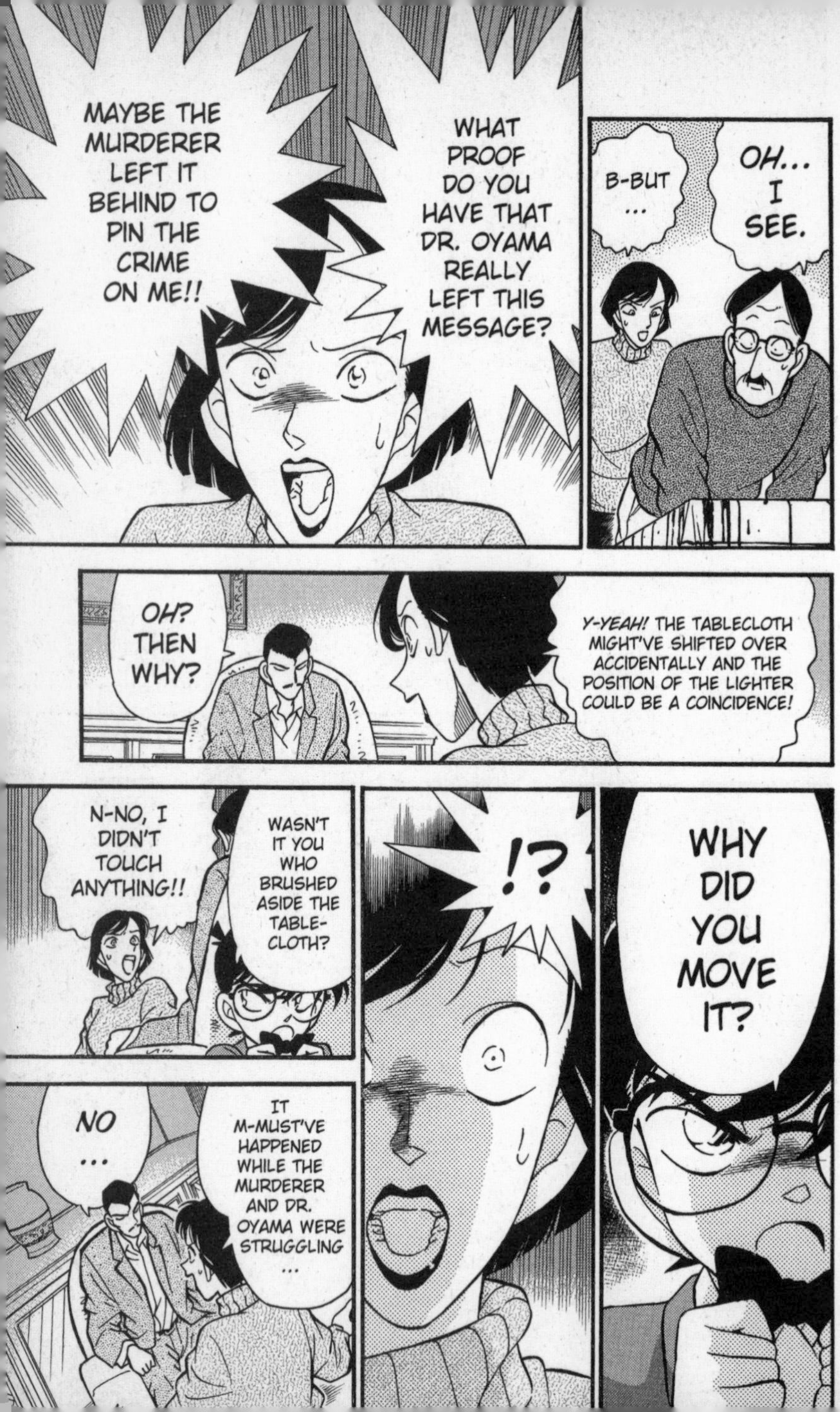

OH... I SEE.
B-BUT ...
WHAT PROOF DO YOU HAVE THAT DR. OYAMA REALLY LEFT THIS MESSAGE?
MAYBE THE MURDERER LEFT IT BEHIND TO PIN THE CRIME ON ME!!
Y-YEAH! THE TABLECLOTH MIGHT'VE SHIFTED OVER ACCIDENTALLY AND THE POSITION OF THE LIGHTER COULD BE A COINCIDENCE!
OH? THEN WHY?
WHY DID YOU MOVE IT?
!?
WASN'T IT YOU WHO BRUSHED ASIDE THE TABLE-CLOTH?
N-NO, I DIDN'T TOUCH ANYTHING!!
IT M-MUST'VE HAPPENED WHILE THE MURDERER AND DR. OYAMA WERE STRUGGLING ...
NO ...

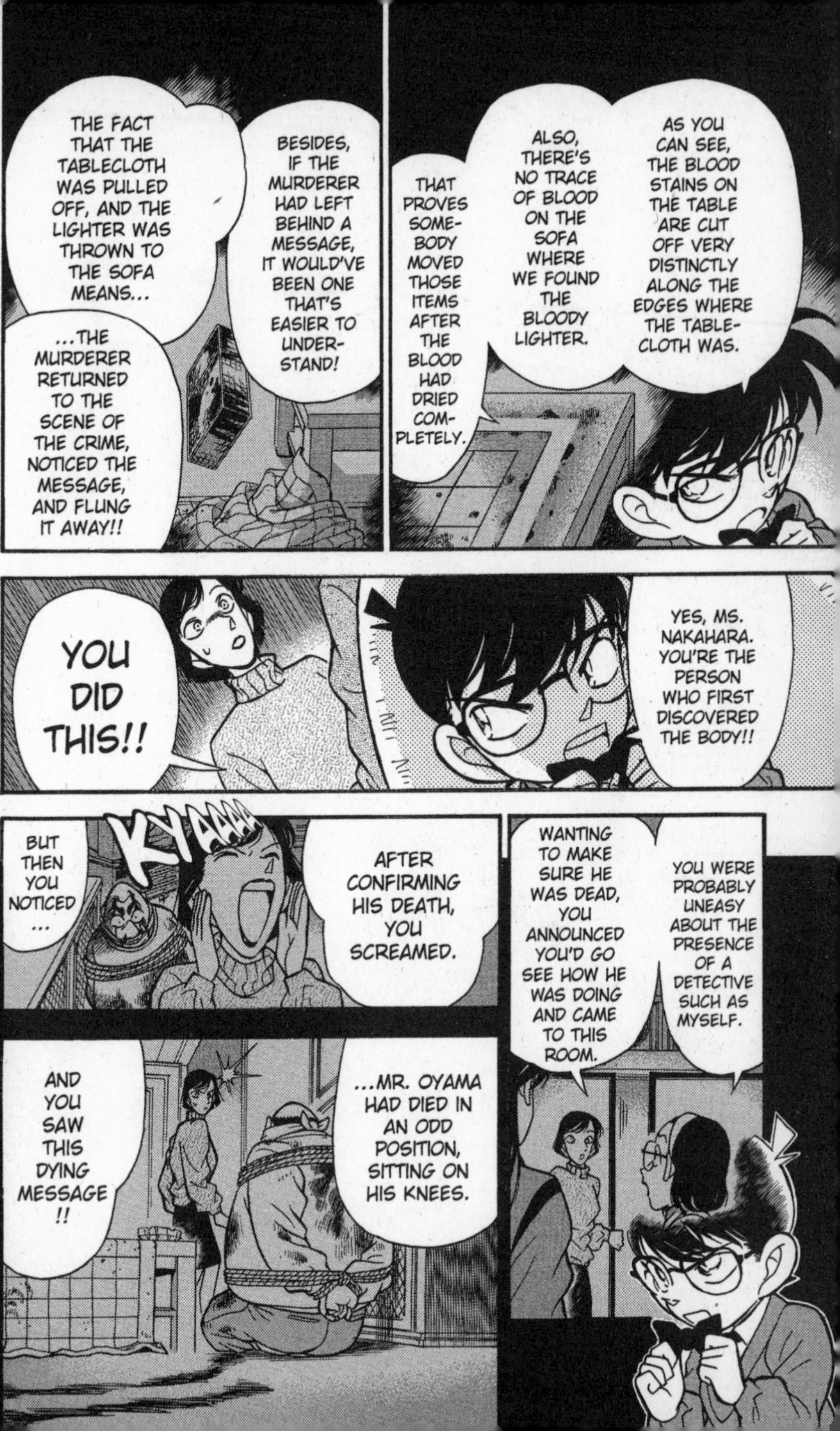
AS YOU CAN SEE, THE BLOOD STAINS ON THE TABLE ARE CUT OFF VERY DISTINCTLY ALONG THE EDGES WHERE THE TABLECLOTH WAS.
ALSO, THERE'S NO TRACE OF BLOOD ON THE SOFA WHERE WE FOUND THE BLOODY LIGHTER.
THAT PROVES SOMEBODY MOVED THOSE ITEMS AFTER THE BLOOD HAD DRIED COMPLETELY.
BESIDES, IF THE MURDERER HAD LEFT BEHIND A MESSAGE, IT WOULD'VE BEEN ONE THAT'S EASIER TO UNDERSTAND!
THE FACT THAT THE TABLECLOTH WAS PULLED OFF, AND THE LIGHTER WAS THROWN TO THE SOFA MEANS...
...THE MURDERER RETURNED TO THE SCENE OF THE CRIME, NOTICED THE MESSAGE, AND FLUNG IT AWAY!!
YES, MS. NAKAHARA. YOU'RE THE PERSON WHO FIRST DISCOVERED THE BODY!!
YOU DID THIS!!
YOU WERE PROBABLY UNEASY ABOUT THE PRESENCE OF A DETECTIVE SUCH AS MYSELF.
WANTING TO MAKE SURE HE WAS DEAD, YOU ANNOUNCED YOU'D GO SEE HOW HE WAS DOING AND CAME TO THIS ROOM.
AFTER CONFIRMING HIS DEATH, YOU SCREAMED.
KYAAA
BUT THEN YOU NOTICED ...
...MR. OYAMA HAD DIED IN AN ODD POSITION, SITTING ON HIS KNEES.
AND YOU SAW THIS DYING MESSAGE!!

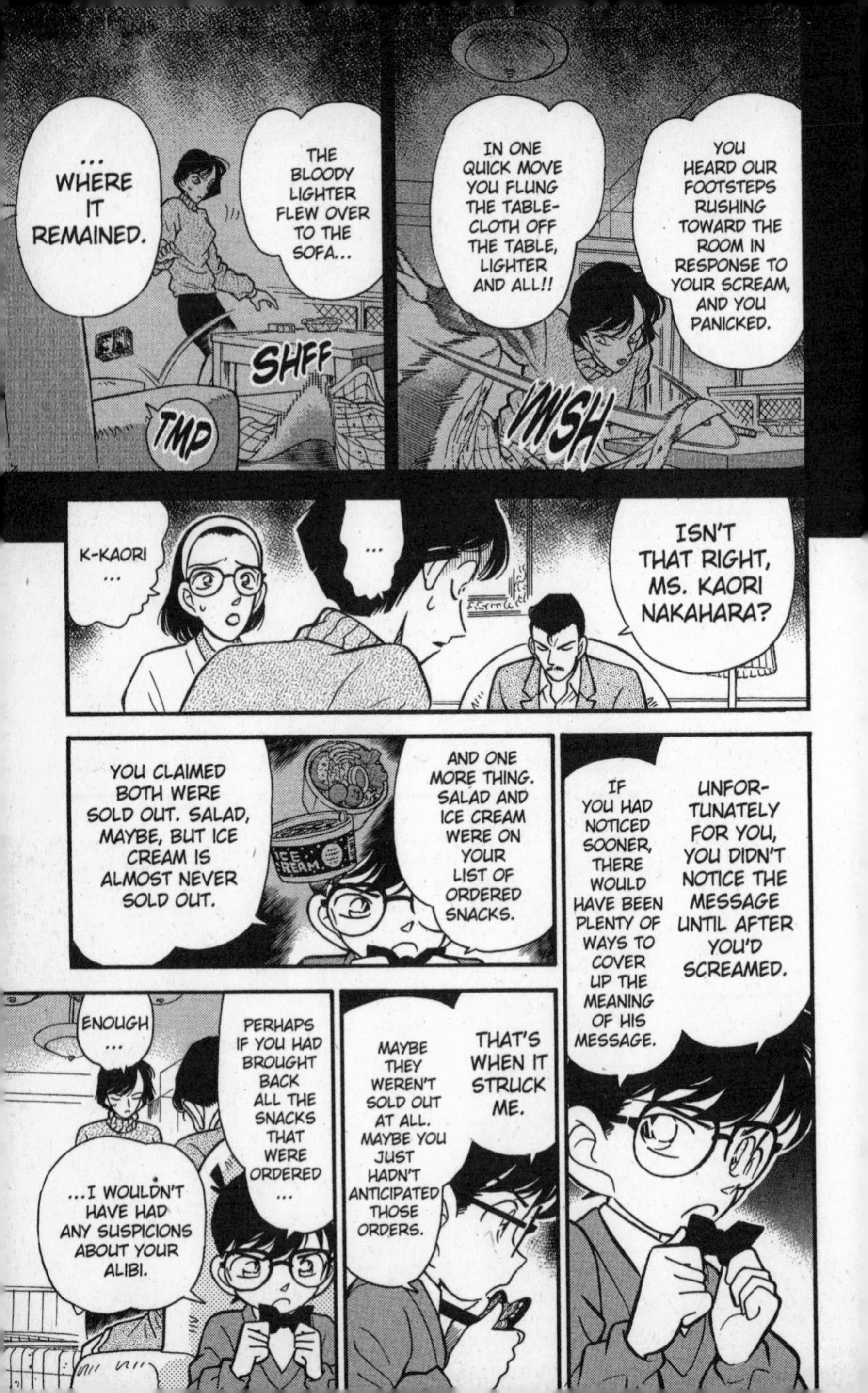
YOU HEARD OUR FOOTSTEPS RUSHING TOWARD THE ROOM IN RESPONSE TO YOUR SCREAM, AND YOU PANICKED.
IN ONE QUICK MOVE YOU FLUNG THE TABLE-CLOTH OFF THE TABLE, LIGHTER AND ALL!!
VWSH
THE BLOODY LIGHTER FLEW OVER TO THE SOFA...
... WHERE IT REMAINED.
SHFF
TMP
ISN'T THAT RIGHT, MS. KAORI NAKAHARA?
...
K-KAORI ...
UNFOR-TUNATELY FOR YOU, YOU DIDN'T NOTICE THE MESSAGE UNTIL AFTER YOU'D SCREAMED.
IF YOU HAD NOTICED SOONER, THERE WOULD HAVE BEEN PLENTY OF WAYS TO COVER UP THE MEANING OF HIS MESSAGE.
AND ONE MORE THING. SALAD AND ICE CREAM WERE ON YOUR LIST OF ORDERED SNACKS.
YOU CLAIMED BOTH WERE SOLD OUT. SALAD, MAYBE, BUT ICE CREAM IS ALMOST NEVER SOLD OUT.
ICE CREAM
THAT'S WHEN IT STRUCK ME.
MAYBE THEY WEREN'T SOLD OUT AT ALL. MAYBE YOU JUST HADN'T ANTICIPATED THOSE ORDERS.
PERHAPS IF YOU HAD BROUGHT BACK ALL THE SNACKS THAT WERE ORDERED ...
ENOUGH ...
...I WOULDN'T HAVE HAD ANY SUSPICIONS ABOUT YOUR ALIBI.

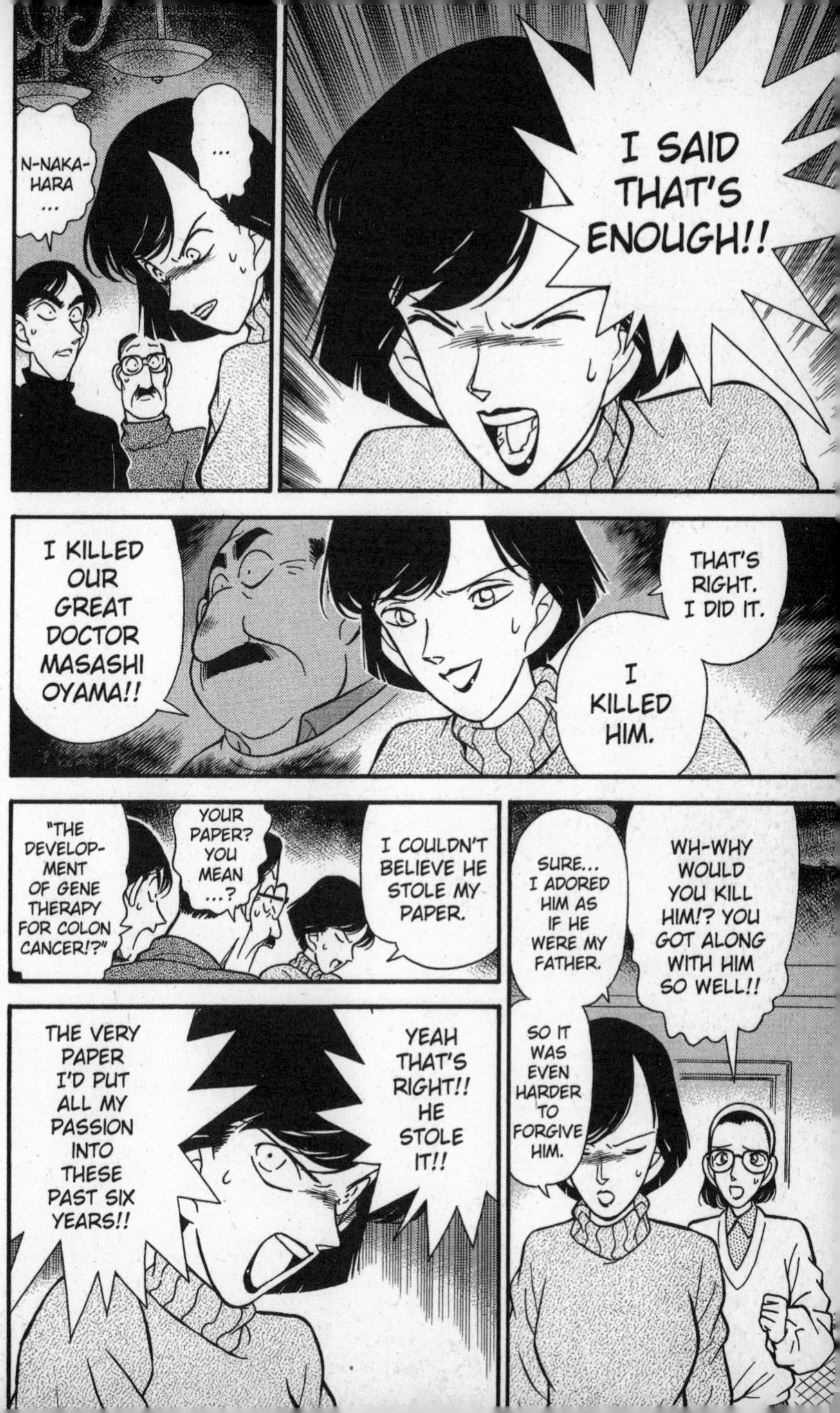
I SAID THAT'S ENOUGH!!
...
N-NAKAHARA ...
THAT'S RIGHT. I DID IT.
I KILLED HIM.
I KILLED OUR GREAT DOCTOR MASASHI OYAMA!!
WH-WHY WOULD YOU KILL HIM!? YOU GOT ALONG WITH HIM SO WELL!!
SURE... I ADORED HIM AS IF HE WERE MY FATHER.
SO IT WAS EVEN HARDER TO FORGIVE HIM.
I COULDN'T BELIEVE HE STOLE MY PAPER.
YOUR PAPER? YOU MEAN ...?
"THE DEVELOPMENT OF GENE THERAPY FOR COLON CANCER!?"
YEAH THAT'S RIGHT!! HE STOLE IT!!
THE VERY PAPER I'D PUT ALL MY PASSION INTO THESE PAST SIX YEARS!!

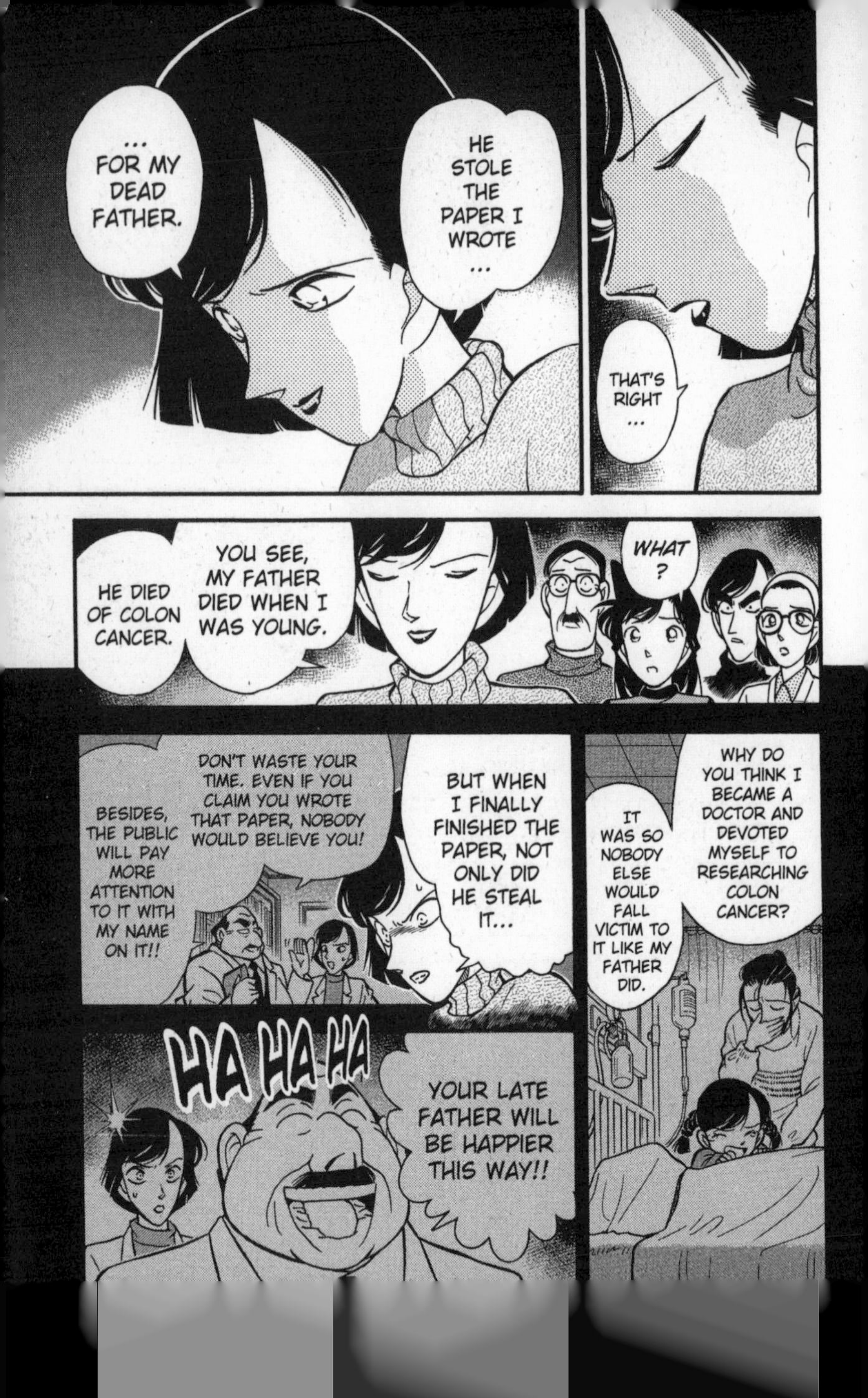
THAT'S RIGHT ...
HE STOLE THE PAPER I WROTE ...
... FOR MY DEAD FATHER.
WHAT?
YOU SEE, MY FATHER DIED WHEN I WAS YOUNG.
HE DIED OF COLON CANCER.
WHY DO YOU THINK I BECAME A DOCTOR AND DEVOTED MYSELF TO RESEARCHING COLON CANCER?
IT WAS SO NOBODY ELSE WOULD FALL VICTIM TO IT LIKE MY FATHER DID.
BUT WHEN I FINALLY FINISHED THE PAPER, NOT ONLY DID HE STEAL IT...
DON'T WASTE YOUR TIME. EVEN IF YOU CLAIM YOU WROTE THAT PAPER, NOBODY WOULD BELIEVE YOU!
BESIDES, THE PUBLIC WILL PAY MORE ATTENTION TO IT WITH MY NAME ON IT!!
HA HA HA
YOUR LATE FATHER WILL BE HAPPIER THIS WAY!!

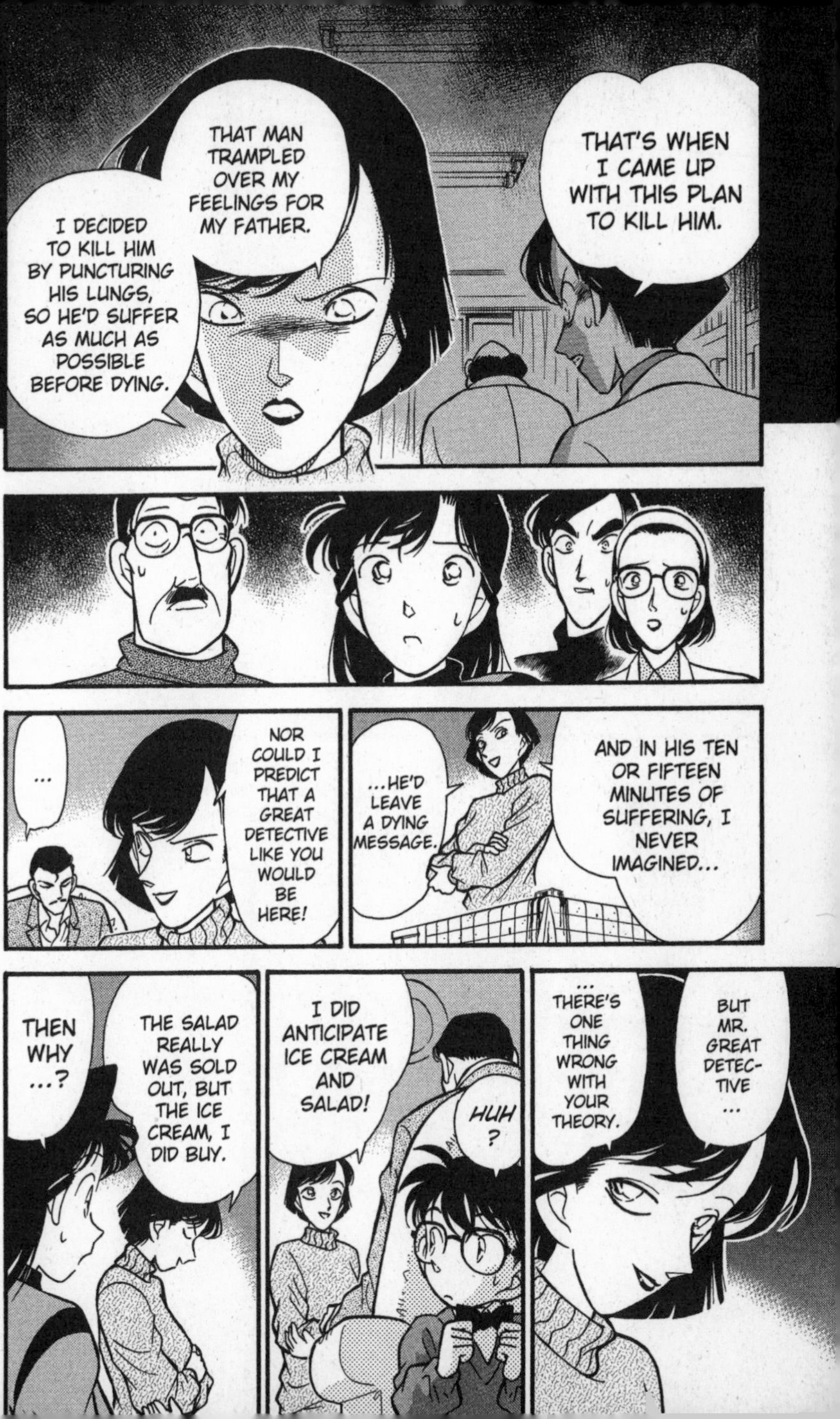
THAT'S WHEN I CAME UP WITH THIS PLAN TO KILL HIM.
THAT MAN TRAMPLED OVER MY FEELINGS FOR MY FATHER.
I DECIDED TO KILL HIM BY PUNCTURING HIS LUNGS, SO HE'D SUFFER AS MUCH AS POSSIBLE BEFORE DYING.
AND IN HIS TEN OR FIFTEEN MINUTES OF SUFFERING, I NEVER IMAGINED...
...HE'D LEAVE A DYING MESSAGE.
NOR COULD I PREDICT THAT A GREAT DETECTIVE LIKE YOU WOULD BE HERE!
...
BUT MR. GREAT DETECTIVE...
...THERE'S ONE THING WRONG WITH YOUR THEORY.
I DID ANTICIPATE ICE CREAM AND SALAD!
HUH?
THE SALAD REALLY WAS SOLD OUT, BUT THE ICE CREAM, I DID BUY.
THEN WHY...?

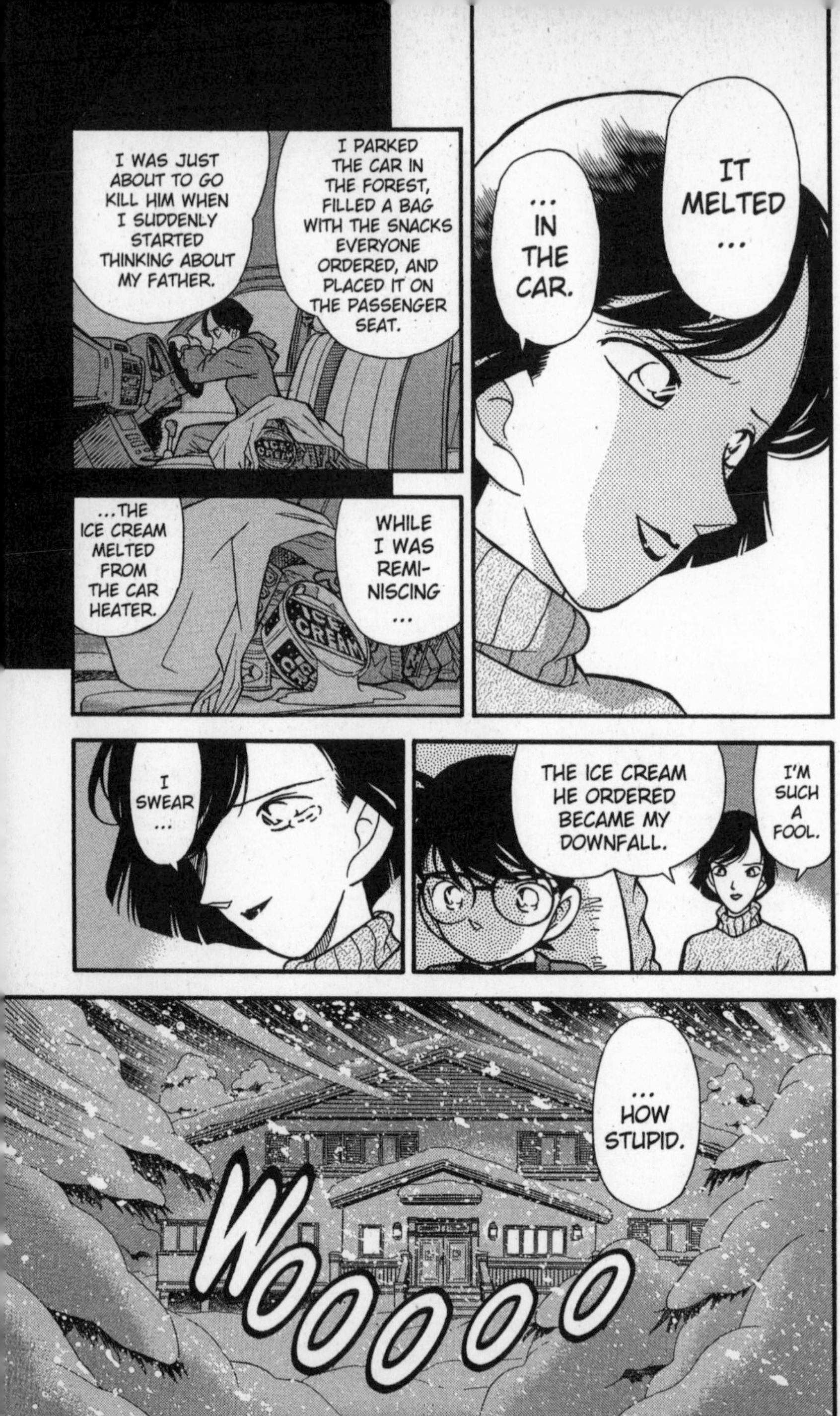
IT MELTED ...
... IN THE CAR.
I PARKED THE CAR IN THE FOREST, FILLED A BAG WITH THE SNACKS EVERYONE ORDERED, AND PLACED IT ON THE PASSENGER SEAT.
I WAS JUST ABOUT TO GO KILL HIM WHEN I SUDDENLY STARTED THINKING ABOUT MY FATHER.
WHILE I WAS REMI-NISCING ...
...THE ICE CREAM MELTED FROM THE CAR HEATER.
I'M SUCH A FOOL.
THE ICE CREAM HE ORDERED BECAME MY DOWNFALL.
I SWEAR ...
... HOW STUPID.
WOOOOOO

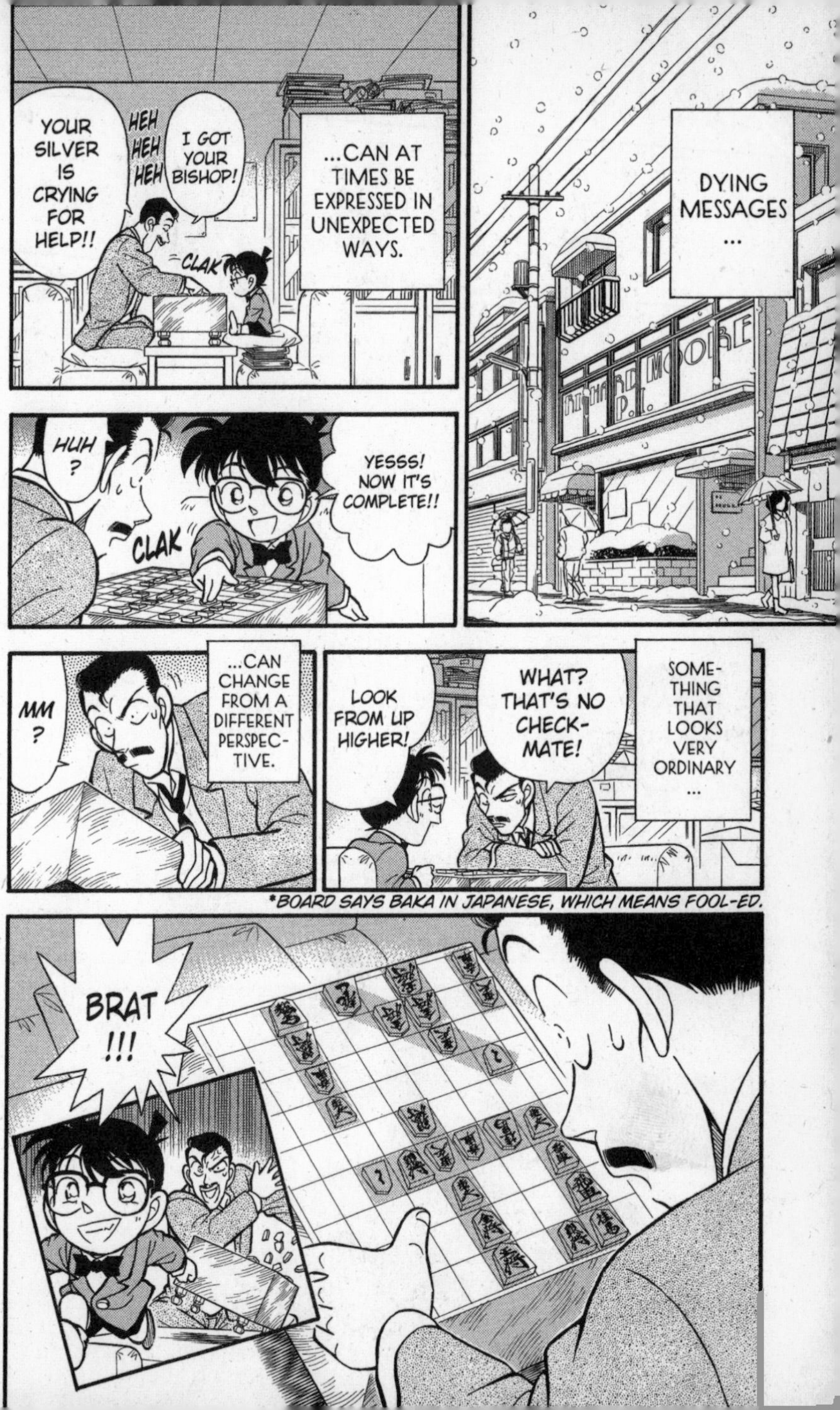
DYING MESSAGES ...
...CAN AT TIMES BE EXPRESSED IN UNEXPECTED WAYS.
I GOT YOUR BISHOP!
HEH HEH HEH
YOUR SILVER IS CRYING FOR HELP!!
CLAK
YESSS! NOW IT'S COMPLETE!!
CLAK
HUH ?
SOMETHING THAT LOOKS VERY ORDINARY ...
WHAT? THAT'S NO CHECKMATE!
LOOK FROM UP HIGHER!
...CAN CHANGE FROM A DIFFERENT PERSPECTIVE.
MM ?
*BOARD SAYS BAKA IN JAPANESE, WHICH MEANS FOOL-ED.
BRAT !!!

FILE 2:
DEATH DURING LIVE BROADCAST

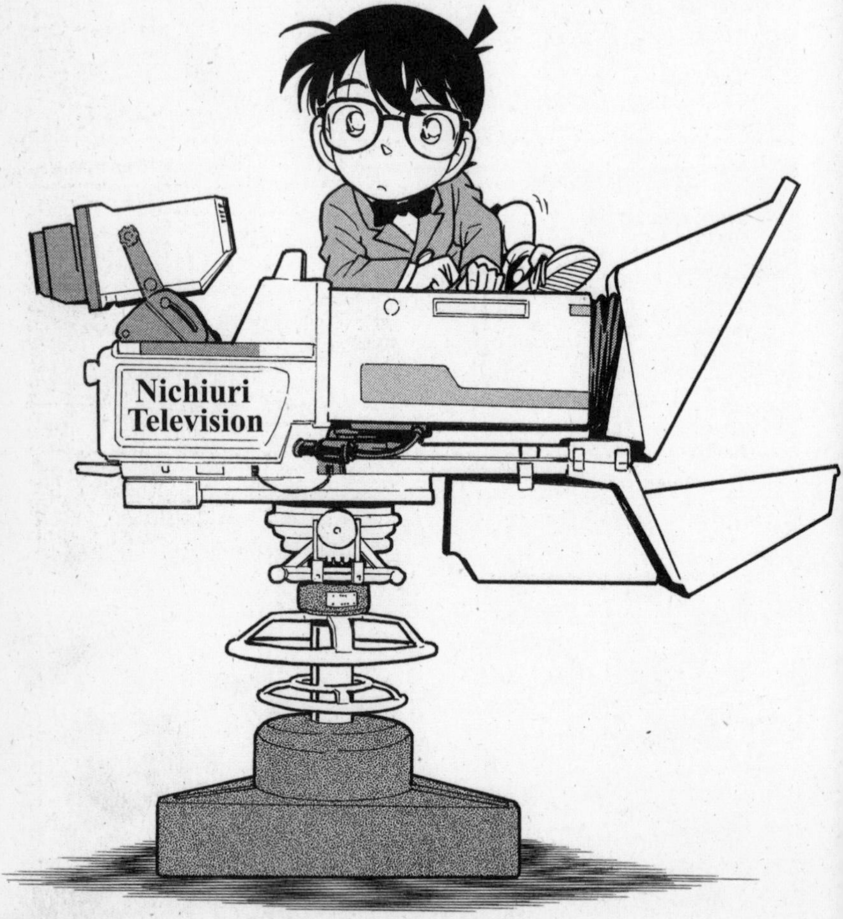
Nichiuri Television

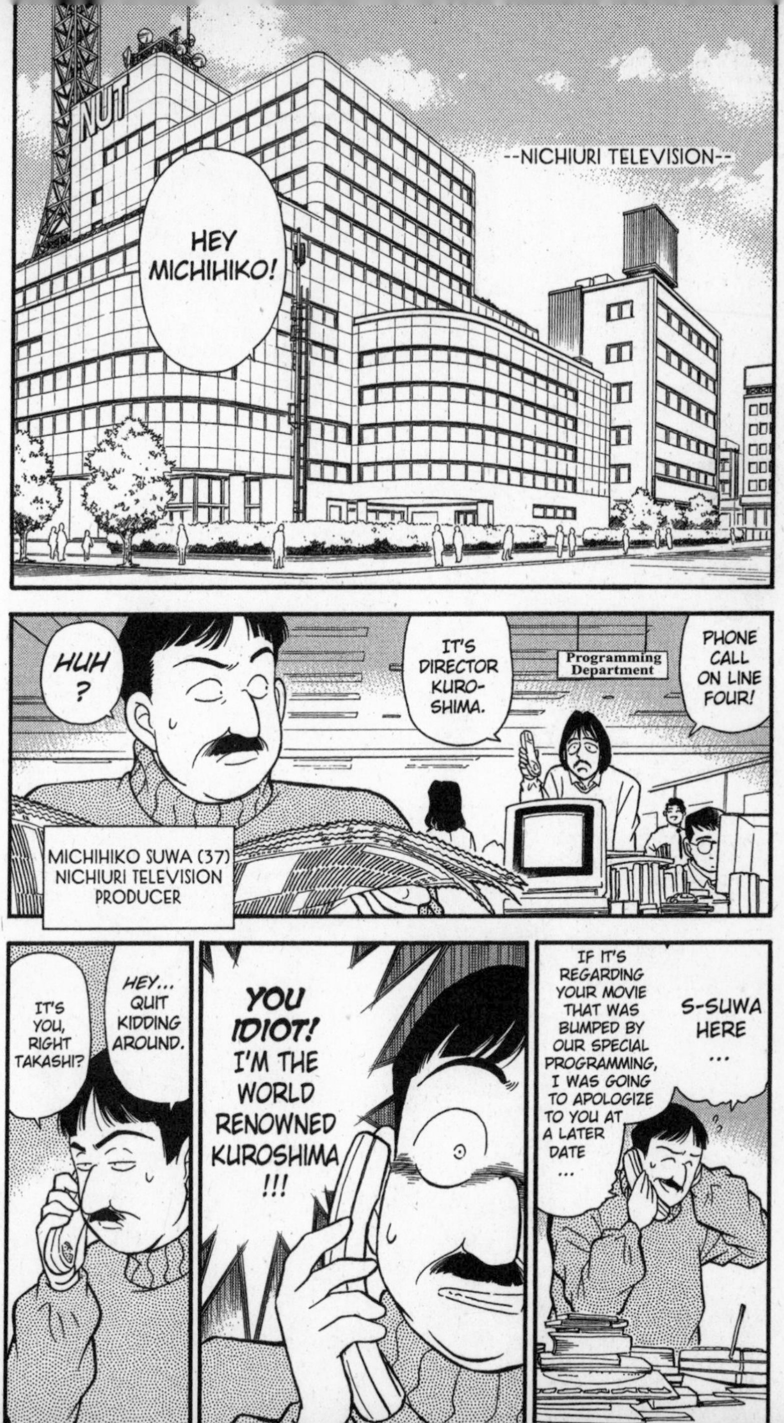
--NICHIURI TELEVISION--
HEY MICHIHIKO!
PHONE CALL ON LINE FOUR!
Programming Department
IT'S DIRECTOR KURO-SHIMA.
HUH?
MICHIHIKO SUWA (37) NICHIURI TELEVISION PRODUCER
S-SUWA HERE ...
IF IT'S REGARDING YOUR MOVIE THAT WAS BUMPED BY OUR SPECIAL PROGRAMMING, I WAS GOING TO APOLOGIZE TO YOU AT A LATER DATE ...
YOU IDIOT! I'M THE WORLD RENOWNED KUROSHIMA!!!
HEY... QUIT KIDDING AROUND.
IT'S YOU, RIGHT TAKASHI?

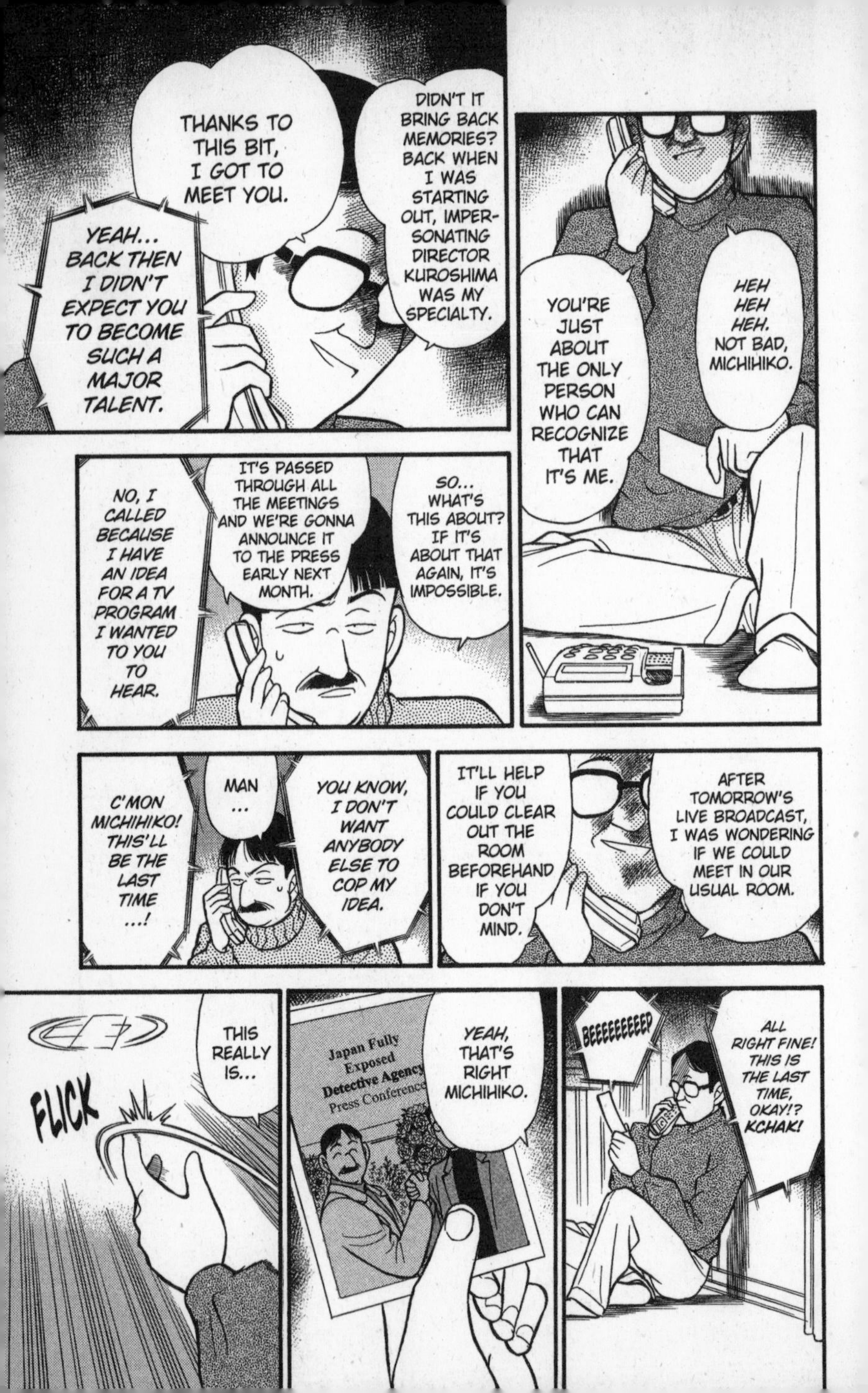
HEH HEH HEH. NOT BAD, MICHIHIKO.
YOU'RE JUST ABOUT THE ONLY PERSON WHO CAN RECOGNIZE THAT IT'S ME.
DIDN'T IT BRING BACK MEMORIES? BACK WHEN I WAS STARTING OUT, IMPER-SONATING DIRECTOR KUROSHIMA WAS MY SPECIALTY.
THANKS TO THIS BIT, I GOT TO MEET YOU.
YEAH... BACK THEN I DIDN'T EXPECT YOU TO BECOME SUCH A MAJOR TALENT.
SO... WHAT'S THIS ABOUT? IF IT'S ABOUT THAT AGAIN, IT'S IMPOSSIBLE.
IT'S PASSED THROUGH ALL THE MEETINGS AND WE'RE GONNA ANNOUNCE IT TO THE PRESS EARLY NEXT MONTH.
NO, I CALLED BECAUSE I HAVE AN IDEA FOR A TV PROGRAM I WANTED TO YOU TO HEAR.
AFTER TOMORROW'S LIVE BROADCAST, I WAS WONDERING IF WE COULD MEET IN OUR USUAL ROOM.
IT'LL HELP IF YOU COULD CLEAR OUT THE ROOM BEFOREHAND IF YOU DON'T MIND.
YOU KNOW, I DON'T WANT ANYBODY ELSE TO COP MY IDEA.
MAN ...
C'MON MICHIHIKO! THIS'LL BE THE LAST TIME ...!
ALL RIGHT FINE! THIS IS THE LAST TIME, OKAY!? KCHAK!
BEEEEEEEEEP
YEAH, THAT'S RIGHT MICHIHIKO.
Japan Fully Exposed Detective Agency Press Conference
THIS REALLY IS...
FLICK

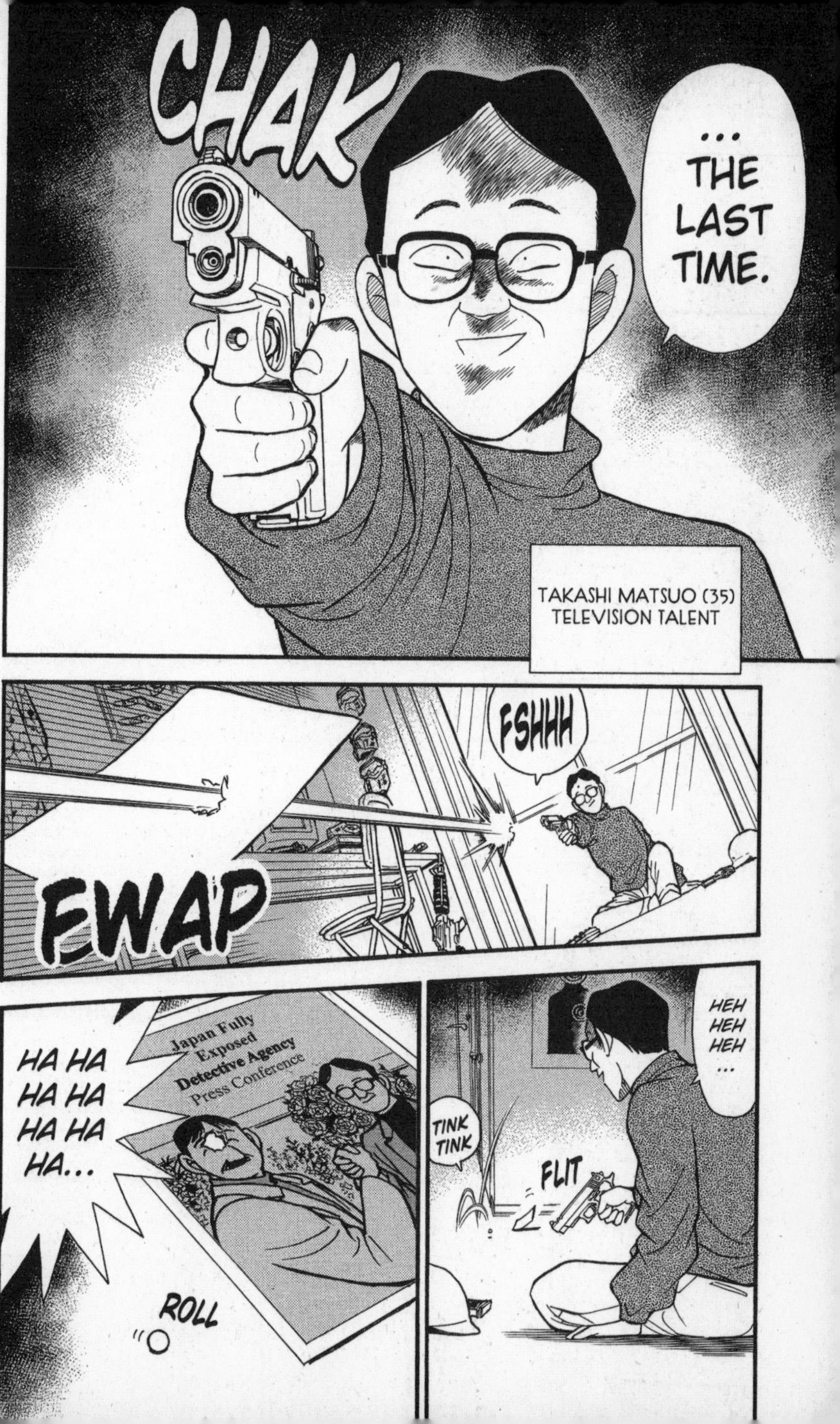
CHAK
... THE LAST TIME.
TAKASHI MATSUO (35) TELEVISION TALENT
FSHHH
FWAP
HEH HEH HEH ...
TINK TINK
FLIT
Japan Fully Exposed Detective Agency Press Conference
HA HA HA HA HA HA HA...
ROLL

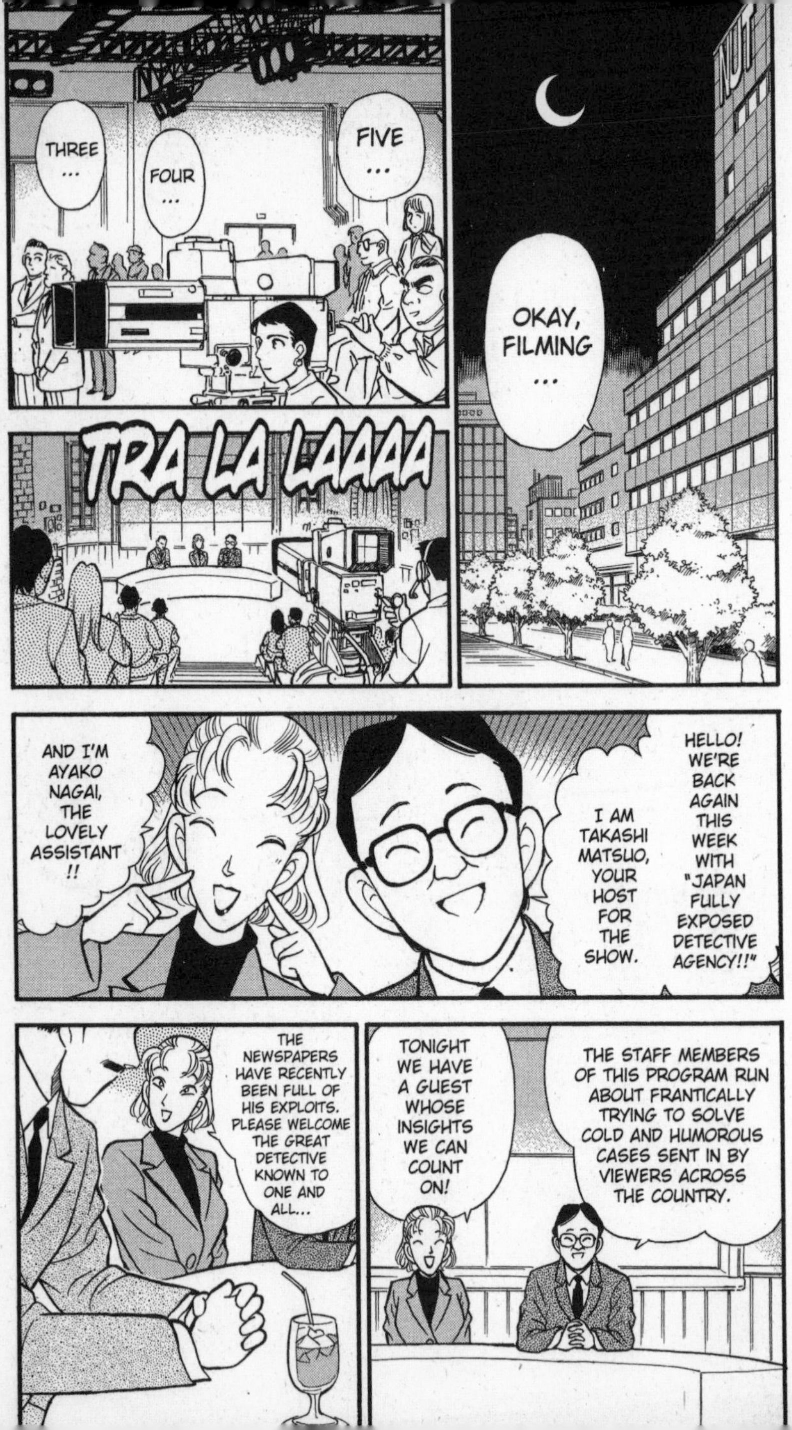
OKAY, FILMING ...
FIVE ...
FOUR ...
THREE ...
TRA LA LAAAA
HELLO! WE'RE BACK AGAIN THIS WEEK WITH "JAPAN FULLY EXPOSED DETECTIVE AGENCY!!"
I AM TAKASHI MATSUO, YOUR HOST FOR THE SHOW.
AND I'M AYAKO NAGAI, THE LOVELY ASSISTANT !!
THE STAFF MEMBERS OF THIS PROGRAM RUN ABOUT FRANTICALLY TRYING TO SOLVE COLD AND HUMOROUS CASES SENT IN BY VIEWERS ACROSS THE COUNTRY.
TONIGHT WE HAVE A GUEST WHOSE INSIGHTS WE CAN COUNT ON!
THE NEWSPAPERS HAVE RECENTLY BEEN FULL OF HIS EXPLOITS. PLEASE WELCOME THE GREAT DETECTIVE KNOWN TO ONE AND ALL...

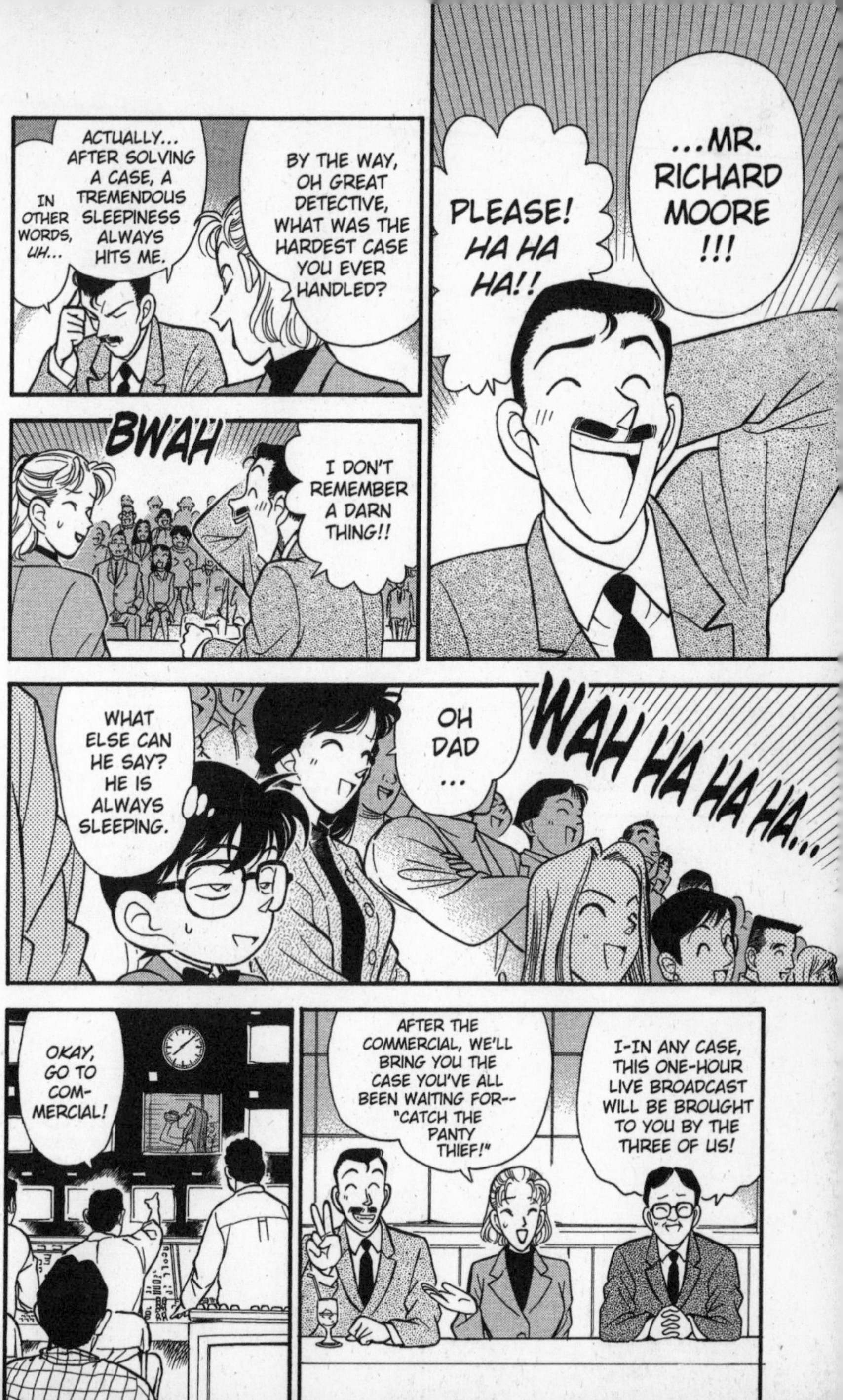
...MR. RICHARD MOORE !!!
PLEASE! HA HA HA!!
BY THE WAY, OH GREAT DETECTIVE, WHAT WAS THE HARDEST CASE YOU EVER HANDLED?
ACTUALLY... AFTER SOLVING A CASE, A TREMENDOUS SLEEPINESS ALWAYS HITS ME.
IN OTHER WORDS, UH...
BWAH
I DON'T REMEMBER A DARN THING!!
WAH HA HA HA HA...
OH DAD ...
WHAT ELSE CAN HE SAY? HE IS ALWAYS SLEEPING.
I-IN ANY CASE, THIS ONE-HOUR LIVE BROADCAST WILL BE BROUGHT TO YOU BY THE THREE OF US!
AFTER THE COMMERCIAL, WE'LL BRING YOU THE CASE YOU'VE ALL BEEN WAITING FOR-- "CATCH THE PANTY THIEF!"
OKAY, GO TO COM-MERCIAL!

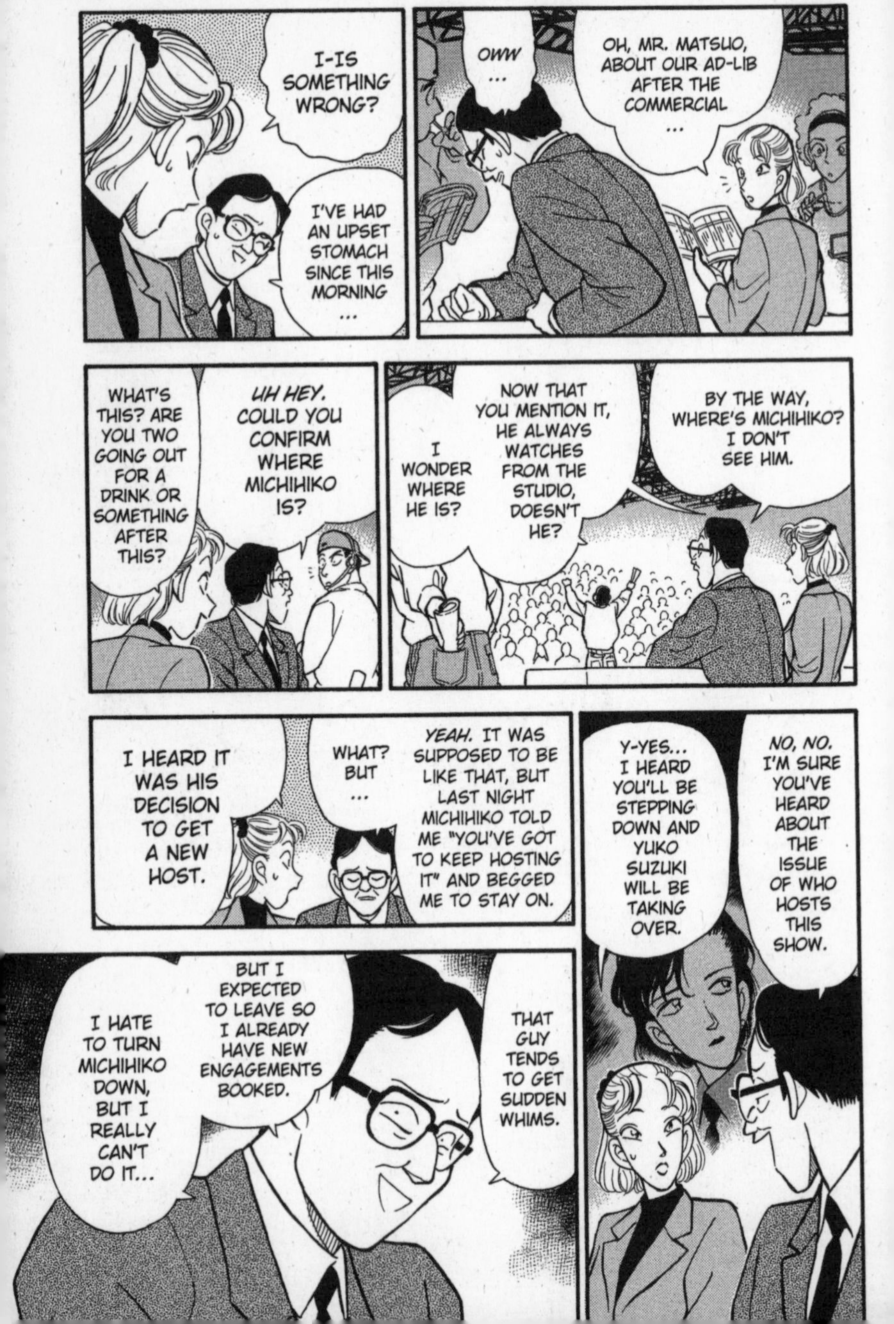
OH, MR. MATSUO, ABOUT OUR AD-LIB AFTER THE COMMERCIAL ...
OWW ...
I-IS SOMETHING WRONG?
I'VE HAD AN UPSET STOMACH SINCE THIS MORNING ...
BY THE WAY, WHERE'S MICHIHIKO? I DON'T SEE HIM.
NOW THAT YOU MENTION IT, HE ALWAYS WATCHES FROM THE STUDIO, DOESN'T HE?
I WONDER WHERE HE IS?
UH HEY. COULD YOU CONFIRM WHERE MICHIHIKO IS?
WHAT'S THIS? ARE YOU TWO GOING OUT FOR A DRINK OR SOMETHING AFTER THIS?
NO, NO. I'M SURE YOU'VE HEARD ABOUT THE ISSUE OF WHO HOSTS THIS SHOW.
Y-YES... I HEARD YOU'LL BE STEPPING DOWN AND YUKO SUZUKI WILL BE TAKING OVER.
YEAH. IT WAS SUPPOSED TO BE LIKE THAT, BUT LAST NIGHT MICHIHIKO TOLD ME "YOU'VE GOT TO KEEP HOSTING IT" AND BEGGED ME TO STAY ON.
WHAT? BUT ...
I HEARD IT WAS HIS DECISION TO GET A NEW HOST.
THAT GUY TENDS TO GET SUDDEN WHIMS.
BUT I EXPECTED TO LEAVE SO I ALREADY HAVE NEW ENGAGEMENTS BOOKED.
I HATE TO TURN MICHIHIKO DOWN, BUT I REALLY CAN'T DO IT...

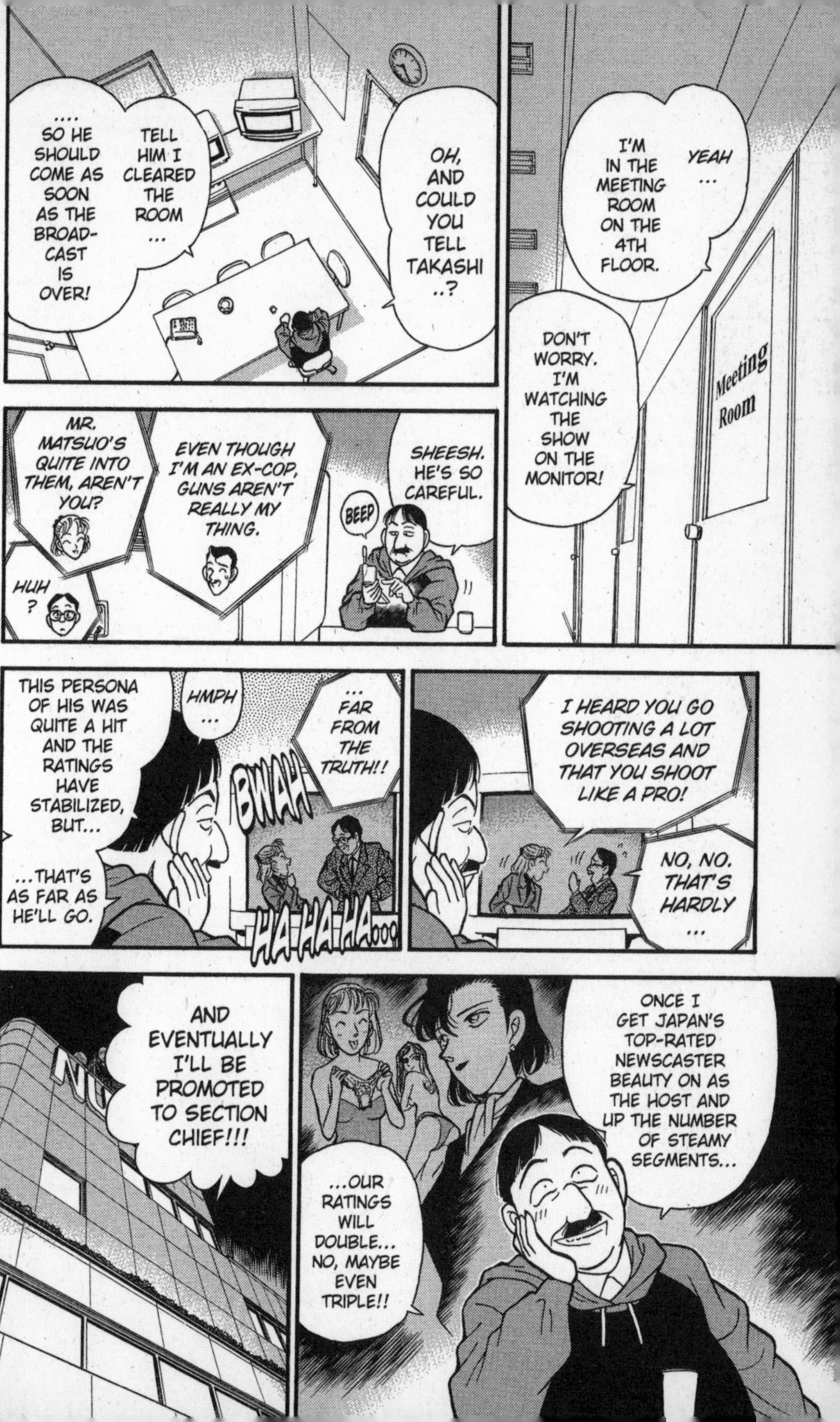
YEAH ...
I'M IN THE MEETING ROOM ON THE 4TH FLOOR.
DON'T WORRY. I'M WATCHING THE SHOW ON THE MONITOR!
Meeting Room
OH, AND COULD YOU TELL TAKASHI ..?
TELL HIM I CLEARED THE ROOM ...
.... SO HE SHOULD COME AS SOON AS THE BROAD-CAST IS OVER!
SHEESH. HE'S SO CAREFUL.
BEEP
EVEN THOUGH I'M AN EX-COP, GUNS AREN'T REALLY MY THING.
MR. MATSUO'S QUITE INTO THEM, AREN'T YOU?
HUH ?
I HEARD YOU GO SHOOTING A LOT OVERSEAS AND THAT YOU SHOOT LIKE A PRO!
NO, NO. THAT'S HARDLY ...
... FAR FROM THE TRUTH!!
BWAH
HA HA HA
HMPH ...
THIS PERSONA OF HIS WAS QUITE A HIT AND THE RATINGS HAVE STABILIZED, BUT...
...THAT'S AS FAR AS HE'LL GO.
ONCE I GET JAPAN'S TOP-RATED NEWSCASTER BEAUTY ON AS THE HOST AND UP THE NUMBER OF STEAMY SEGMENTS...
...OUR RATINGS WILL DOUBLE... NO, MAYBE EVEN TRIPLE!!
AND EVENTUALLY I'LL BE PROMOTED TO SECTION CHIEF!!!

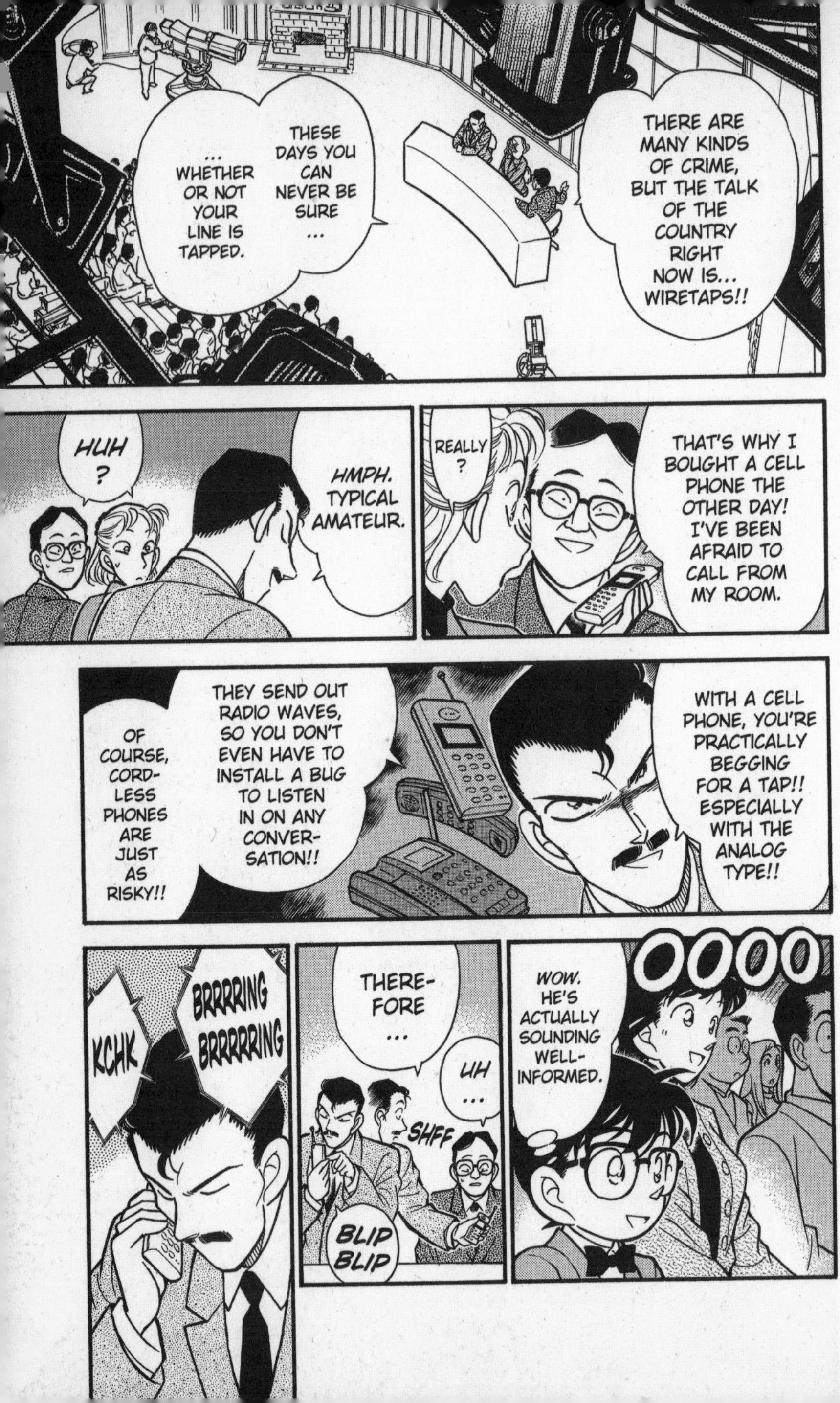
THERE ARE MANY KINDS OF CRIME, BUT THE TALK OF THE COUNTRY RIGHT NOW IS... WIRETAPS!!
THESE DAYS YOU CAN NEVER BE SURE ...
... WHETHER OR NOT YOUR LINE IS TAPPED.
THAT'S WHY I BOUGHT A CELL PHONE THE OTHER DAY! I'VE BEEN AFRAID TO CALL FROM MY ROOM.
REALLY ?
HMPH. TYPICAL AMATEUR.
HUH ?
WITH A CELL PHONE, YOU'RE PRACTICALLY BEGGING FOR A TAP!! ESPECIALLY WITH THE ANALOG TYPE!!
THEY SEND OUT RADIO WAVES, SO YOU DON'T EVEN HAVE TO INSTALL A BUG TO LISTEN IN ON ANY CONVER-SATION!!
OF COURSE, CORD-LESS PHONES ARE JUST AS RISKY!!
OOOO
WOW. HE'S ACTUALLY SOUNDING WELL-INFORMED.
THERE-FORE ...
UH ...
SHFF
BLIP BLIP
BRRRRING BRRRRRING
KCHK

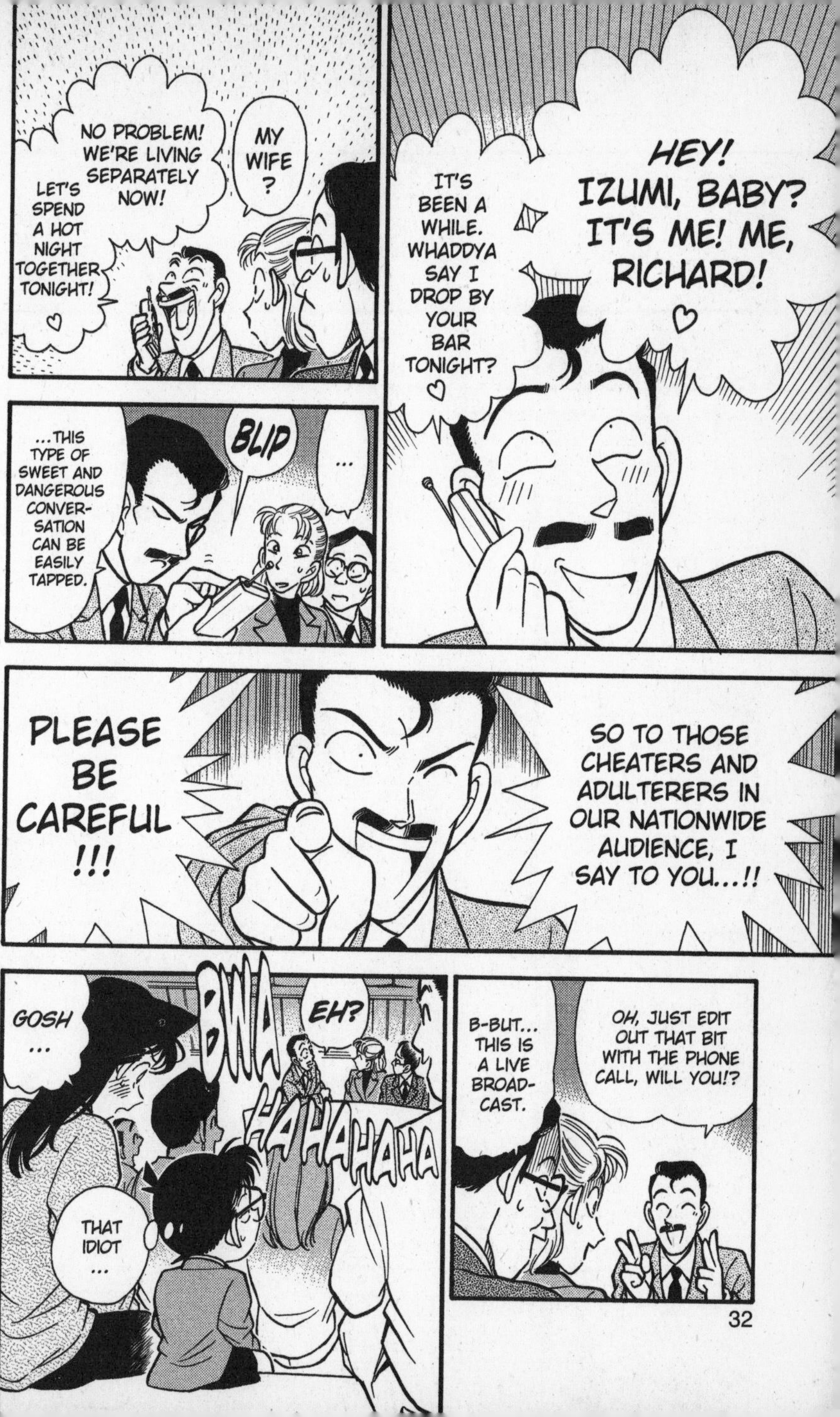
HEY! IZUMI, BABY? IT'S ME! ME, RICHARD! ♡
IT'S BEEN A WHILE. WHADDYA SAY I DROP BY YOUR BAR TONIGHT? ♡
MY WIFE?
NO PROBLEM! WE'RE LIVING SEPARATELY NOW!
LET'S SPEND A HOT NIGHT TOGETHER TONIGHT! ♡
...
BLIP
...THIS TYPE OF SWEET AND DANGEROUS CONVERSATION CAN BE EASILY TAPPED.
SO TO THOSE CHEATERS AND ADULTERERS IN OUR NATIONWIDE AUDIENCE, I SAY TO YOU...!!
PLEASE BE CAREFUL!!!
OH, JUST EDIT OUT THAT BIT WITH THE PHONE CALL, WILL YOU!?
B-BUT... THIS IS A LIVE BROADCAST.
EH?
BWAHAHAHAHA
GOSH...
THAT IDIOT...

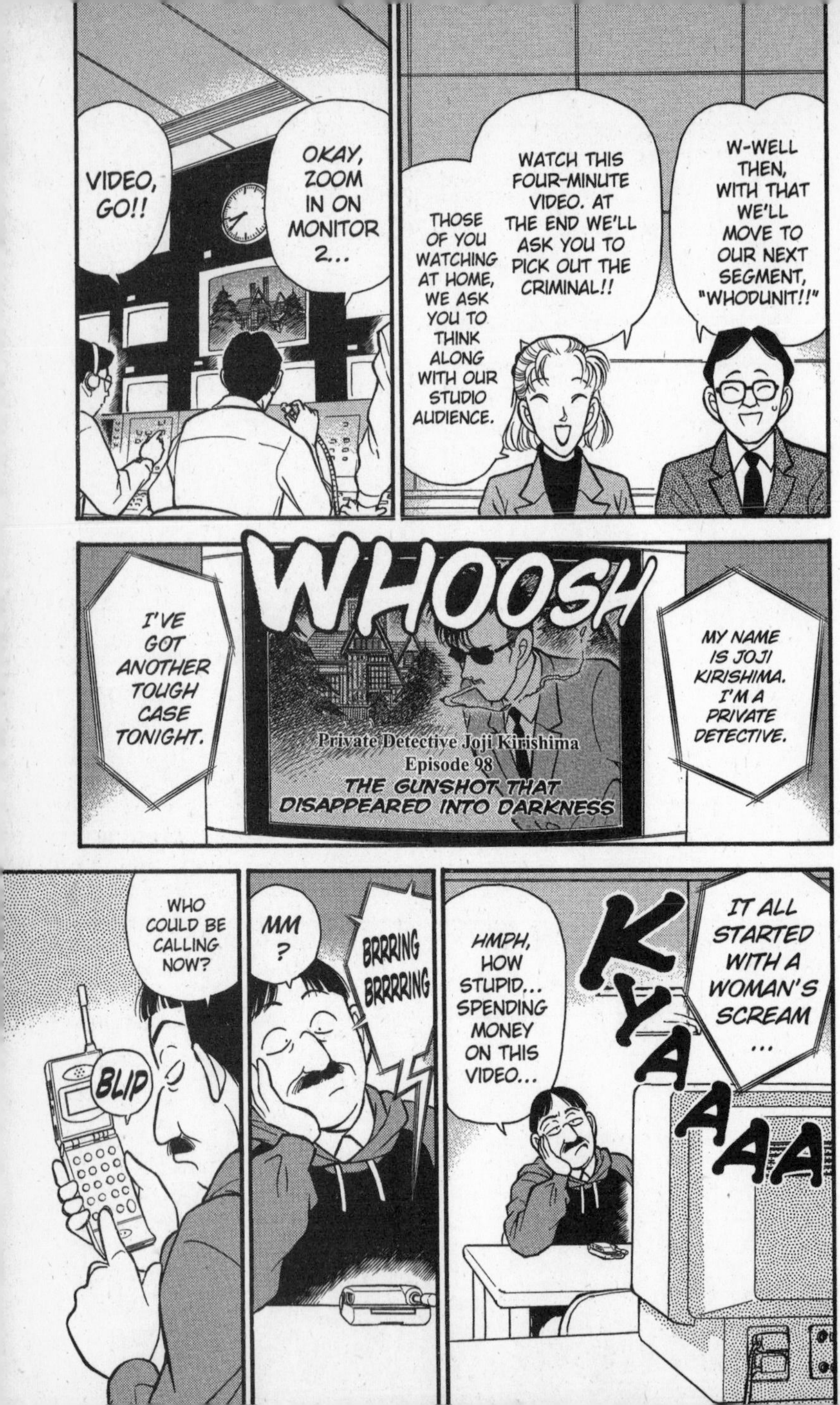
W-WELL THEN, WITH THAT WE'LL MOVE TO OUR NEXT SEGMENT, "WHODUNIT!!"
WATCH THIS FOUR-MINUTE VIDEO. AT THE END WE'LL ASK YOU TO PICK OUT THE CRIMINAL!!
THOSE OF YOU WATCHING AT HOME, WE ASK YOU TO THINK ALONG WITH OUR STUDIO AUDIENCE.
OKAY, ZOOM IN ON MONITOR 2...
VIDEO, GO!!
MY NAME IS JOJI KIRISHIMA. I'M A PRIVATE DETECTIVE.
WHOOSH
Private Detective Joji Kirishima
Episode 98
THE GUNSHOT THAT DISAPPEARED INTO DARKNESS
I'VE GOT ANOTHER TOUGH CASE TONIGHT.
IT ALL STARTED WITH A WOMAN'S SCREAM...
KYAAAAA
HMPH, HOW STUPID... SPENDING MONEY ON THIS VIDEO...
BRRRING BRRRRING
MM?
WHO COULD BE CALLING NOW?
BLIP

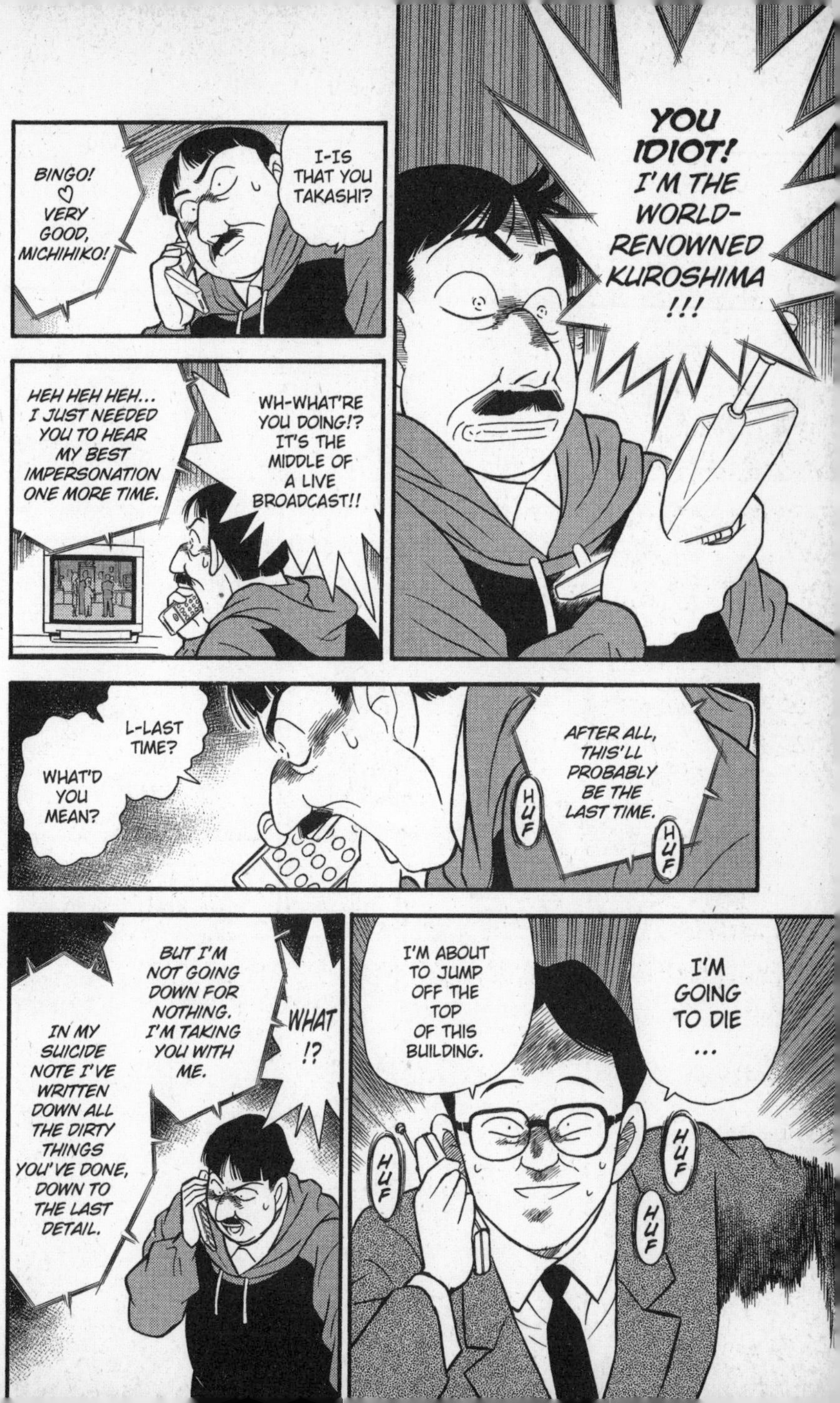
YOU IDIOT! I'M THE WORLD-RENOWNED KUROSHIMA!!!
I-IS THAT YOU TAKASHI?
BINGO! ♡ VERY GOOD, MICHIHIKO!
WH-WHAT'RE YOU DOING!? IT'S THE MIDDLE OF A LIVE BROADCAST!!
HEH HEH HEH... I JUST NEEDED YOU TO HEAR MY BEST IMPERSONATION ONE MORE TIME.
HUF
AFTER ALL, THIS'LL PROBABLY BE THE LAST TIME.
HUF
L-LAST TIME?
WHAT'D YOU MEAN?
I'M GOING TO DIE ...
I'M ABOUT TO JUMP OFF THE TOP OF THIS BUILDING.
HUF
HUF
HUF
WHAT !?
BUT I'M NOT GOING DOWN FOR NOTHING. I'M TAKING YOU WITH ME.
IN MY SUICIDE NOTE I'VE WRITTEN DOWN ALL THE DIRTY THINGS YOU'VE DONE, DOWN TO THE LAST DETAIL.

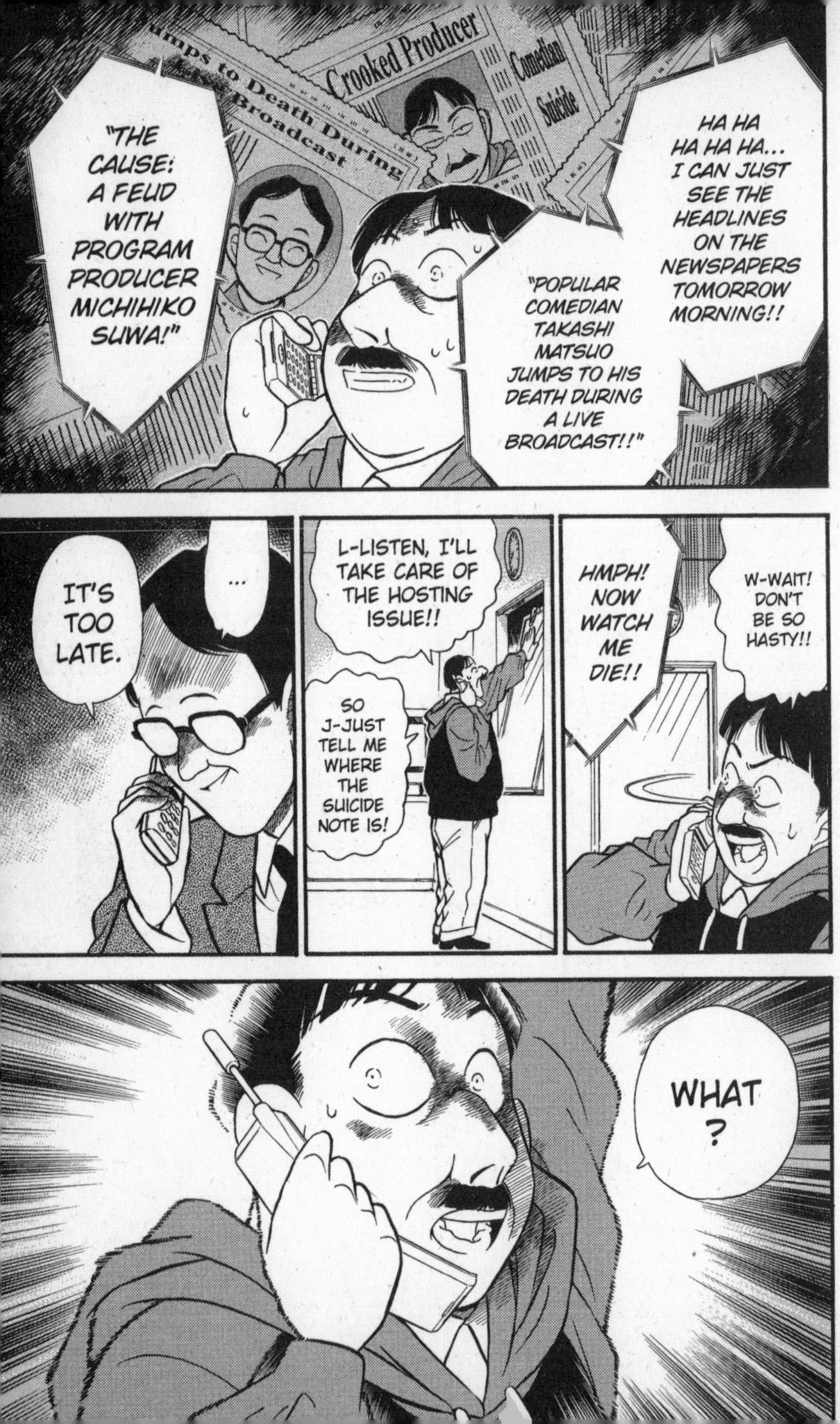
Crooked Producer
Comedian Suicide
umps to Death During
Broadcast
HA HA HA HA HA... I CAN JUST SEE THE HEADLINES ON THE NEWSPAPERS TOMORROW MORNING!!
"POPULAR COMEDIAN TAKASHI MATSUO JUMPS TO HIS DEATH DURING A LIVE BROADCAST!!"
"THE CAUSE: A FEUD WITH PROGRAM PRODUCER MICHIHIKO SUWA!"
W-WAIT! DON'T BE SO HASTY!!
HMPH! NOW WATCH ME DIE!!
L-LISTEN, I'LL TAKE CARE OF THE HOSTING ISSUE!!
SO J-JUST TELL ME WHERE THE SUICIDE NOTE IS!
...
IT'S TOO LATE.
WHAT?

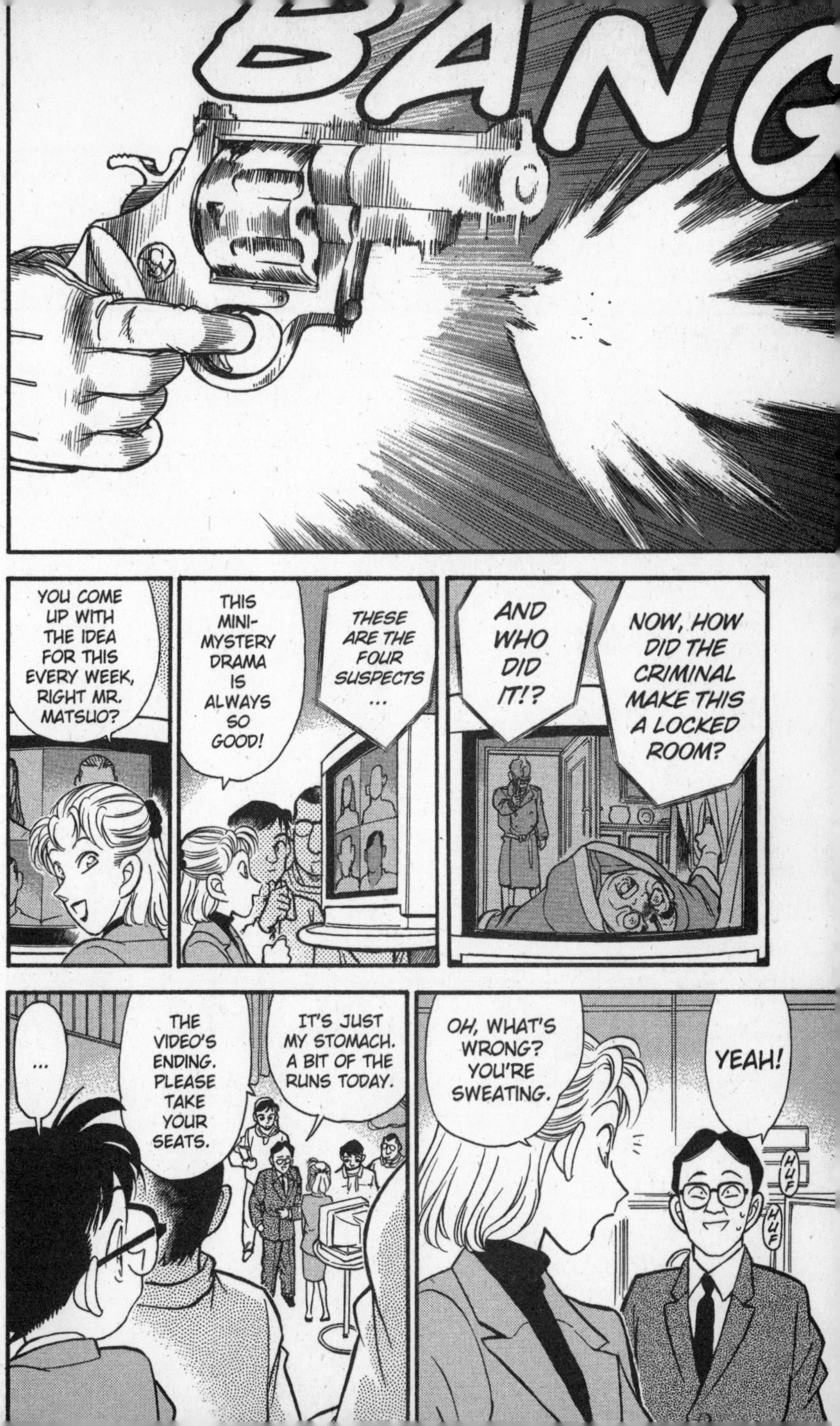
BANG
NOW, HOW DID THE CRIMINAL MAKE THIS A LOCKED ROOM?
AND WHO DID IT!?
THESE ARE THE FOUR SUSPECTS...
THIS MINI-MYSTERY DRAMA IS ALWAYS SO GOOD!
YOU COME UP WITH THE IDEA FOR THIS EVERY WEEK, RIGHT MR. MATSUO?
YEAH!
HUF
HUF
OH, WHAT'S WRONG? YOU'RE SWEATING.
IT'S JUST MY STOMACH. A BIT OF THE RUNS TODAY.
THE VIDEO'S ENDING. PLEASE TAKE YOUR SEATS.
...

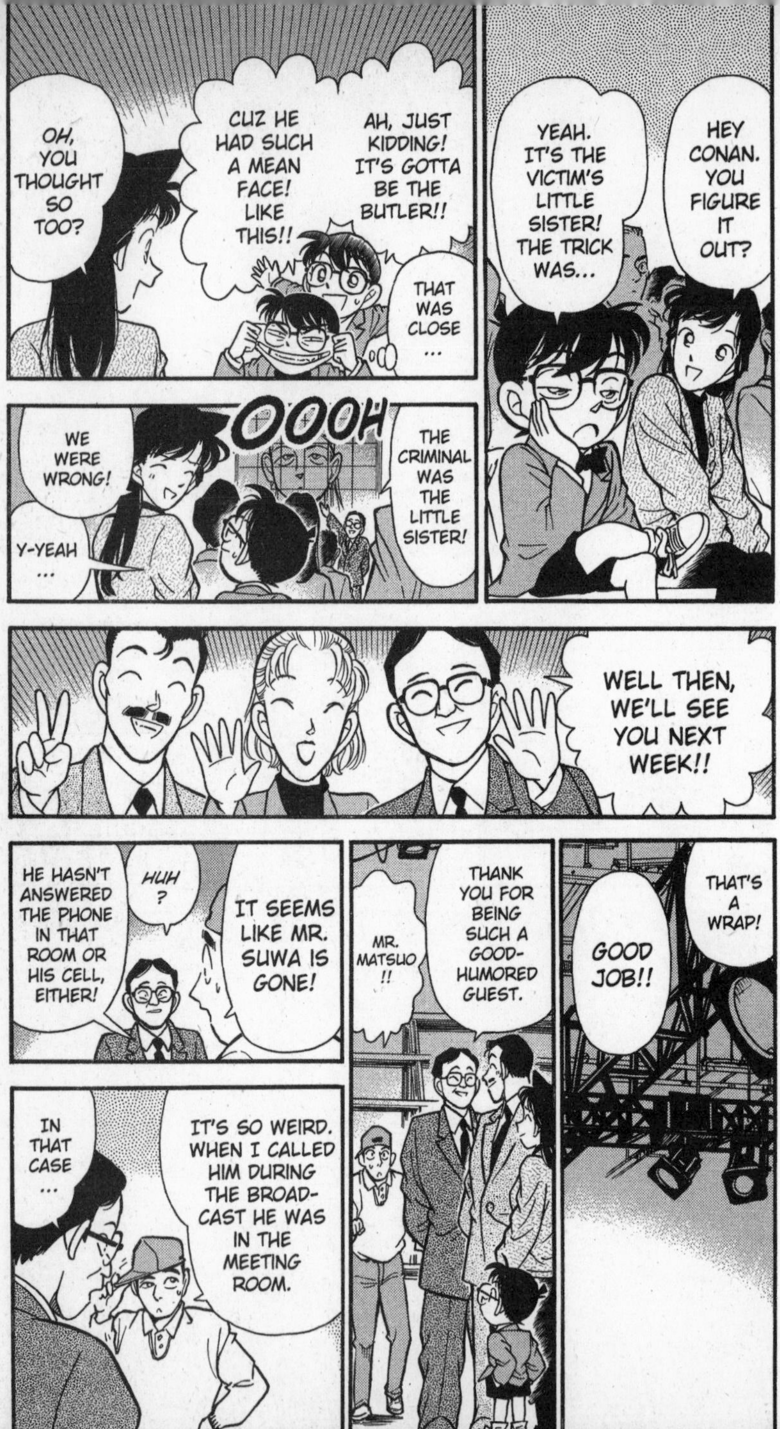
HEY CONAN. YOU FIGURE IT OUT?
YEAH. IT'S THE VICTIM'S LITTLE SISTER! THE TRICK WAS...
AH, JUST KIDDING! IT'S GOTTA BE THE BUTLER!!
CUZ HE HAD SUCH A MEAN FACE! LIKE THIS!!
OH, YOU THOUGHT SO TOO?
THAT WAS CLOSE ...
OOOH
THE CRIMINAL WAS THE LITTLE SISTER!
WE WERE WRONG!
Y-YEAH ...
WELL THEN, WE'LL SEE YOU NEXT WEEK!!
THAT'S A WRAP!
GOOD JOB!!
THANK YOU FOR BEING SUCH A GOOD-HUMORED GUEST.
MR. MATSUO !!
IT SEEMS LIKE MR. SUWA IS GONE!
HUH ?
HE HASN'T ANSWERED THE PHONE IN THAT ROOM OR HIS CELL, EITHER!
IT'S SO WEIRD. WHEN I CALLED HIM DURING THE BROAD-CAST HE WAS IN THE MEETING ROOM.
IN THAT CASE ...

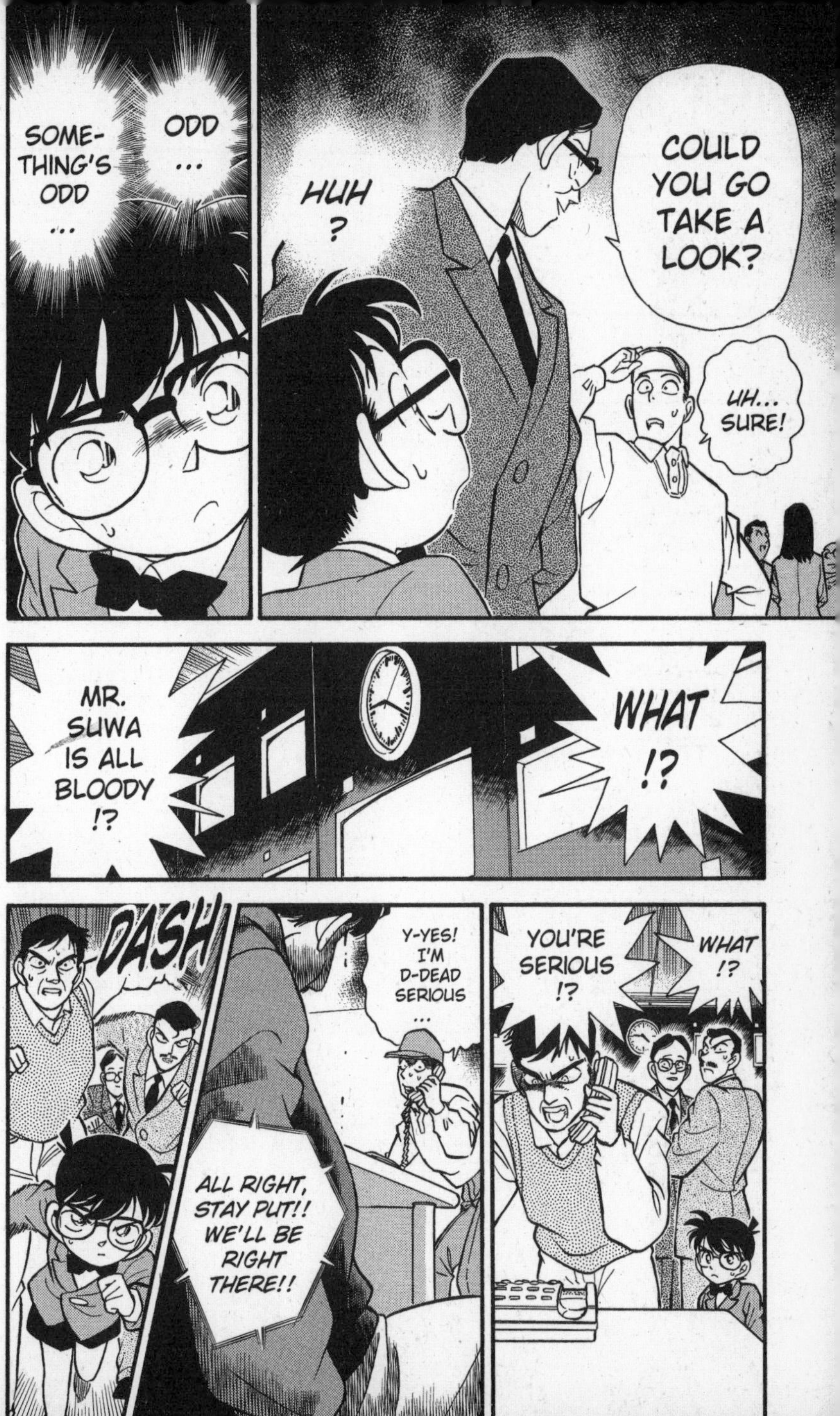
COULD YOU GO TAKE A LOOK?
UH... SURE!
HUH ?
ODD ...
SOME-THING'S ODD ...
WHAT !?
MR. SUWA IS ALL BLOODY !?
WHAT !?
YOU'RE SERIOUS !?
Y-YES! I'M D-DEAD SERIOUS ...
ALL RIGHT, STAY PUT!! WE'LL BE RIGHT THERE!!
DASH

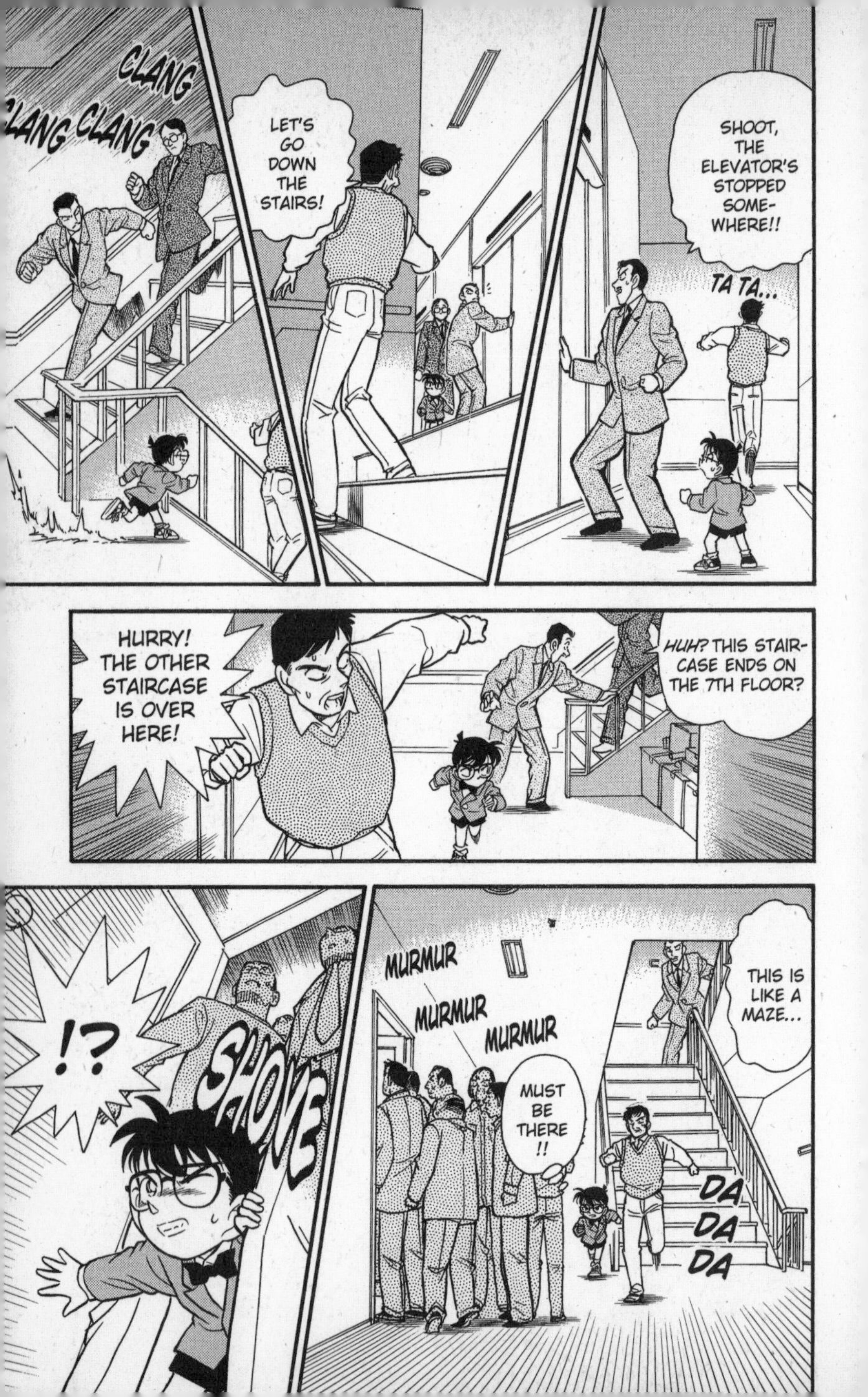
SHOOT, THE ELEVATOR'S STOPPED SOME-WHERE!!
TA TA...
LET'S GO DOWN THE STAIRS!
CLANG
CLANG CLANG
HUH? THIS STAIR-CASE ENDS ON THE 7TH FLOOR?
HURRY! THE OTHER STAIRCASE IS OVER HERE!
THIS IS LIKE A MAZE...
MURMUR
MURMUR
MURMUR
MUST BE THERE!!
DA
DA
DA
SHOVE
!?

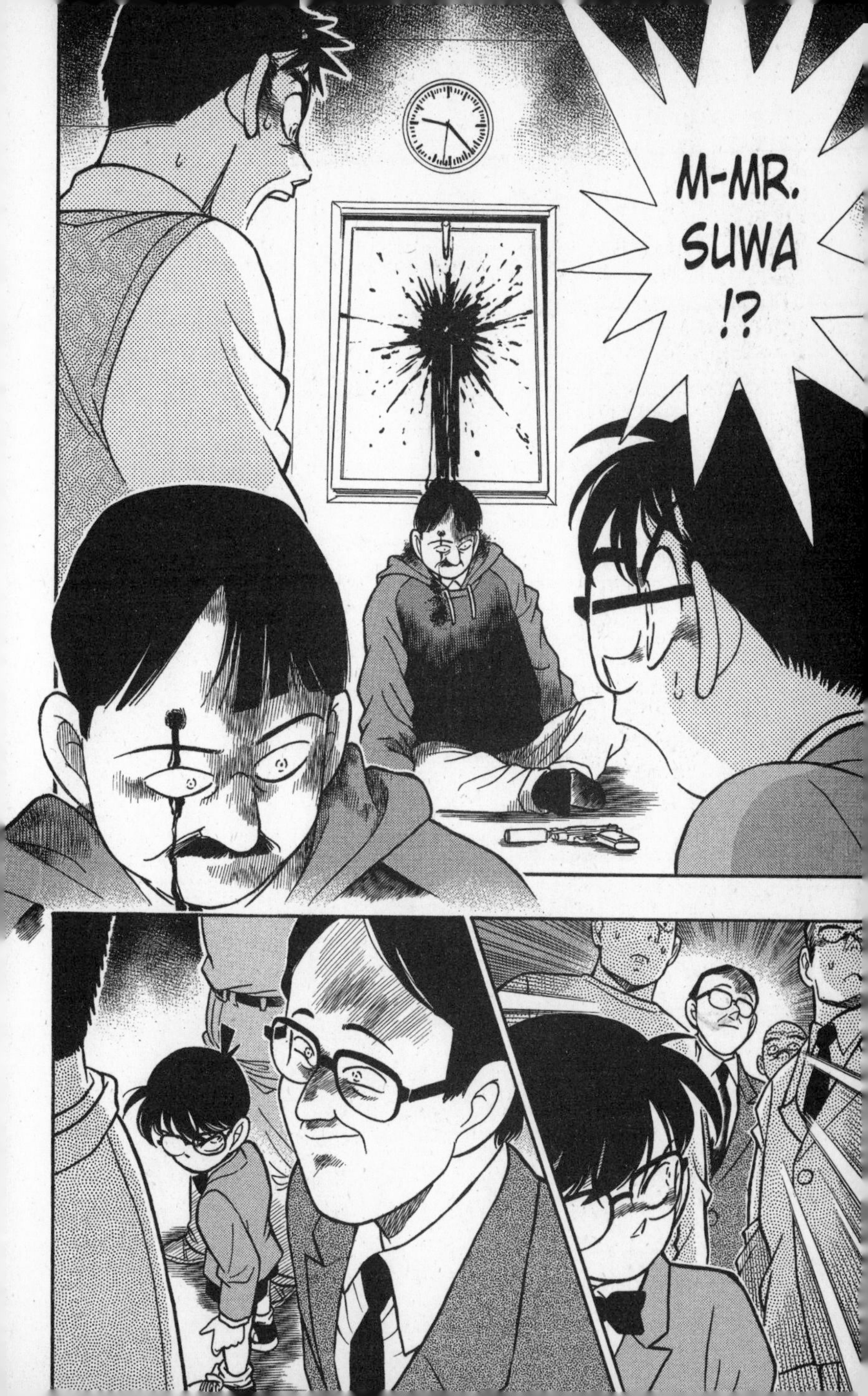
M-MR. SUWA !?

FILE 3: THE SECRET PATH

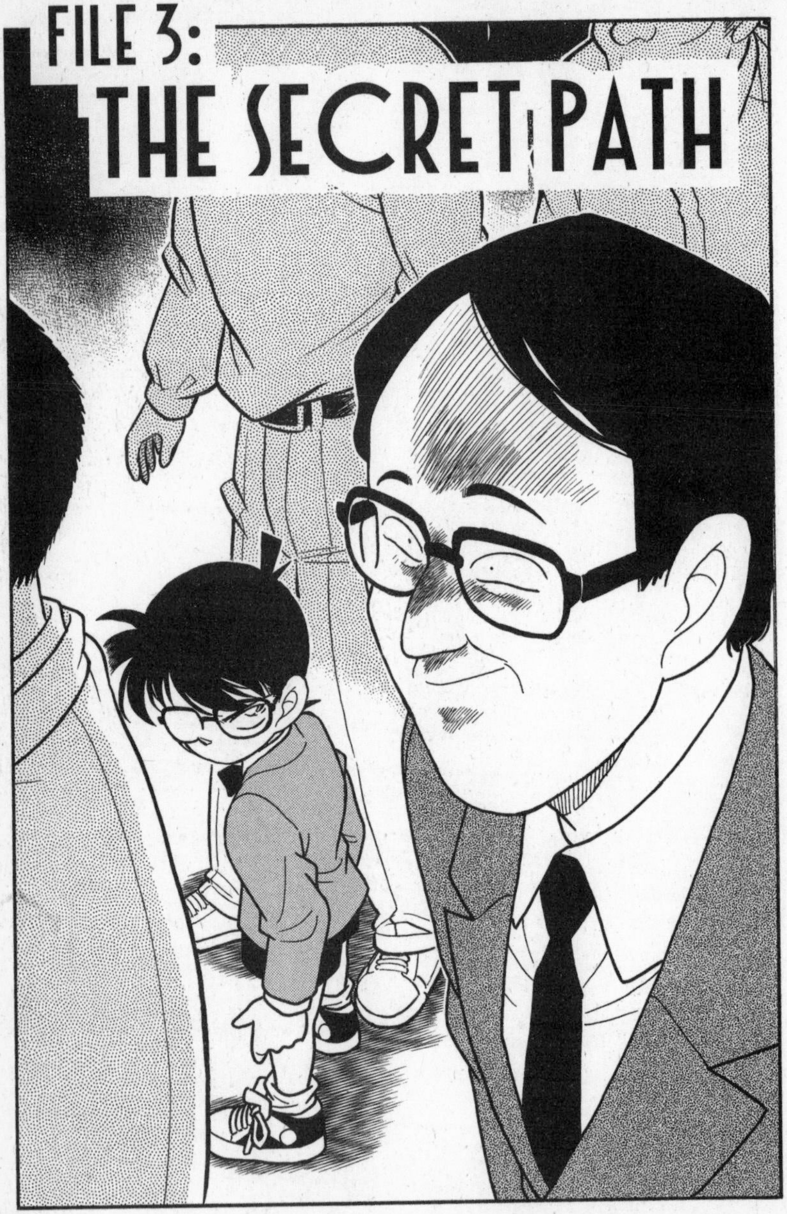

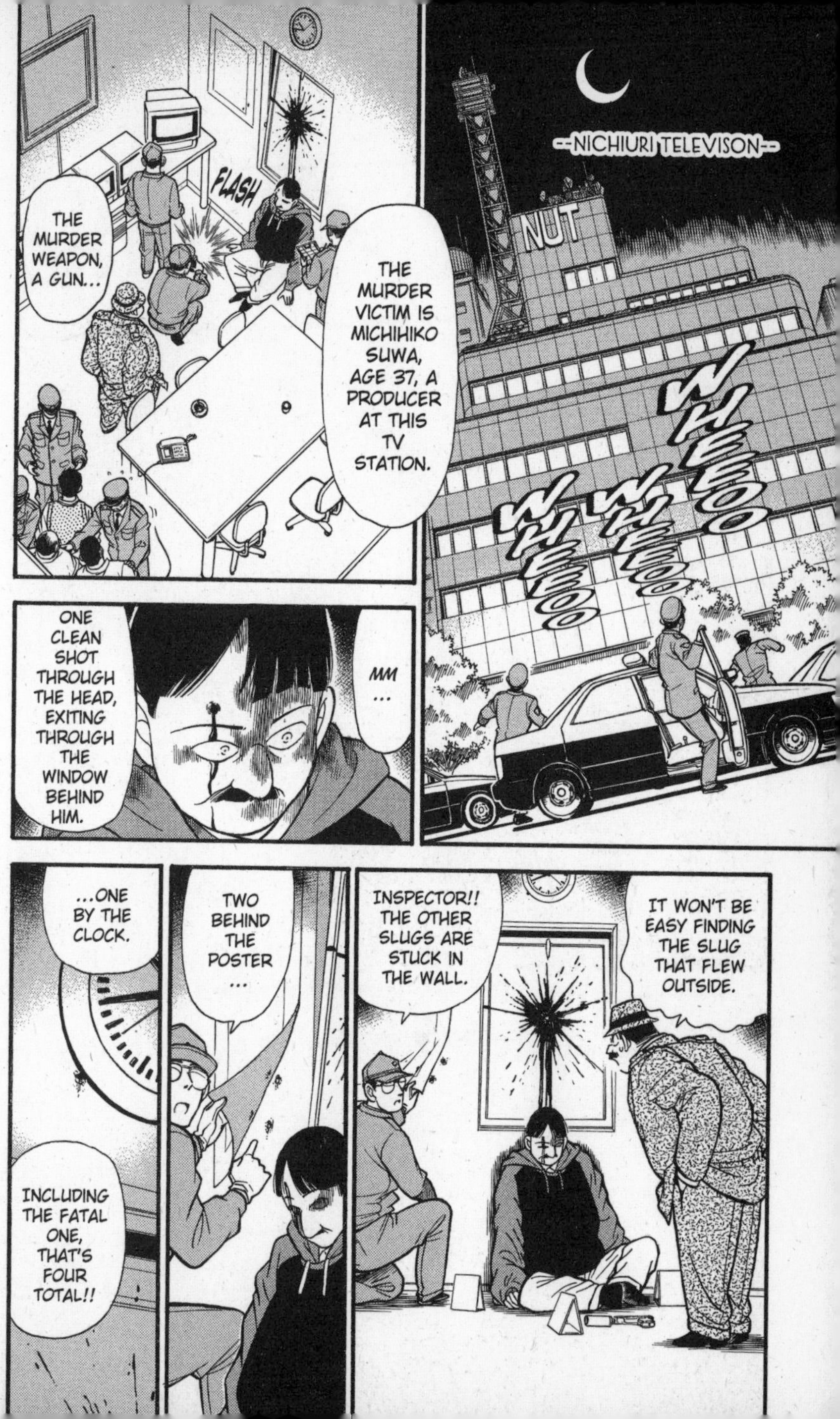
--NICHIURI TELEVISON--
NUT
WHEEOO
WHEEOO
WHEEOO
THE MURDER VICTIM IS MICHIHIKO SUWA, AGE 37, A PRODUCER AT THIS TV STATION.
FLASH
THE MURDER WEAPON, A GUN...
MM ...
ONE CLEAN SHOT THROUGH THE HEAD, EXITING THROUGH THE WINDOW BEHIND HIM.
IT WON'T BE EASY FINDING THE SLUG THAT FLEW OUTSIDE.
INSPECTOR!! THE OTHER SLUGS ARE STUCK IN THE WALL.
TWO BEHIND THE POSTER ...
...ONE BY THE CLOCK.
INCLUDING THE FATAL ONE, THAT'S FOUR TOTAL!!

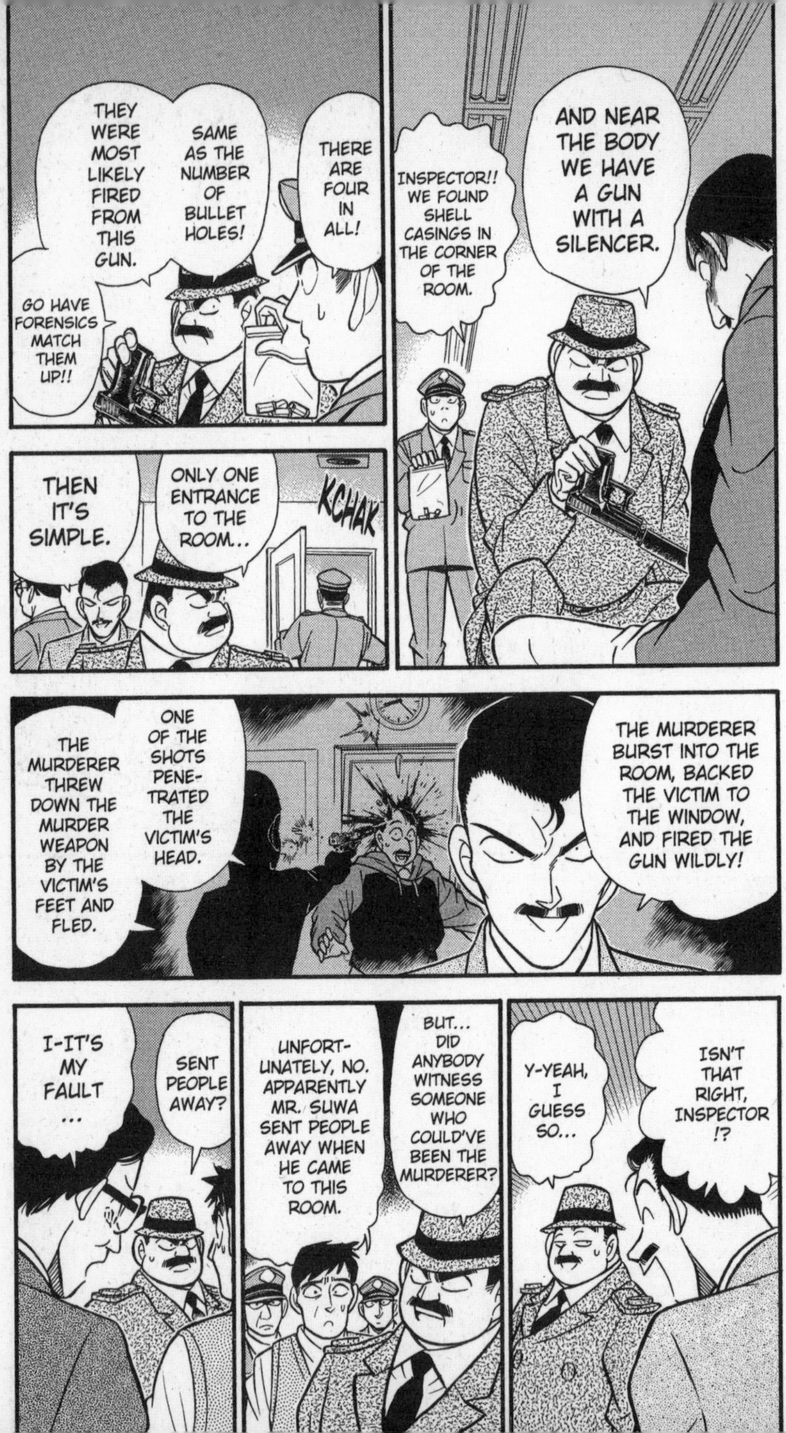
AND NEAR THE BODY WE HAVE A GUN WITH A SILENCER.
INSPECTOR!! WE FOUND SHELL CASINGS IN THE CORNER OF THE ROOM.
THERE ARE FOUR IN ALL!
SAME AS THE NUMBER OF BULLET HOLES!
THEY WERE MOST LIKELY FIRED FROM THIS GUN.
GO HAVE FORENSICS MATCH THEM UP!!
KCHAK
ONLY ONE ENTRANCE TO THE ROOM...
THEN IT'S SIMPLE.
THE MURDERER BURST INTO THE ROOM, BACKED THE VICTIM TO THE WINDOW, AND FIRED THE GUN WILDLY!
ONE OF THE SHOTS PENE-TRATED THE VICTIM'S HEAD.
THE MURDERER THREW DOWN THE MURDER WEAPON BY THE VICTIM'S FEET AND FLED.
ISN'T THAT RIGHT, INSPECTOR!?
Y-YEAH, I GUESS SO...
BUT... DID ANYBODY WITNESS SOMEONE WHO COULD'VE BEEN THE MURDERER?
UNFORT-UNATELY, NO. APPARENTLY MR. SUWA SENT PEOPLE AWAY WHEN HE CAME TO THIS ROOM.
SENT PEOPLE AWAY?
I-IT'S MY FAULT ...

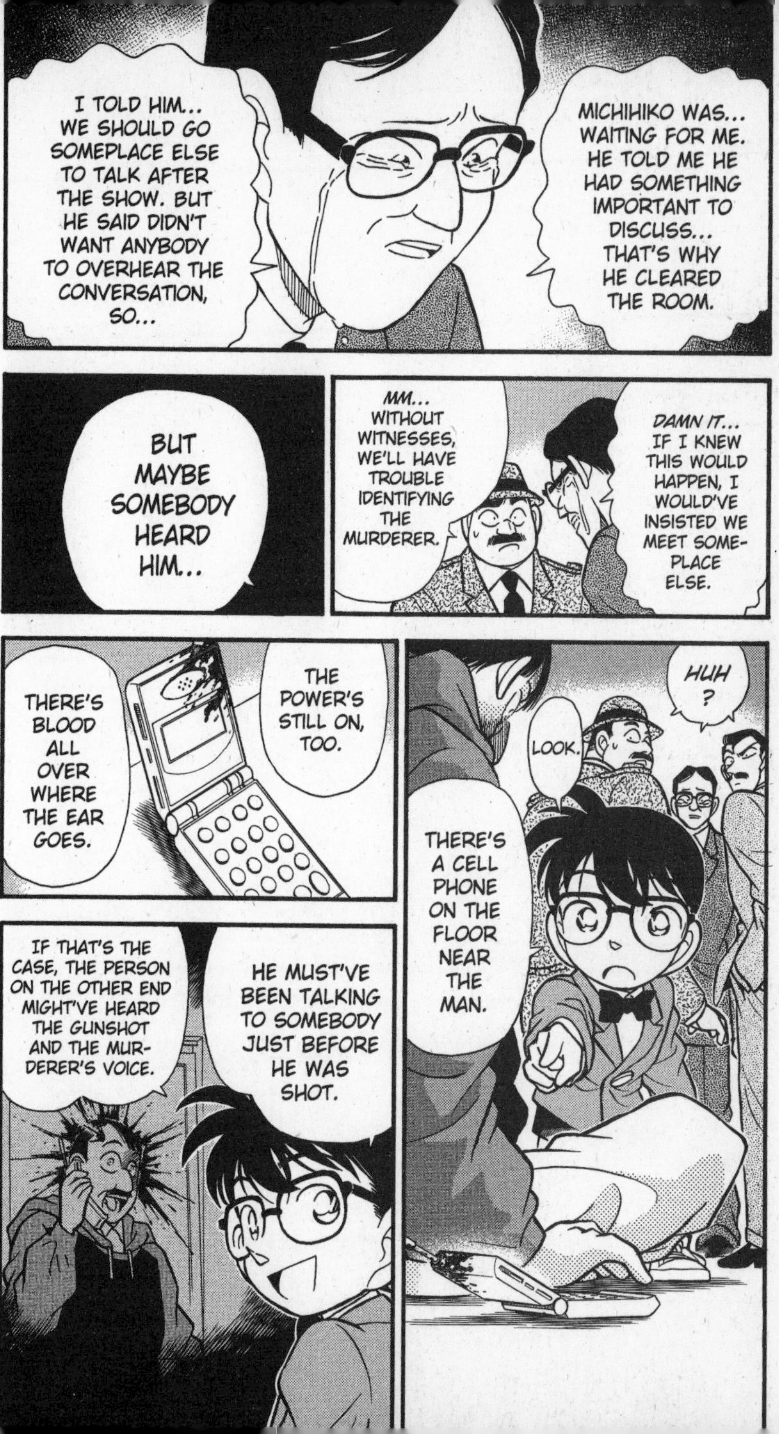
MICHIHIKO WAS... WAITING FOR ME. HE TOLD ME HE HAD SOMETHING IMPORTANT TO DISCUSS... THAT'S WHY HE CLEARED THE ROOM.
I TOLD HIM... WE SHOULD GO SOMEPLACE ELSE TO TALK AFTER THE SHOW. BUT HE SAID DIDN'T WANT ANYBODY TO OVERHEAR THE CONVERSATION, SO...
DAMN IT... IF I KNEW THIS WOULD HAPPEN, I WOULD'VE INSISTED WE MEET SOME-PLACE ELSE.
MM... WITHOUT WITNESSES, WE'LL HAVE TROUBLE IDENTIFYING THE MURDERER.
BUT MAYBE SOMEBODY HEARD HIM...
HUH?
LOOK.
THERE'S A CELL PHONE ON THE FLOOR NEAR THE MAN.
THE POWER'S STILL ON, TOO.
THERE'S BLOOD ALL OVER WHERE THE EAR GOES.
HE MUST'VE BEEN TALKING TO SOMEBODY JUST BEFORE HE WAS SHOT.
IF THAT'S THE CASE, THE PERSON ON THE OTHER END MIGHT'VE HEARD THE GUNSHOT AND THE MUR-DERER'S VOICE.

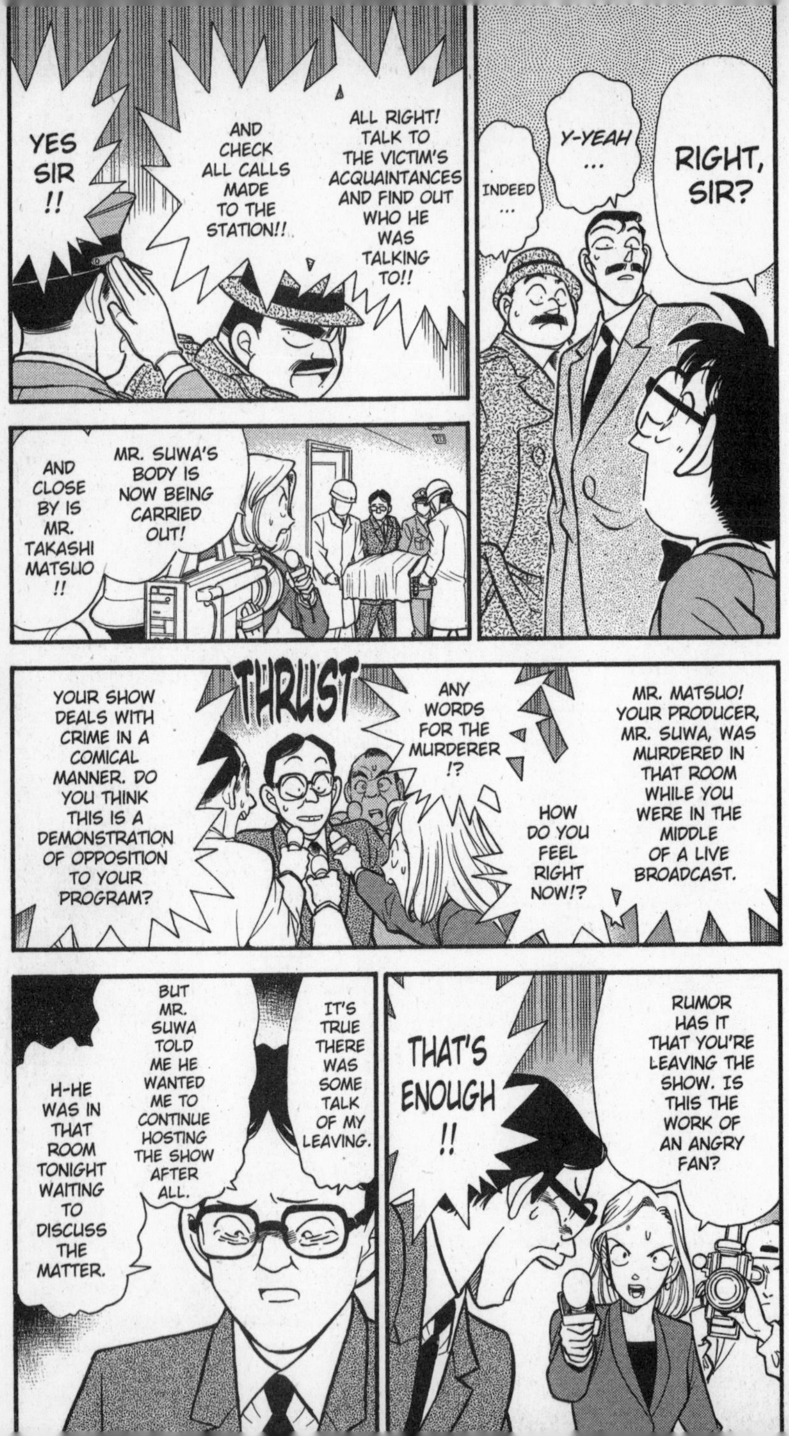
RIGHT, SIR?
Y-YEAH ...
INDEED ...
ALL RIGHT! TALK TO THE VICTIM'S ACQUAINTANCES AND FIND OUT WHO HE WAS TALKING TO!!
AND CHECK ALL CALLS MADE TO THE STATION!!
YES SIR !!
MR. SUWA'S BODY IS NOW BEING CARRIED OUT!
AND CLOSE BY IS MR. TAKASHI MATSUO !!
MR. MATSUO! YOUR PRODUCER, MR. SUWA, WAS MURDERED IN THAT ROOM WHILE YOU WERE IN THE MIDDLE OF A LIVE BROADCAST.
HOW DO YOU FEEL RIGHT NOW!?
ANY WORDS FOR THE MURDERER !?
THRUST
YOUR SHOW DEALS WITH CRIME IN A COMICAL MANNER. DO YOU THINK THIS IS A DEMONSTRATION OF OPPOSITION TO YOUR PROGRAM?
RUMOR HAS IT THAT YOU'RE LEAVING THE SHOW. IS THIS THE WORK OF AN ANGRY FAN?
THAT'S ENOUGH !!
IT'S TRUE THERE WAS SOME TALK OF MY LEAVING.
BUT MR. SUWA TOLD ME HE WANTED ME TO CONTINUE HOSTING THE SHOW AFTER ALL.
H-HE WAS IN THAT ROOM TONIGHT WAITING TO DISCUSS THE MATTER.

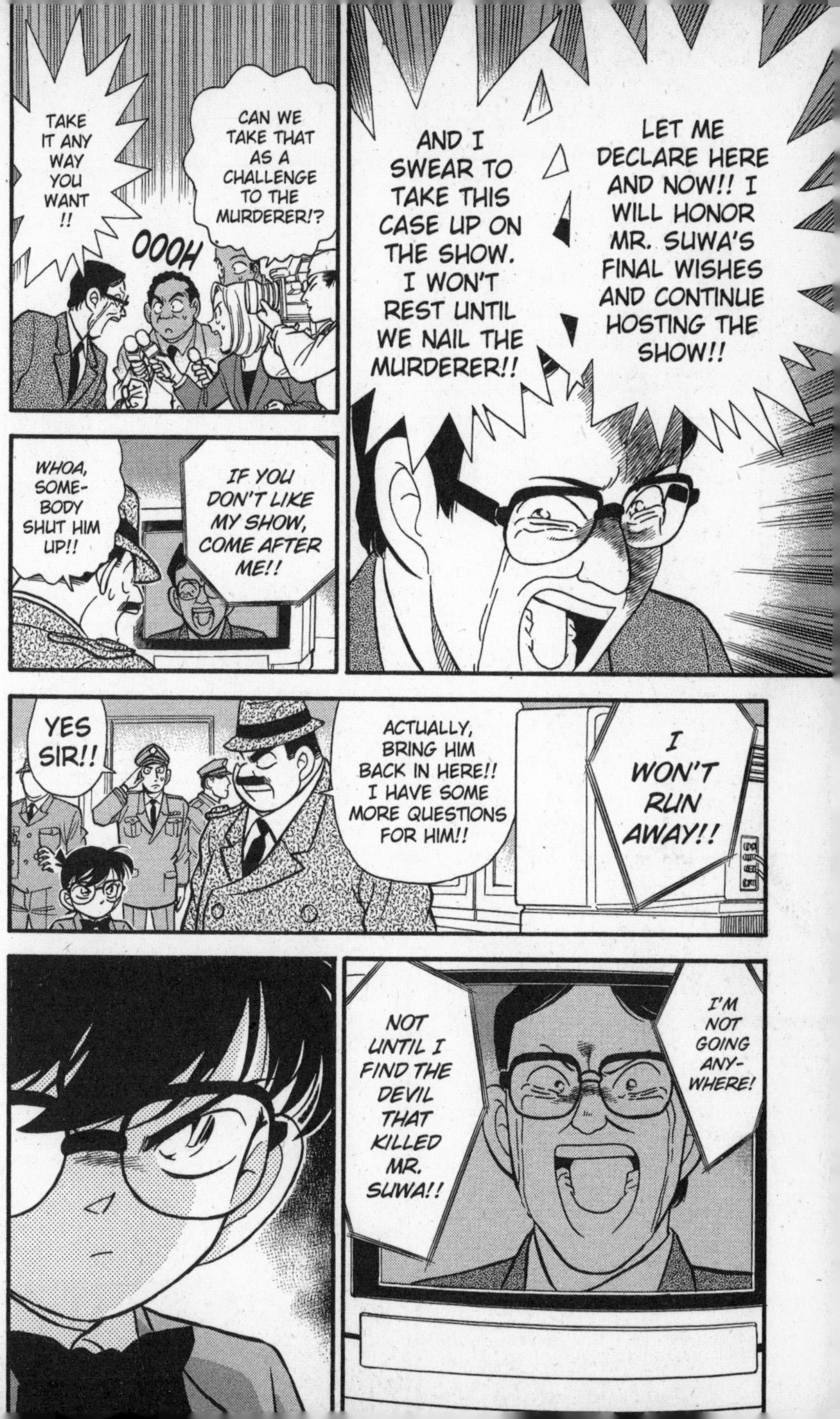
LET ME DECLARE HERE AND NOW!! I WILL HONOR MR. SUWA'S FINAL WISHES AND CONTINUE HOSTING THE SHOW!!
AND I SWEAR TO TAKE THIS CASE UP ON THE SHOW. I WON'T REST UNTIL WE NAIL THE MURDERER!!
CAN WE TAKE THAT AS A CHALLENGE TO THE MURDERER!?
TAKE IT ANY WAY YOU WANT !!
OOOH
IF YOU DON'T LIKE MY SHOW, COME AFTER ME!!
WHOA, SOME-BODY SHUT HIM UP!!
I WON'T RUN AWAY!!
ACTUALLY, BRING HIM BACK IN HERE!! I HAVE SOME MORE QUESTIONS FOR HIM!!
YES SIR!!
I'M NOT GOING ANY-WHERE!
NOT UNTIL I FIND THE DEVIL THAT KILLED MR. SUWA!!

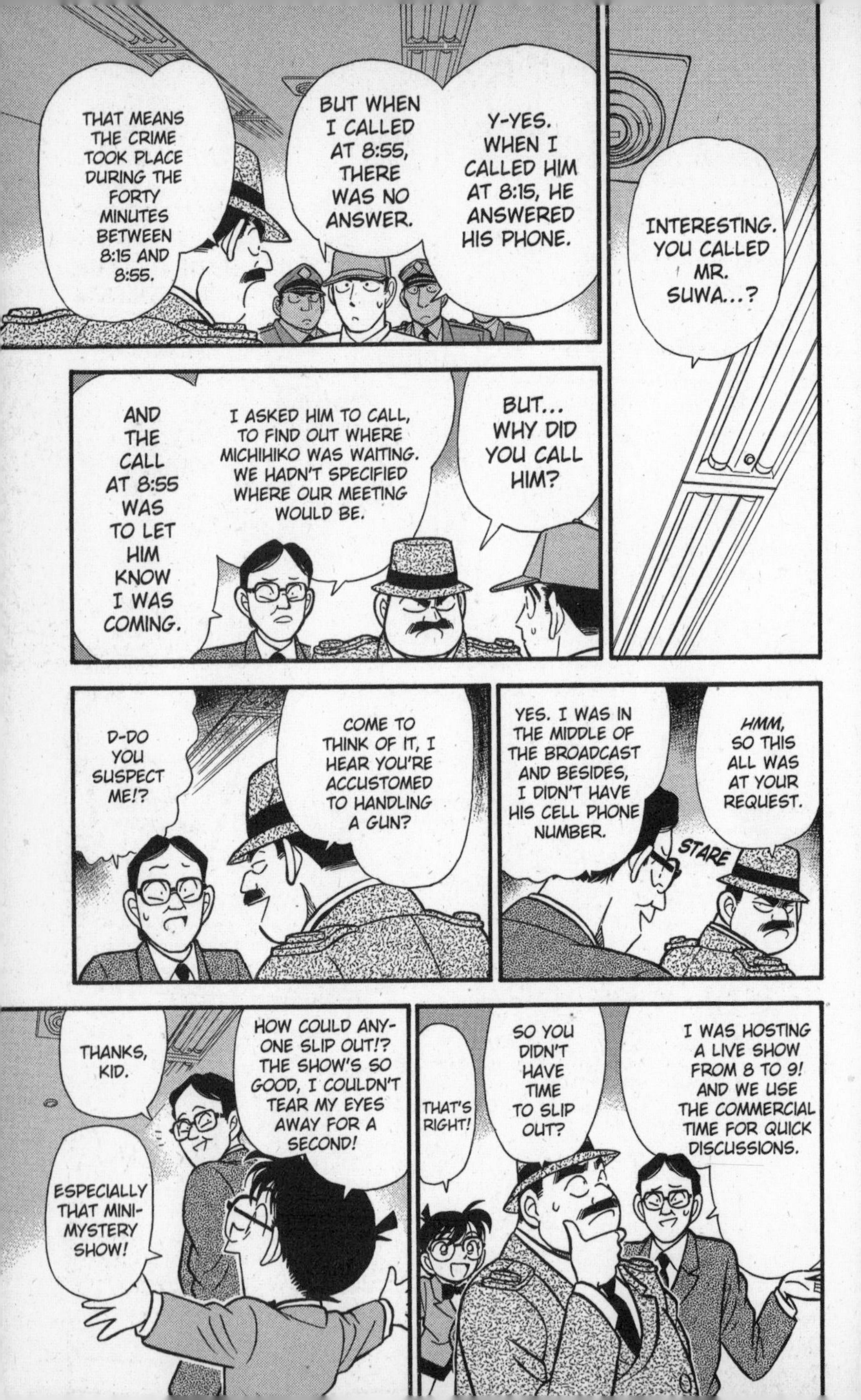
INTERESTING. YOU CALLED MR. SUWA...?
Y-YES. WHEN I CALLED HIM AT 8:15, HE ANSWERED HIS PHONE.
BUT WHEN I CALLED AT 8:55, THERE WAS NO ANSWER.
THAT MEANS THE CRIME TOOK PLACE DURING THE FORTY MINUTES BETWEEN 8:15 AND 8:55.
BUT... WHY DID YOU CALL HIM?
I ASKED HIM TO CALL, TO FIND OUT WHERE MICHIHIKO WAS WAITING. WE HADN'T SPECIFIED WHERE OUR MEETING WOULD BE.
AND THE CALL AT 8:55 WAS TO LET HIM KNOW I WAS COMING.
HMM, SO THIS ALL WAS AT YOUR REQUEST.
STARE
YES. I WAS IN THE MIDDLE OF THE BROADCAST AND BESIDES, I DIDN'T HAVE HIS CELL PHONE NUMBER.
COME TO THINK OF IT, I HEAR YOU'RE ACCUSTOMED TO HANDLING A GUN?
D-DO YOU SUSPECT ME!?
I WAS HOSTING A LIVE SHOW FROM 8 TO 9! AND WE USE THE COMMERCIAL TIME FOR QUICK DISCUSSIONS.
SO YOU DIDN'T HAVE TIME TO SLIP OUT?
THAT'S RIGHT!
HOW COULD ANY-ONE SLIP OUT!? THE SHOW'S SO GOOD, I COULDN'T TEAR MY EYES AWAY FOR A SECOND!
THANKS, KID.
ESPECIALLY THAT MINI-MYSTERY SHOW!

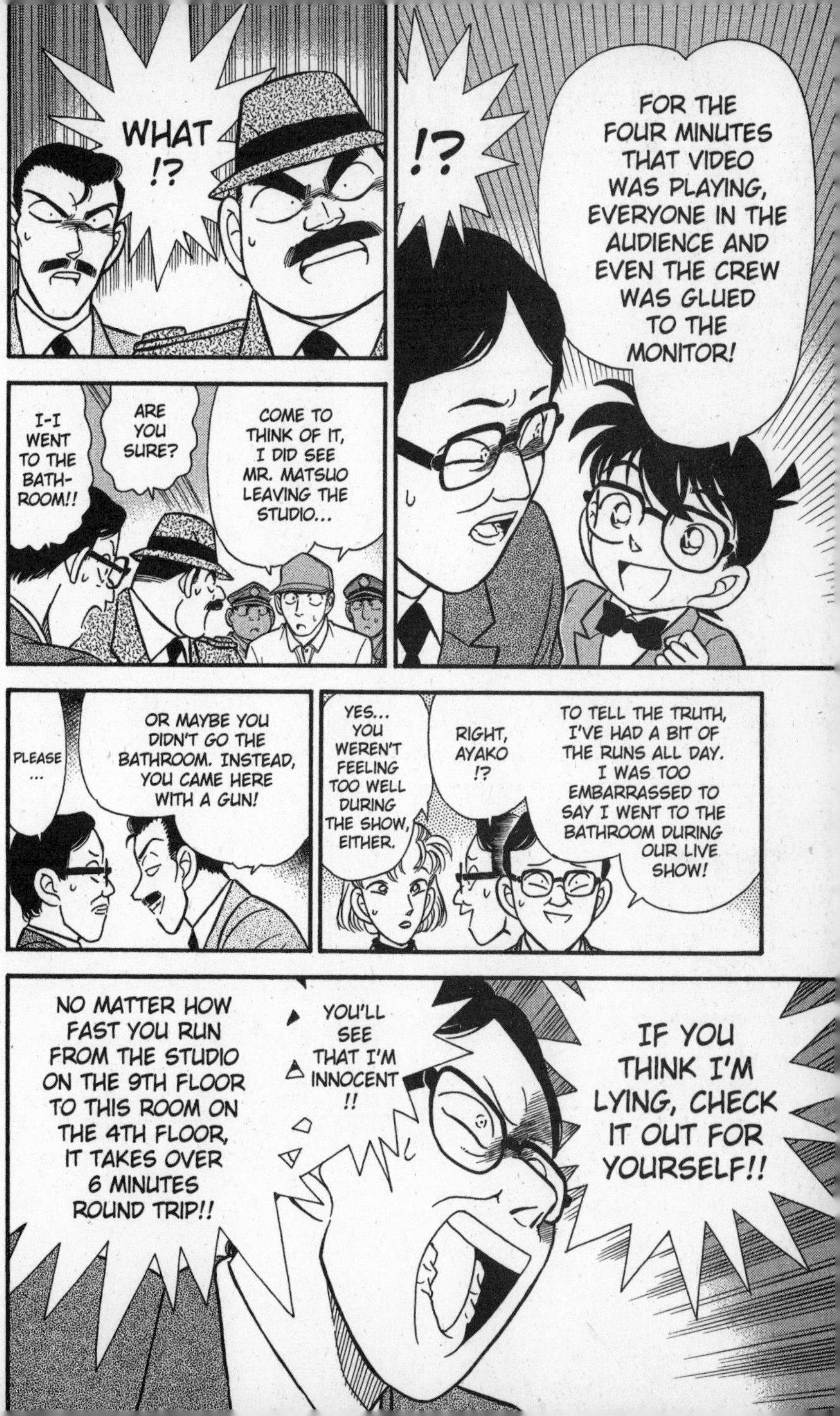
FOR THE FOUR MINUTES THAT VIDEO WAS PLAYING, EVERYONE IN THE AUDIENCE AND EVEN THE CREW WAS GLUED TO THE MONITOR!
!?
WHAT !?
COME TO THINK OF IT, I DID SEE MR. MATSUO LEAVING THE STUDIO...
ARE YOU SURE?
I-I WENT TO THE BATH-ROOM!!
TO TELL THE TRUTH, I'VE HAD A BIT OF THE RUNS ALL DAY. I WAS TOO EMBARRASSED TO SAY I WENT TO THE BATHROOM DURING OUR LIVE SHOW!
RIGHT, AYAKO !?
YES... YOU WEREN'T FEELING TOO WELL DURING THE SHOW, EITHER.
OR MAYBE YOU DIDN'T GO THE BATHROOM. INSTEAD, YOU CAME HERE WITH A GUN!
PLEASE ...
IF YOU THINK I'M LYING, CHECK IT OUT FOR YOURSELF!!
YOU'LL SEE THAT I'M INNOCENT !!
NO MATTER HOW FAST YOU RUN FROM THE STUDIO ON THE 9TH FLOOR TO THIS ROOM ON THE 4TH FLOOR, IT TAKES OVER 6 MINUTES ROUND TRIP!!

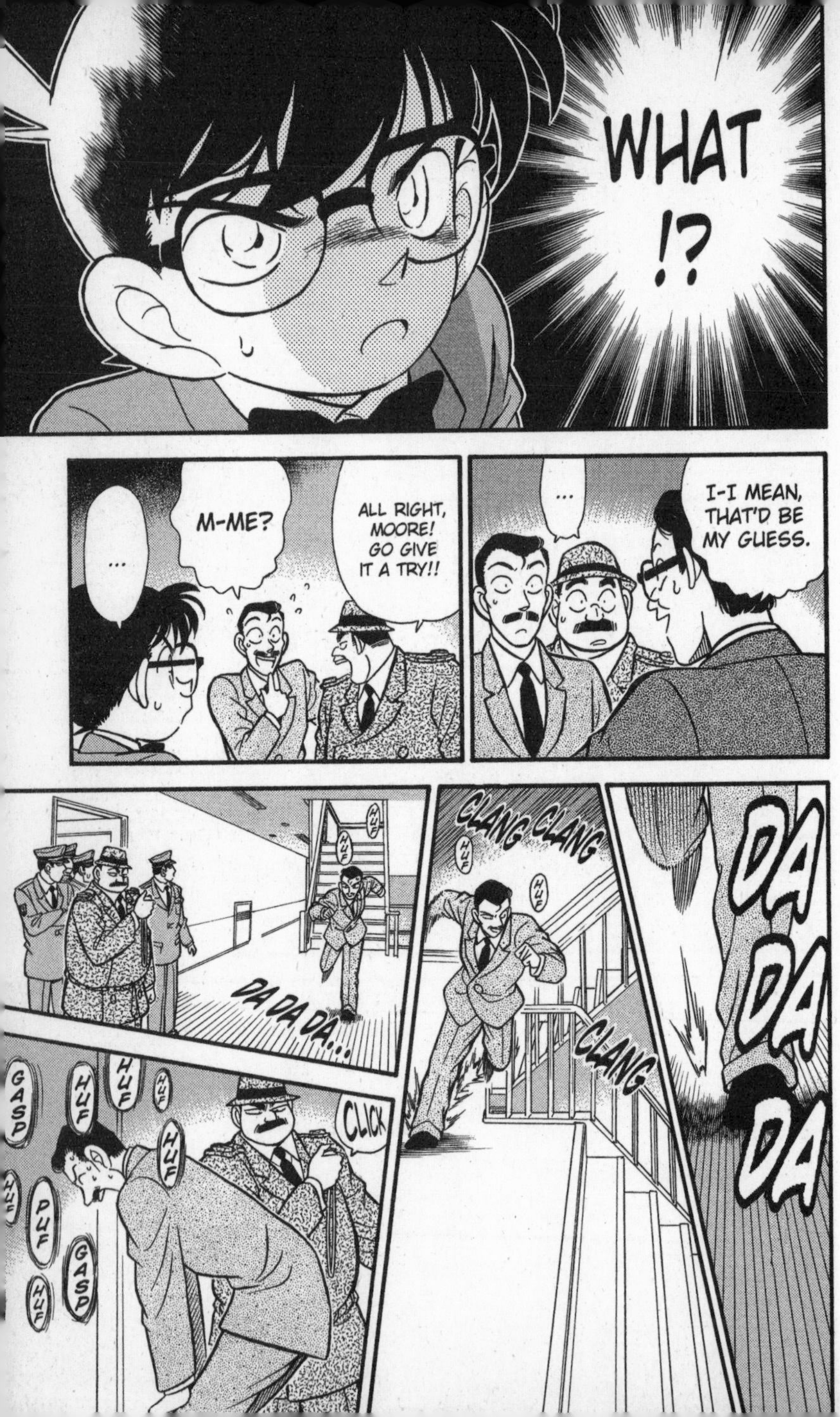
WHAT !?
I-I MEAN, THAT'D BE MY GUESS.
...
ALL RIGHT, MOORE! GO GIVE IT A TRY!!
M-ME?
...
DA DA DA DA
CLANG CLANG
HUF
HUF
CLANG
HUF
HUF
DA DA DA...
CLICK
HUF
HUF
HUF
GASP
HUF
PUF
GASP
HUF
HUF

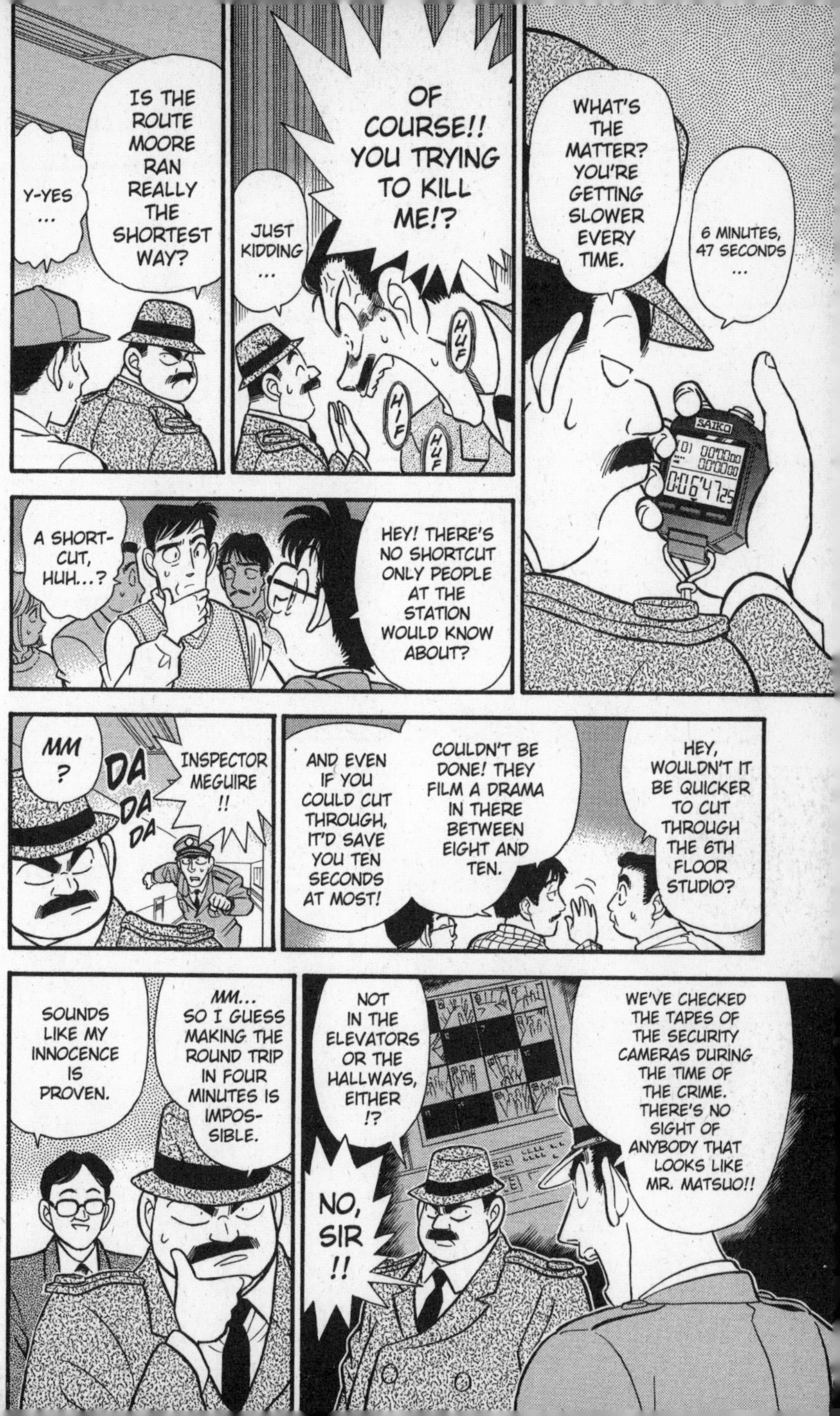
6 MINUTES, 47 SECONDS ...
WHAT'S THE MATTER? YOU'RE GETTING SLOWER EVERY TIME.
SAIKO
OF COURSE!! YOU TRYING TO KILL ME!?
JUST KIDDING ...
HUF
HIF
HUF
IS THE ROUTE MOORE RAN REALLY THE SHORTEST WAY?
Y-YES ...
HEY! THERE'S NO SHORTCUT ONLY PEOPLE AT THE STATION WOULD KNOW ABOUT?
A SHORT-CUT, HUH...?
HEY, WOULDN'T IT BE QUICKER TO CUT THROUGH THE 6TH FLOOR STUDIO?
COULDN'T BE DONE! THEY FILM A DRAMA IN THERE BETWEEN EIGHT AND TEN.
AND EVEN IF YOU COULD CUT THROUGH, IT'D SAVE YOU TEN SECONDS AT MOST!
INSPECTOR MEGUIRE !!
DA DA DA
MM ?
WE'VE CHECKED THE TAPES OF THE SECURITY CAMERAS DURING THE TIME OF THE CRIME. THERE'S NO SIGHT OF ANYBODY THAT LOOKS LIKE MR. MATSUO!!
NOT IN THE ELEVATORS OR THE HALLWAYS, EITHER !?
NO, SIR !!
MM... SO I GUESS MAKING THE ROUND TRIP IN FOUR MINUTES IS IMPOSSIBLE.
SOUNDS LIKE MY INNOCENCE IS PROVEN.

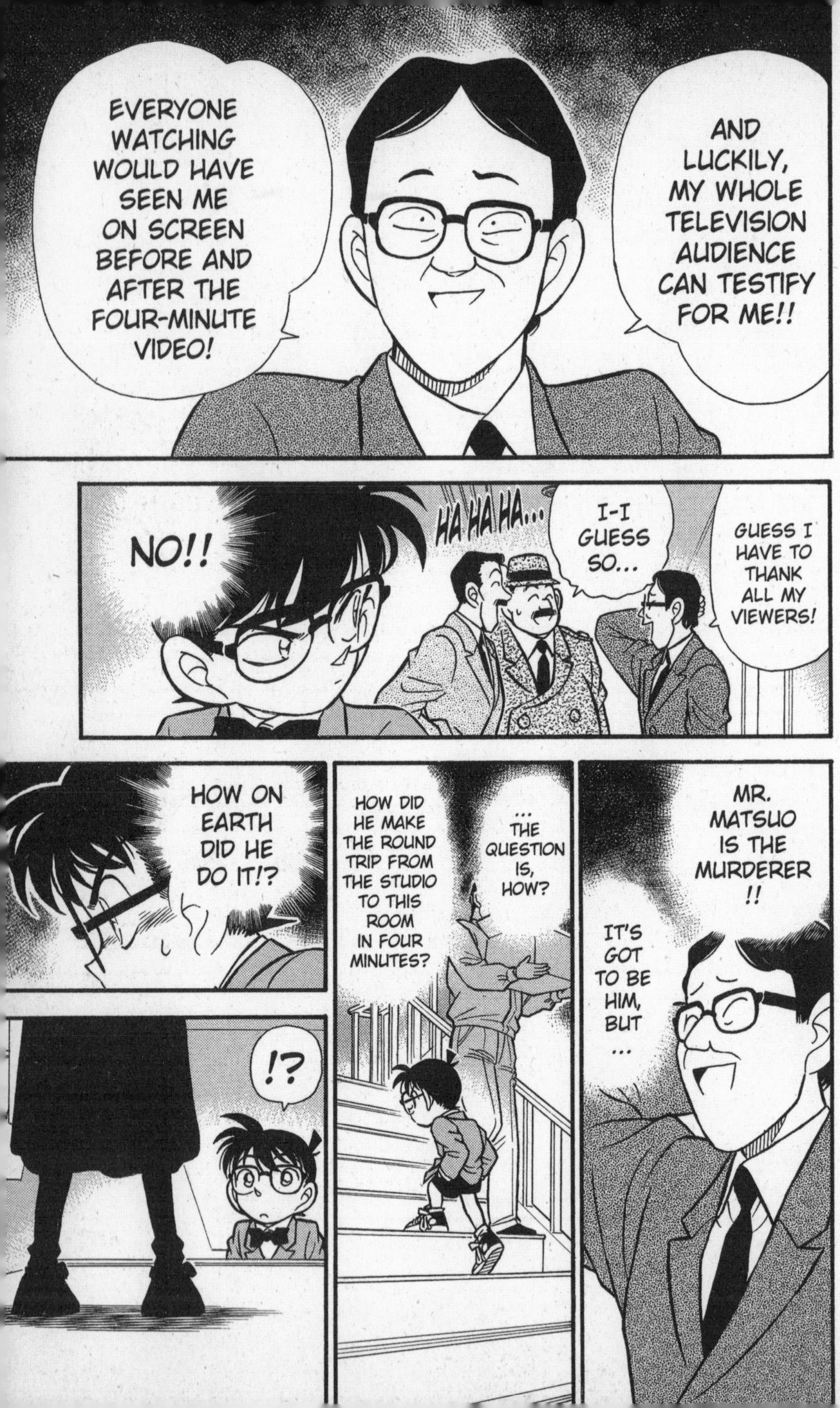
EVERYONE WATCHING WOULD HAVE SEEN ME ON SCREEN BEFORE AND AFTER THE FOUR-MINUTE VIDEO!
AND LUCKILY, MY WHOLE TELEVISION AUDIENCE CAN TESTIFY FOR ME!!
GUESS I HAVE TO THANK ALL MY VIEWERS!
I-I GUESS SO...
HA HA HA...
NO!!
MR. MATSUO IS THE MURDERER !!
IT'S GOT TO BE HIM, BUT ...
... THE QUESTION IS, HOW?
HOW DID HE MAKE THE ROUND TRIP FROM THE STUDIO TO THIS ROOM IN FOUR MINUTES?
HOW ON EARTH DID HE DO IT!?
!?

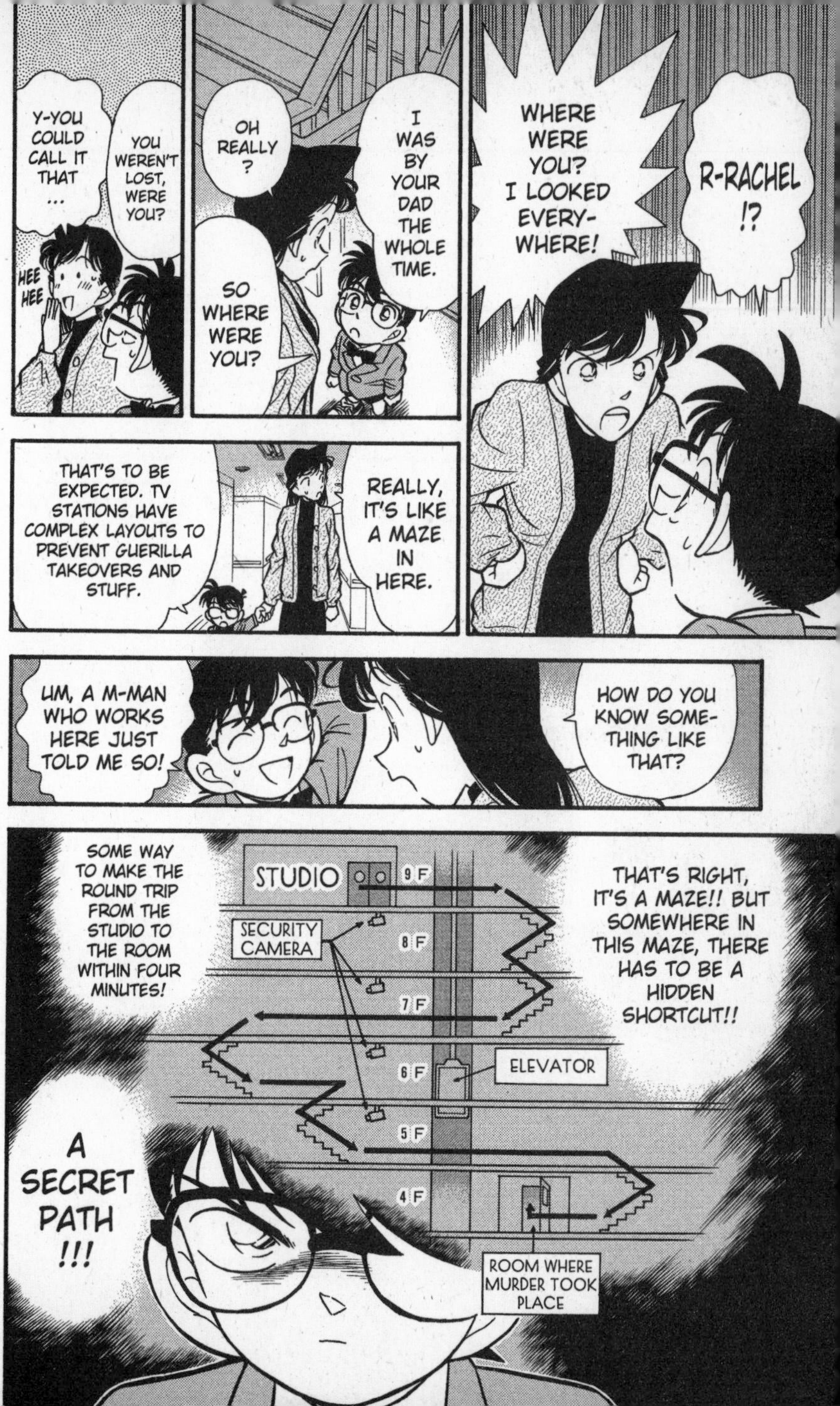
R-RACHEL !?
WHERE WERE YOU? I LOOKED EVERY-WHERE!
I WAS BY YOUR DAD THE WHOLE TIME.
OH REALLY?
SO WHERE WERE YOU?
YOU WEREN'T LOST, WERE YOU?
Y-YOU COULD CALL IT THAT ...
HEE HEE
REALLY, IT'S LIKE A MAZE IN HERE.
THAT'S TO BE EXPECTED. TV STATIONS HAVE COMPLEX LAYOUTS TO PREVENT GUERILLA TAKEOVERS AND STUFF.
HOW DO YOU KNOW SOME-THING LIKE THAT?
UM, A M-MAN WHO WORKS HERE JUST TOLD ME SO!
THAT'S RIGHT, IT'S A MAZE!! BUT SOMEWHERE IN THIS MAZE, THERE HAS TO BE A HIDDEN SHORTCUT!!
STUDIO
9 F
8 F
7 F
6 F
5 F
4 F
SECURITY CAMERA
ELEVATOR
ROOM WHERE MURDER TOOK PLACE
SOME WAY TO MAKE THE ROUND TRIP FROM THE STUDIO TO THE ROOM WITHIN FOUR MINUTES!
A SECRET PATH !!!

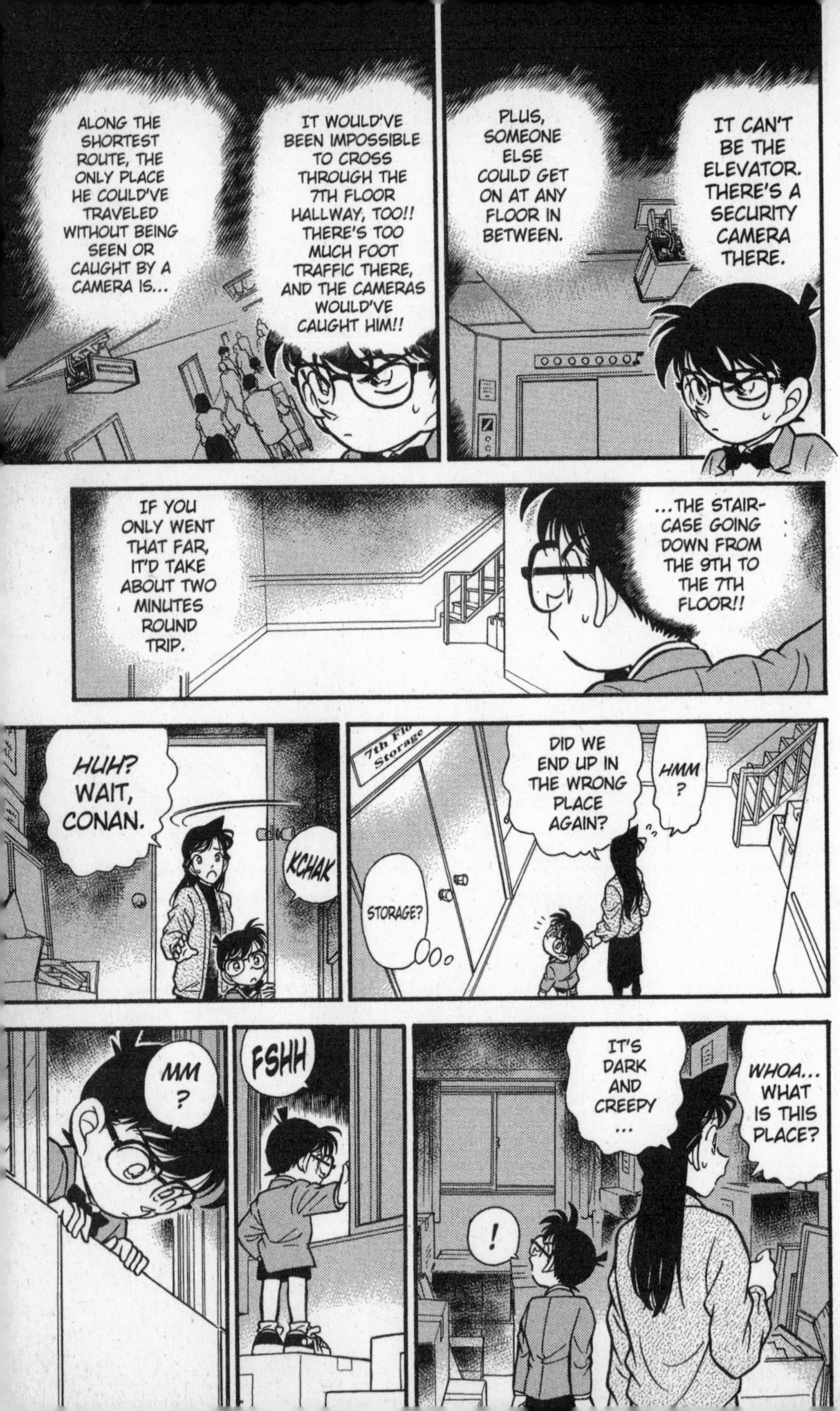
IT CAN'T BE THE ELEVATOR. THERE'S A SECURITY CAMERA THERE.
PLUS, SOMEONE ELSE COULD GET ON AT ANY FLOOR IN BETWEEN.
IT WOULD'VE BEEN IMPOSSIBLE TO CROSS THROUGH THE 7TH FLOOR HALLWAY, TOO!! THERE'S TOO MUCH FOOT TRAFFIC THERE, AND THE CAMERAS WOULD'VE CAUGHT HIM!!
ALONG THE SHORTEST ROUTE, THE ONLY PLACE HE COULD'VE TRAVELED WITHOUT BEING SEEN OR CAUGHT BY A CAMERA IS...
...THE STAIR-CASE GOING DOWN FROM THE 9TH TO THE 7TH FLOOR!!
IF YOU ONLY WENT THAT FAR, IT'D TAKE ABOUT TWO MINUTES ROUND TRIP.
HMM ?
DID WE END UP IN THE WRONG PLACE AGAIN?
STORAGE?
KCHAK
HUH? WAIT, CONAN.
WHOA... WHAT IS THIS PLACE?
IT'S DARK AND CREEPY ...
!
FSHH
MM ?

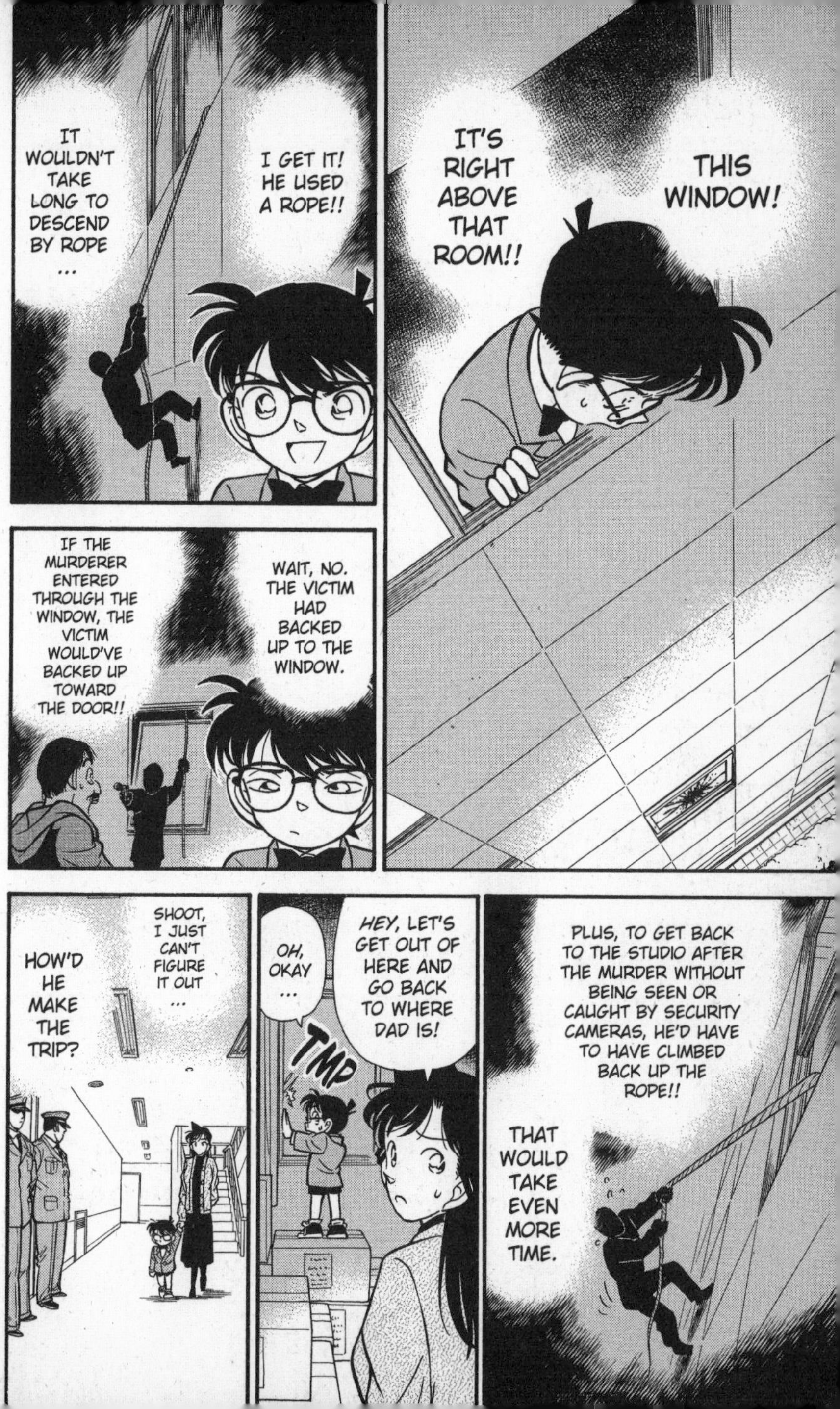
THIS WINDOW!
IT'S RIGHT ABOVE THAT ROOM!!
I GET IT! HE USED A ROPE!!
IT WOULDN'T TAKE LONG TO DESCEND BY ROPE ...
WAIT, NO. THE VICTIM HAD BACKED UP TO THE WINDOW.
IF THE MURDERER ENTERED THROUGH THE WINDOW, THE VICTIM WOULD'VE BACKED UP TOWARD THE DOOR!!
PLUS, TO GET BACK TO THE STUDIO AFTER THE MURDER WITHOUT BEING SEEN OR CAUGHT BY SECURITY CAMERAS, HE'D HAVE TO HAVE CLIMBED BACK UP THE ROPE!!
THAT WOULD TAKE EVEN MORE TIME.
HEY, LET'S GET OUT OF HERE AND GO BACK TO WHERE DAD IS!
TMP
OH, OKAY ...
SHOOT, I JUST CAN'T FIGURE IT OUT ...
HOW'D HE MAKE THE TRIP?

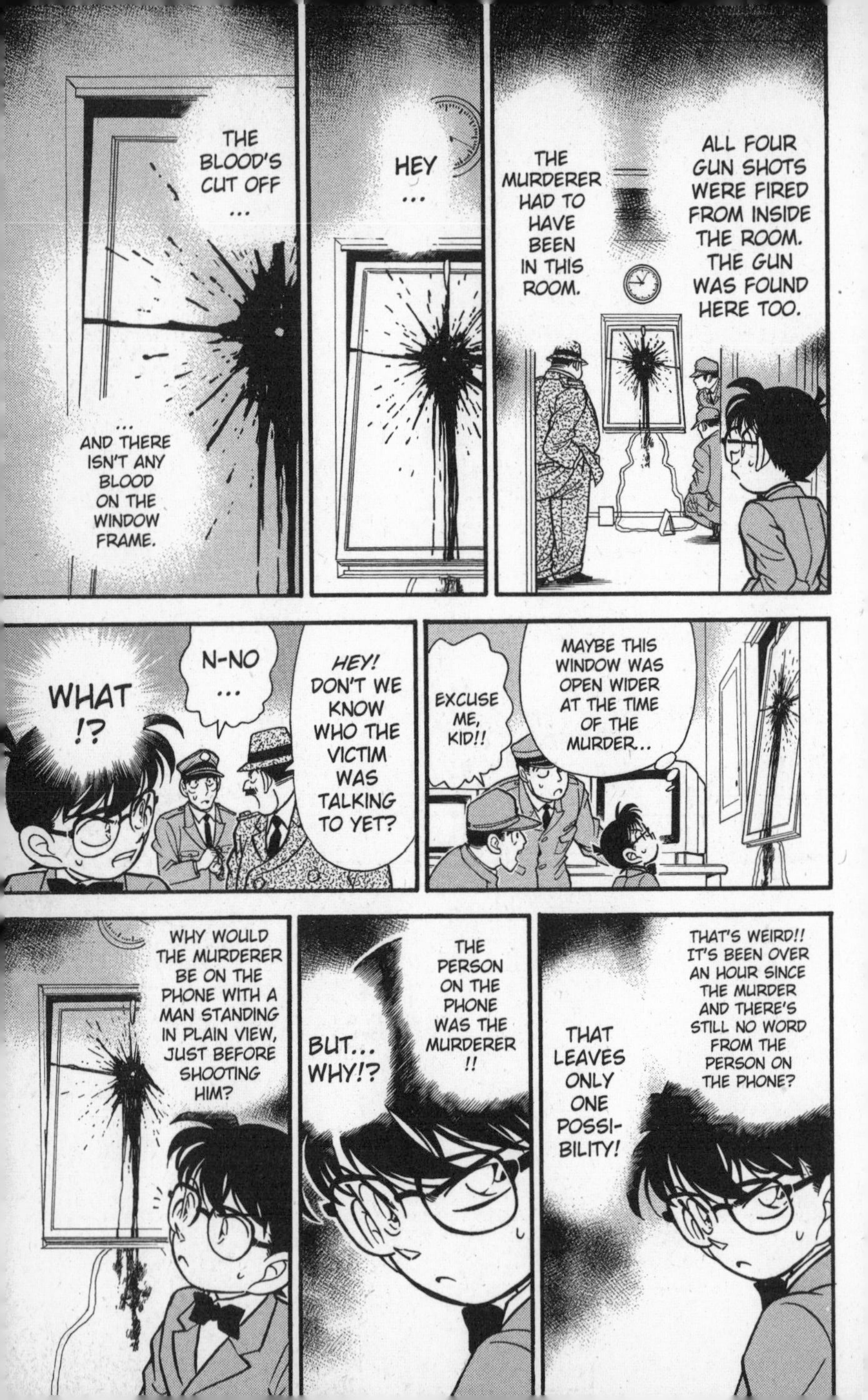
ALL FOUR GUN SHOTS WERE FIRED FROM INSIDE THE ROOM. THE GUN WAS FOUND HERE TOO.
THE MURDERER HAD TO HAVE BEEN IN THIS ROOM.
HEY ...
THE BLOOD'S CUT OFF ...
... AND THERE ISN'T ANY BLOOD ON THE WINDOW FRAME.
MAYBE THIS WINDOW WAS OPEN WIDER AT THE TIME OF THE MURDER...
EXCUSE ME, KID!!
HEY! DON'T WE KNOW WHO THE VICTIM WAS TALKING TO YET?
N-NO ...
WHAT !?
THAT'S WEIRD!! IT'S BEEN OVER AN HOUR SINCE THE MURDER AND THERE'S STILL NO WORD FROM THE PERSON ON THE PHONE?
THAT LEAVES ONLY ONE POSSIBILITY!
THE PERSON ON THE PHONE WAS THE MURDERER !!
BUT... WHY!?
WHY WOULD THE MURDERER BE ON THE PHONE WITH A MAN STANDING IN PLAIN VIEW, JUST BEFORE SHOOTING HIM?

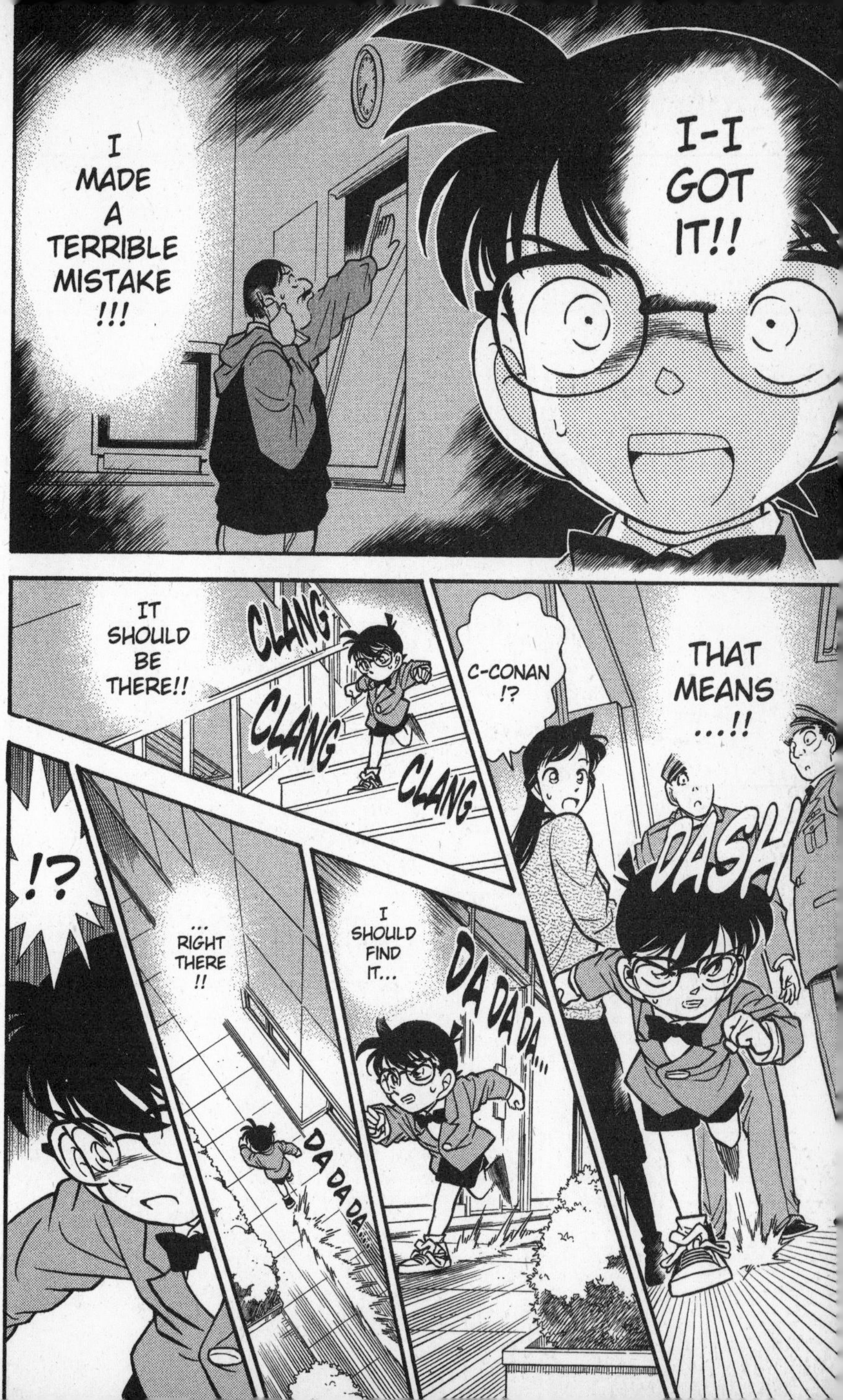
I-I GOT IT!!
I MADE A TERRIBLE MISTAKE!!!
THAT MEANS...!!
C-CONAN!?
DASH
IT SHOULD BE THERE!!
CLANG
CLANG
CLANG
I SHOULD FIND IT...
DA DA DA...
...RIGHT THERE!!
DA DA DA...
!?

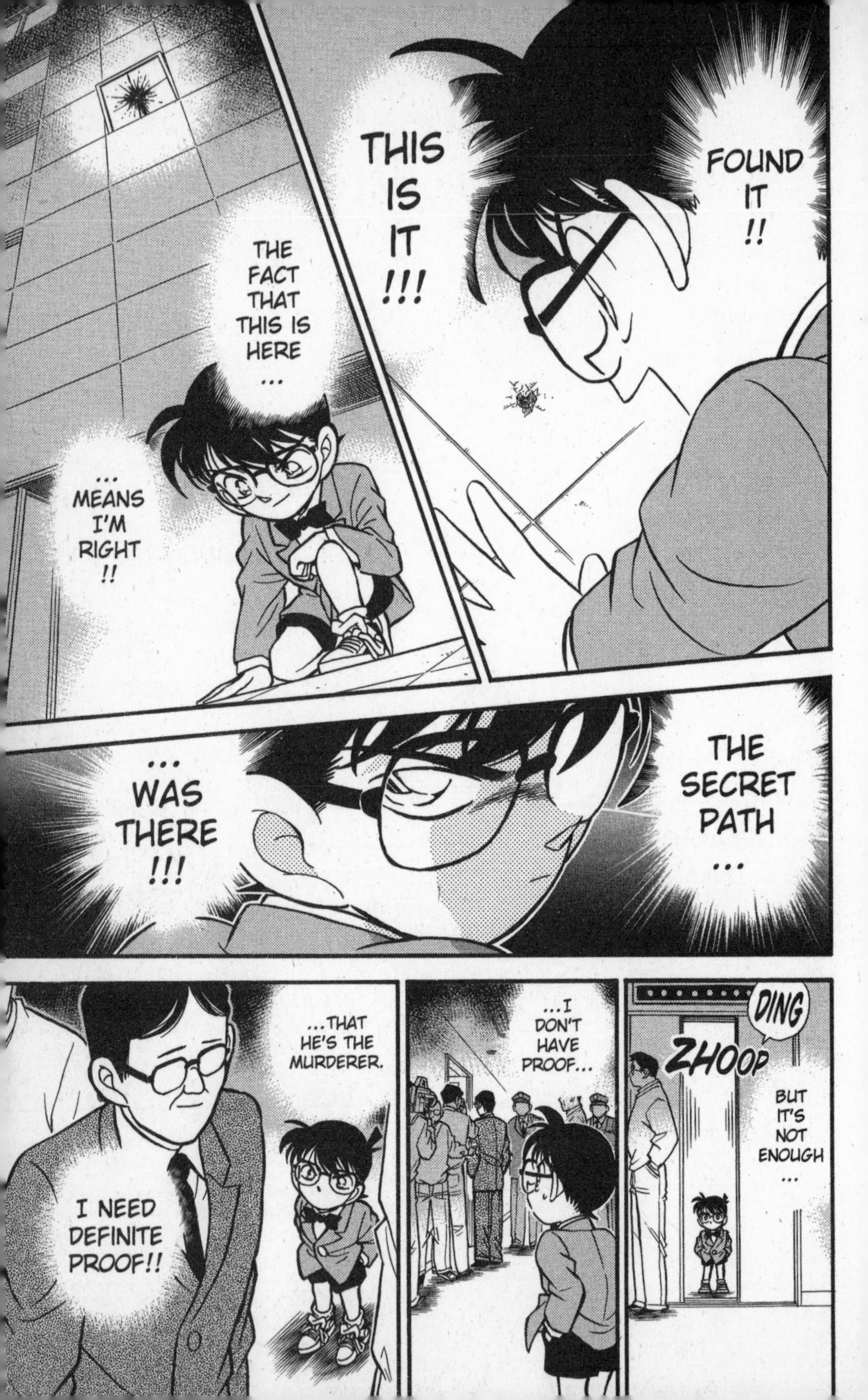
FOUND IT!!
THIS IS IT!!!
THE FACT THAT THIS IS HERE...
...MEANS I'M RIGHT!!
THE SECRET PATH...
...WAS THERE!!!
DING
ZHOOP
BUT IT'S NOT ENOUGH...
...I DON'T HAVE PROOF...
...THAT HE'S THE MURDERER.
I NEED DEFINITE PROOF!!

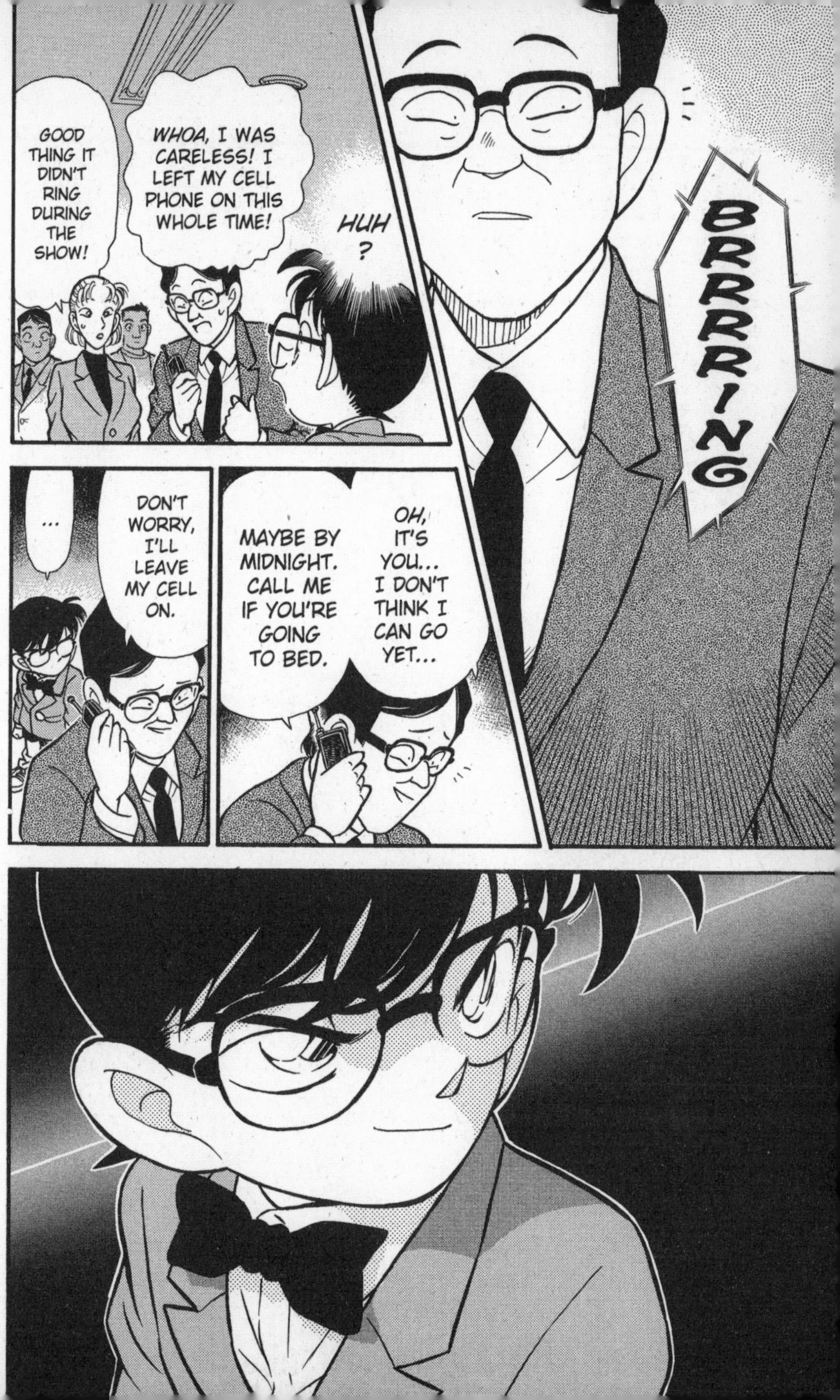
BRRRRING
HUH ?
WHOA, I WAS CARELESS! I LEFT MY CELL PHONE ON THIS WHOLE TIME!
GOOD THING IT DIDN'T RING DURING THE SHOW!
OH, IT'S YOU... I DON'T THINK I CAN GO YET...
MAYBE BY MIDNIGHT. CALL ME IF YOU'RE GOING TO BED.
DON'T WORRY, I'LL LEAVE MY CELL ON.
...

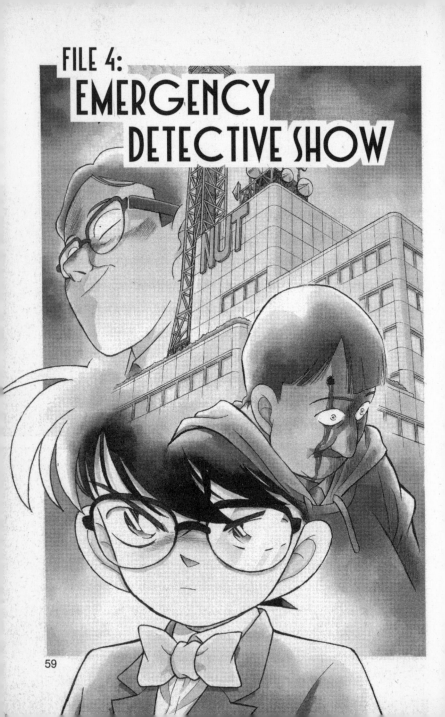

FILE 4: EMERGENCY DETECTIVE SHOW

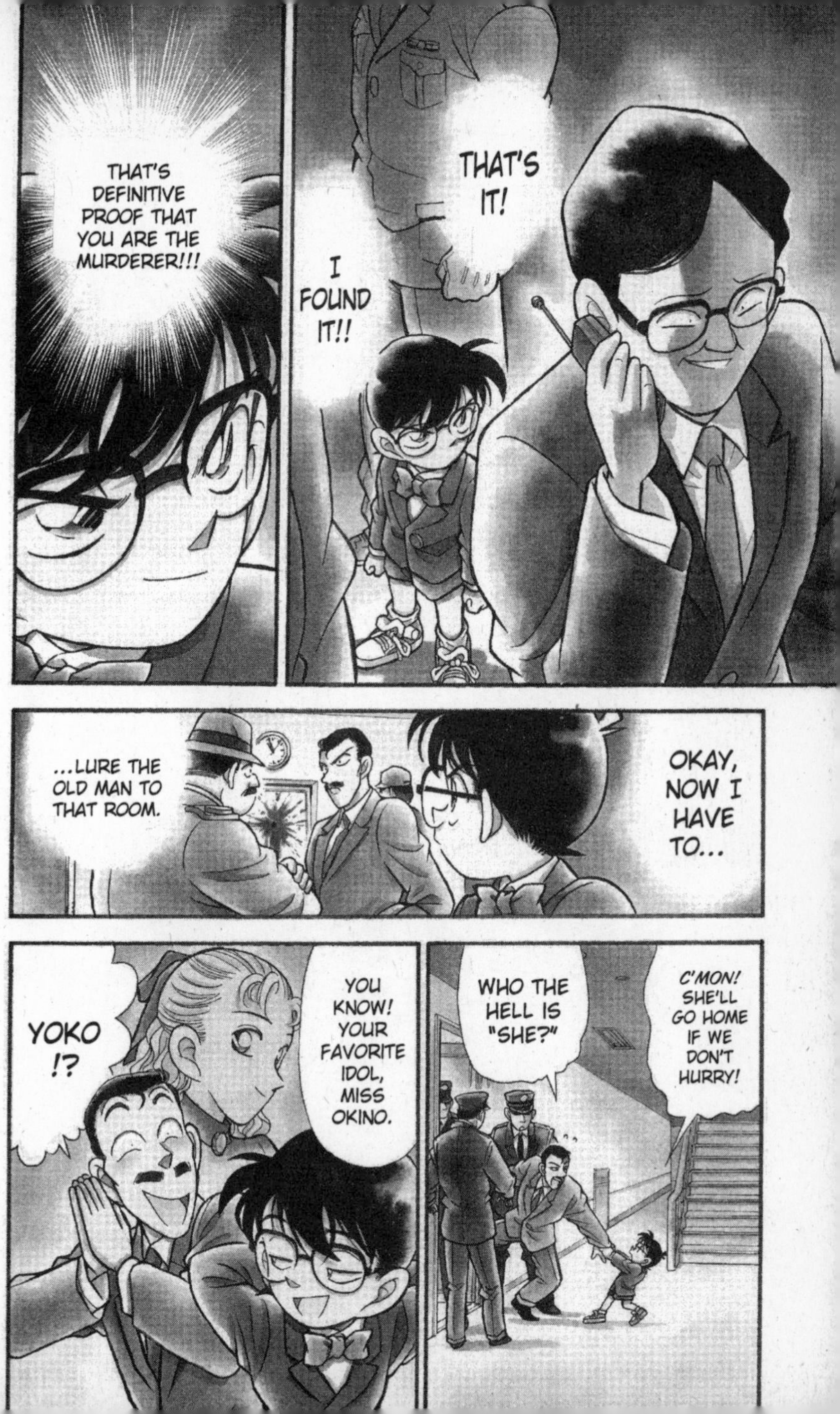
THAT'S IT!
I FOUND IT!!
THAT'S DEFINITIVE PROOF THAT YOU ARE THE MURDERER!!!
OKAY, NOW I HAVE TO...
...LURE THE OLD MAN TO THAT ROOM.
C'MON! SHE'LL GO HOME IF WE DON'T HURRY!
WHO THE HELL IS "SHE?"
YOU KNOW! YOUR FAVORITE IDOL, MISS OKINO.
YOKO !?

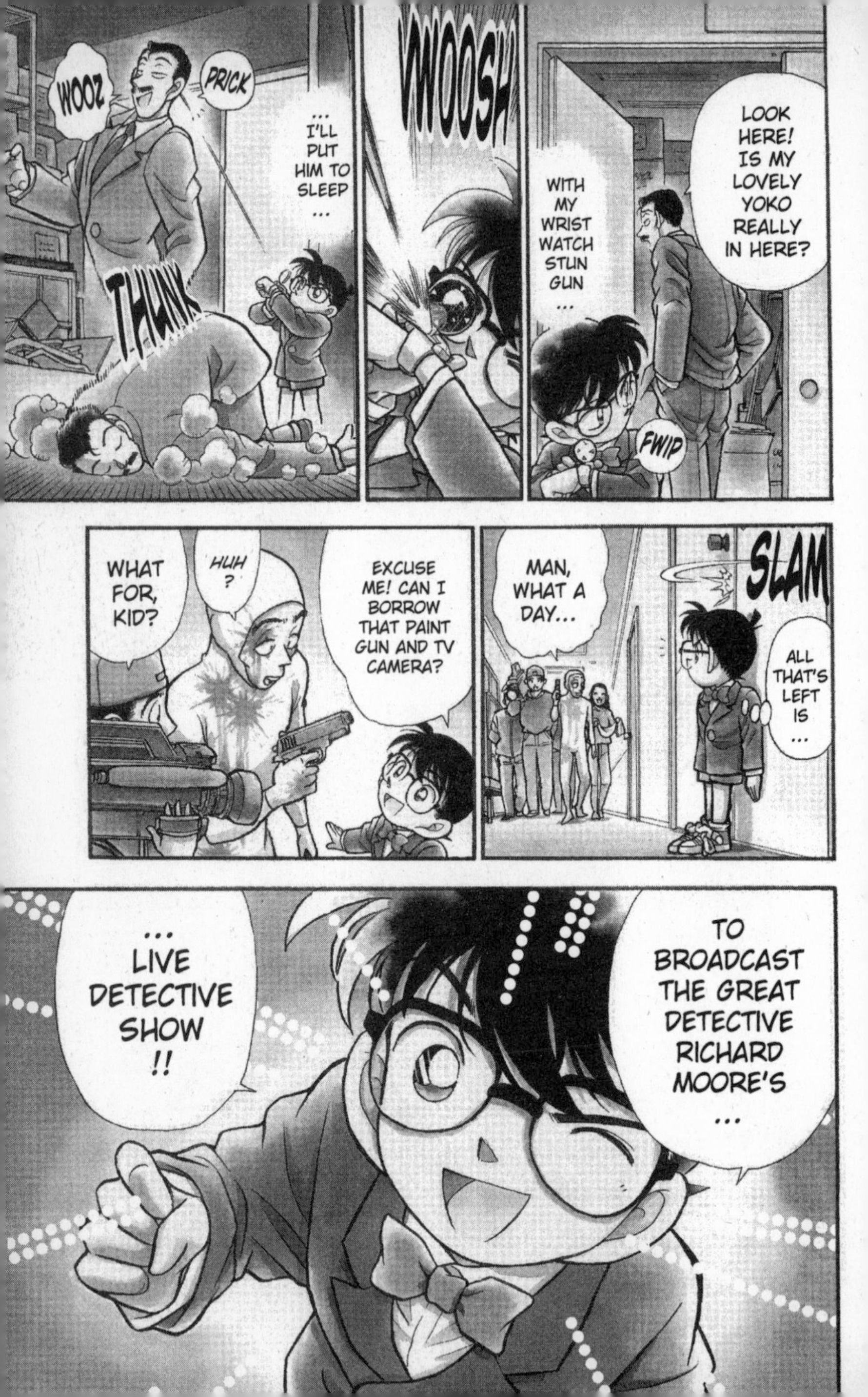

LOOK HERE! IS MY LOVELY YOKO REALLY IN HERE?
WITH MY WRIST WATCH STUN GUN ...
FWIP
VWOOSH
... I'LL PUT HIM TO SLEEP ...
PRICK
WOOZ
THUNK
SLAM
ALL THAT'S LEFT IS ...
MAN, WHAT A DAY...
EXCUSE ME! CAN I BORROW THAT PAINT GUN AND TV CAMERA?
HUH ?
WHAT FOR, KID?
TO BROADCAST THE GREAT DETECTIVE RICHARD MOORE'S ...
... LIVE DETECTIVE SHOW !!

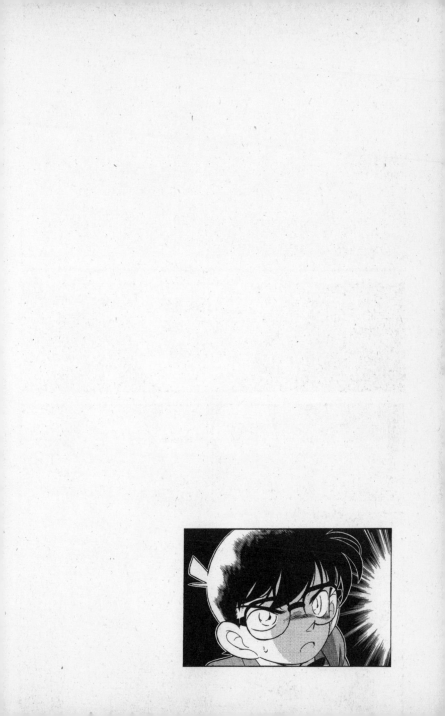

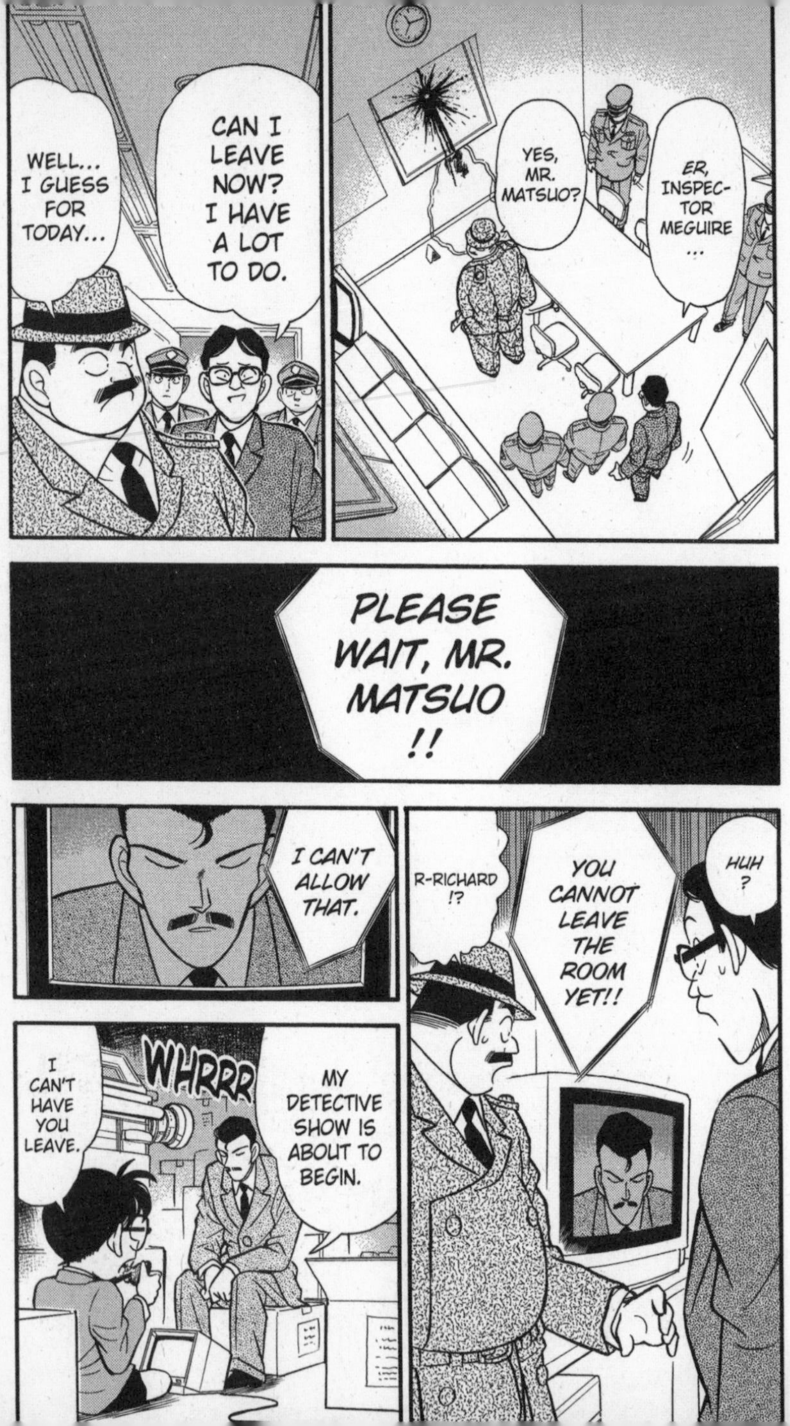
ER, INSPEC-TOR MEGUIRE...
YES, MR. MATSUO?
CAN I LEAVE NOW? I HAVE A LOT TO DO.
WELL... I GUESS FOR TODAY...
PLEASE WAIT, MR. MATSUO!!
HUH?
YOU CANNOT LEAVE THE ROOM YET!!
R-RICHARD!?
I CAN'T ALLOW THAT.
MY DETECTIVE SHOW IS ABOUT TO BEGIN.
WHRRR
I CAN'T HAVE YOU LEAVE.

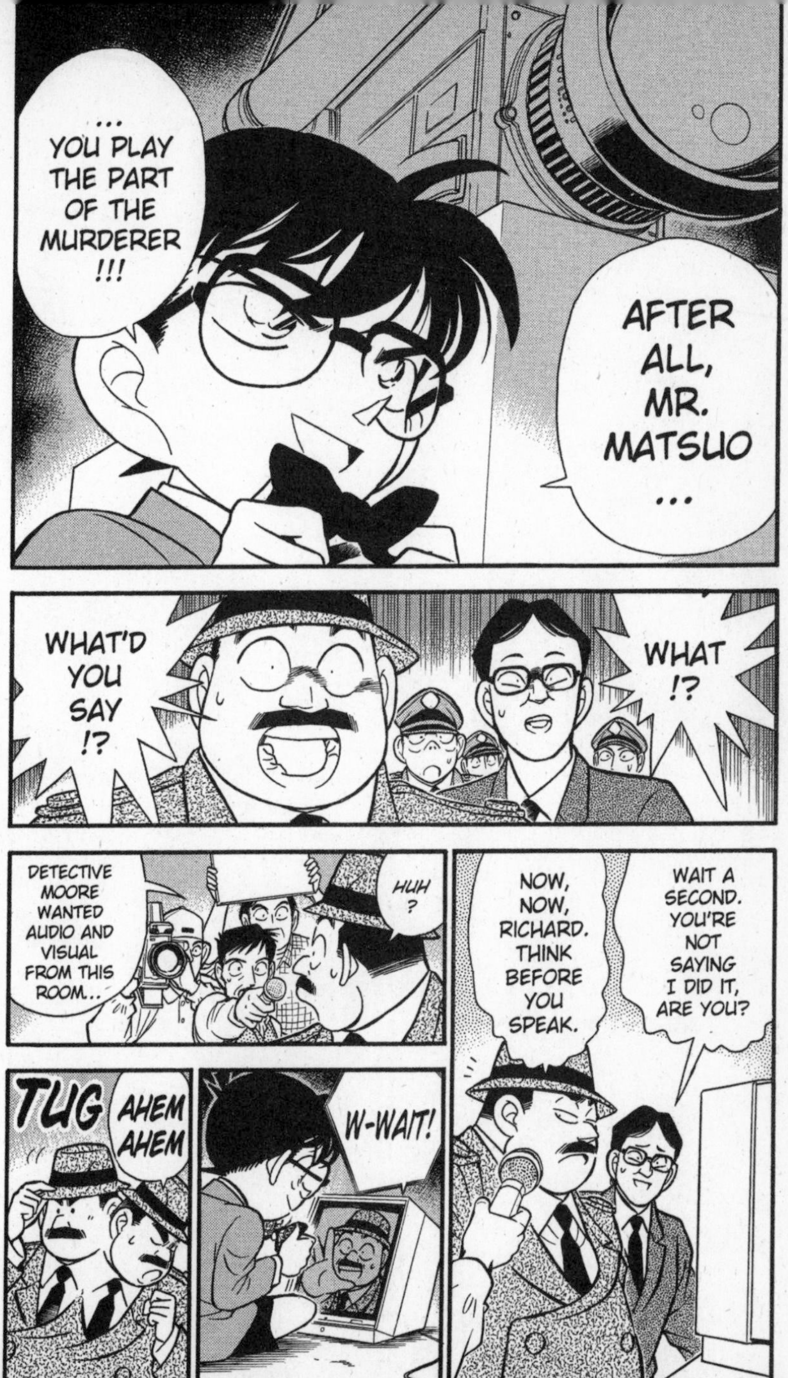
AFTER ALL, MR. MATSUO ...
... YOU PLAY THE PART OF THE MURDERER !!!
WHAT !?
WHAT'D YOU SAY !?
WAIT A SECOND. YOU'RE NOT SAYING I DID IT, ARE YOU?
NOW, NOW, RICHARD. THINK BEFORE YOU SPEAK.
HUH ?
DETECTIVE MOORE WANTED AUDIO AND VISUAL FROM THIS ROOM...
W-WAIT!
TUG
AHEM AHEM

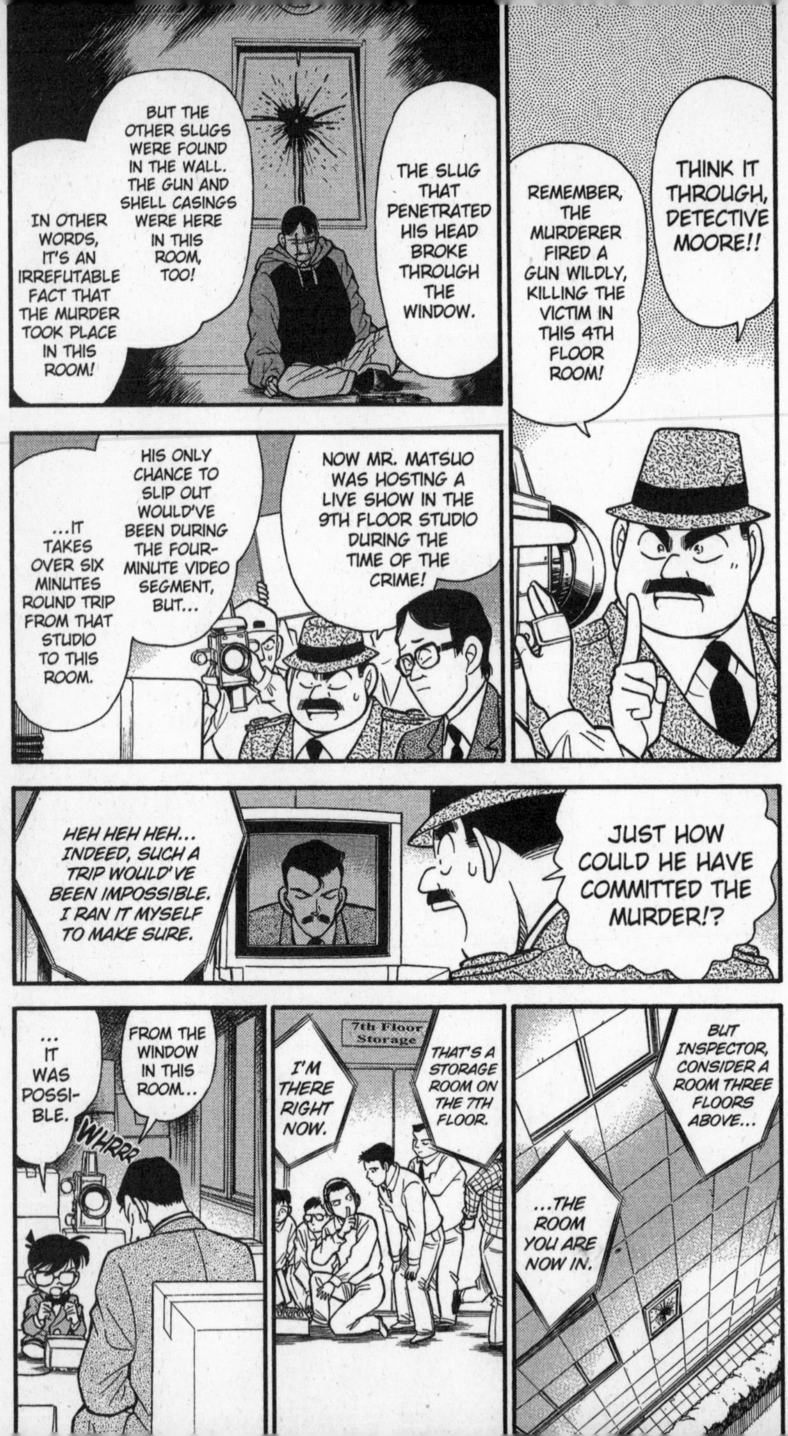
THINK IT THROUGH, DETECTIVE MOORE!!
REMEMBER, THE MURDERER FIRED A GUN WILDLY, KILLING THE VICTIM IN THIS 4TH FLOOR ROOM!
THE SLUG THAT PENETRATED HIS HEAD BROKE THROUGH THE WINDOW.
BUT THE OTHER SLUGS WERE FOUND IN THE WALL. THE GUN AND SHELL CASINGS WERE HERE IN THIS ROOM, TOO!
IN OTHER WORDS, IT'S AN IRREFUTABLE FACT THAT THE MURDER TOOK PLACE IN THIS ROOM!
NOW MR. MATSUO WAS HOSTING A LIVE SHOW IN THE 9TH FLOOR STUDIO DURING THE TIME OF THE CRIME!
HIS ONLY CHANCE TO SLIP OUT WOULD'VE BEEN DURING THE FOUR-MINUTE VIDEO SEGMENT, BUT...
...IT TAKES OVER SIX MINUTES ROUND TRIP FROM THAT STUDIO TO THIS ROOM.
JUST HOW COULD HE HAVE COMMITTED THE MURDER!?
HEH HEH HEH... INDEED, SUCH A TRIP WOULD'VE BEEN IMPOSSIBLE. I RAN IT MYSELF TO MAKE SURE.
BUT INSPECTOR, CONSIDER A ROOM THREE FLOORS ABOVE...
...THE ROOM YOU ARE NOW IN.
7th Floor Storage
THAT'S A STORAGE ROOM ON THE 7TH FLOOR.
I'M THERE RIGHT NOW.
FROM THE WINDOW IN THIS ROOM...
...IT WAS POSSIBLE.
WHRRR

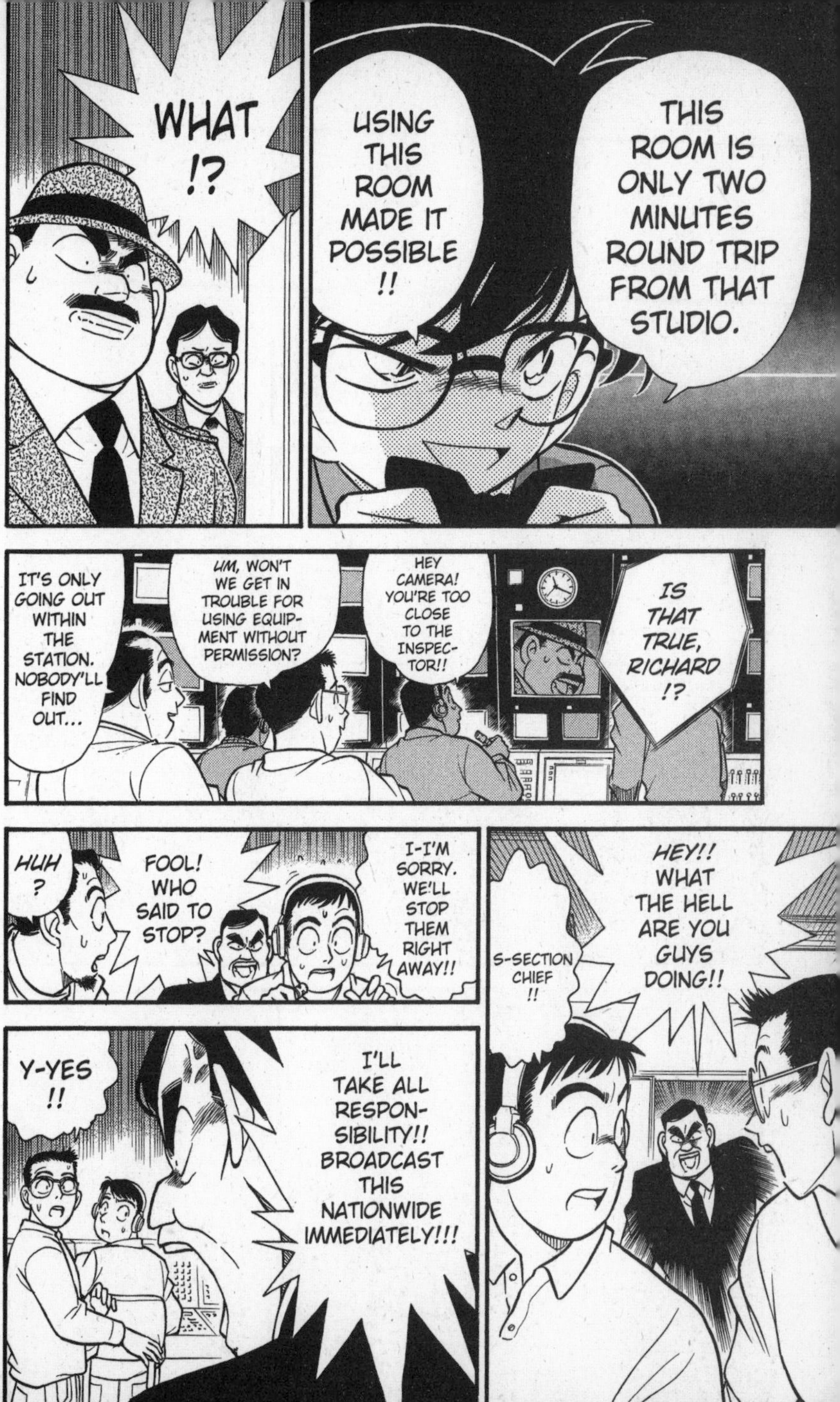
THIS ROOM IS ONLY TWO MINUTES ROUND TRIP FROM THAT STUDIO.
USING THIS ROOM MADE IT POSSIBLE!!
WHAT !?
IS THAT TRUE, RICHARD !?
HEY CAMERA! YOU'RE TOO CLOSE TO THE INSPECTOR!!
UM, WON'T WE GET IN TROUBLE FOR USING EQUIPMENT WITHOUT PERMISSION?
IT'S ONLY GOING OUT WITHIN THE STATION. NOBODY'LL FIND OUT...
HEY!! WHAT THE HELL ARE YOU GUYS DOING!!
S-SECTION CHIEF !!
I-I'M SORRY. WE'LL STOP THEM RIGHT AWAY!!
FOOL! WHO SAID TO STOP?
HUH ?
I'LL TAKE ALL RESPONSIBILITY!! BROADCAST THIS NATIONWIDE IMMEDIATELY!!!
Y-YES !!

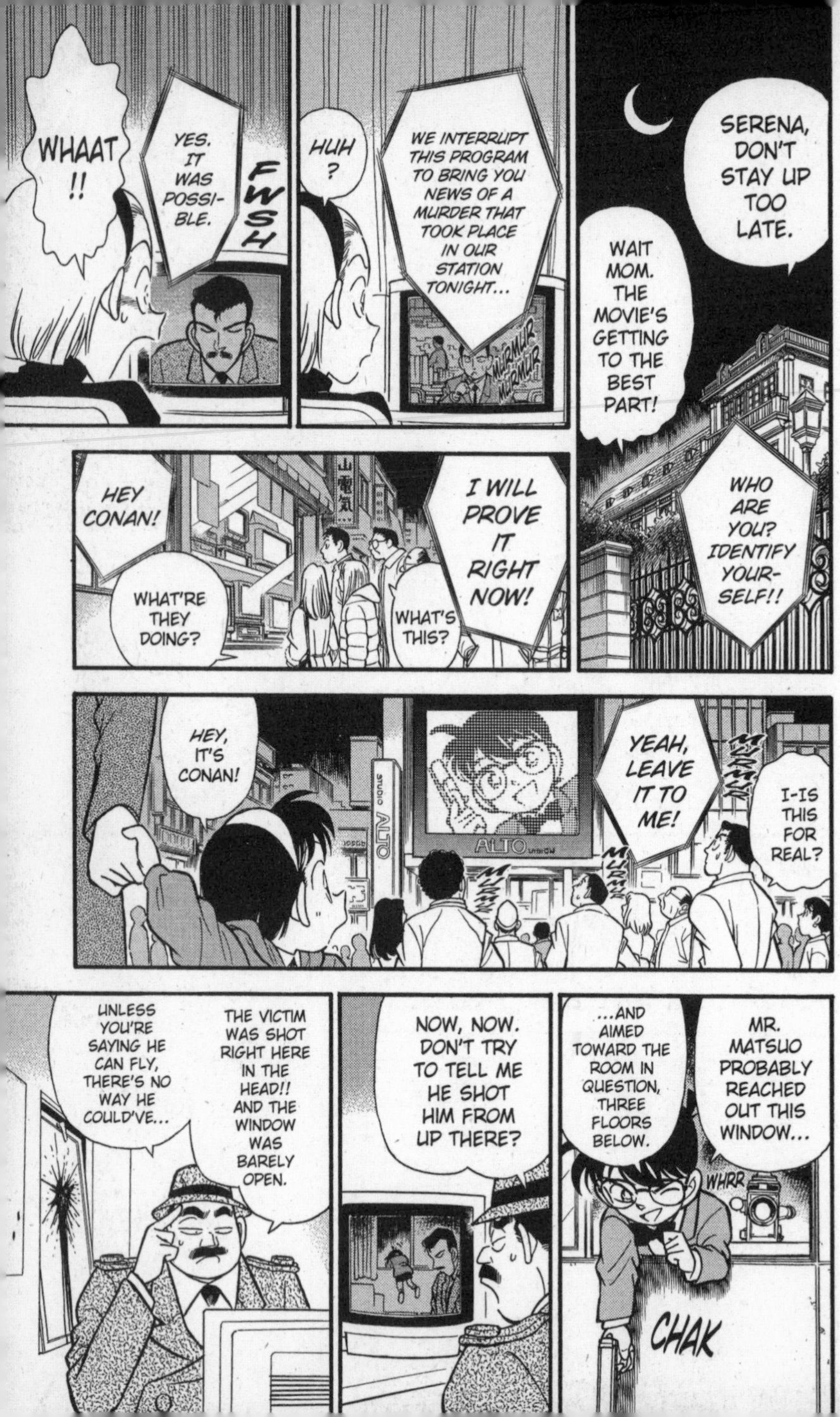
SERENA, DON'T STAY UP TOO LATE.
WAIT MOM. THE MOVIE'S GETTING TO THE BEST PART!
WHO ARE YOU? IDENTIFY YOURSELF!!
WE INTERRUPT THIS PROGRAM TO BRING YOU NEWS OF A MURDER THAT TOOK PLACE IN OUR STATION TONIGHT...
MURMUR MURMUR
HUH?
YES. IT WAS POSSIBLE.
FWSH
WHAAT!!
I WILL PROVE IT RIGHT NOW!
WHAT'S THIS?
HEY CONAN!
WHAT'RE THEY DOING?
YEAH, LEAVE IT TO ME!
I-IS THIS FOR REAL?
MURMUR
MURMUR
MURMUR
HEY, IT'S CONAN!
MR. MATSUO PROBABLY REACHED OUT THIS WINDOW...
...AND AIMED TOWARD THE ROOM IN QUESTION, THREE FLOORS BELOW.
WHRR
CHAK
NOW, NOW. DON'T TRY TO TELL ME HE SHOT HIM FROM UP THERE?
THE VICTIM WAS SHOT RIGHT HERE IN THE HEAD!! AND THE WINDOW WAS BARELY OPEN.
UNLESS YOU'RE SAYING HE CAN FLY, THERE'S NO WAY HE COULD'VE...

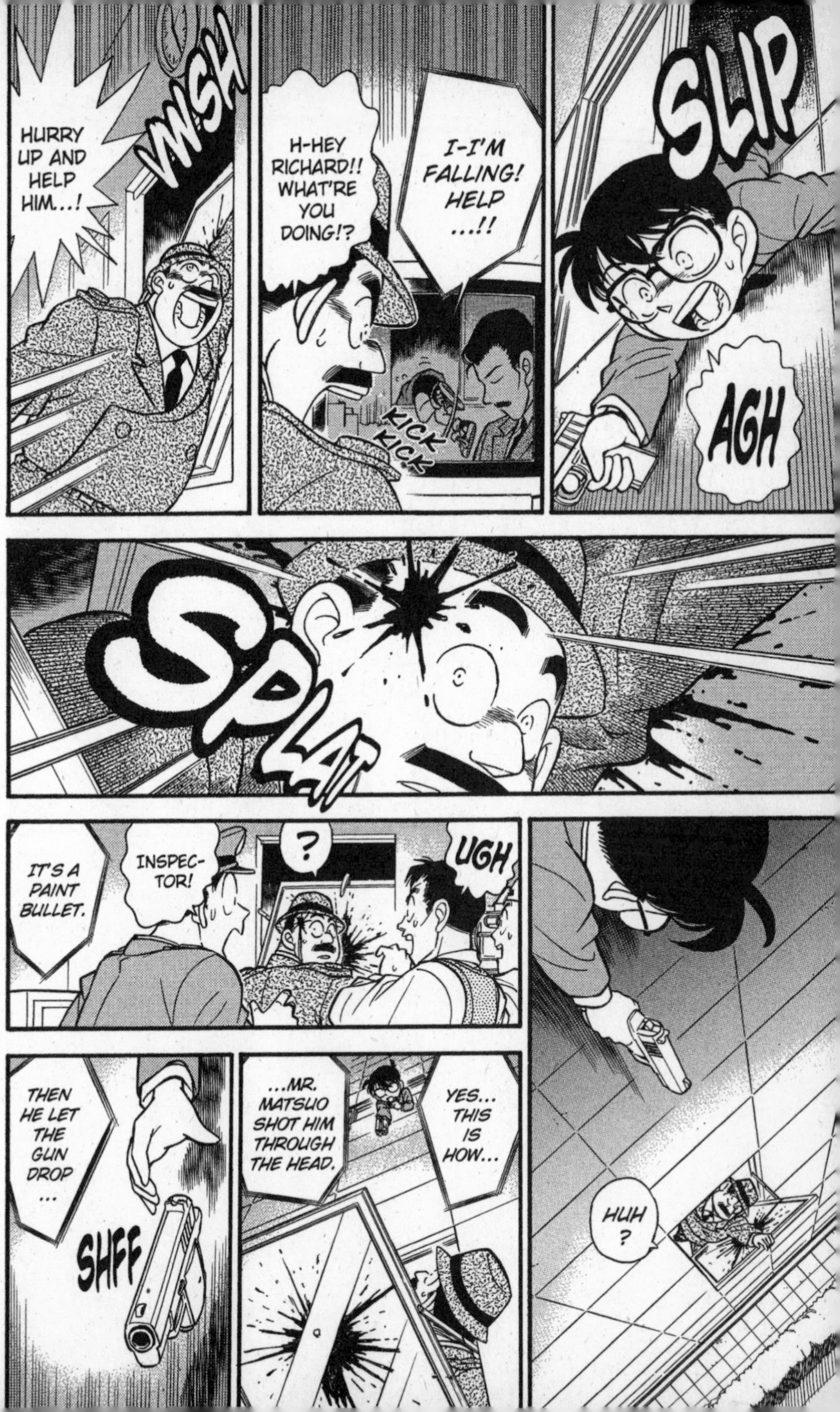
SLIP
AGH
I-I'M FALLING! HELP ...!!
H-HEY RICHARD!! WHAT'RE YOU DOING!?
KICK KICK
VWSH
HURRY UP AND HELP HIM...!
SPLAT
HUH ?
UGH
?
INSPECTOR!
IT'S A PAINT BULLET.
YES... THIS IS HOW...
...MR. MATSUO SHOT HIM THROUGH THE HEAD.
THEN HE LET THE GUN DROP ...
SHFF

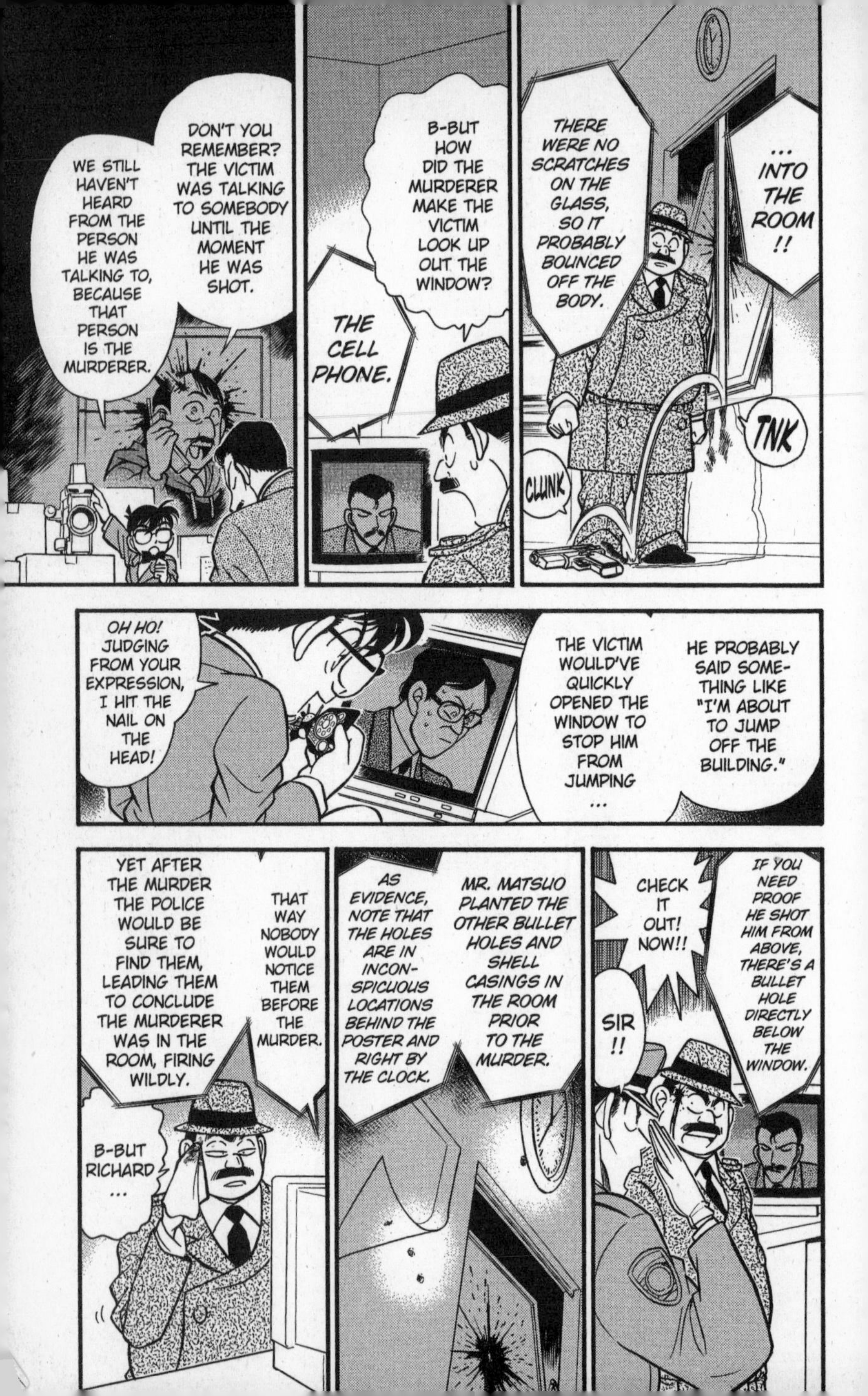
... INTO THE ROOM !!
THERE WERE NO SCRATCHES ON THE GLASS, SO IT PROBABLY BOUNCED OFF THE BODY.
TNK
CLUNK
B-BUT HOW DID THE MURDERER MAKE THE VICTIM LOOK UP OUT THE WINDOW?
THE CELL PHONE.
DON'T YOU REMEMBER? THE VICTIM WAS TALKING TO SOMEBODY UNTIL THE MOMENT HE WAS SHOT.
WE STILL HAVEN'T HEARD FROM THE PERSON HE WAS TALKING TO, BECAUSE THAT PERSON IS THE MURDERER.
HE PROBABLY SAID SOME-THING LIKE "I'M ABOUT TO JUMP OFF THE BUILDING."
THE VICTIM WOULD'VE QUICKLY OPENED THE WINDOW TO STOP HIM FROM JUMPING ...
OH HO! JUDGING FROM YOUR EXPRESSION, I HIT THE NAIL ON THE HEAD!
IF YOU NEED PROOF HE SHOT HIM FROM ABOVE, THERE'S A BULLET HOLE DIRECTLY BELOW THE WINDOW.
CHECK IT OUT! NOW!!
SIR !!
MR. MATSUO PLANTED THE OTHER BULLET HOLES AND SHELL CASINGS IN THE ROOM PRIOR TO THE MURDER.
AS EVIDENCE, NOTE THAT THE HOLES ARE IN INCON-SPICUOUS LOCATIONS BEHIND THE POSTER AND RIGHT BY THE CLOCK.
THAT WAY NOBODY WOULD NOTICE THEM BEFORE THE MURDER.
YET AFTER THE MURDER THE POLICE WOULD BE SURE TO FIND THEM, LEADING THEM TO CONCLUDE THE MURDERER WAS IN THE ROOM, FIRING WILDLY.
B-BUT RICHARD ...

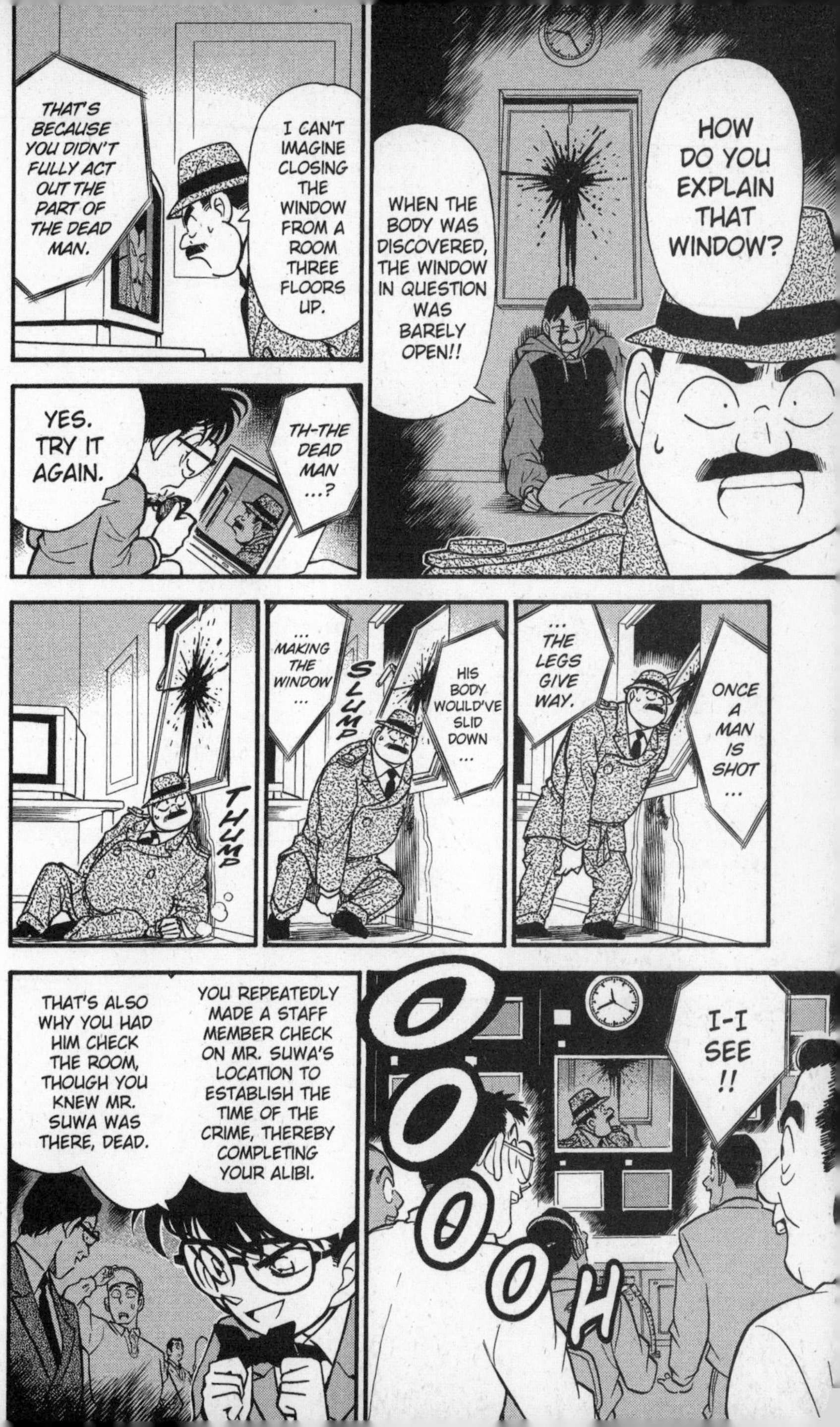
HOW DO YOU EXPLAIN THAT WINDOW?
WHEN THE BODY WAS DISCOVERED, THE WINDOW IN QUESTION WAS BARELY OPEN!!
I CAN'T IMAGINE CLOSING THE WINDOW FROM A ROOM THREE FLOORS UP.
THAT'S BECAUSE YOU DIDN'T FULLY ACT OUT THE PART OF THE DEAD MAN.
TH-THE DEAD MAN ...?
YES. TRY IT AGAIN.
ONCE A MAN IS SHOT ...
... THE LEGS GIVE WAY.
HIS BODY WOULD'VE SLID DOWN ...
SLUMP
... MAKING THE WINDOW ...
THUMP
I-I SEE !!
OOOOOH
YOU REPEATEDLY MADE A STAFF MEMBER CHECK ON MR. SUWA'S LOCATION TO ESTABLISH THE TIME OF THE CRIME, THEREBY COMPLETING YOUR ALIBI.
THAT'S ALSO WHY YOU HAD HIM CHECK THE ROOM, THOUGH YOU KNEW MR. SUWA WAS THERE, DEAD.

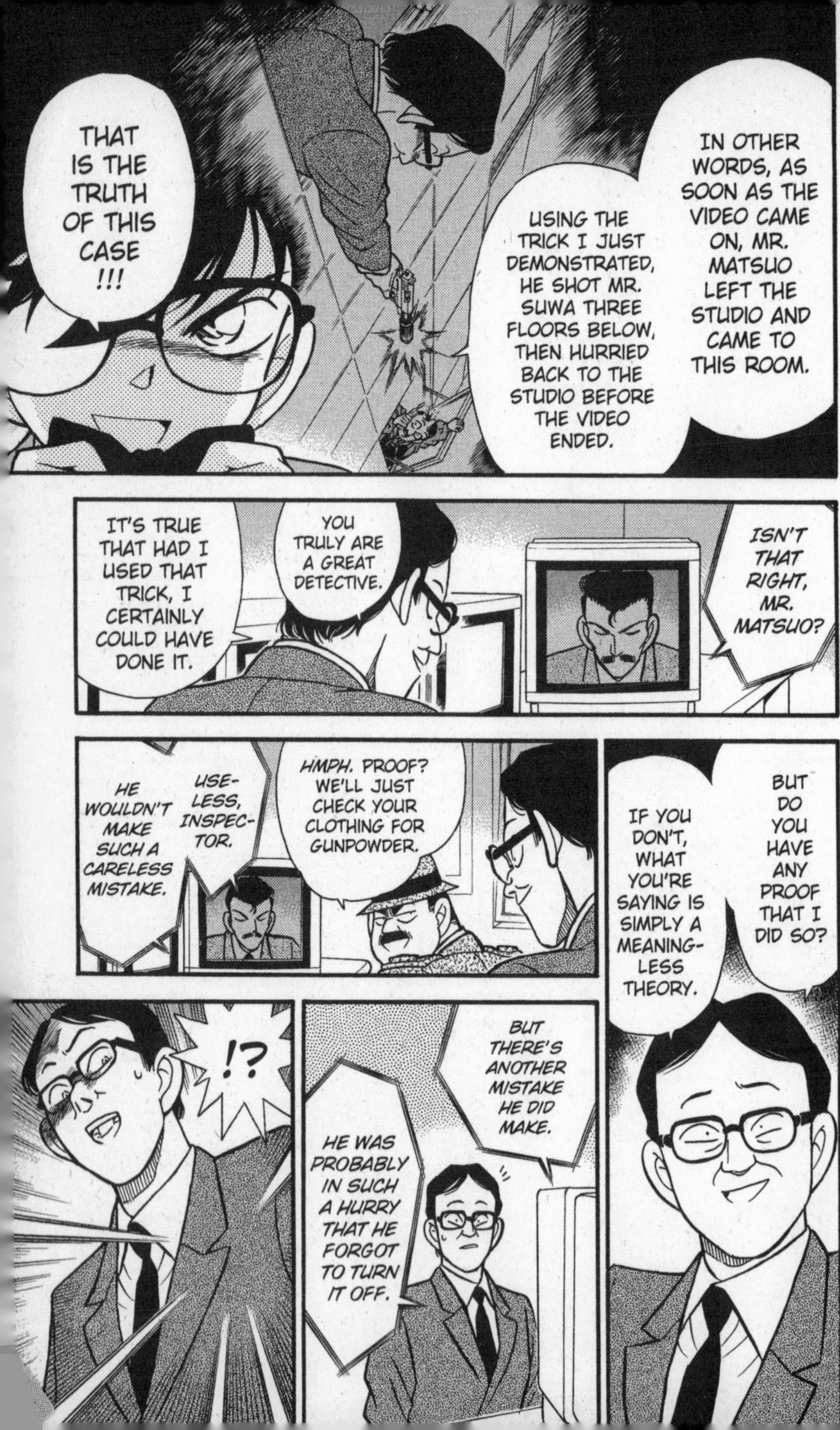
IN OTHER WORDS, AS SOON AS THE VIDEO CAME ON, MR. MATSUO LEFT THE STUDIO AND CAME TO THIS ROOM.
USING THE TRICK I JUST DEMONSTRATED, HE SHOT MR. SUWA THREE FLOORS BELOW, THEN HURRIED BACK TO THE STUDIO BEFORE THE VIDEO ENDED.
THAT IS THE TRUTH OF THIS CASE !!!
ISN'T THAT RIGHT, MR. MATSUO?
YOU TRULY ARE A GREAT DETECTIVE.
IT'S TRUE THAT HAD I USED THAT TRICK, I CERTAINLY COULD HAVE DONE IT.
BUT DO YOU HAVE ANY PROOF THAT I DID SO?
IF YOU DON'T, WHAT YOU'RE SAYING IS SIMPLY A MEANING-LESS THEORY.
HMPH. PROOF? WE'LL JUST CHECK YOUR CLOTHING FOR GUNPOWDER.
USE-LESS, INSPEC-TOR.
HE WOULDN'T MAKE SUCH A CARELESS MISTAKE.
BUT THERE'S ANOTHER MISTAKE HE DID MAKE.
HE WAS PROBABLY IN SUCH A HURRY THAT HE FORGOT TO TURN IT OFF.
!?

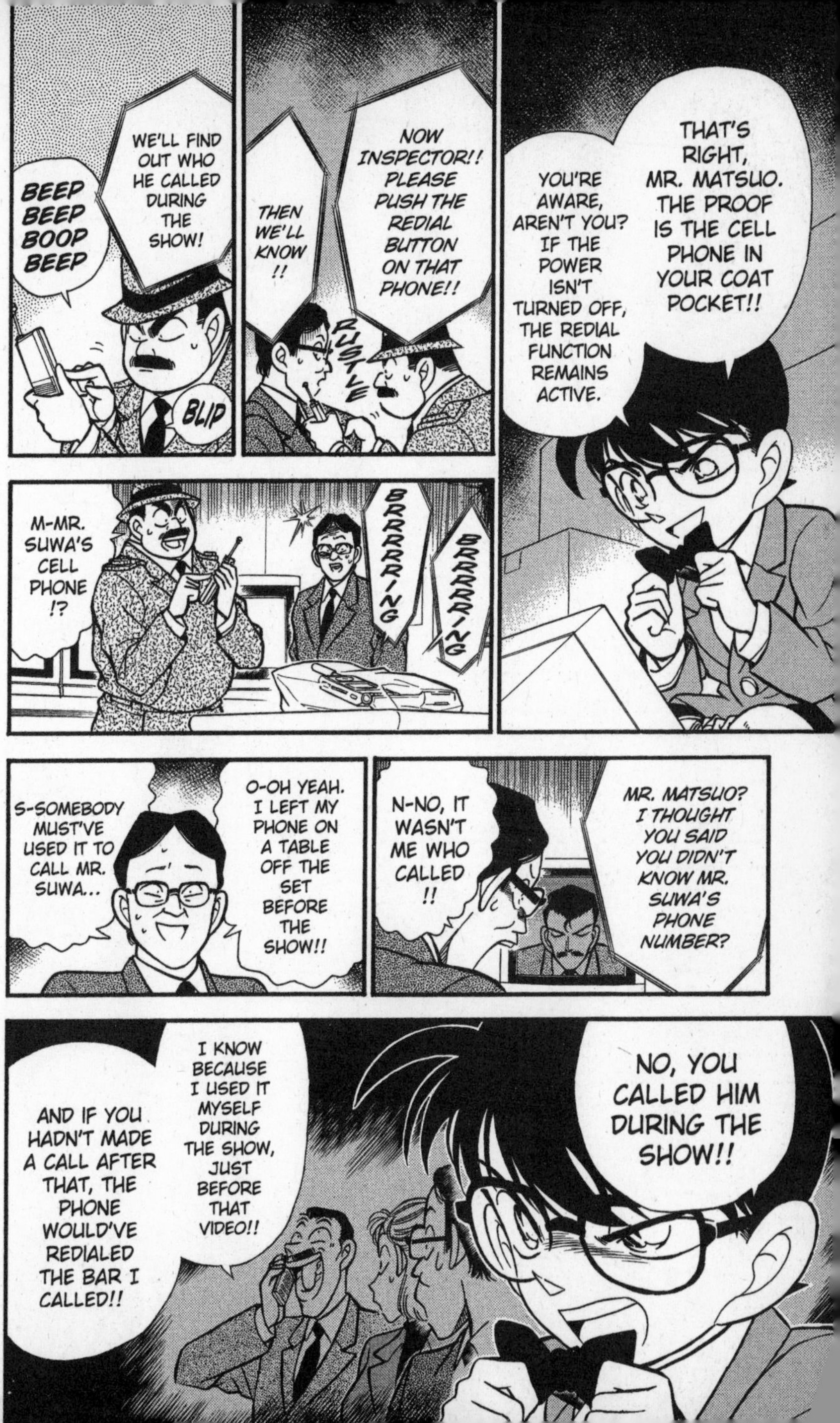
THAT'S RIGHT, MR. MATSUO. THE PROOF IS THE CELL PHONE IN YOUR COAT POCKET!!
YOU'RE AWARE, AREN'T YOU? IF THE POWER ISN'T TURNED OFF, THE REDIAL FUNCTION REMAINS ACTIVE.
NOW INSPECTOR!! PLEASE PUSH THE REDIAL BUTTON ON THAT PHONE!!
THEN WE'LL KNOW !!
RUSTLE
WE'LL FIND OUT WHO HE CALLED DURING THE SHOW!
BEEP BEEP BOOP BEEP
BLIP
BRRRRING
BRRRRING
M-MR. SUWA'S CELL PHONE !?
MR. MATSUO? I THOUGHT YOU SAID YOU DIDN'T KNOW MR. SUWA'S PHONE NUMBER?
N-NO, IT WASN'T ME WHO CALLED !!
O-OH YEAH. I LEFT MY PHONE ON A TABLE OFF THE SET BEFORE THE SHOW!!
S-SOMEBODY MUST'VE USED IT TO CALL MR. SUWA...
NO, YOU CALLED HIM DURING THE SHOW!!
I KNOW BECAUSE I USED IT MYSELF DURING THE SHOW, JUST BEFORE THAT VIDEO!!
AND IF YOU HADN'T MADE A CALL AFTER THAT, THE PHONE WOULD'VE REDIALED THE BAR I CALLED!!

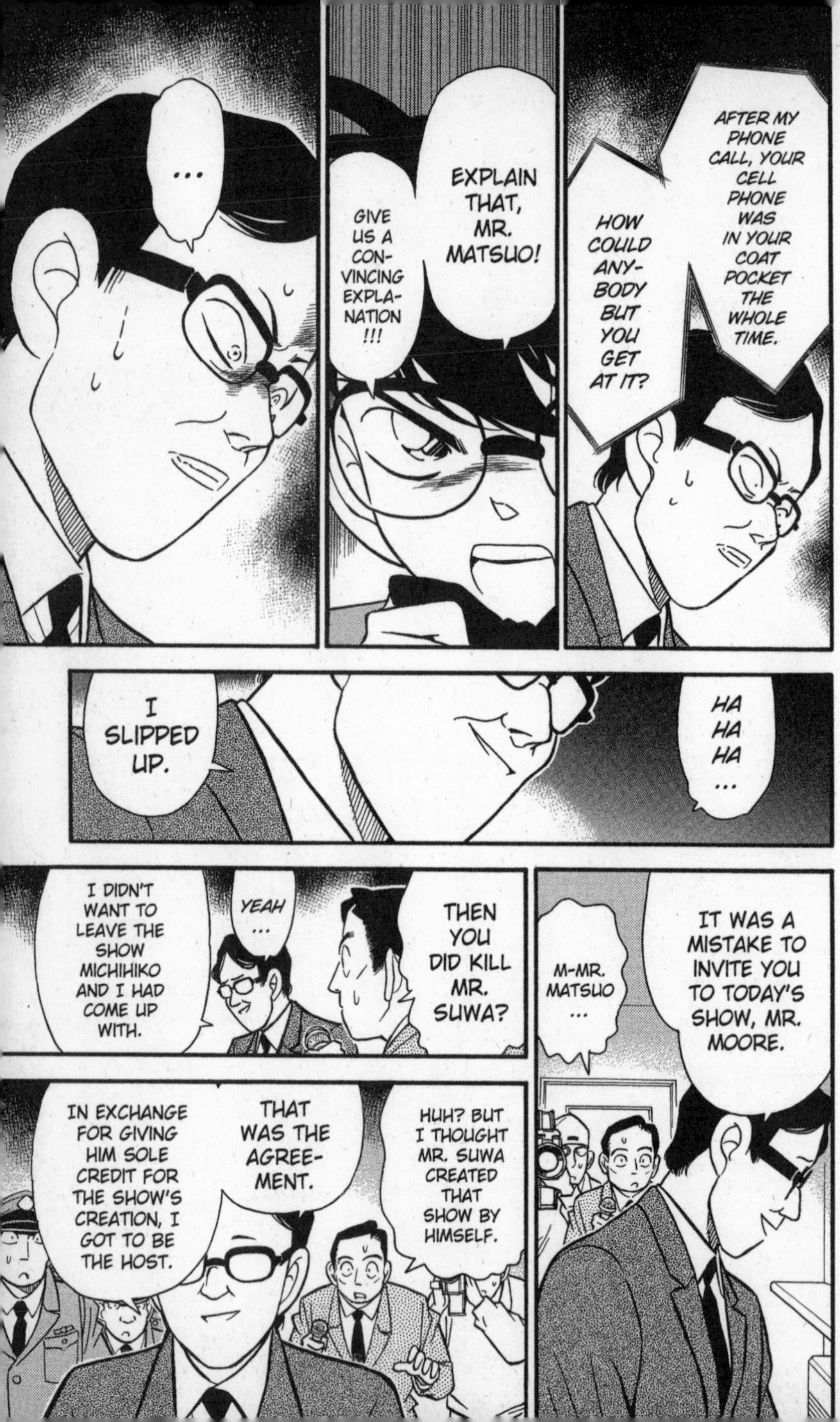
AFTER MY PHONE CALL, YOUR CELL PHONE WAS IN YOUR COAT POCKET THE WHOLE TIME.
HOW COULD ANYBODY BUT YOU GET AT IT?
EXPLAIN THAT, MR. MATSUO!
GIVE US A CONVINCING EXPLANATION!!!
...
HA HA HA ...
I SLIPPED UP.
IT WAS A MISTAKE TO INVITE YOU TO TODAY'S SHOW, MR. MOORE.
M-MR. MATSUO ...
THEN YOU DID KILL MR. SUWA?
YEAH ...
I DIDN'T WANT TO LEAVE THE SHOW MICHIHIKO AND I HAD COME UP WITH.
HUH? BUT I THOUGHT MR. SUWA CREATED THAT SHOW BY HIMSELF.
THAT WAS THE AGREEMENT.
IN EXCHANGE FOR GIVING HIM SOLE CREDIT FOR THE SHOW'S CREATION, I GOT TO BE THE HOST.

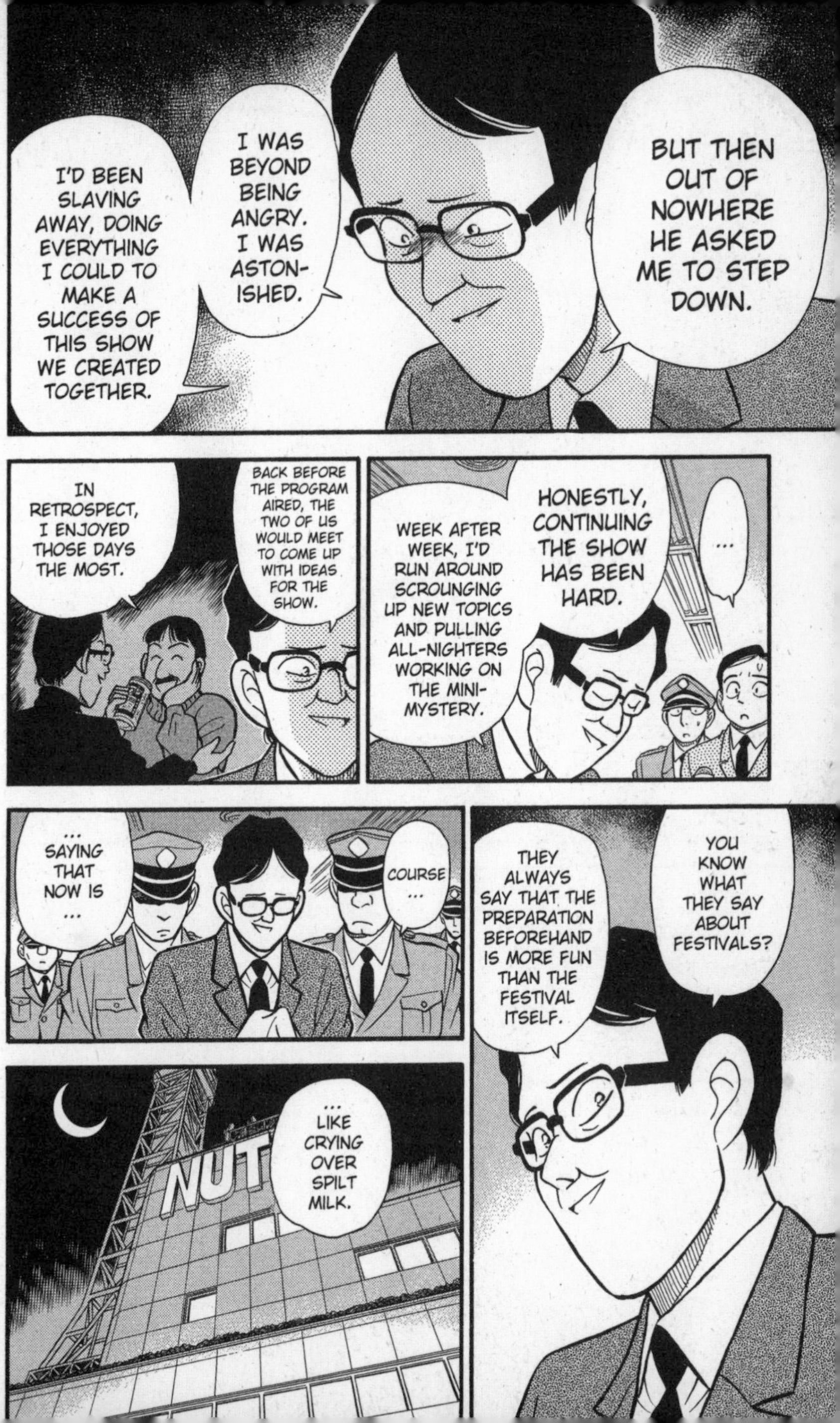
BUT THEN OUT OF NOWHERE HE ASKED ME TO STEP DOWN.
I WAS BEYOND BEING ANGRY. I WAS ASTONISHED.
I'D BEEN SLAVING AWAY, DOING EVERYTHING I COULD TO MAKE A SUCCESS OF THIS SHOW WE CREATED TOGETHER.
...
HONESTLY, CONTINUING THE SHOW HAS BEEN HARD.
WEEK AFTER WEEK, I'D RUN AROUND SCROUNGING UP NEW TOPICS AND PULLING ALL-NIGHTERS WORKING ON THE MINI-MYSTERY.
BACK BEFORE THE PROGRAM AIRED, THE TWO OF US WOULD MEET TO COME UP WITH IDEAS FOR THE SHOW.
IN RETROSPECT, I ENJOYED THOSE DAYS THE MOST.
YOU KNOW WHAT THEY SAY ABOUT FESTIVALS?
THEY ALWAYS SAY THAT THE PREPARATION BEFOREHAND IS MORE FUN THAN THE FESTIVAL ITSELF.
COURSE ...
... SAYING THAT NOW IS ...
NUT
... LIKE CRYING OVER SPILT MILK.

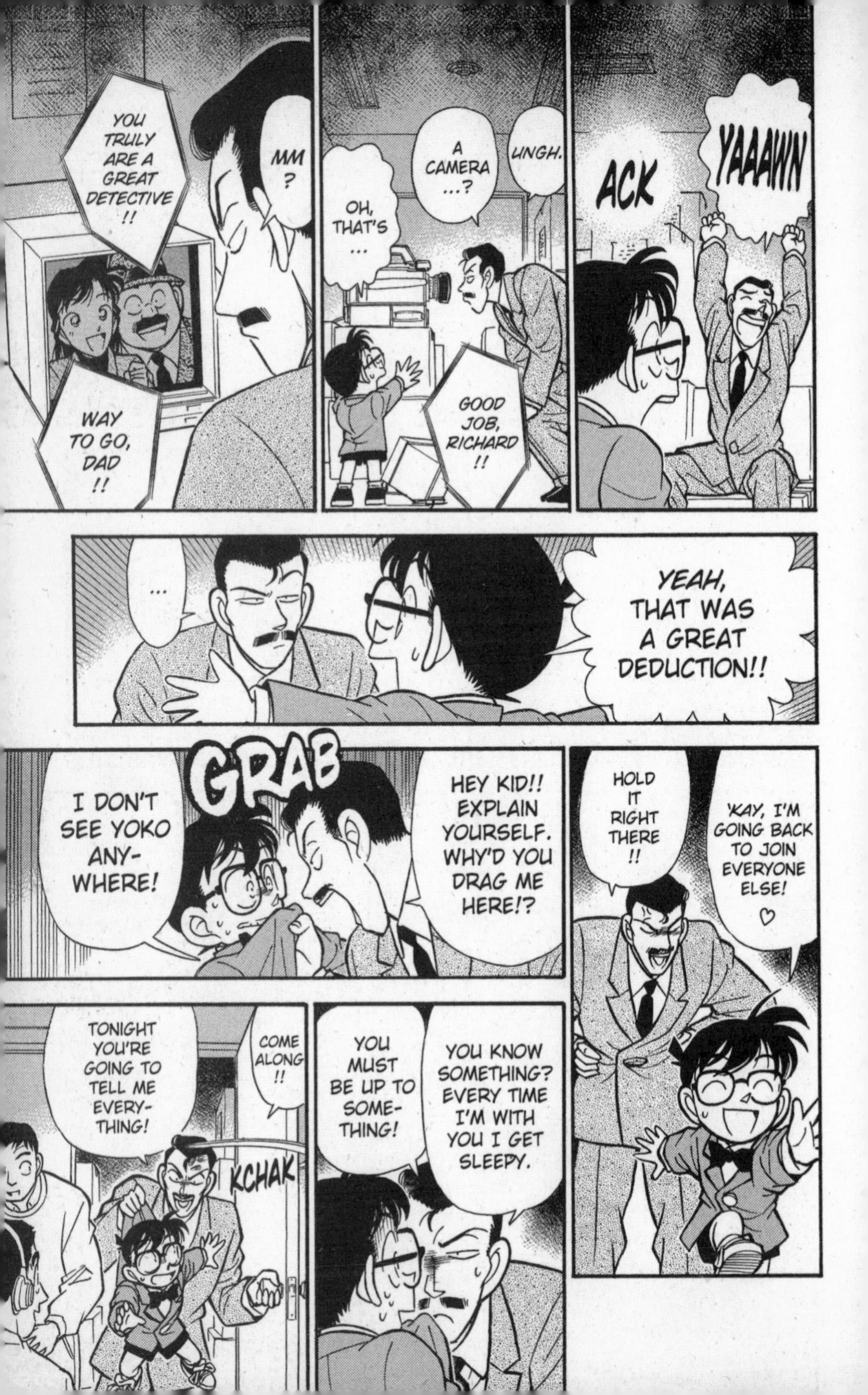
YAAAWN
ACK
UNGH.
A CAMERA ...?
OH, THAT'S ...
GOOD JOB, RICHARD !!
MM ?
YOU TRULY ARE A GREAT DETECTIVE !!
WAY TO GO, DAD !!
YEAH, THAT WAS A GREAT DEDUCTION!!
...
'KAY, I'M GOING BACK TO JOIN EVERYONE ELSE! ♡
HOLD IT RIGHT THERE !!
HEY KID!! EXPLAIN YOURSELF. WHY'D YOU DRAG ME HERE!?
GRAB
I DON'T SEE YOKO ANY-WHERE!
YOU KNOW SOMETHING? EVERY TIME I'M WITH YOU I GET SLEEPY.
YOU MUST BE UP TO SOME-THING!
COME ALONG !!
TONIGHT YOU'RE GOING TO TELL ME EVERY-THING!
KCHAK

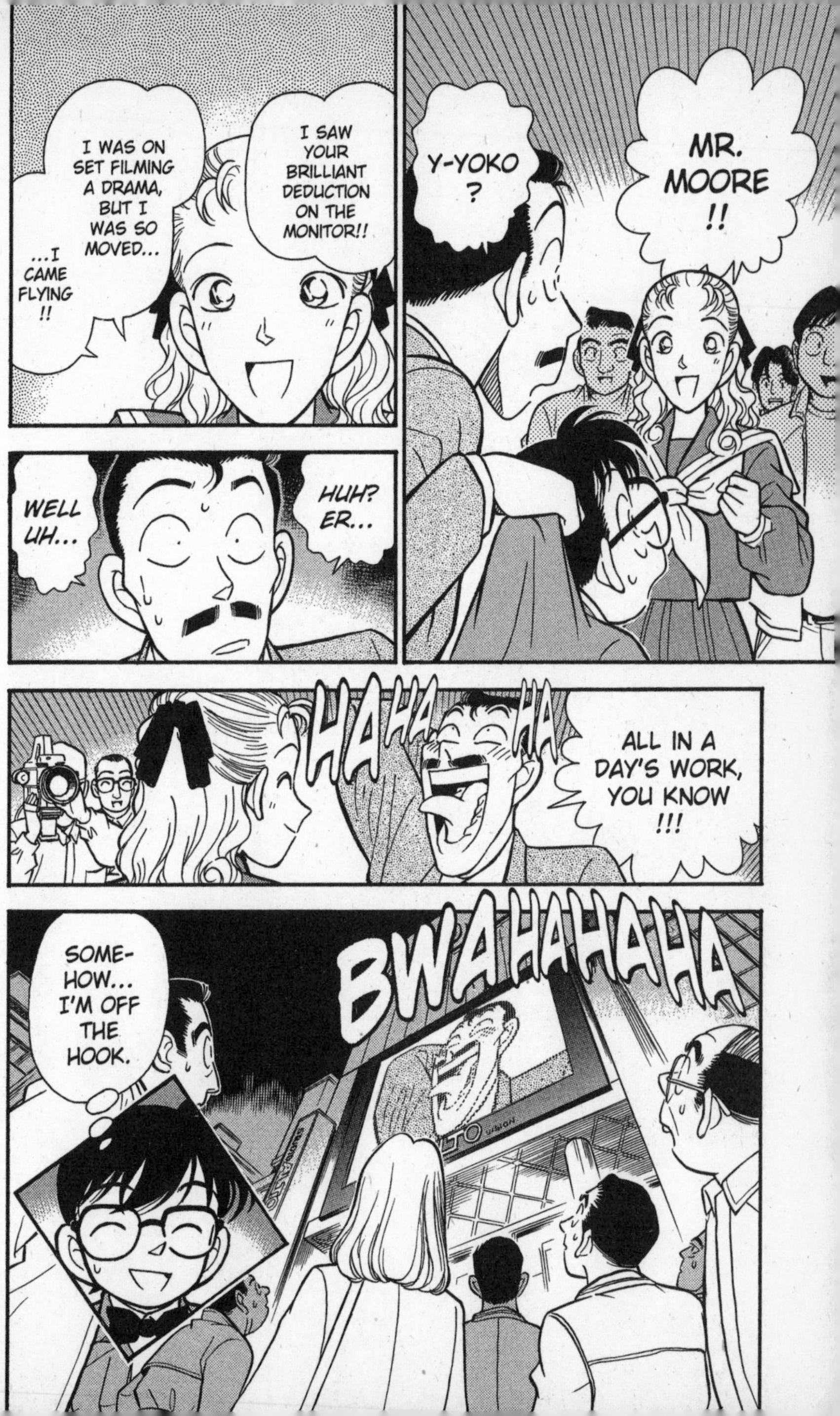
MR. MOORE !!
Y-YOKO ?
I SAW YOUR BRILLIANT DEDUCTION ON THE MONITOR!!
I WAS ON SET FILMING A DRAMA, BUT I WAS SO MOVED...
...I CAME FLYING !!
HUH? ER...
WELL UH...
ALL IN A DAY'S WORK, YOU KNOW !!!
HAHA HA
BWAHAHAHAHA
SOME-HOW... I'M OFF THE HOOK.

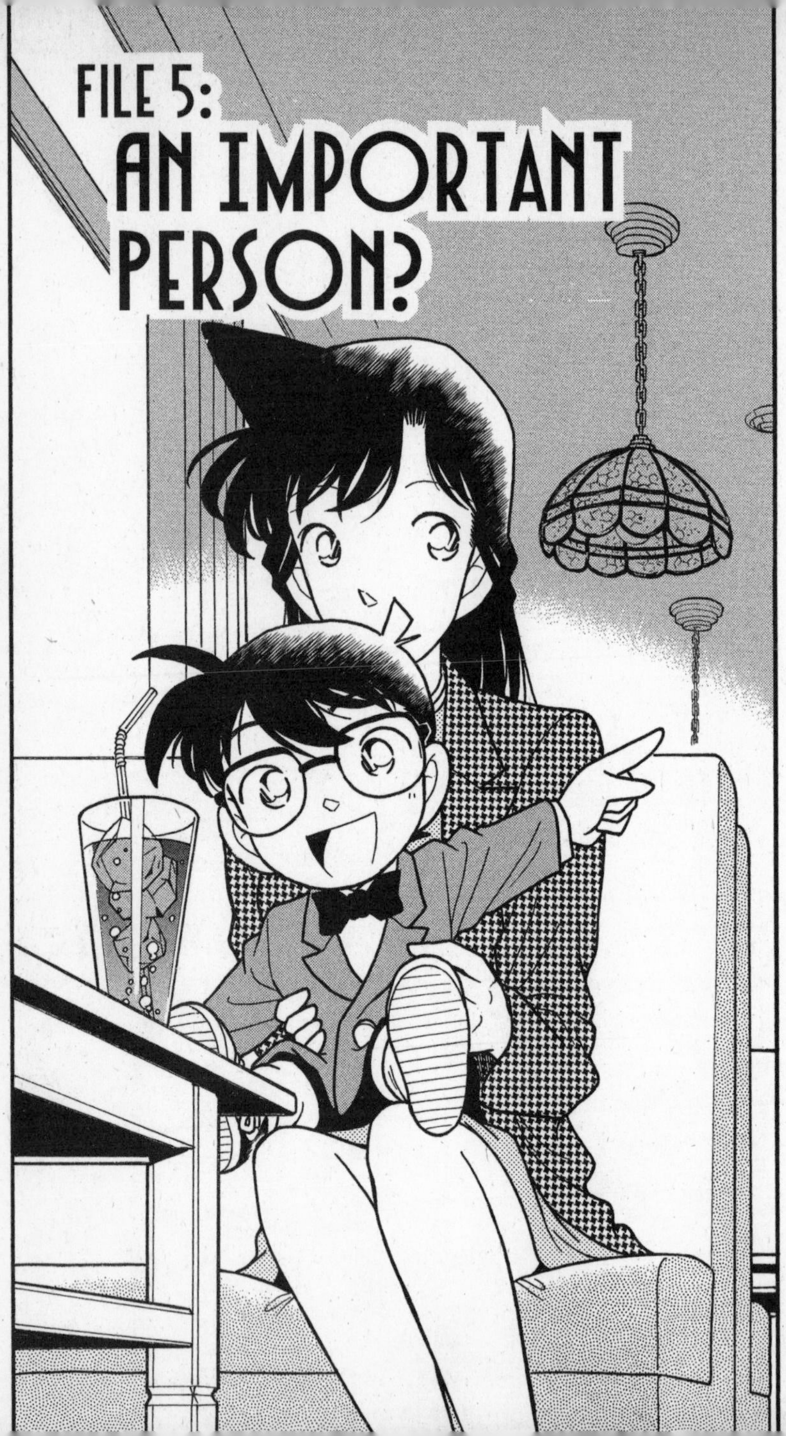
FILE 5:
AN IMPORTANT PERSON?

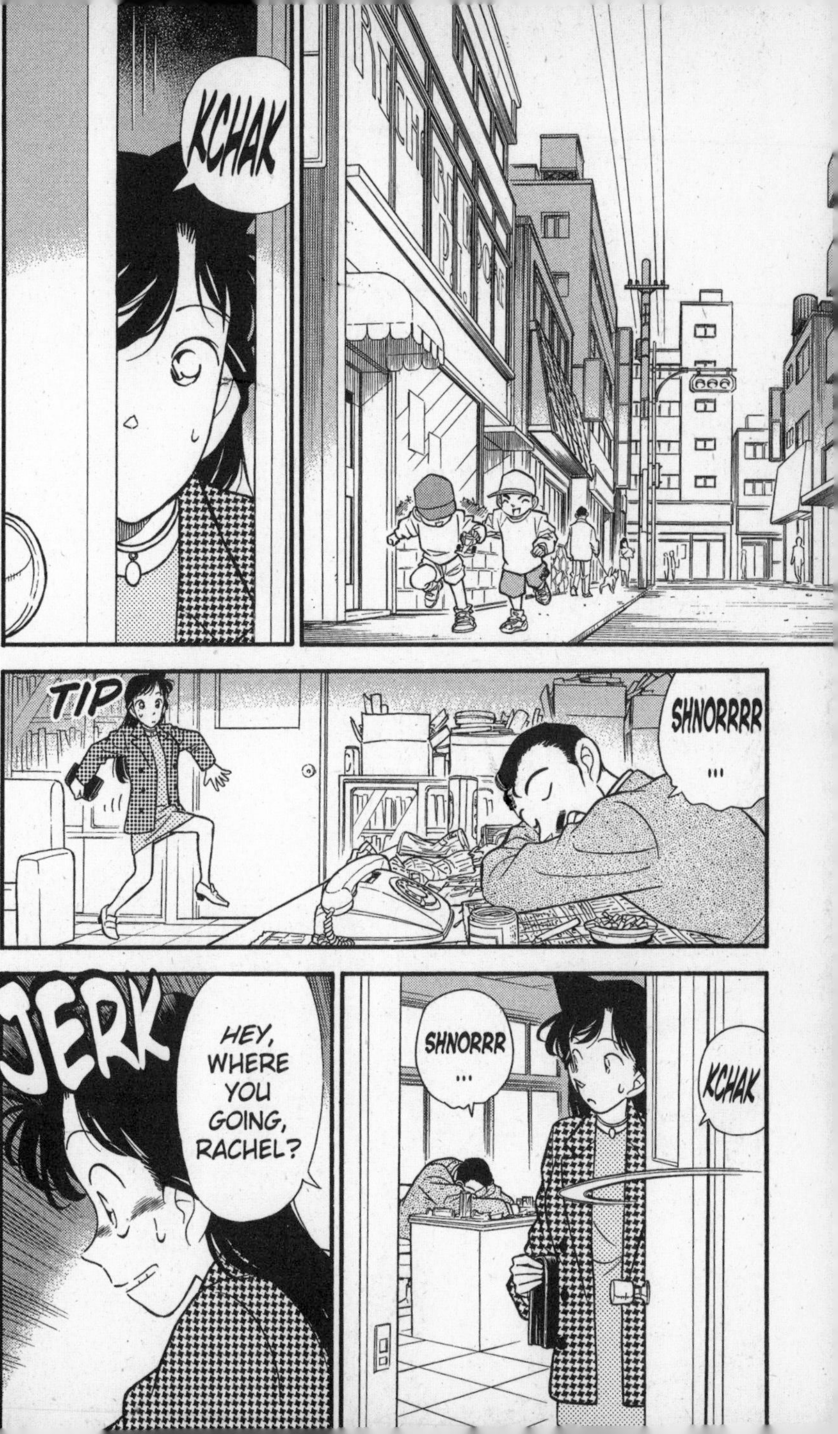
KCHAK
SHNORRRR ...
TIP
KCHAK
SHNORRR ...
JERK
HEY, WHERE YOU GOING, RACHEL?

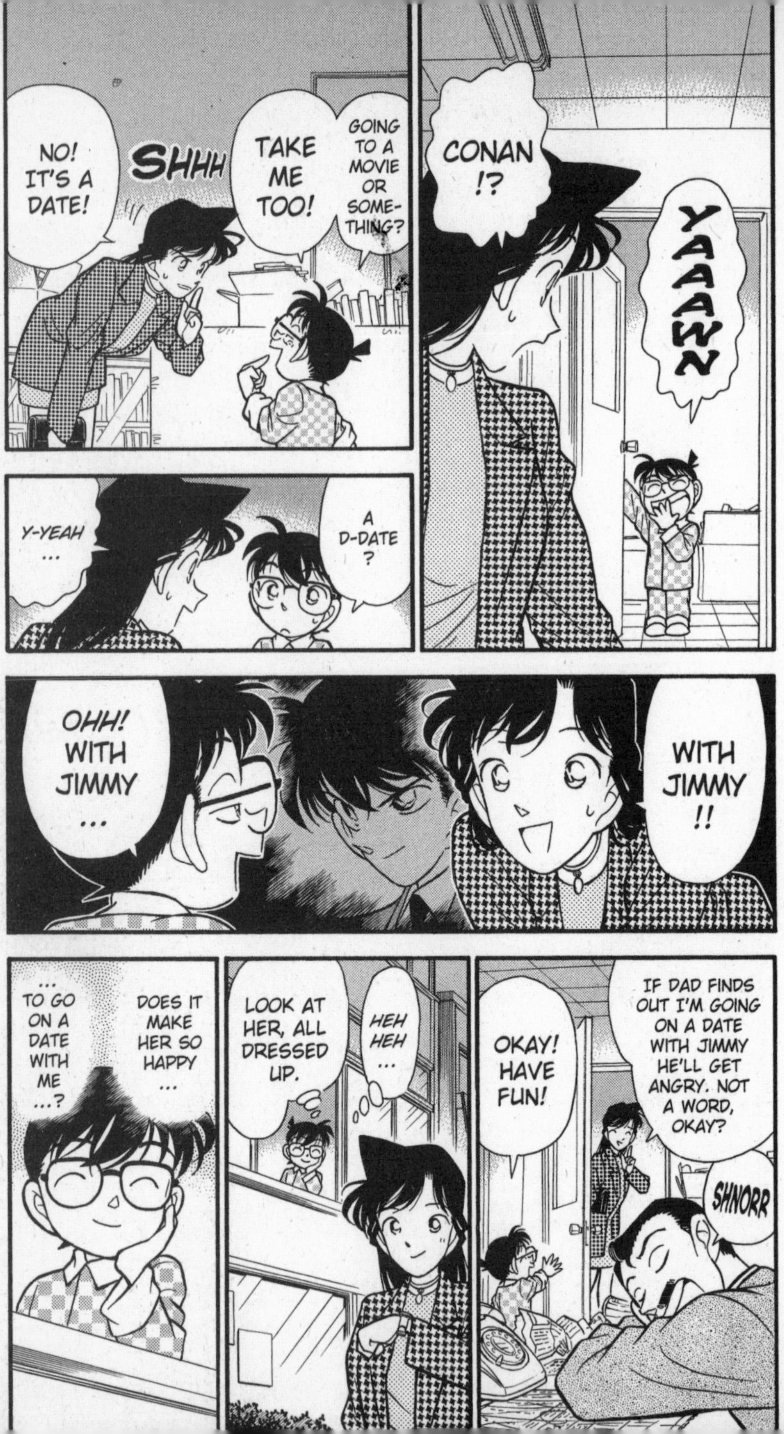
YAAAWN
CONAN !?
GOING TO A MOVIE OR SOME-THING?
TAKE ME TOO!
SHHH
NO! IT'S A DATE!
A D-DATE ?
Y-YEAH ...
WITH JIMMY !!
OHH! WITH JIMMY ...
IF DAD FINDS OUT I'M GOING ON A DATE WITH JIMMY HE'LL GET ANGRY. NOT A WORD, OKAY?
SHNORR
OKAY! HAVE FUN!
HEH HEH ...
LOOK AT HER, ALL DRESSED UP.
DOES IT MAKE HER SO HAPPY ...
... TO GO ON A DATE WITH ME ...?

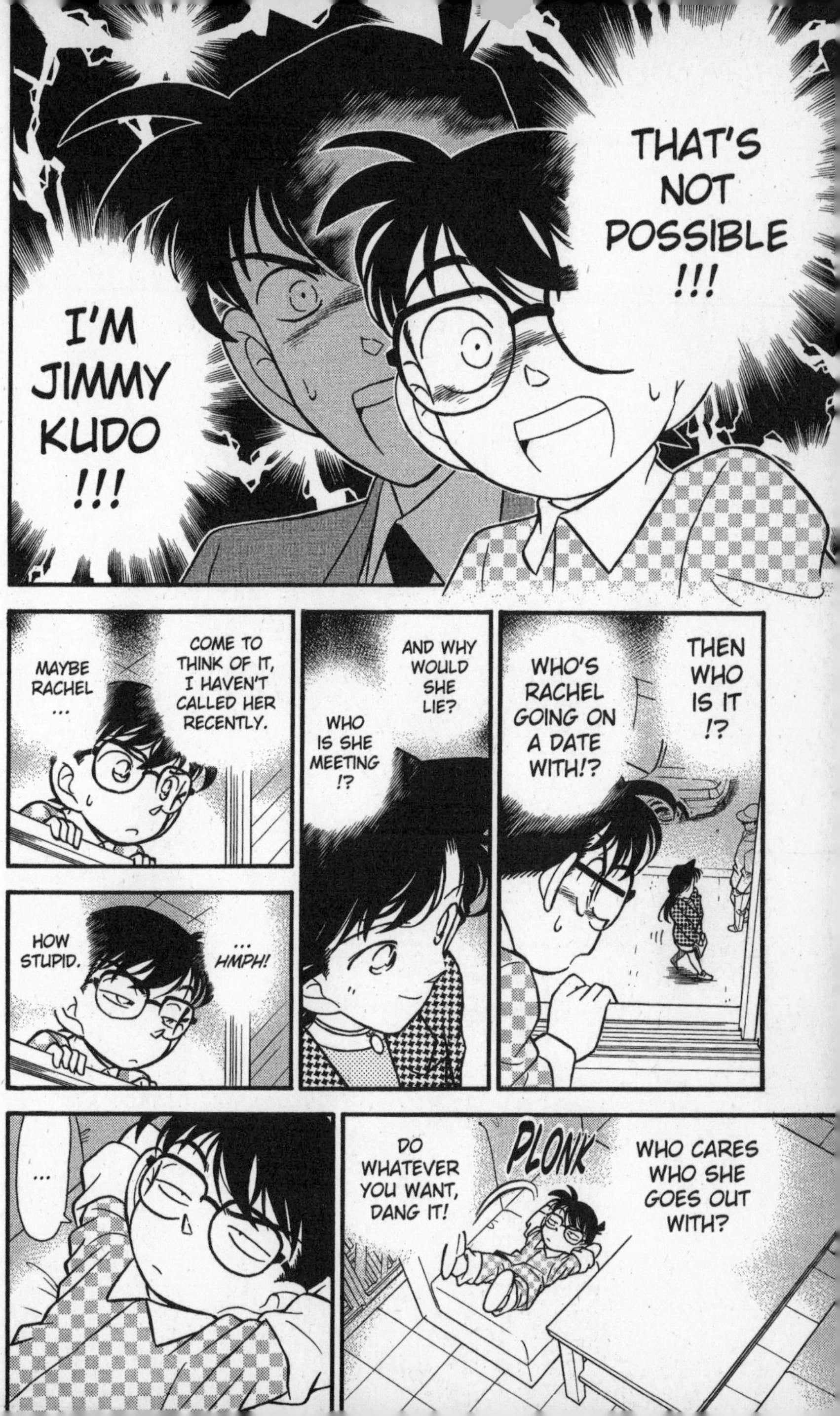
THAT'S NOT POSSIBLE !!!
I'M JIMMY KUDO !!!
THEN WHO IS IT !?
WHO'S RACHEL GOING ON A DATE WITH!?
AND WHY WOULD SHE LIE?
WHO IS SHE MEETING !?
COME TO THINK OF IT, I HAVEN'T CALLED HER RECENTLY.
MAYBE RACHEL ...
... HMPH!
HOW STUPID.
WHO CARES WHO SHE GOES OUT WITH?
PLONK
DO WHATEVER YOU WANT, DANG IT!
...

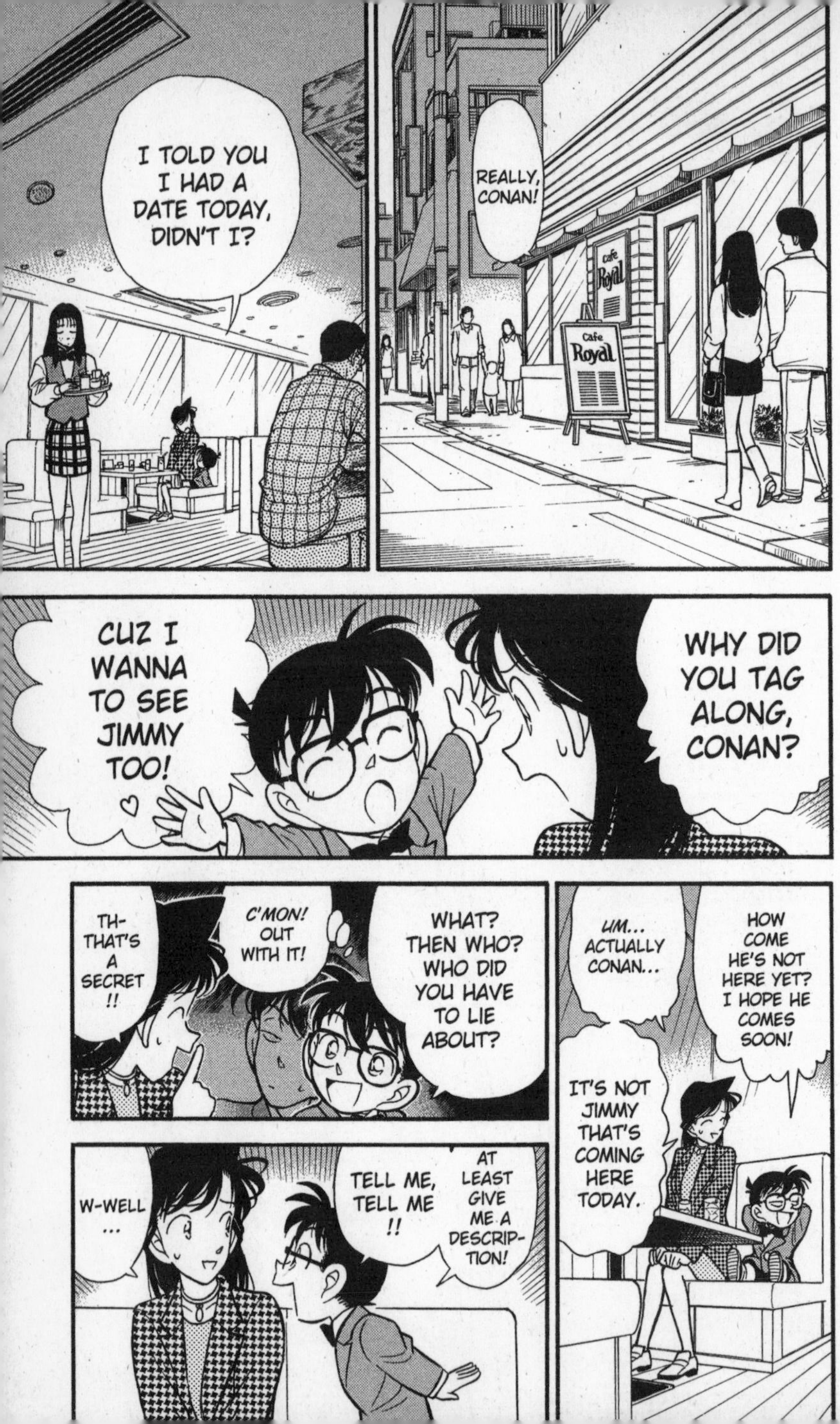
REALLY, CONAN!
I TOLD YOU I HAD A DATE TODAY, DIDN'T I?
WHY DID YOU TAG ALONG, CONAN?
CUZ I WANNA TO SEE JIMMY TOO! ♡
HOW COME HE'S NOT HERE YET? I HOPE HE COMES SOON!
UM... ACTUALLY CONAN...
IT'S NOT JIMMY THAT'S COMING HERE TODAY.
WHAT? THEN WHO? WHO DID YOU HAVE TO LIE ABOUT?
C'MON! OUT WITH IT!
TH- THAT'S A SECRET !!
AT LEAST GIVE ME A DESCRIPTION!
TELL ME, TELL ME !!
W-WELL ...

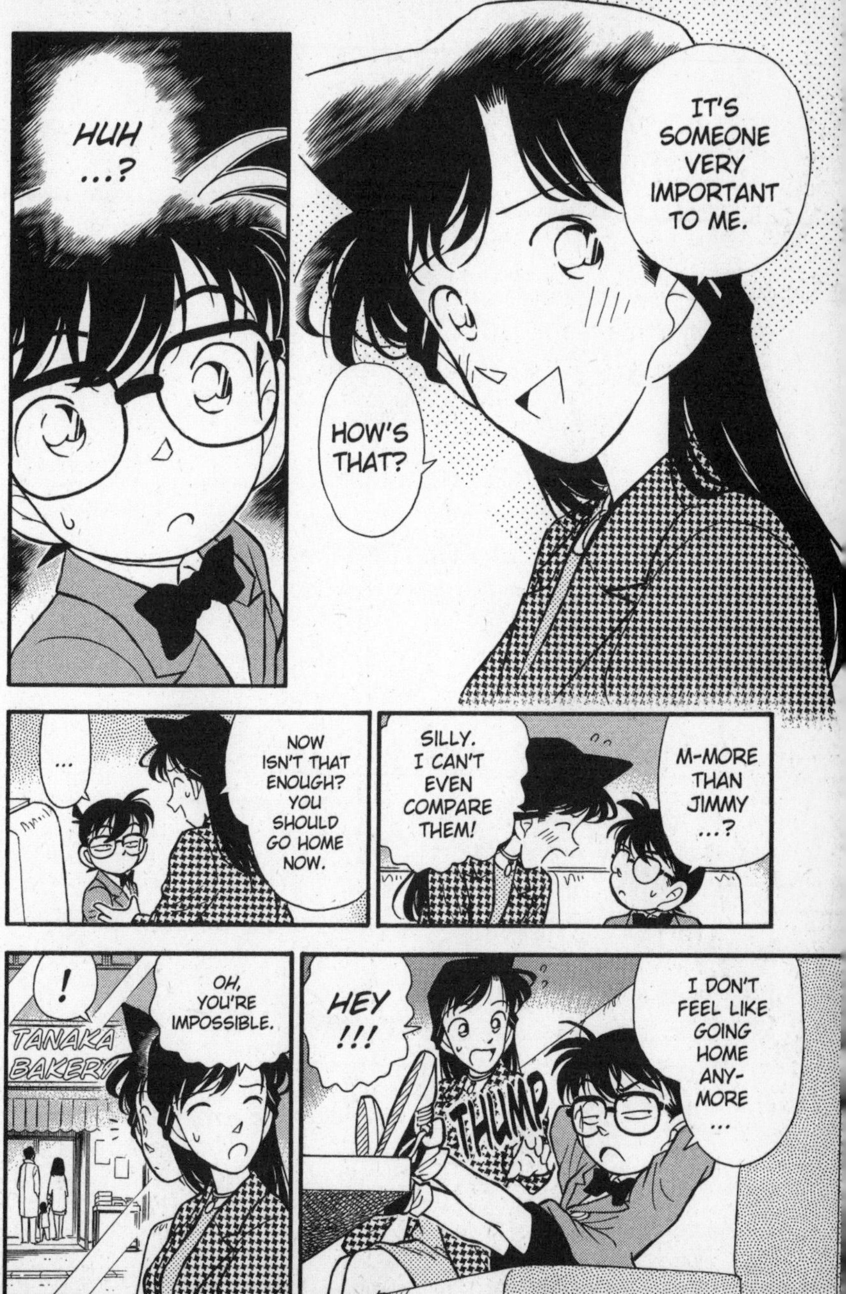
IT'S SOMEONE VERY IMPORTANT TO ME.
HOW'S THAT?
HUH ...?
M-MORE THAN JIMMY ...?
SILLY. I CAN'T EVEN COMPARE THEM!
NOW ISN'T THAT ENOUGH? YOU SHOULD GO HOME NOW.
...
I DON'T FEEL LIKE GOING HOME ANY-MORE ...
THUMP
HEY !!!
OH, YOU'RE IMPOSSIBLE.
!
TANAKA BAKERY

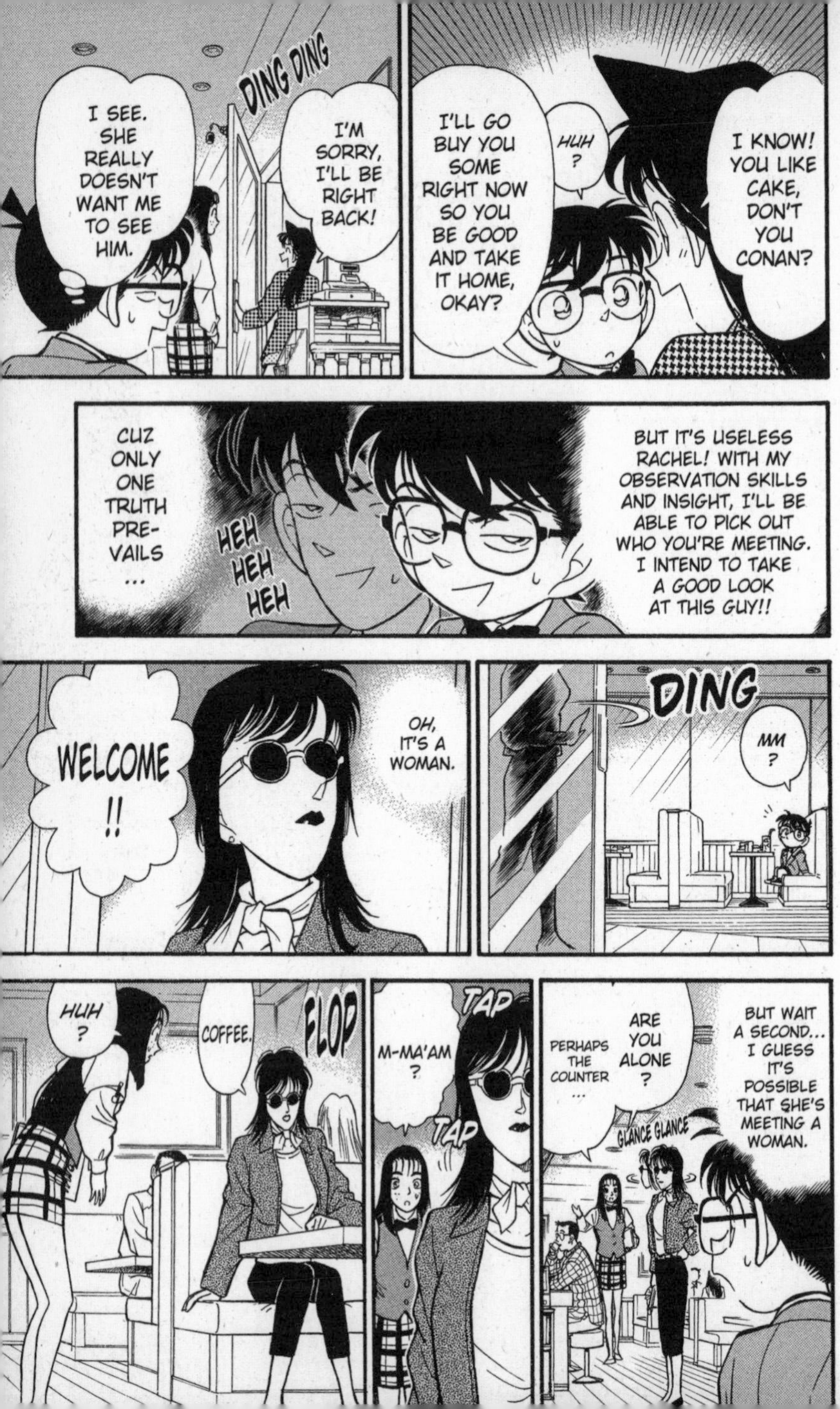
I KNOW! YOU LIKE CAKE, DON'T YOU CONAN?
HUH?
I'LL GO BUY YOU SOME RIGHT NOW SO YOU BE GOOD AND TAKE IT HOME, OKAY?
DING DING
I'M SORRY, I'LL BE RIGHT BACK!
I SEE. SHE REALLY DOESN'T WANT ME TO SEE HIM.
BUT IT'S USELESS RACHEL! WITH MY OBSERVATION SKILLS AND INSIGHT, I'LL BE ABLE TO PICK OUT WHO YOU'RE MEETING. I INTEND TO TAKE A GOOD LOOK AT THIS GUY!!
HEH HEH HEH
CUZ ONLY ONE TRUTH PRE-VAILS ...
DING
MM?
OH, IT'S A WOMAN.
WELCOME!!
BUT WAIT A SECOND... I GUESS IT'S POSSIBLE THAT SHE'S MEETING A WOMAN.
ARE YOU ALONE?
PERHAPS THE COUNTER ...
GLANCE GLANCE
TAP
M-MA'AM?
TAP
FLOP
COFFEE.
HUH?

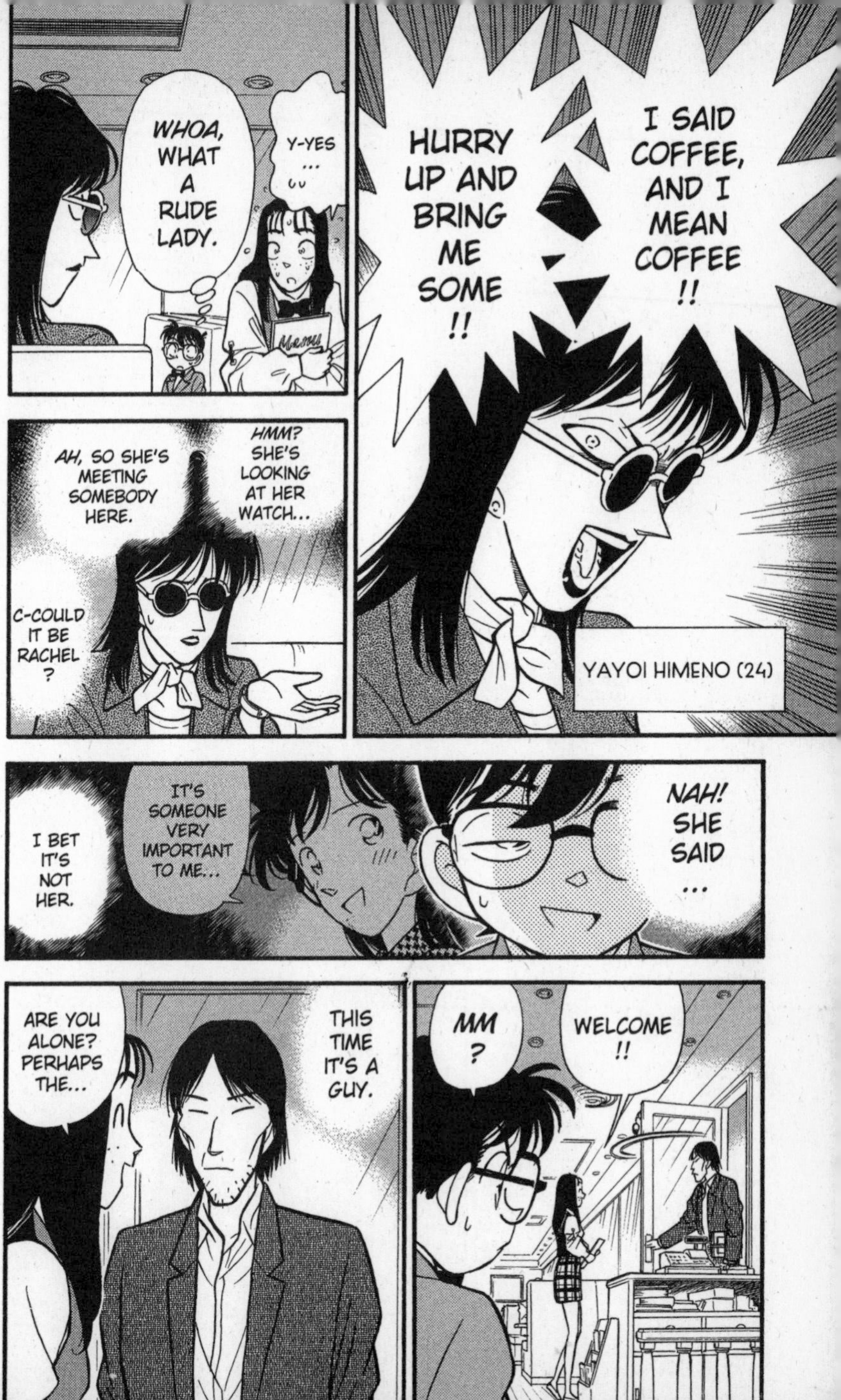
I SAID COFFEE, AND I MEAN COFFEE!!
HURRY UP AND BRING ME SOME!!
YAYOI HIMENO (24)
Y-YES...
WHOA, WHAT A RUDE LADY.
HMM? SHE'S LOOKING AT HER WATCH...
AH, SO SHE'S MEETING SOMEBODY HERE.
C-COULD IT BE RACHEL?
NAH! SHE SAID...
IT'S SOMEONE VERY IMPORTANT TO ME...
I BET IT'S NOT HER.
WELCOME!!
MM?
THIS TIME IT'S A GUY.
ARE YOU ALONE? PERHAPS THE...

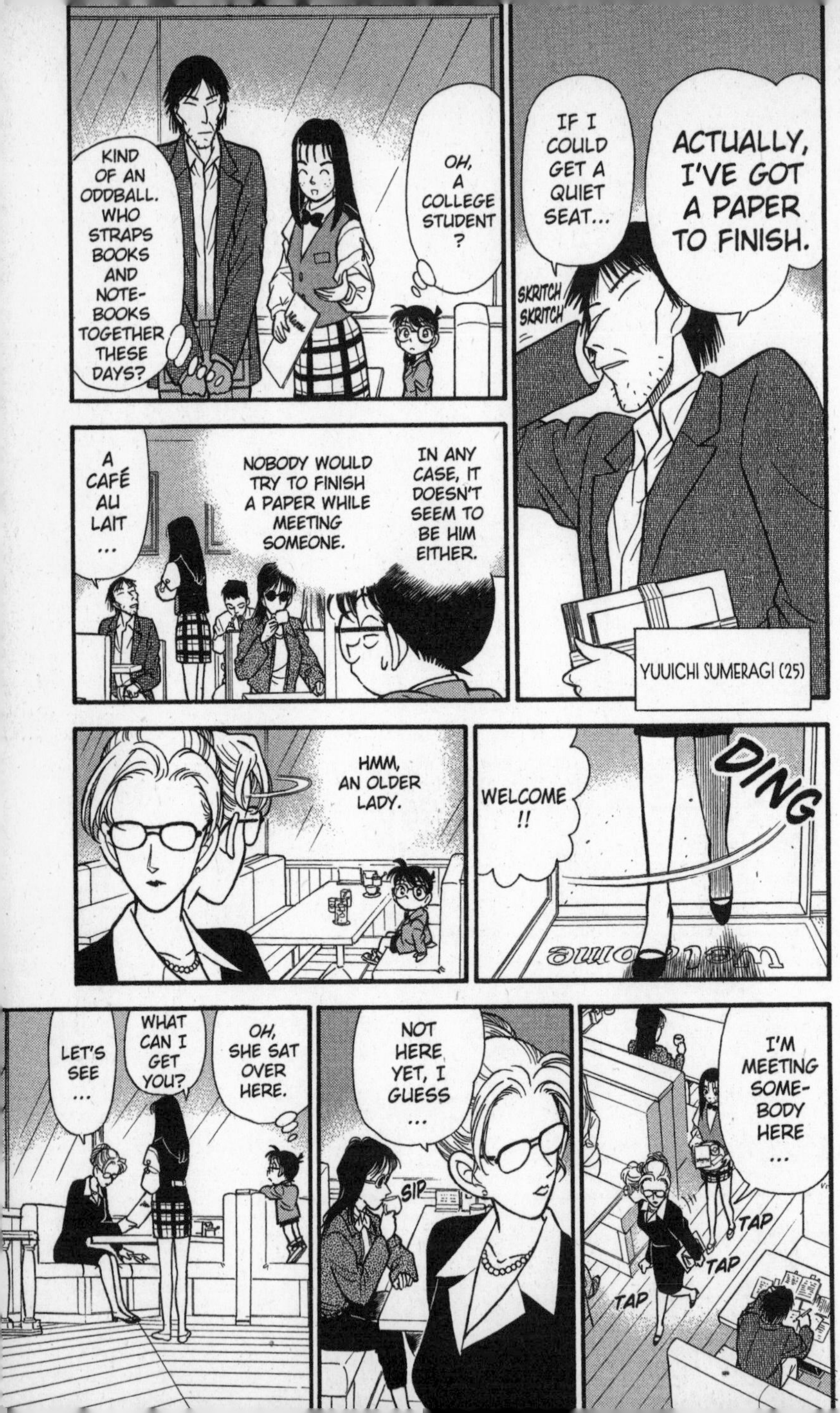
ACTUALLY, I'VE GOT A PAPER TO FINISH.
IF I COULD GET A QUIET SEAT...
SKRITCH SKRITCH
YUUICHI SUMERAGI (25)
OH, A COLLEGE STUDENT?
KIND OF AN ODDBALL. WHO STRAPS BOOKS AND NOTE-BOOKS TOGETHER THESE DAYS?
IN ANY CASE, IT DOESN'T SEEM TO BE HIM EITHER.
NOBODY WOULD TRY TO FINISH A PAPER WHILE MEETING SOMEONE.
A CAFÉ AU LAIT...
DING
WELCOME!!
HMM, AN OLDER LADY.
I'M MEETING SOME-BODY HERE...
TAP
TAP
TAP
NOT HERE YET, I GUESS...
SIP
OH, SHE SAT OVER HERE.
WHAT CAN I GET YOU?
LET'S SEE...

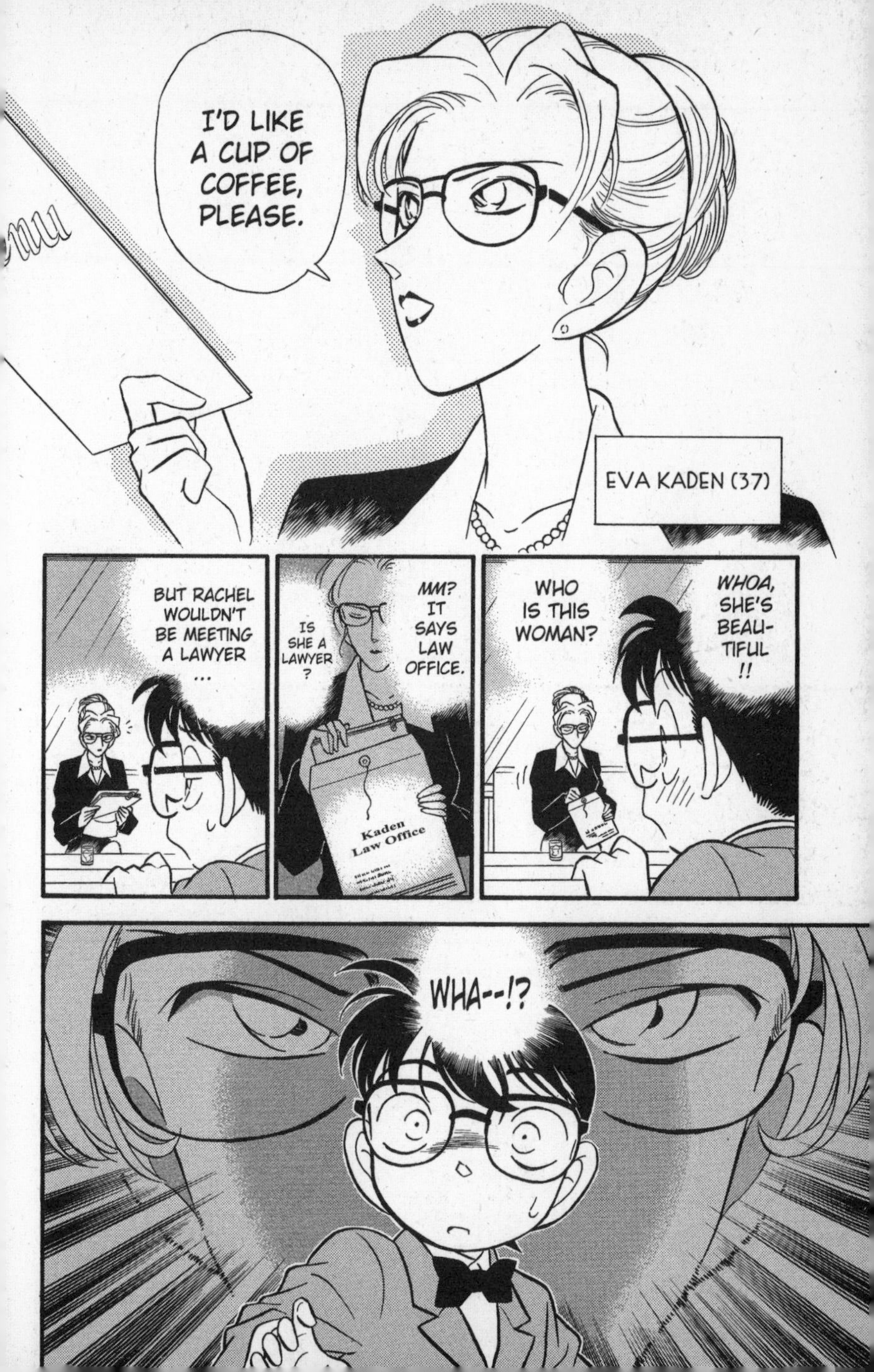
I'D LIKE A CUP OF COFFEE, PLEASE.
EVA KADEN (37)
WHOA, SHE'S BEAU-TIFUL !!
WHO IS THIS WOMAN?
MM? IT SAYS LAW OFFICE.
IS SHE A LAWYER ?
Kaden Law Office
BUT RACHEL WOULDN'T BE MEETING A LAWYER ...
WHA--!?

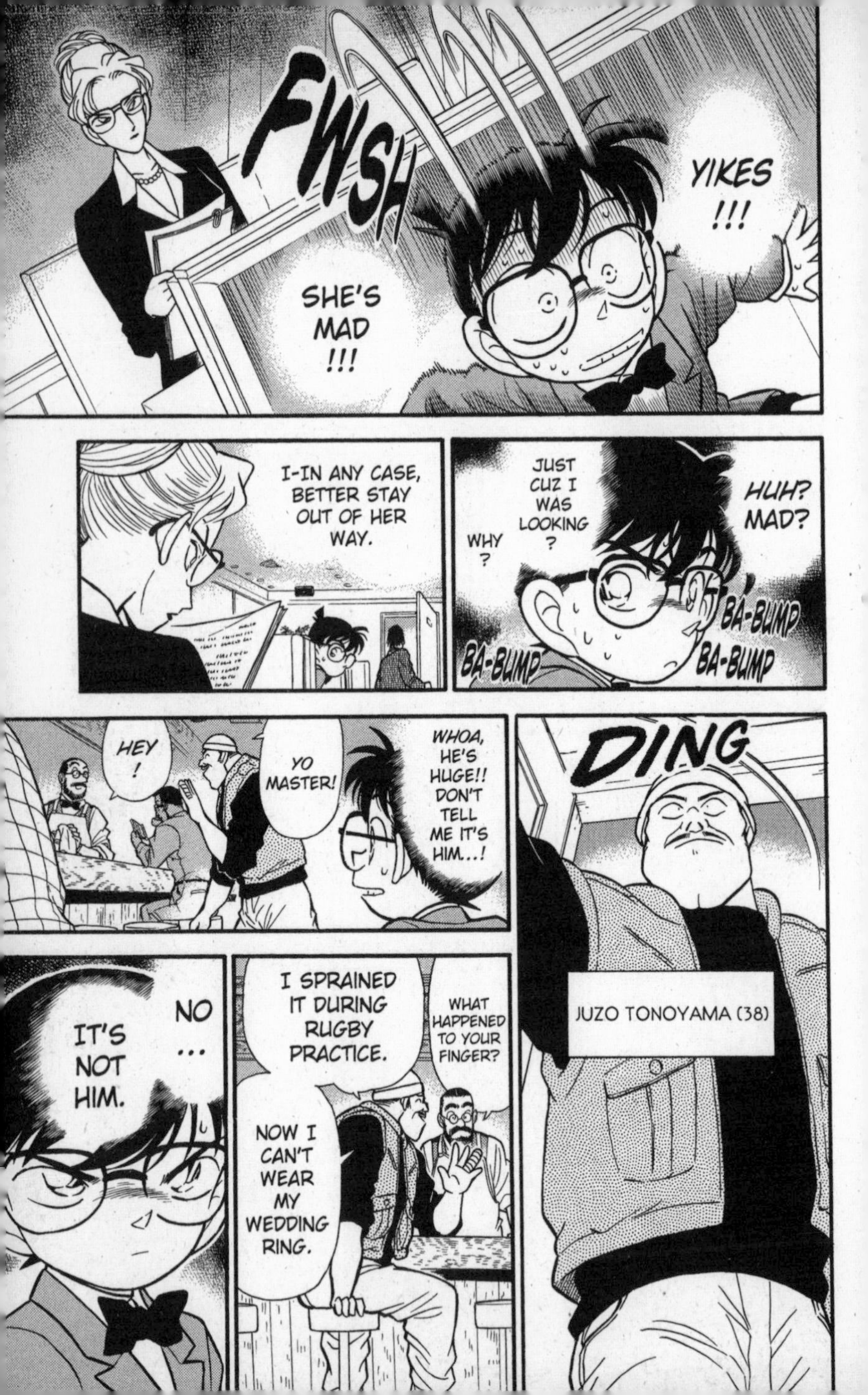
YIKES !!!
FWSH
SHE'S MAD !!!
HUH? MAD?
JUST CUZ I WAS LOOKING ?
WHY ?
BA-BUMP
BA-BUMP
BA-BUMP
I-IN ANY CASE, BETTER STAY OUT OF HER WAY.
DING
JUZO TONOYAMA (38)
WHOA, HE'S HUGE!! DON'T TELL ME IT'S HIM...!
YO MASTER!
HEY !
WHAT HAPPENED TO YOUR FINGER?
I SPRAINED IT DURING RUGBY PRACTICE.
NOW I CAN'T WEAR MY WEDDING RING.
NO ...
IT'S NOT HIM.

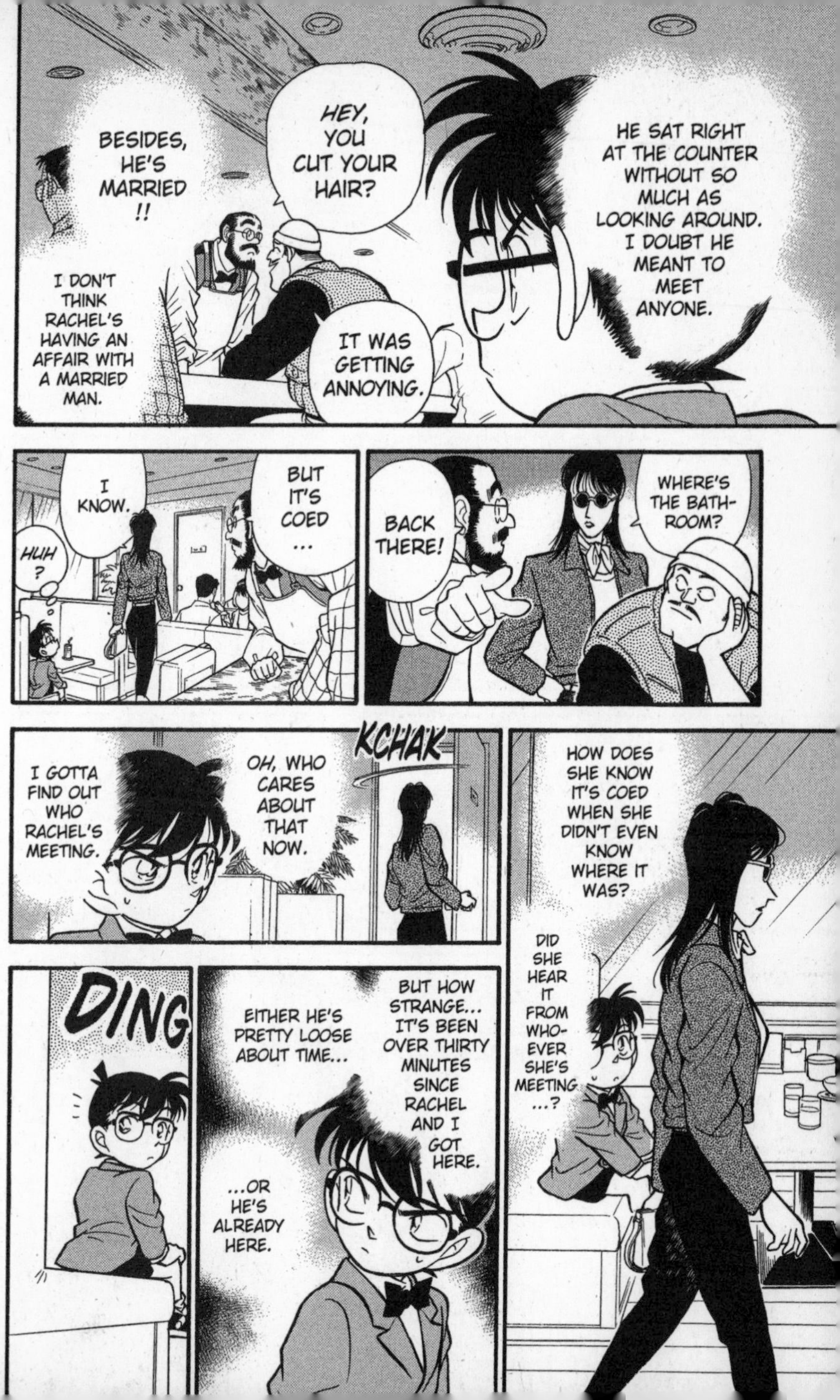

HE SAT RIGHT AT THE COUNTER WITHOUT SO MUCH AS LOOKING AROUND. I DOUBT HE MEANT TO MEET ANYONE.
HEY, YOU CUT YOUR HAIR?
BESIDES, HE'S MARRIED !!
IT WAS GETTING ANNOYING.
I DON'T THINK RACHEL'S HAVING AN AFFAIR WITH A MARRIED MAN.
WHERE'S THE BATH-ROOM?
BACK THERE!
BUT IT'S COED ...
I KNOW.
HUH ?
HOW DOES SHE KNOW IT'S COED WHEN SHE DIDN'T EVEN KNOW WHERE IT WAS?
DID SHE HEAR IT FROM WHO-EVER SHE'S MEETING ...?
KCHAK
OH, WHO CARES ABOUT THAT NOW.
I GOTTA FIND OUT WHO RACHEL'S MEETING.
BUT HOW STRANGE... IT'S BEEN OVER THIRTY MINUTES SINCE RACHEL AND I GOT HERE.
EITHER HE'S PRETTY LOOSE ABOUT TIME...
...OR HE'S ALREADY HERE.
DING

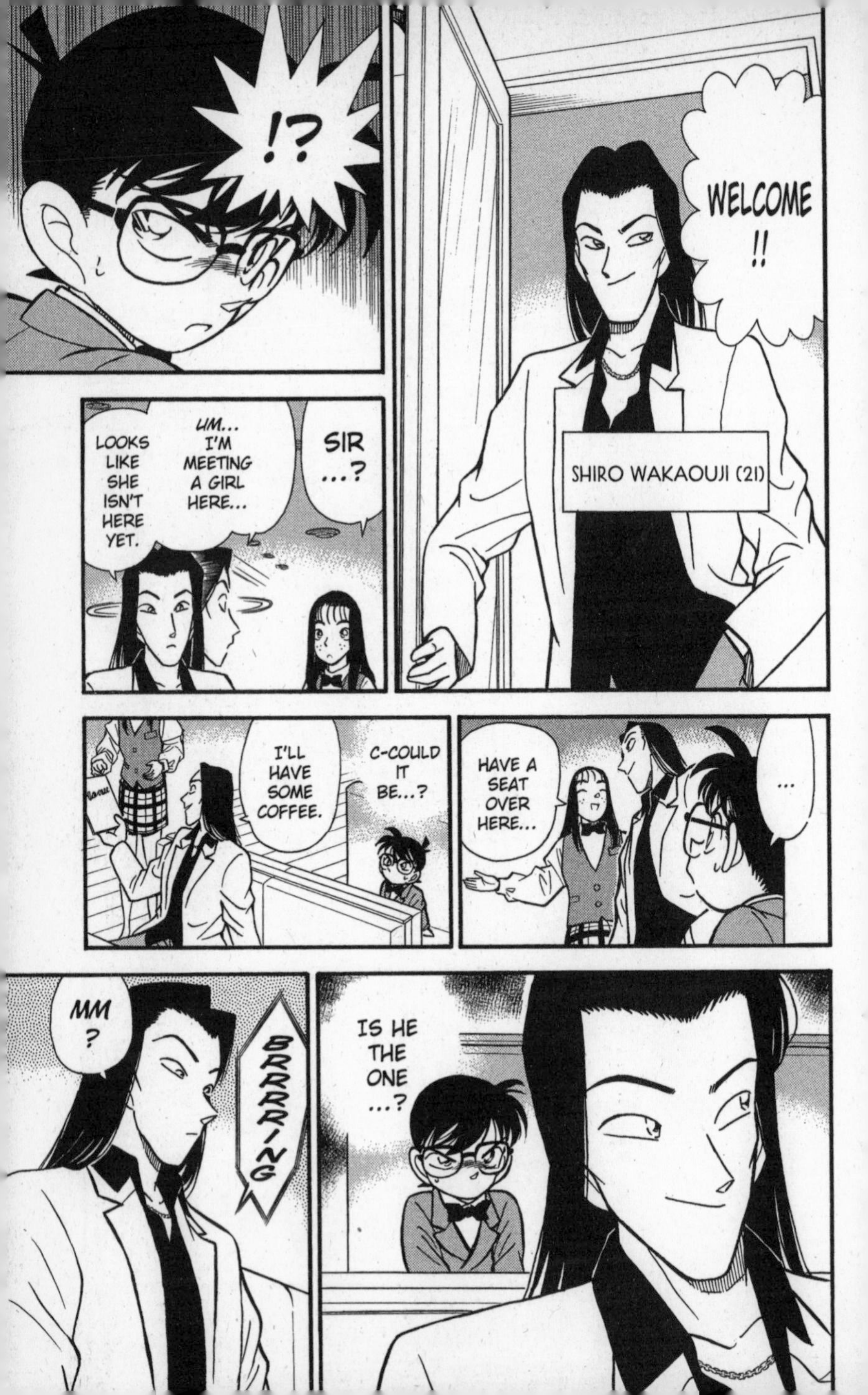
WELCOME!!
SHIRO WAKAOUJI (21)
!?
SIR...?
UM... I'M MEETING A GIRL HERE...
LOOKS LIKE SHE ISN'T HERE YET.
...
HAVE A SEAT OVER HERE...
C-COULD IT BE...?
I'LL HAVE SOME COFFEE.
IS HE THE ONE...?
MM?
BRRRRING

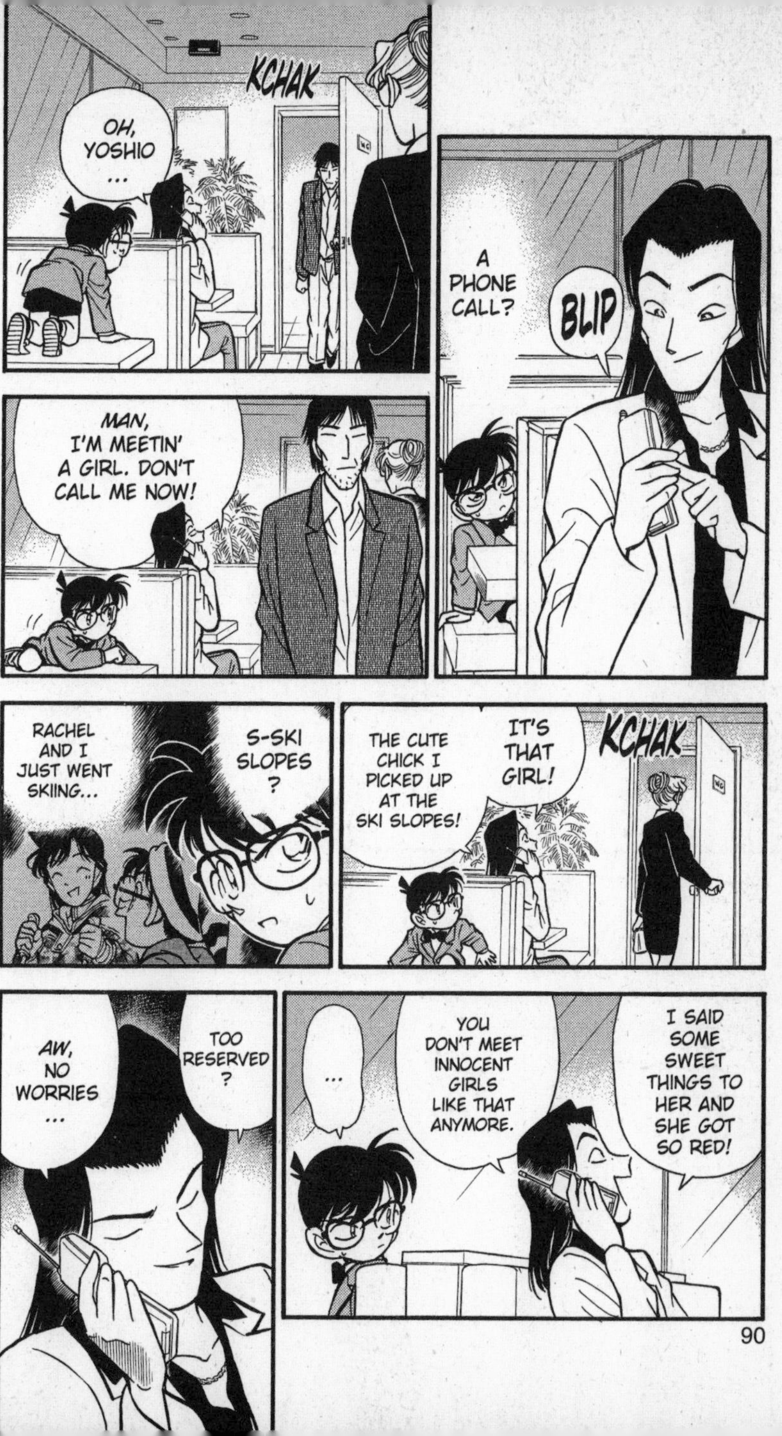
KCHAK
OH, YOSHIO ...
A PHONE CALL?
BLIP
MAN, I'M MEETIN' A GIRL. DON'T CALL ME NOW!
KCHAK
IT'S THAT GIRL!
THE CUTE CHICK I PICKED UP AT THE SKI SLOPES!
S-SKI SLOPES ?
RACHEL AND I JUST WENT SKIING...
I SAID SOME SWEET THINGS TO HER AND SHE GOT SO RED!
YOU DON'T MEET INNOCENT GIRLS LIKE THAT ANYMORE.
...
TOO RESERVED ?
AW, NO WORRIES ...

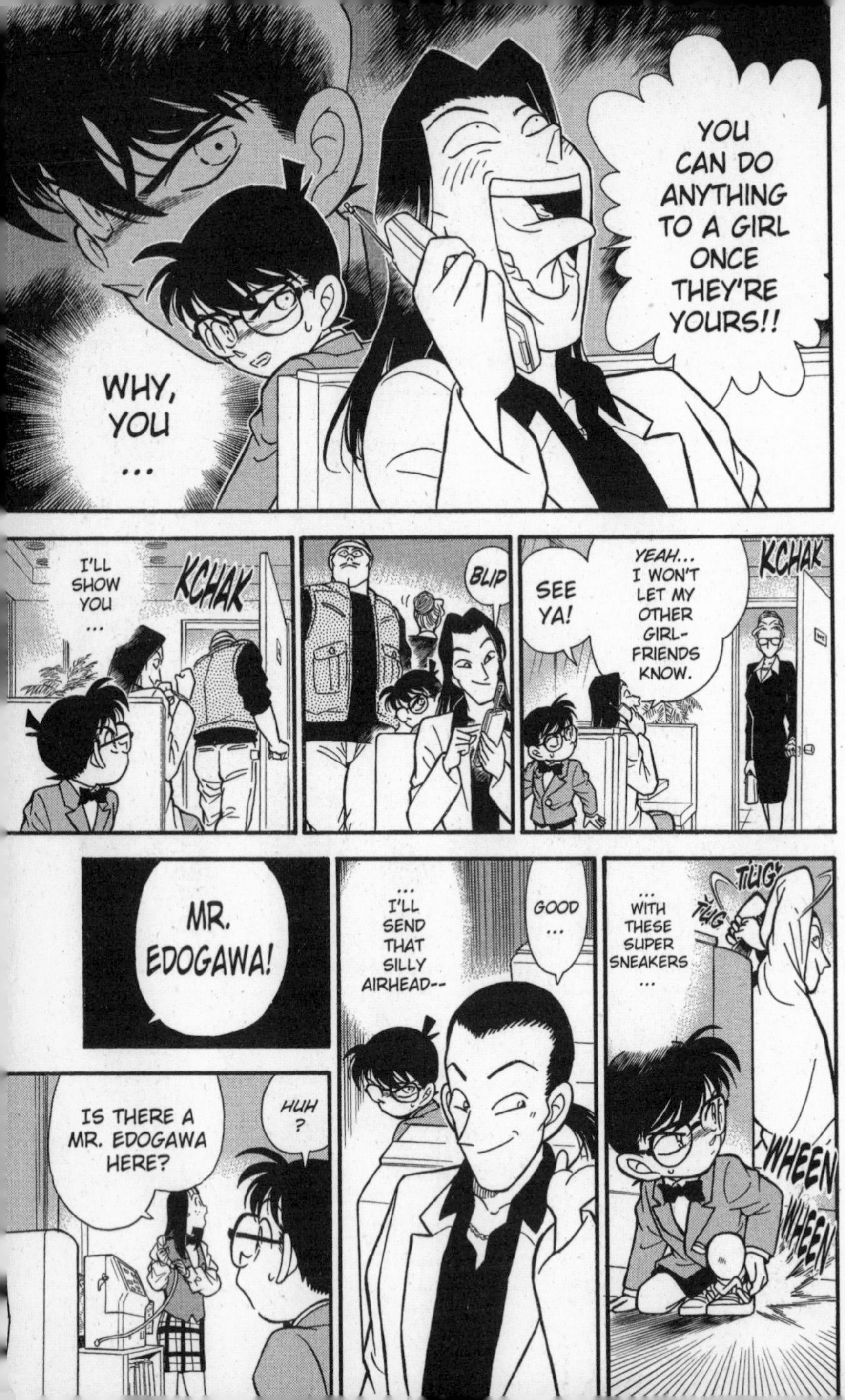
YOU CAN DO ANYTHING TO A GIRL ONCE THEY'RE YOURS!!
WHY, YOU ...
KCHAK
YEAH... I WON'T LET MY OTHER GIRL-FRIENDS KNOW.
SEE YA!
BLIP
KCHAK
I'LL SHOW YOU ...
TUG
TUG
... WITH THESE SUPER SNEAKERS ...
WHEEN
WHEEN
GOOD ...
... I'LL SEND THAT SILLY AIRHEAD--
MR. EDOGAWA!
HUH ?
IS THERE A MR. EDOGAWA HERE?

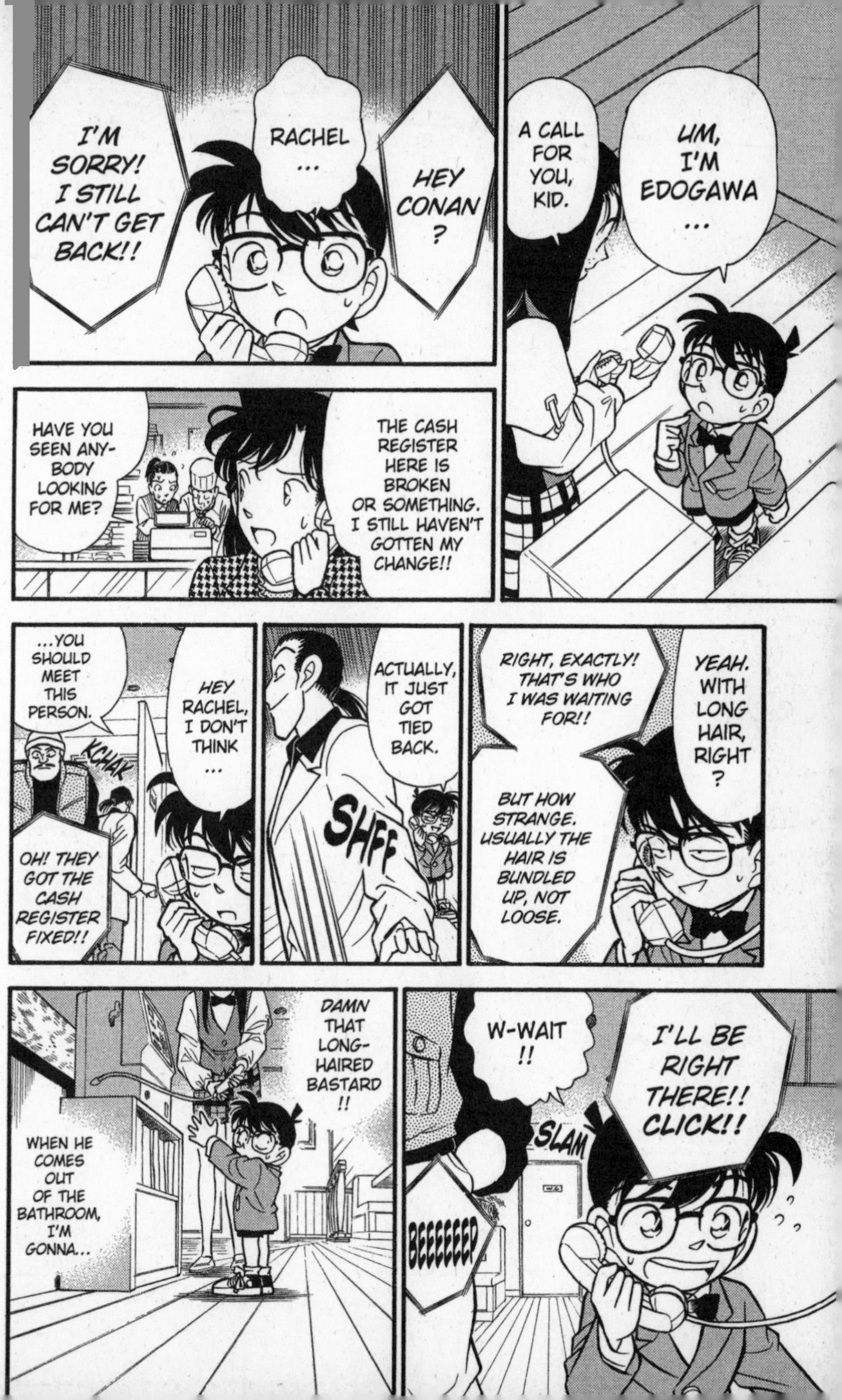
UM, I'M EDOGAWA ...
A CALL FOR YOU, KID.
HEY CONAN ?
RACHEL ...
I'M SORRY! I STILL CAN'T GET BACK!!
THE CASH REGISTER HERE IS BROKEN OR SOMETHING. I STILL HAVEN'T GOTTEN MY CHANGE!!
HAVE YOU SEEN ANY-BODY LOOKING FOR ME?
YEAH. WITH LONG HAIR, RIGHT ?
RIGHT, EXACTLY! THAT'S WHO I WAS WAITING FOR!!
BUT HOW STRANGE. USUALLY THE HAIR IS BUNDLED UP, NOT LOOSE.
ACTUALLY, IT JUST GOT TIED BACK.
SHFF
HEY RACHEL, I DON'T THINK ...
...YOU SHOULD MEET THIS PERSON.
KCHAK
OH! THEY GOT THE CASH REGISTER FIXED!!
I'LL BE RIGHT THERE!! CLICK!!
W-WAIT !!
SLAM
BEEEEEEP
DAMN THAT LONG-HAIRED BASTARD !!
WHEN HE COMES OUT OF THE BATHROOM, I'M GONNA...

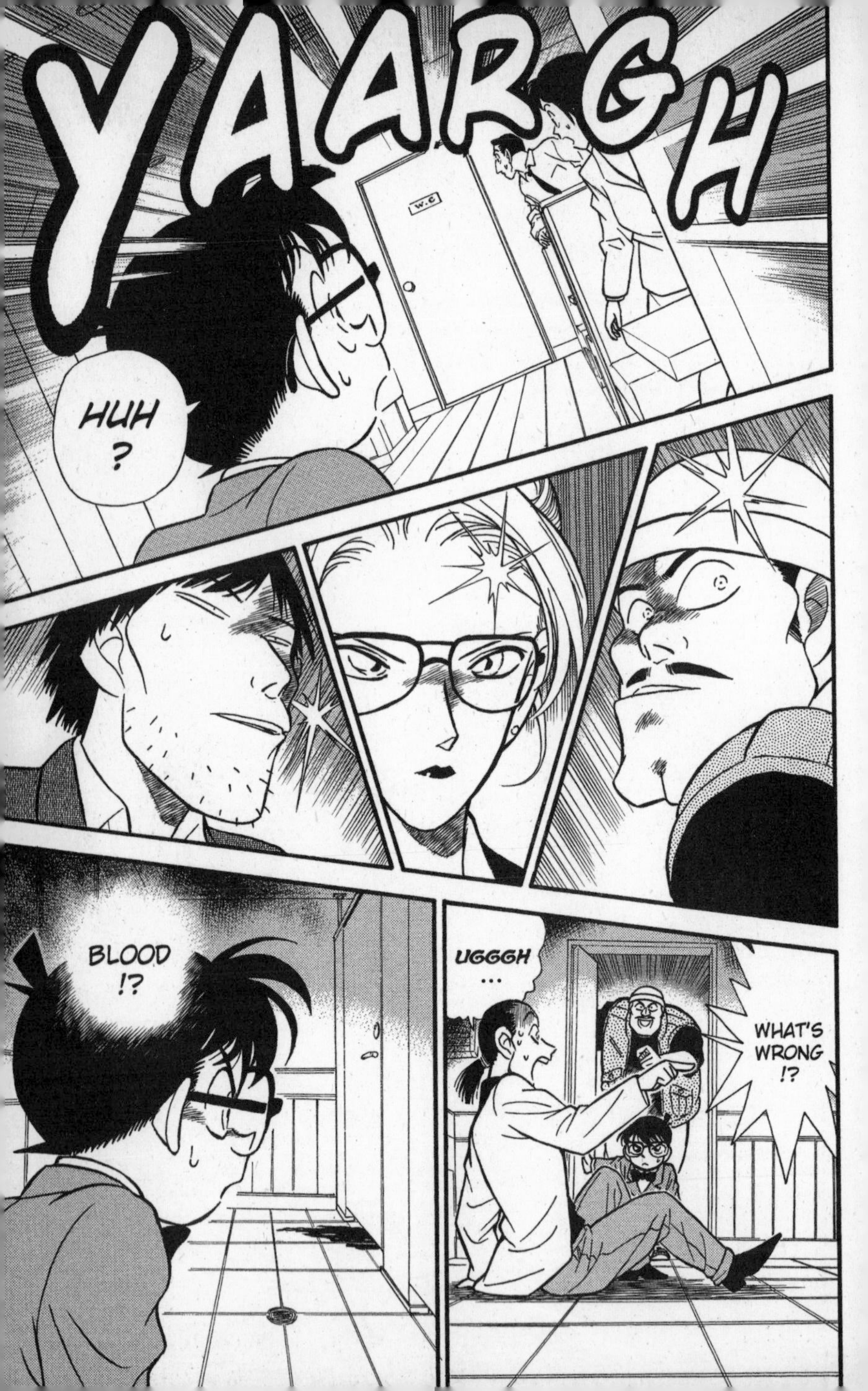
YAARGH
HUH?
WHAT'S WRONG!?
UGGGH...
BLOOD!?

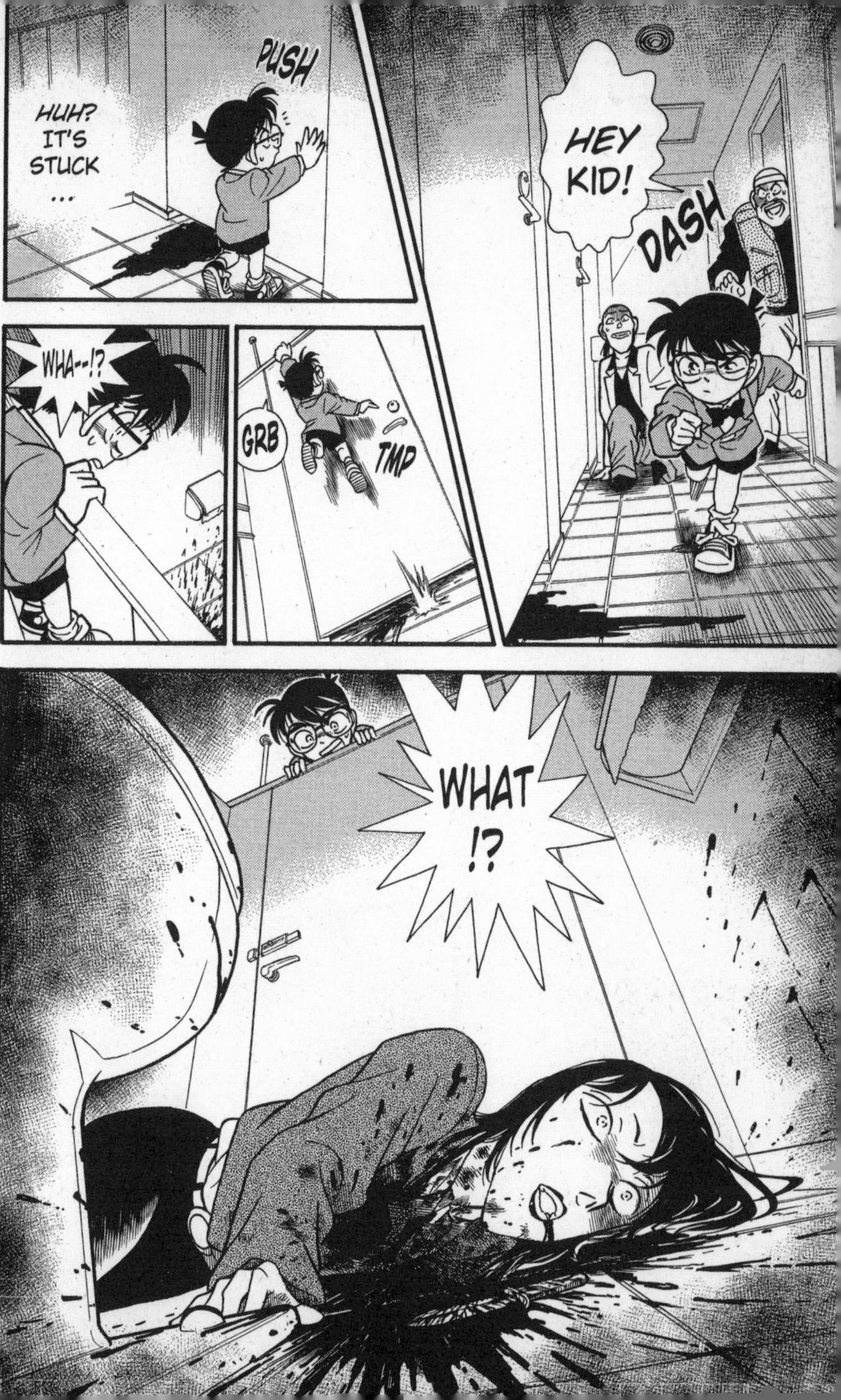
HEY KID!
DASH
PUSH
HUH? IT'S STUCK ...
GRB
TMP
WHA--!?
WHAT !?

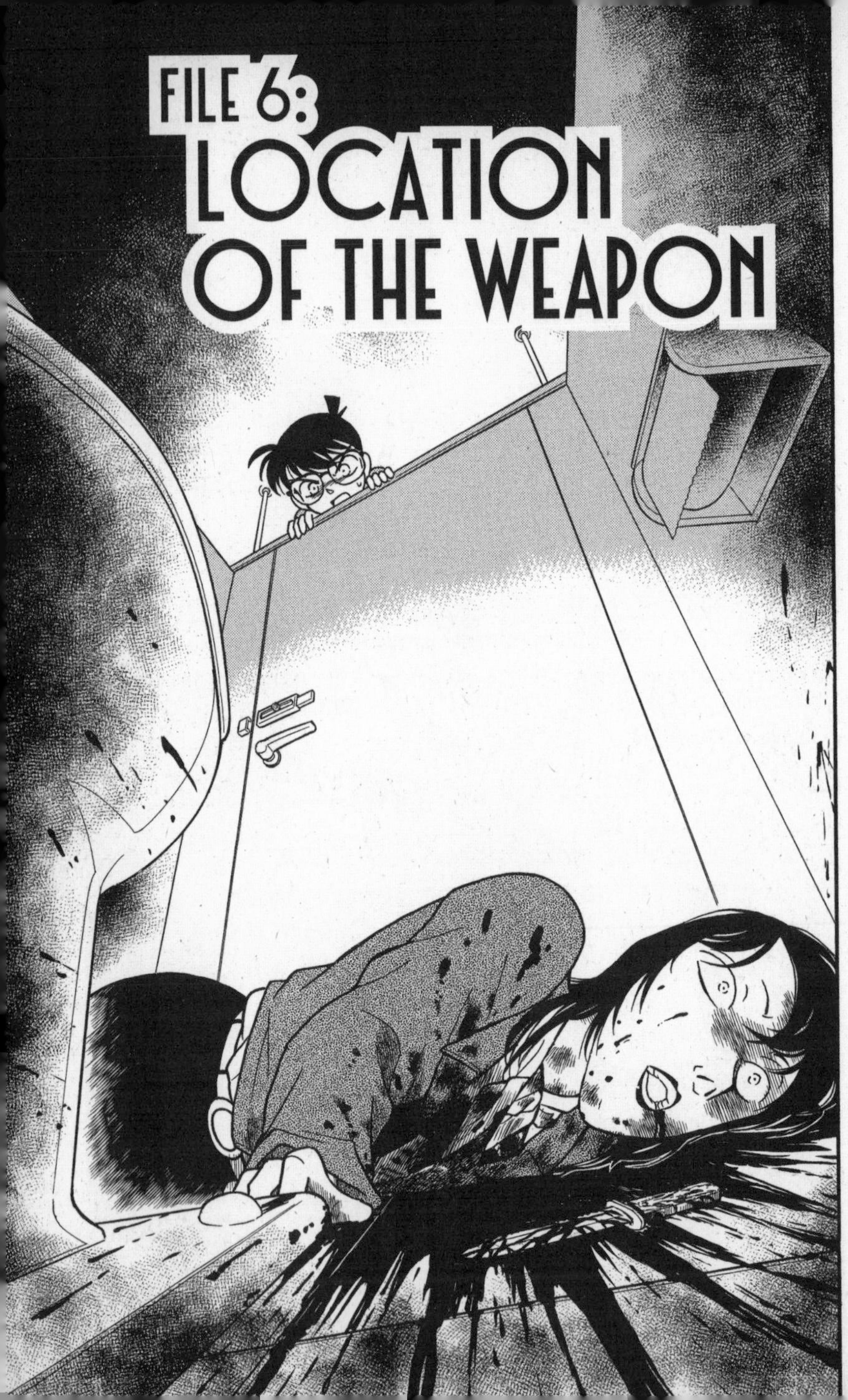
FILE 6:
LOCATION OF THE WEAPON

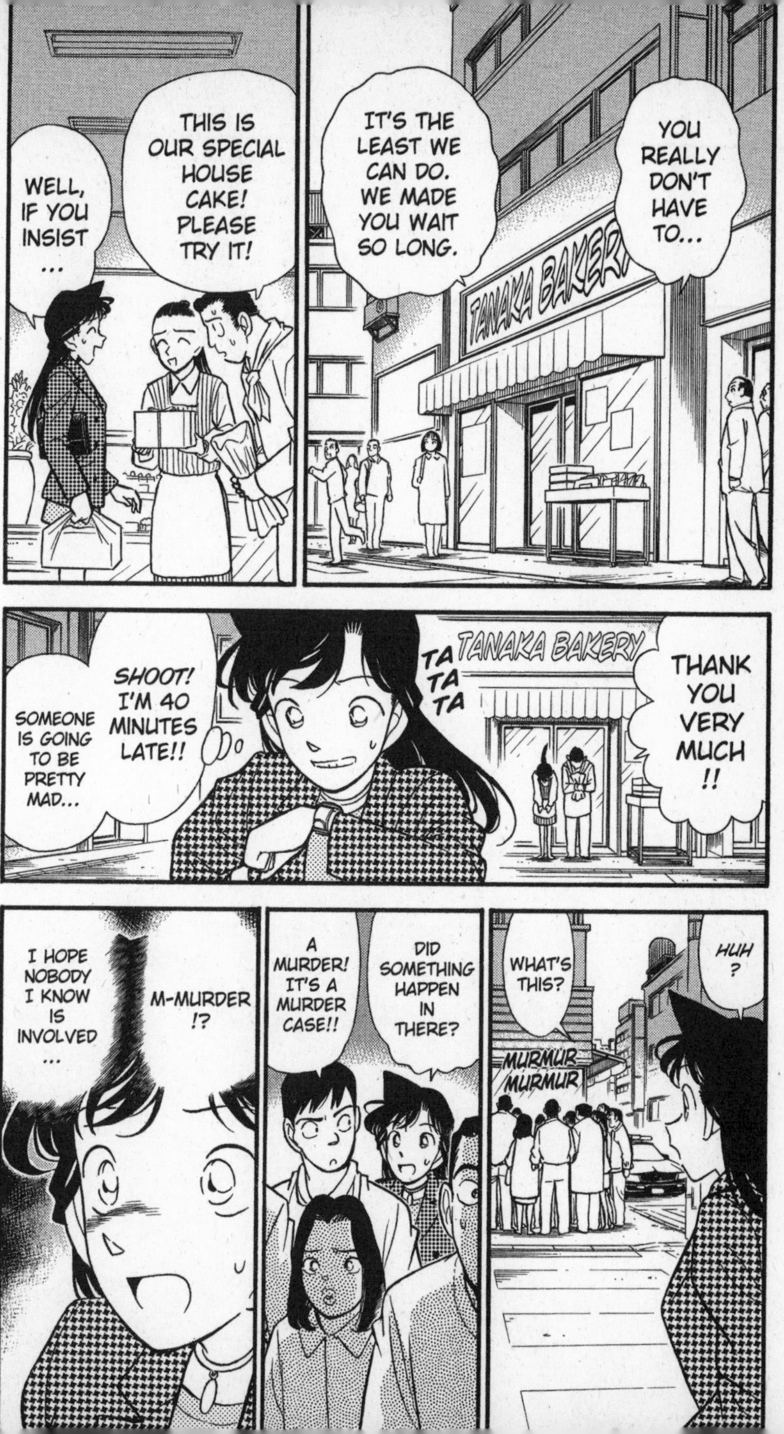
YOU REALLY DON'T HAVE TO...
TANAKA BAKERY
IT'S THE LEAST WE CAN DO. WE MADE YOU WAIT SO LONG.
THIS IS OUR SPECIAL HOUSE CAKE! PLEASE TRY IT!
WELL, IF YOU INSIST...
THANK YOU VERY MUCH!!
TANAKA BAKERY
TA TA TA
SHOOT! I'M 40 MINUTES LATE!!
SOMEONE IS GOING TO BE PRETTY MAD...
HUH?
WHAT'S THIS?
MURMUR MURMUR
DID SOMETHING HAPPEN IN THERE?
A MURDER! IT'S A MURDER CASE!!
M-MURDER!?
I HOPE NOBODY I KNOW IS INVOLVED...

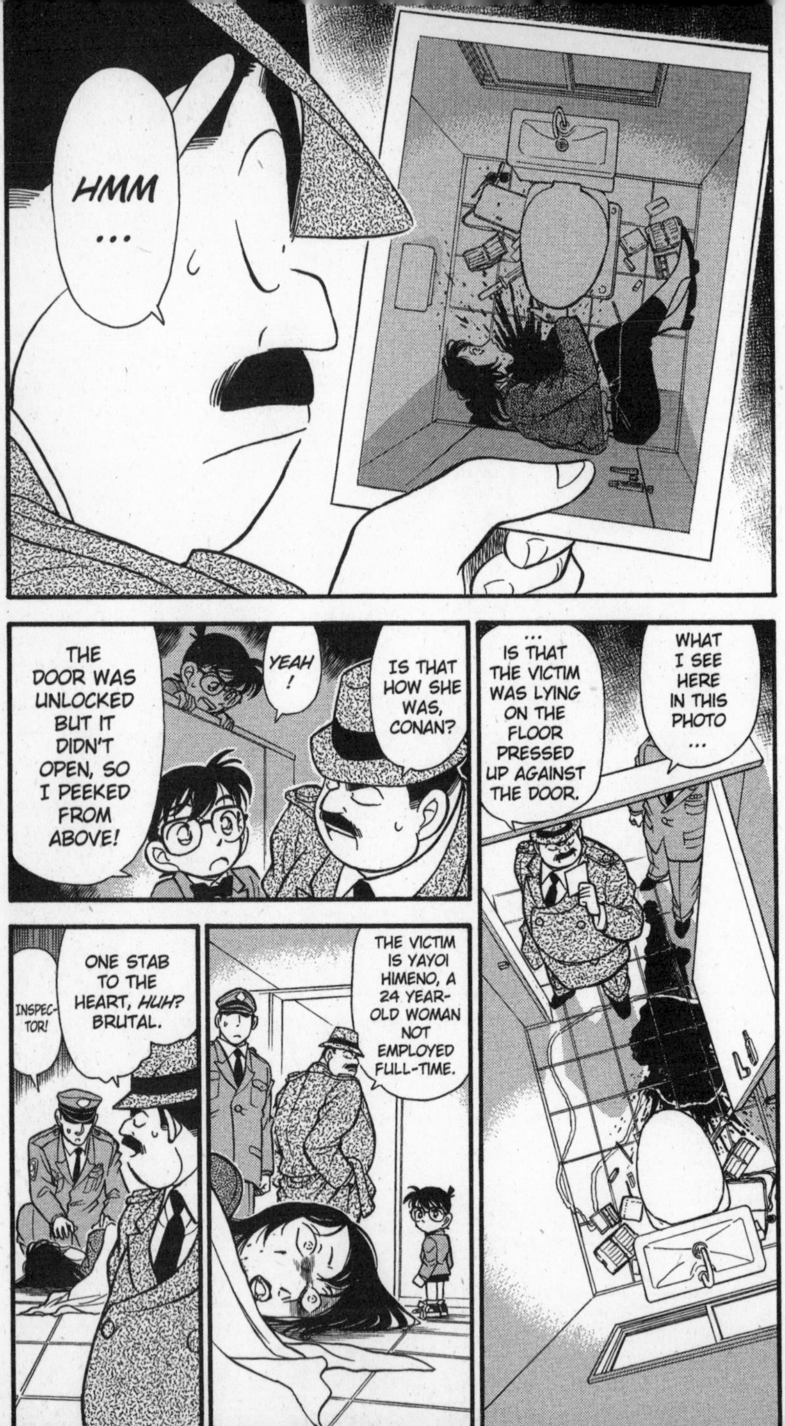
HMM ...
WHAT I SEE HERE IN THIS PHOTO ...
... IS THAT THE VICTIM WAS LYING ON THE FLOOR PRESSED UP AGAINST THE DOOR.
IS THAT HOW SHE WAS, CONAN?
YEAH!
THE DOOR WAS UNLOCKED BUT IT DIDN'T OPEN, SO I PEEKED FROM ABOVE!
THE VICTIM IS YAYOI HIMENO, A 24 YEAR-OLD WOMAN NOT EMPLOYED FULL-TIME.
ONE STAB TO THE HEART, *HUH?* BRUTAL.
INSPEC-TOR!

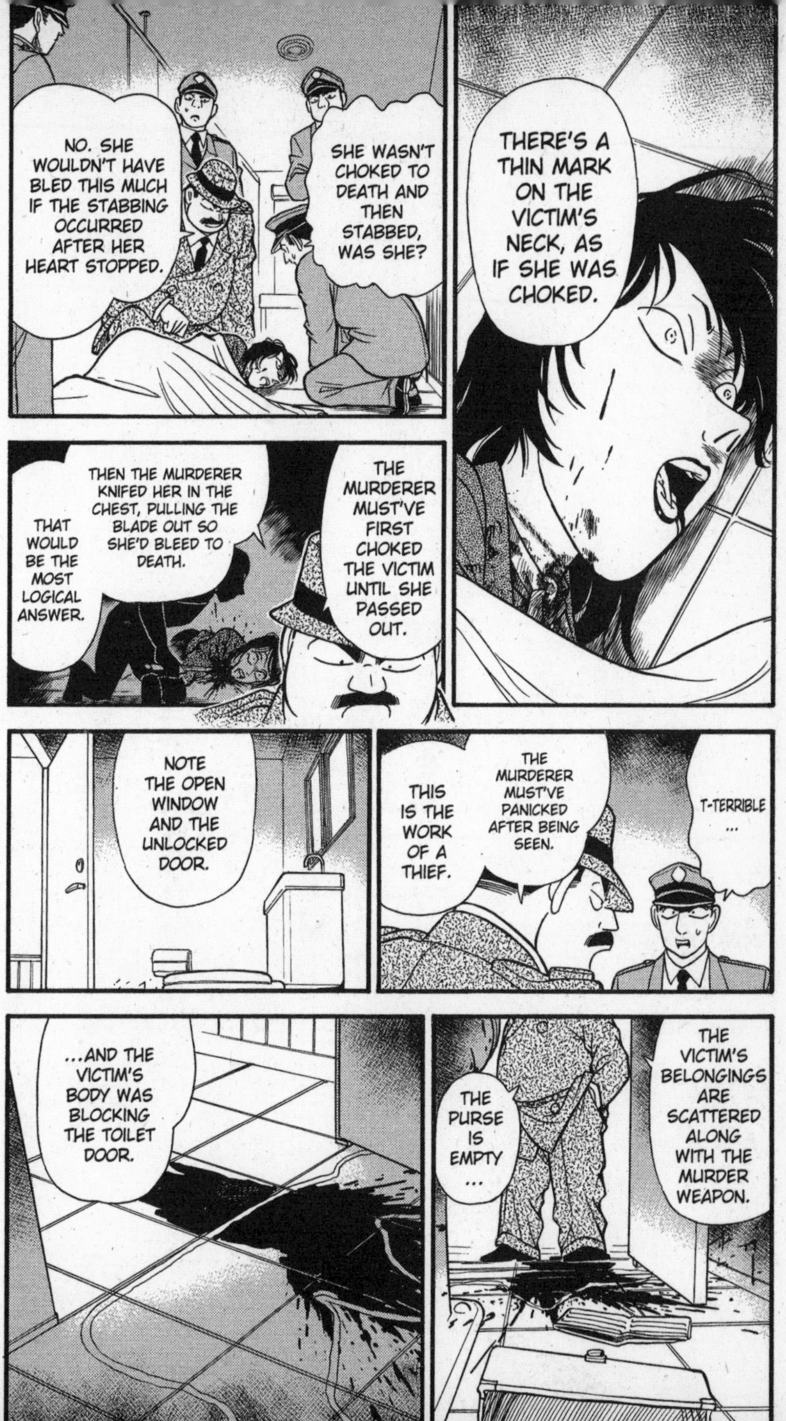
THERE'S A THIN MARK ON THE VICTIM'S NECK, AS IF SHE WAS CHOKED.
SHE WASN'T CHOKED TO DEATH AND THEN STABBED, WAS SHE?
NO. SHE WOULDN'T HAVE BLED THIS MUCH IF THE STABBING OCCURRED AFTER HER HEART STOPPED.
THE MURDERER MUST'VE FIRST CHOKED THE VICTIM UNTIL SHE PASSED OUT.
THEN THE MURDERER KNIFED HER IN THE CHEST, PULLING THE BLADE OUT SO SHE'D BLEED TO DEATH.
THAT WOULD BE THE MOST LOGICAL ANSWER.
T-TERRIBLE...
THE MURDERER MUST'VE PANICKED AFTER BEING SEEN.
THIS IS THE WORK OF A THIEF.
NOTE THE OPEN WINDOW AND THE UNLOCKED DOOR.
THE VICTIM'S BELONGINGS ARE SCATTERED ALONG WITH THE MURDER WEAPON.
THE PURSE IS EMPTY...
...AND THE VICTIM'S BODY WAS BLOCKING THE TOILET DOOR.

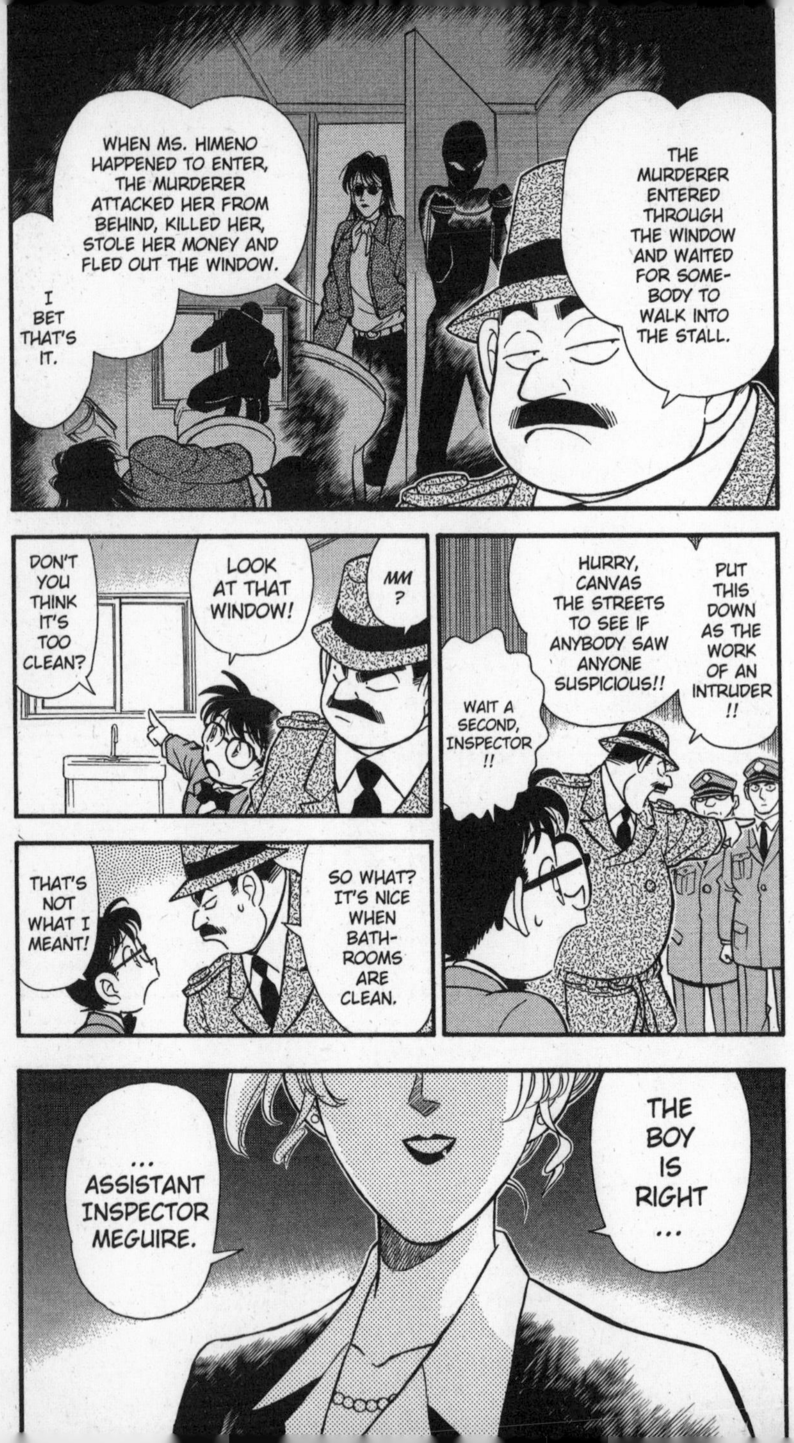
THE MURDERER ENTERED THROUGH THE WINDOW AND WAITED FOR SOMEBODY TO WALK INTO THE STALL.
WHEN MS. HIMENO HAPPENED TO ENTER, THE MURDERER ATTACKED HER FROM BEHIND, KILLED HER, STOLE HER MONEY AND FLED OUT THE WINDOW.
I BET THAT'S IT.
PUT THIS DOWN AS THE WORK OF AN INTRUDER!!
HURRY, CANVAS THE STREETS TO SEE IF ANYBODY SAW ANYONE SUSPICIOUS!!
WAIT A SECOND, INSPECTOR!!
MM?
LOOK AT THAT WINDOW!
DON'T YOU THINK IT'S TOO CLEAN?
SO WHAT? IT'S NICE WHEN BATHROOMS ARE CLEAN.
THAT'S NOT WHAT I MEANT!
THE BOY IS RIGHT...
...ASSISTANT INSPECTOR MEGUIRE.

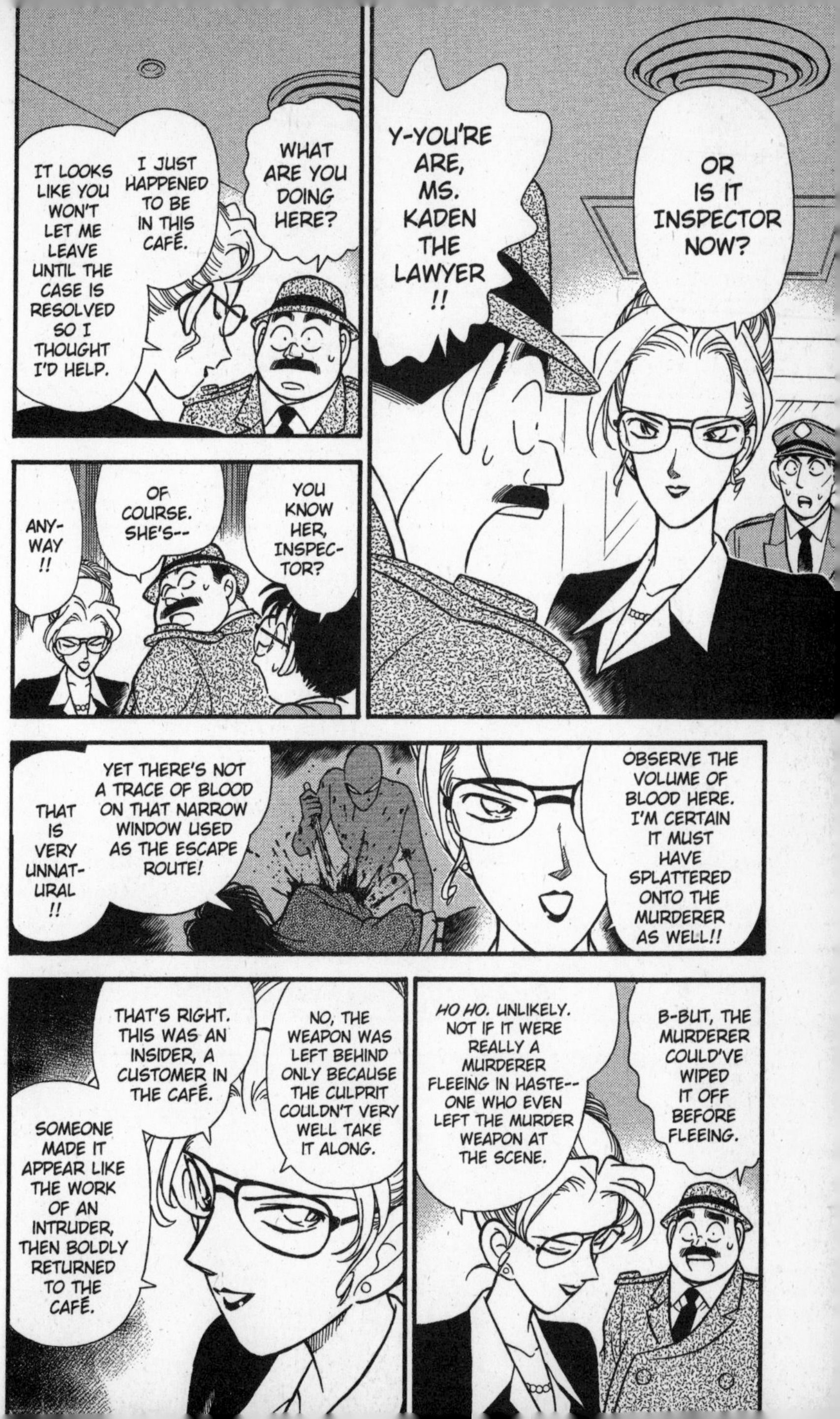
OR IS IT INSPECTOR NOW?
Y-YOU'RE ARE, MS. KADEN THE LAWYER !!
WHAT ARE YOU DOING HERE?
I JUST HAPPENED TO BE IN THIS CAFÉ.
IT LOOKS LIKE YOU WON'T LET ME LEAVE UNTIL THE CASE IS RESOLVED SO I THOUGHT I'D HELP.
YOU KNOW HER, INSPECTOR?
OF COURSE. SHE'S--
ANY-WAY !!
OBSERVE THE VOLUME OF BLOOD HERE. I'M CERTAIN IT MUST HAVE SPLATTERED ONTO THE MURDERER AS WELL!!
YET THERE'S NOT A TRACE OF BLOOD ON THAT NARROW WINDOW USED AS THE ESCAPE ROUTE!
THAT IS VERY UNNAT-URAL !!
B-BUT, THE MURDERER COULD'VE WIPED IT OFF BEFORE FLEEING.
HO HO. UNLIKELY. NOT IF IT WERE REALLY A MURDERER FLEEING IN HASTE-- ONE WHO EVEN LEFT THE MURDER WEAPON AT THE SCENE.
NO, THE WEAPON WAS LEFT BEHIND ONLY BECAUSE THE CULPRIT COULDN'T VERY WELL TAKE IT ALONG.
THAT'S RIGHT. THIS WAS AN INSIDER, A CUSTOMER IN THE CAFÉ.
SOMEONE MADE IT APPEAR LIKE THE WORK OF AN INTRUDER, THEN BOLDLY RETURNED TO THE CAFÉ.

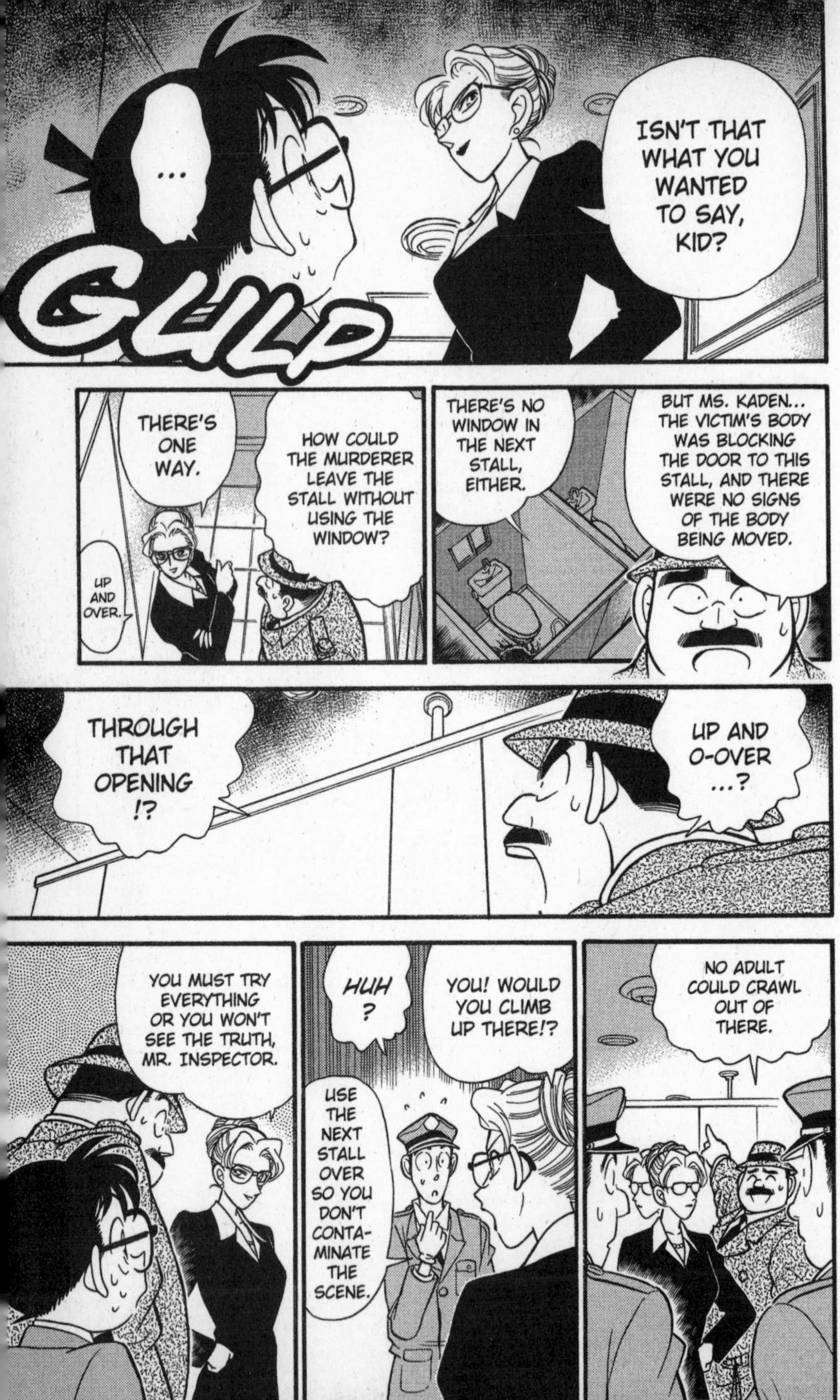
ISN'T THAT WHAT YOU WANTED TO SAY, KID?
...
GULP
BUT MS. KADEN... THE VICTIM'S BODY WAS BLOCKING THE DOOR TO THIS STALL, AND THERE WERE NO SIGNS OF THE BODY BEING MOVED.
THERE'S NO WINDOW IN THE NEXT STALL, EITHER.
HOW COULD THE MURDERER LEAVE THE STALL WITHOUT USING THE WINDOW?
THERE'S ONE WAY.
UP AND OVER.
UP AND O-OVER ...?
THROUGH THAT OPENING !?
NO ADULT COULD CRAWL OUT OF THERE.
YOU! WOULD YOU CLIMB UP THERE!?
HUH ?
USE THE NEXT STALL OVER SO YOU DON'T CONTA-MINATE THE SCENE.
YOU MUST TRY EVERYTHING OR YOU WON'T SEE THE TRUTH, MR. INSPECTOR.

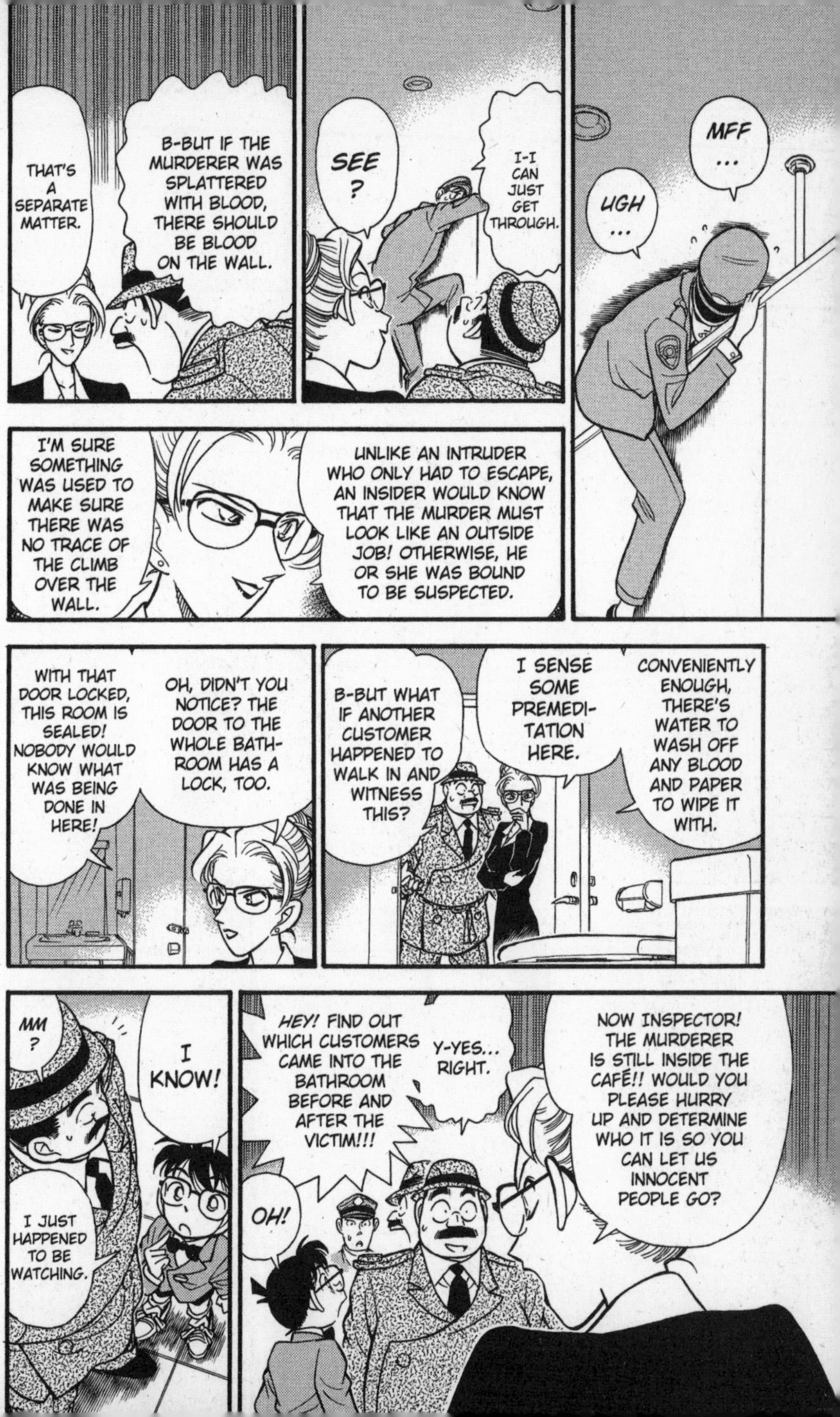
MFF ...
UGH ...
I-I CAN JUST GET THROUGH.
SEE ?
B-BUT IF THE MURDERER WAS SPLATTERED WITH BLOOD, THERE SHOULD BE BLOOD ON THE WALL.
THAT'S A SEPARATE MATTER.
UNLIKE AN INTRUDER WHO ONLY HAD TO ESCAPE, AN INSIDER WOULD KNOW THAT THE MURDER MUST LOOK LIKE AN OUTSIDE JOB! OTHERWISE, HE OR SHE WAS BOUND TO BE SUSPECTED.
I'M SURE SOMETHING WAS USED TO MAKE SURE THERE WAS NO TRACE OF THE CLIMB OVER THE WALL.
CONVENIENTLY ENOUGH, THERE'S WATER TO WASH OFF ANY BLOOD AND PAPER TO WIPE IT WITH.
I SENSE SOME PREMEDI-TATION HERE.
B-BUT WHAT IF ANOTHER CUSTOMER HAPPENED TO WALK IN AND WITNESS THIS?
OH, DIDN'T YOU NOTICE? THE DOOR TO THE WHOLE BATH-ROOM HAS A LOCK, TOO.
WITH THAT DOOR LOCKED, THIS ROOM IS SEALED! NOBODY WOULD KNOW WHAT WAS BEING DONE IN HERE!
NOW INSPECTOR! THE MURDERER IS STILL INSIDE THE CAFÉ!! WOULD YOU PLEASE HURRY UP AND DETERMINE WHO IT IS SO YOU CAN LET US INNOCENT PEOPLE GO?
Y-YES... RIGHT.
HEY! FIND OUT WHICH CUSTOMERS CAME INTO THE BATHROOM BEFORE AND AFTER THE VICTIM!!!
OH!
I KNOW!
MM ?
I JUST HAPPENED TO BE WATCHING.

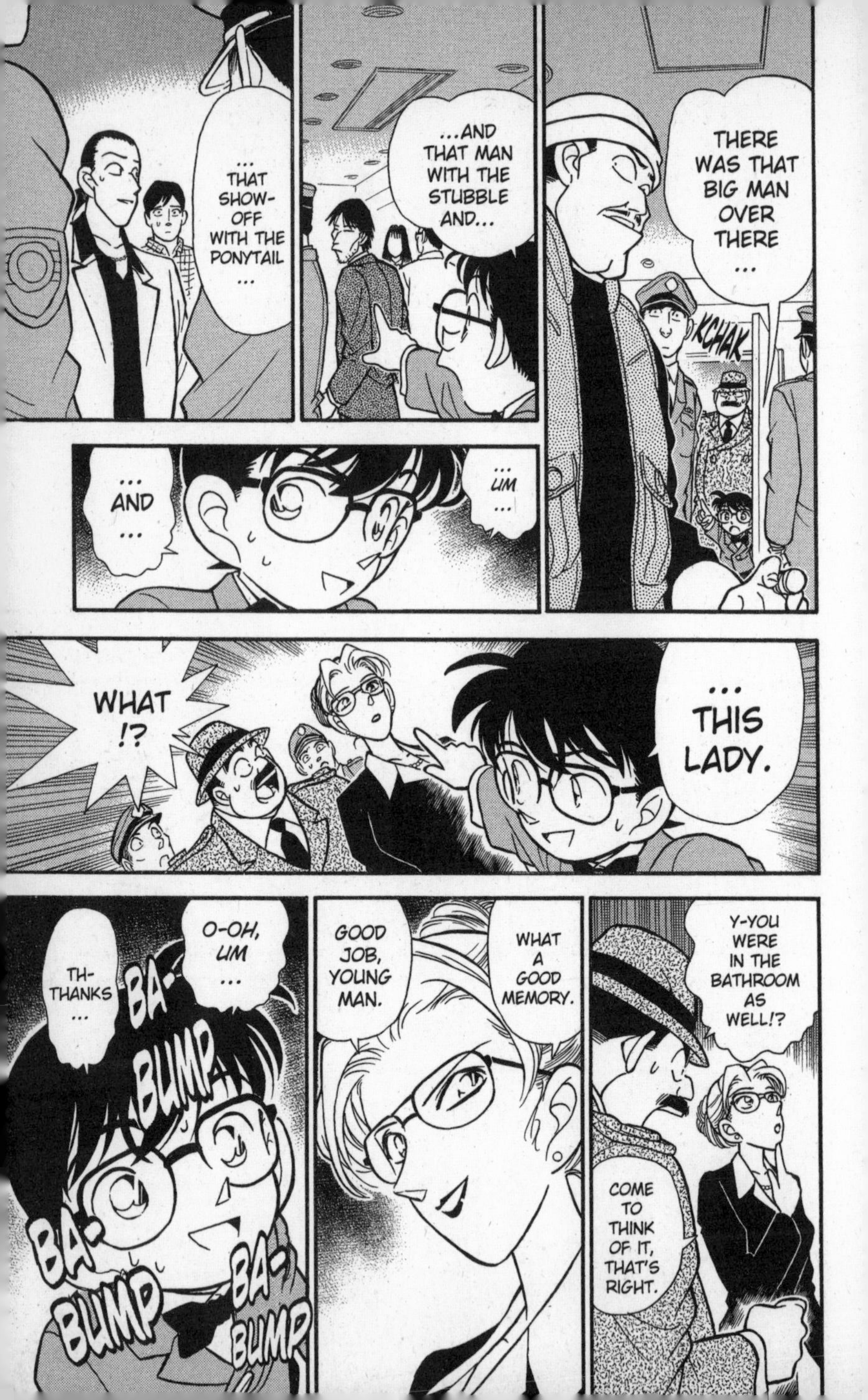
THERE WAS THAT BIG MAN OVER THERE ...
KCHAK
...AND THAT MAN WITH THE STUBBLE AND...
... THAT SHOW-OFF WITH THE PONYTAIL ...
... UM ...
... AND ...
... THIS LADY.
WHAT !?
Y-YOU WERE IN THE BATHROOM AS WELL!?
COME TO THINK OF IT, THAT'S RIGHT.
WHAT A GOOD MEMORY.
GOOD JOB, YOUNG MAN.
O-OH, UM ...
TH-THANKS ...
BA-BUMP
BA-BUMP
BA-BUMP

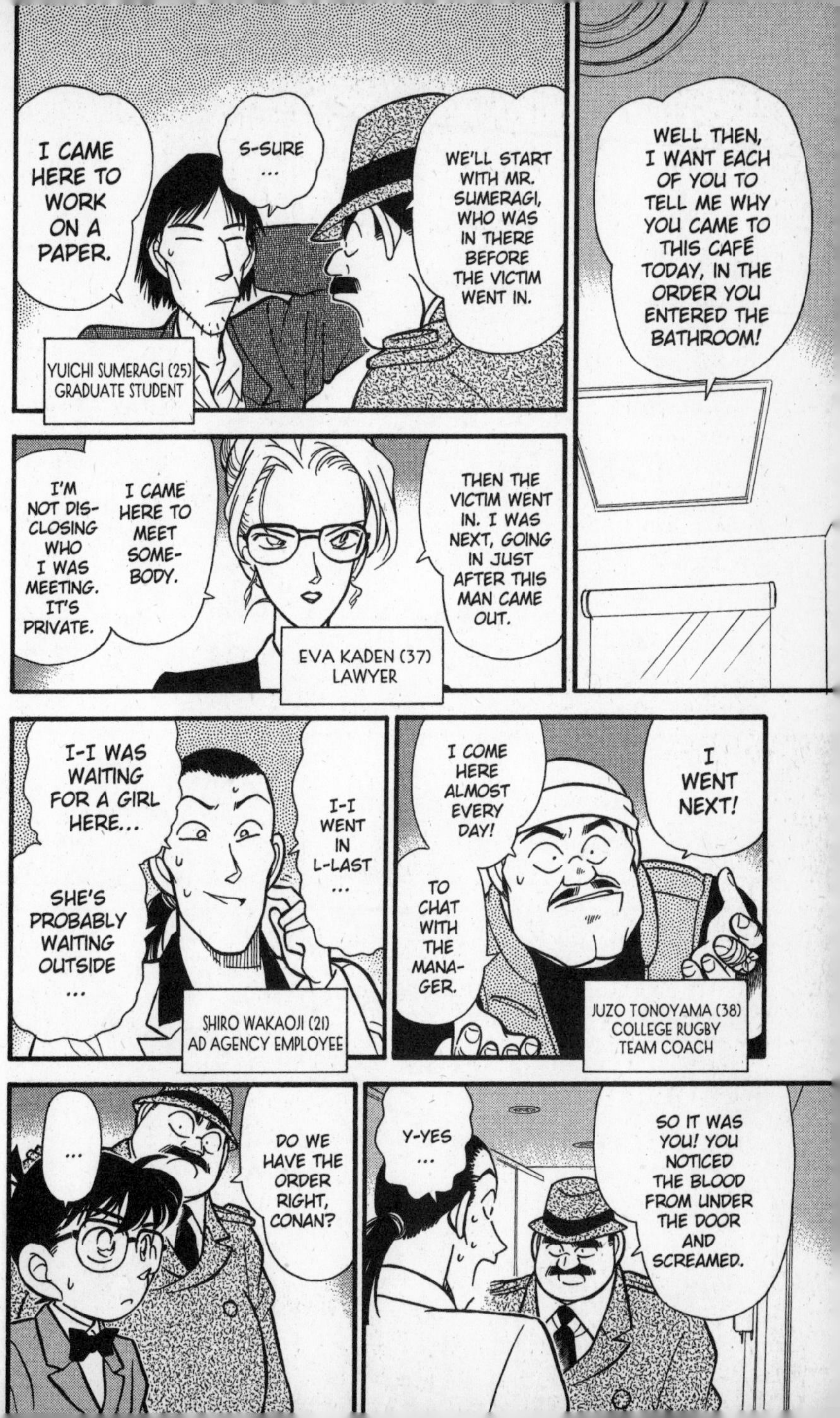
WELL THEN, I WANT EACH OF YOU TO TELL ME WHY YOU CAME TO THIS CAFÉ TODAY, IN THE ORDER YOU ENTERED THE BATHROOM!
WE'LL START WITH MR. SUMERAGI, WHO WAS IN THERE BEFORE THE VICTIM WENT IN.
S-SURE ...
I CAME HERE TO WORK ON A PAPER.
YUICHI SUMERAGI (25) GRADUATE STUDENT
THEN THE VICTIM WENT IN. I WAS NEXT, GOING IN JUST AFTER THIS MAN CAME OUT.
I CAME HERE TO MEET SOMEBODY.
I'M NOT DISCLOSING WHO I WAS MEETING. IT'S PRIVATE.
EVA KADEN (37) LAWYER
I WENT NEXT!
I COME HERE ALMOST EVERY DAY!
TO CHAT WITH THE MANAGER.
JUZO TONOYAMA (38) COLLEGE RUGBY TEAM COACH
I-I WENT IN L-LAST ...
I-I WAS WAITING FOR A GIRL HERE...
SHE'S PROBABLY WAITING OUTSIDE ...
SHIRO WAKAOJI (21) AD AGENCY EMPLOYEE
SO IT WAS YOU! YOU NOTICED THE BLOOD FROM UNDER THE DOOR AND SCREAMED.
Y-YES ...
DO WE HAVE THE ORDER RIGHT, CONAN?
...

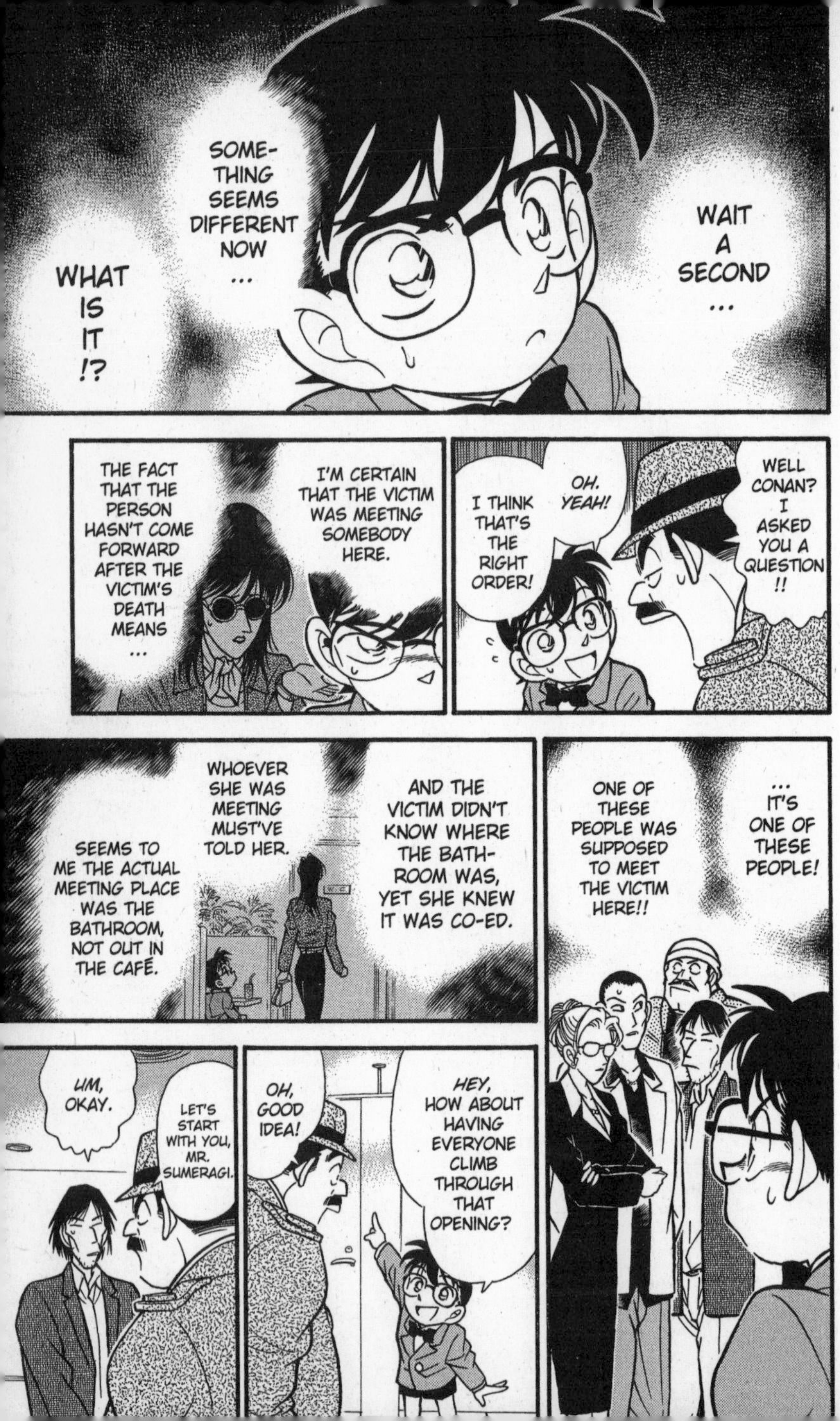
WAIT A SECOND ...
SOME-THING SEEMS DIFFERENT NOW ...
WHAT IS IT !?
WELL CONAN? I ASKED YOU A QUESTION !!
OH. YEAH!
I THINK THAT'S THE RIGHT ORDER!
I'M CERTAIN THAT THE VICTIM WAS MEETING SOMEBODY HERE.
THE FACT THAT THE PERSON HASN'T COME FORWARD AFTER THE VICTIM'S DEATH MEANS ...
... IT'S ONE OF THESE PEOPLE!
ONE OF THESE PEOPLE WAS SUPPOSED TO MEET THE VICTIM HERE!!
AND THE VICTIM DIDN'T KNOW WHERE THE BATH-ROOM WAS, YET SHE KNEW IT WAS CO-ED.
WHOEVER SHE WAS MEETING MUST'VE TOLD HER.
SEEMS TO ME THE ACTUAL MEETING PLACE WAS THE BATHROOM, NOT OUT IN THE CAFÉ.
HEY, HOW ABOUT HAVING EVERYONE CLIMB THROUGH THAT OPENING?
OH, GOOD IDEA!
LET'S START WITH YOU, MR. SUMERAGI.
UM, OKAY.

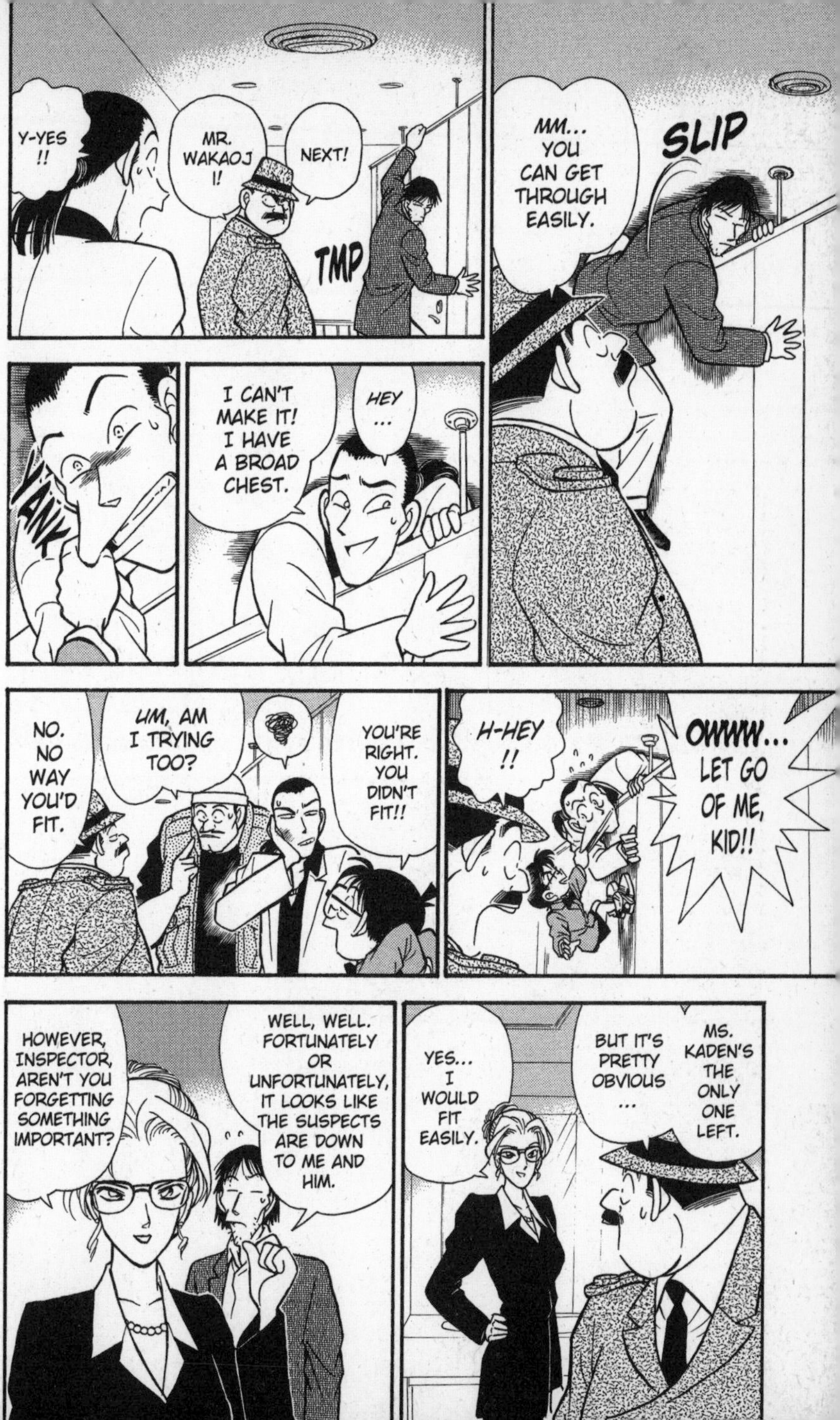
MM... YOU CAN GET THROUGH EASILY.
SLIP
NEXT!
TMP
MR. WAKAOJ I!
Y-YES !!
HEY ...
I CAN'T MAKE IT! I HAVE A BROAD CHEST.
YANK
OWWW... LET GO OF ME, KID!!
H-HEY !!
YOU'RE RIGHT. YOU DIDN'T FIT!!
UM, AM I TRYING TOO?
NO. NO WAY YOU'D FIT.
MS. KADEN'S THE ONLY ONE LEFT.
BUT IT'S PRETTY OBVIOUS ...
YES... I WOULD FIT EASILY.
WELL, WELL. FORTUNATELY OR UNFORTUNATELY, IT LOOKS LIKE THE SUSPECTS ARE DOWN TO ME AND HIM.
HOWEVER, INSPECTOR, AREN'T YOU FORGETTING SOMETHING IMPORTANT?

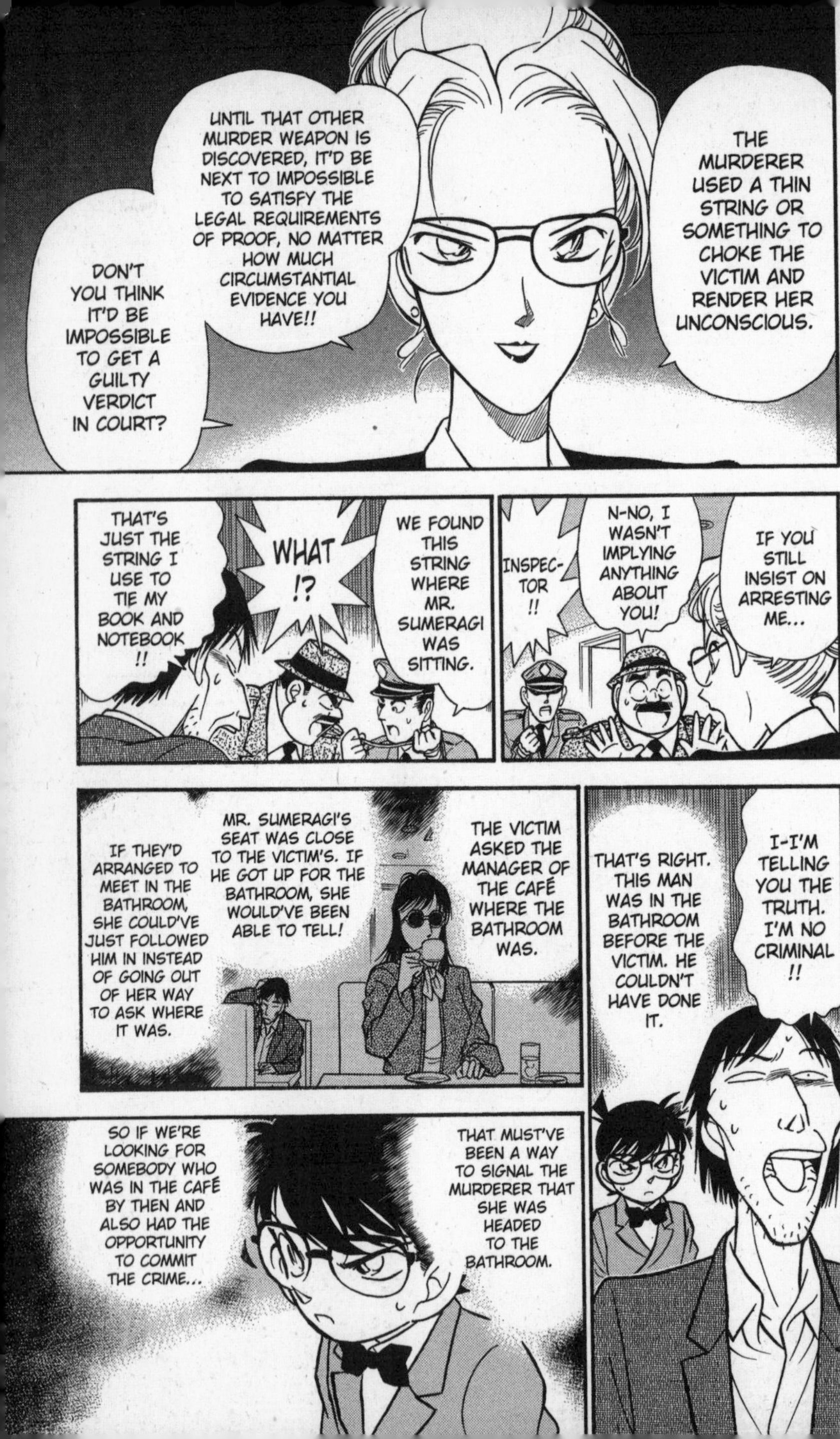
THE MURDERER USED A THIN STRING OR SOMETHING TO CHOKE THE VICTIM AND RENDER HER UNCONSCIOUS.
UNTIL THAT OTHER MURDER WEAPON IS DISCOVERED, IT'D BE NEXT TO IMPOSSIBLE TO SATISFY THE LEGAL REQUIREMENTS OF PROOF, NO MATTER HOW MUCH CIRCUMSTANTIAL EVIDENCE YOU HAVE!!
DON'T YOU THINK IT'D BE IMPOSSIBLE TO GET A GUILTY VERDICT IN COURT?
IF YOU STILL INSIST ON ARRESTING ME...
N-NO, I WASN'T IMPLYING ANYTHING ABOUT YOU!
INSPEC-TOR!!
WE FOUND THIS STRING WHERE MR. SUMERAGI WAS SITTING.
WHAT!?
THAT'S JUST THE STRING I USE TO TIE MY BOOK AND NOTEBOOK!!
I-I'M TELLING YOU THE TRUTH. I'M NO CRIMINAL!!
THAT'S RIGHT. THIS MAN WAS IN THE BATHROOM BEFORE THE VICTIM. HE COULDN'T HAVE DONE IT.
THE VICTIM ASKED THE MANAGER OF THE CAFÉ WHERE THE BATHROOM WAS.
MR. SUMERAGI'S SEAT WAS CLOSE TO THE VICTIM'S. IF HE GOT UP FOR THE BATHROOM, SHE WOULD'VE BEEN ABLE TO TELL!
IF THEY'D ARRANGED TO MEET IN THE BATHROOM, SHE COULD'VE JUST FOLLOWED HIM IN INSTEAD OF GOING OUT OF HER WAY TO ASK WHERE IT WAS.
THAT MUST'VE BEEN A WAY TO SIGNAL THE MURDERER THAT SHE WAS HEADED TO THE BATHROOM.
SO IF WE'RE LOOKING FOR SOMEBODY WHO WAS IN THE CAFÉ BY THEN AND ALSO HAD THE OPPORTUNITY TO COMMIT THE CRIME...

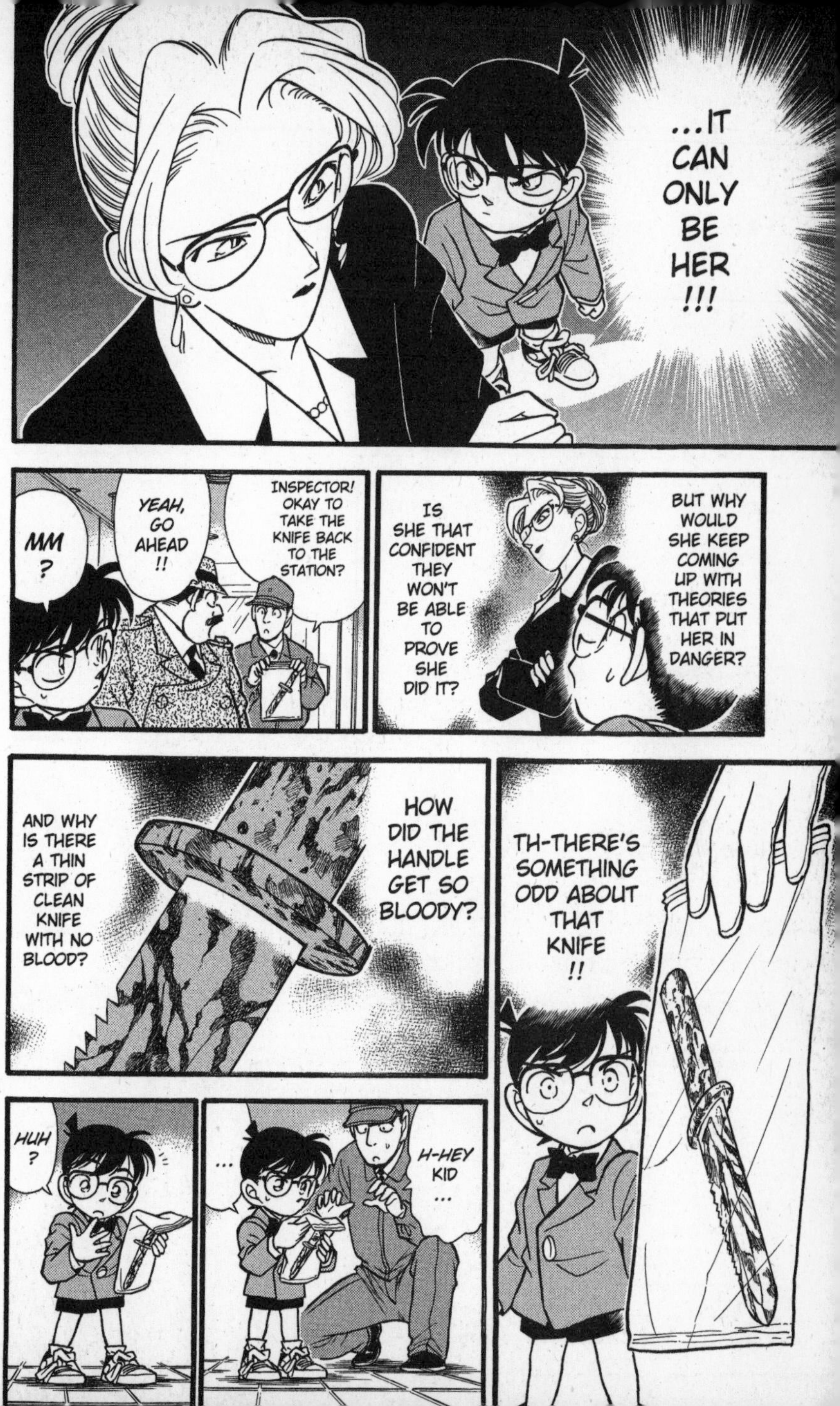
...IT CAN ONLY BE HER !!!
BUT WHY WOULD SHE KEEP COMING UP WITH THEORIES THAT PUT HER IN DANGER?
IS SHE THAT CONFIDENT THEY WON'T BE ABLE TO PROVE SHE DID IT?
INSPECTOR! OKAY TO TAKE THE KNIFE BACK TO THE STATION?
YEAH, GO AHEAD !!
MM ?
TH-THERE'S SOMETHING ODD ABOUT THAT KNIFE !!
HOW DID THE HANDLE GET SO BLOODY?
AND WHY IS THERE A THIN STRIP OF CLEAN KNIFE WITH NO BLOOD?
H-HEY KID ...
...
HUH ?

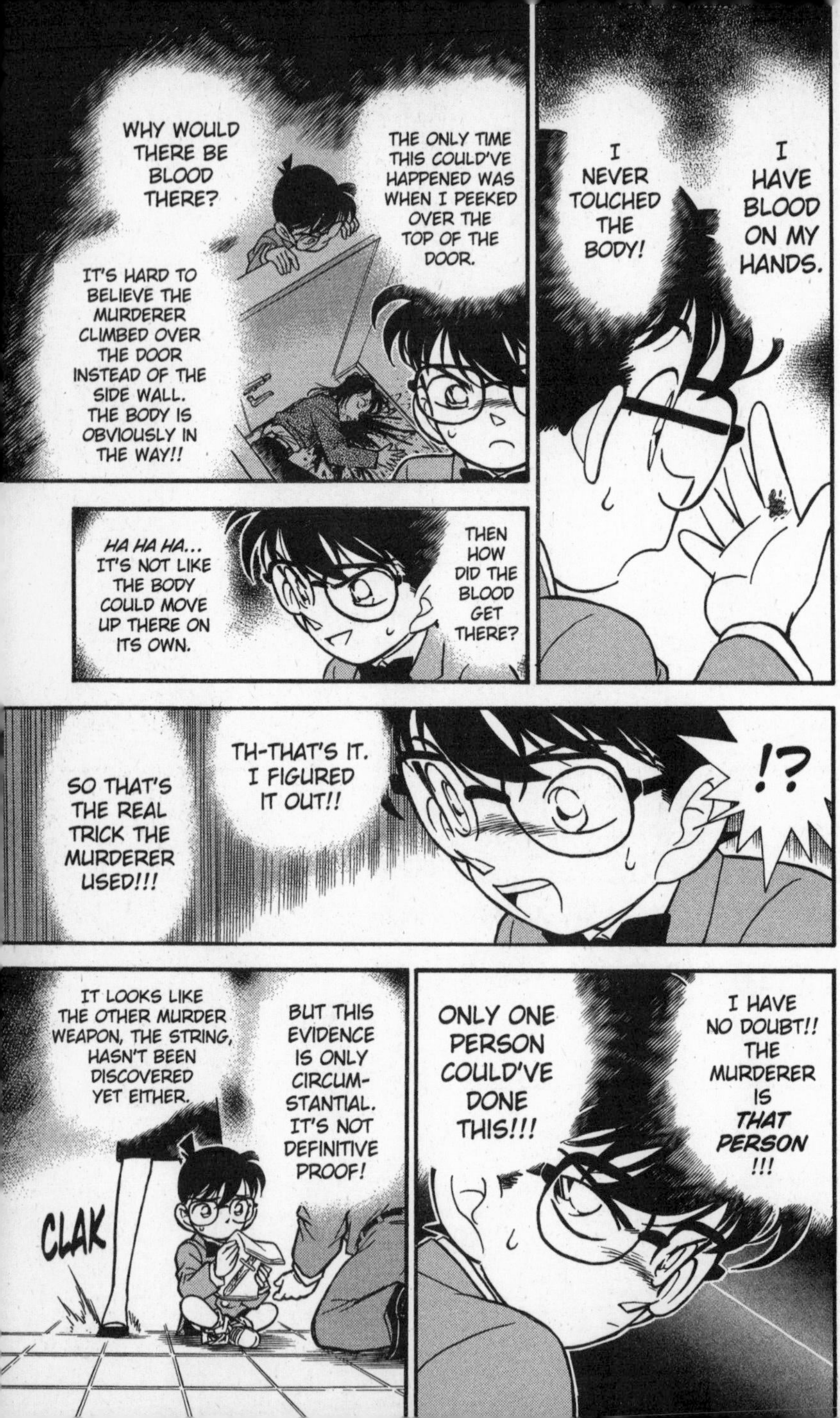
I HAVE BLOOD ON MY HANDS.
I NEVER TOUCHED THE BODY!
THE ONLY TIME THIS COULD'VE HAPPENED WAS WHEN I PEEKED OVER THE TOP OF THE DOOR.
WHY WOULD THERE BE BLOOD THERE?
IT'S HARD TO BELIEVE THE MURDERER CLIMBED OVER THE DOOR INSTEAD OF THE SIDE WALL. THE BODY IS OBVIOUSLY IN THE WAY!!
THEN HOW DID THE BLOOD GET THERE?
HA HA HA... IT'S NOT LIKE THE BODY COULD MOVE UP THERE ON ITS OWN.
!?
TH-THAT'S IT. I FIGURED IT OUT!!
SO THAT'S THE REAL TRICK THE MURDERER USED!!!
I HAVE NO DOUBT!! THE MURDERER IS *THAT PERSON* !!!
ONLY ONE PERSON COULD'VE DONE THIS!!!
BUT THIS EVIDENCE IS ONLY CIRCUM-STANTIAL. IT'S NOT DEFINITIVE PROOF!
IT LOOKS LIKE THE OTHER MURDER WEAPON, THE STRING, HASN'T BEEN DISCOVERED YET EITHER.
CLAK

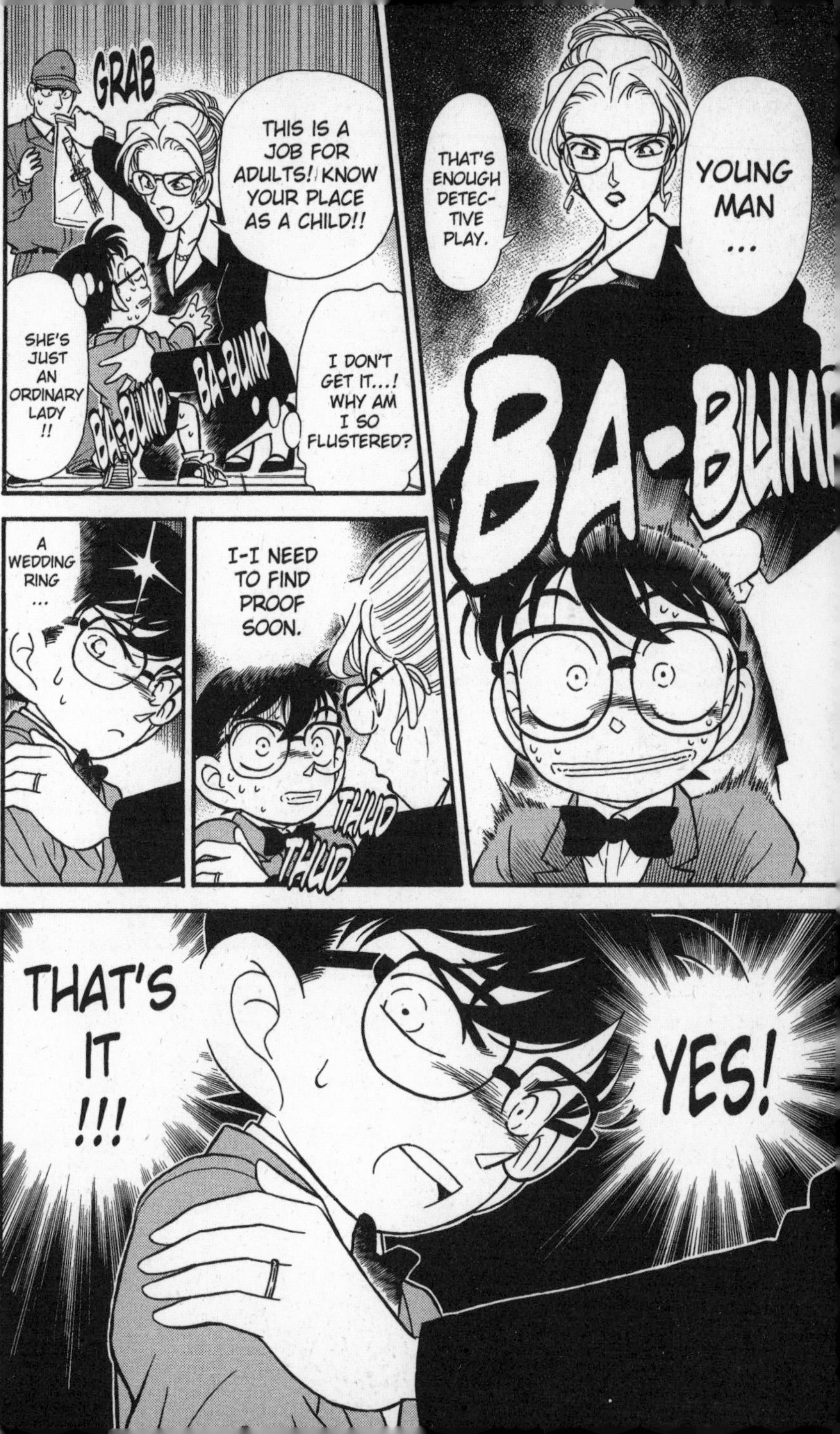
YOUNG MAN ...
THAT'S ENOUGH DETECTIVE PLAY.
BA-BUMP
THIS IS A JOB FOR ADULTS!! KNOW YOUR PLACE AS A CHILD!!
GRAB
I DON'T GET IT...! WHY AM I SO FLUSTERED?
BA-BUMP
SHE'S JUST AN ORDINARY LADY !!
BA-BUMP
I-I NEED TO FIND PROOF SOON.
THUD
THUD
A WEDDING RING ...
YES!
THAT'S IT !!!

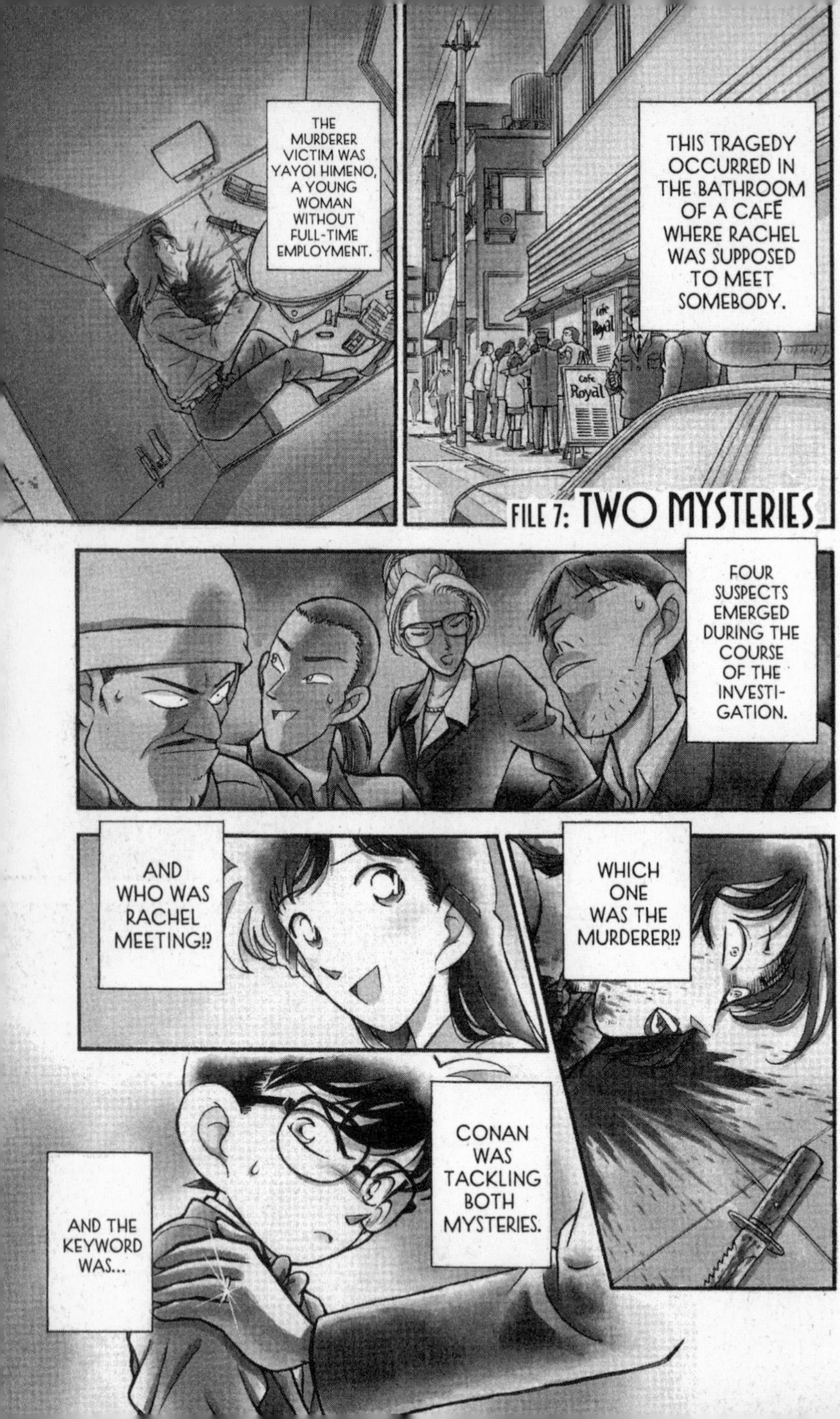
THIS TRAGEDY OCCURRED IN THE BATHROOM OF A CAFÉ WHERE RACHEL WAS SUPPOSED TO MEET SOMEBODY.
Cafe Royal
Cafe Royal
FILE 7: TWO MYSTERIES
THE MURDERER VICTIM WAS YAYOI HIMENO, A YOUNG WOMAN WITHOUT FULL-TIME EMPLOYMENT.
FOUR SUSPECTS EMERGED DURING THE COURSE OF THE INVESTI-GATION.
WHICH ONE WAS THE MURDERER!?
AND WHO WAS RACHEL MEETING!?
CONAN WAS TACKLING BOTH MYSTERIES.
AND THE KEYWORD WAS...

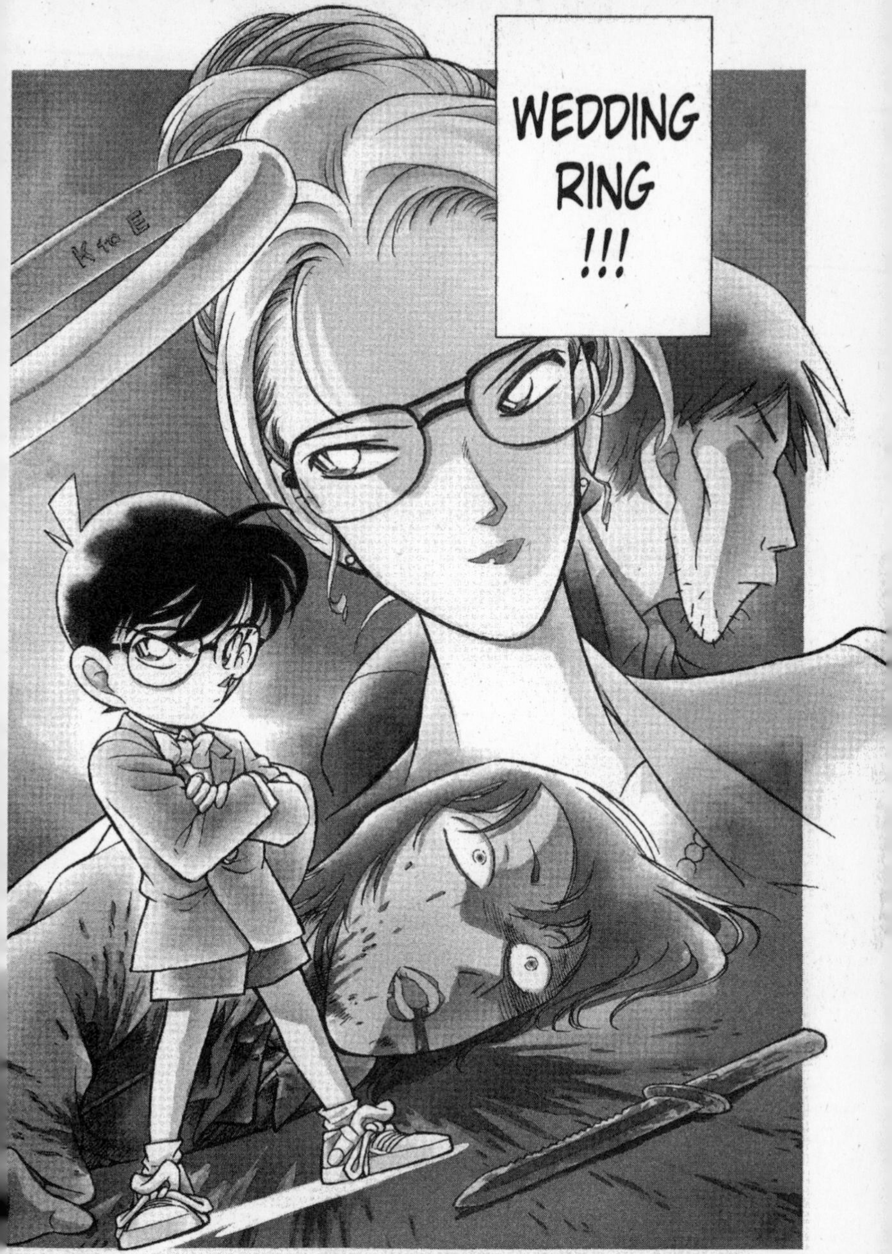
WEDDING RING !!!
K to E

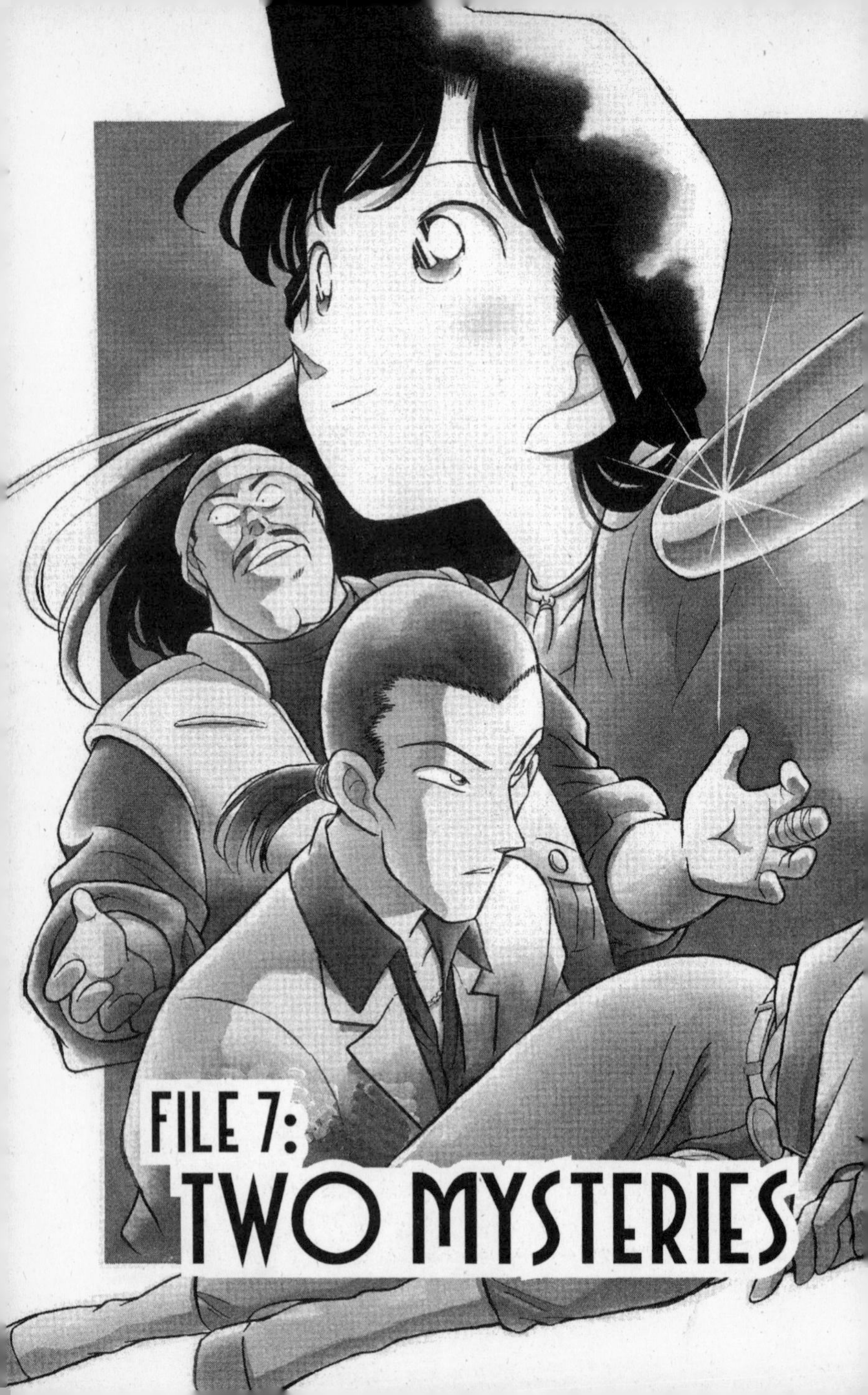
FILE 7:
TWO MYSTERIES

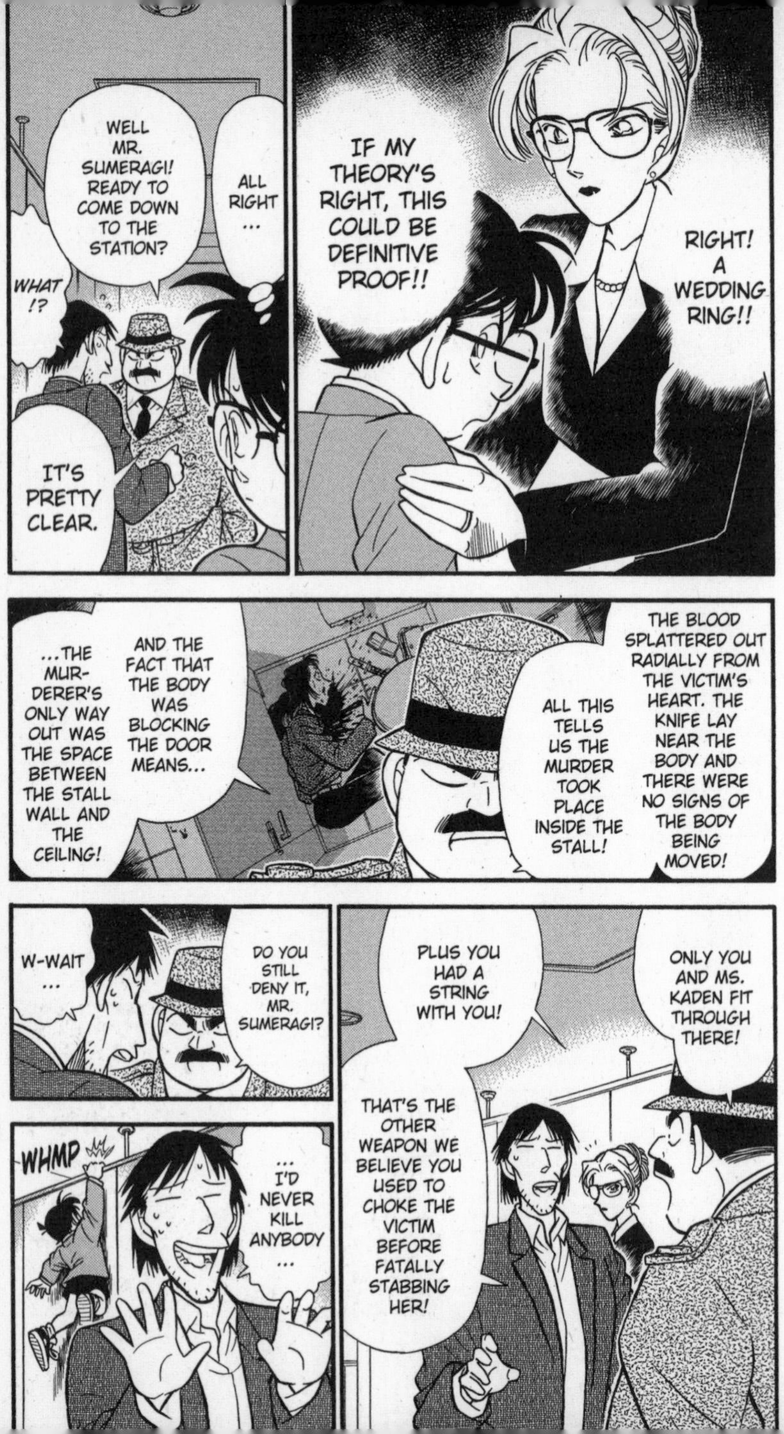
RIGHT! A WEDDING RING!!
IF MY THEORY'S RIGHT, THIS COULD BE DEFINITIVE PROOF!!
ALL RIGHT ...
WELL MR. SUMERAGI! READY TO COME DOWN TO THE STATION?
WHAT !?
IT'S PRETTY CLEAR.
THE BLOOD SPLATTERED OUT RADIALLY FROM THE VICTIM'S HEART. THE KNIFE LAY NEAR THE BODY AND THERE WERE NO SIGNS OF THE BODY BEING MOVED!
ALL THIS TELLS US THE MURDER TOOK PLACE INSIDE THE STALL!
AND THE FACT THAT THE BODY WAS BLOCKING THE DOOR MEANS...
...THE MUR-DERER'S ONLY WAY OUT WAS THE SPACE BETWEEN THE STALL WALL AND THE CEILING!
ONLY YOU AND MS. KADEN FIT THROUGH THERE!
PLUS YOU HAD A STRING WITH YOU!
THAT'S THE OTHER WEAPON WE BELIEVE YOU USED TO CHOKE THE VICTIM BEFORE FATALLY STABBING HER!
DO YOU STILL DENY IT, MR. SUMERAGI?
W-WAIT ...
... I'D NEVER KILL ANYBODY ...
WHMP

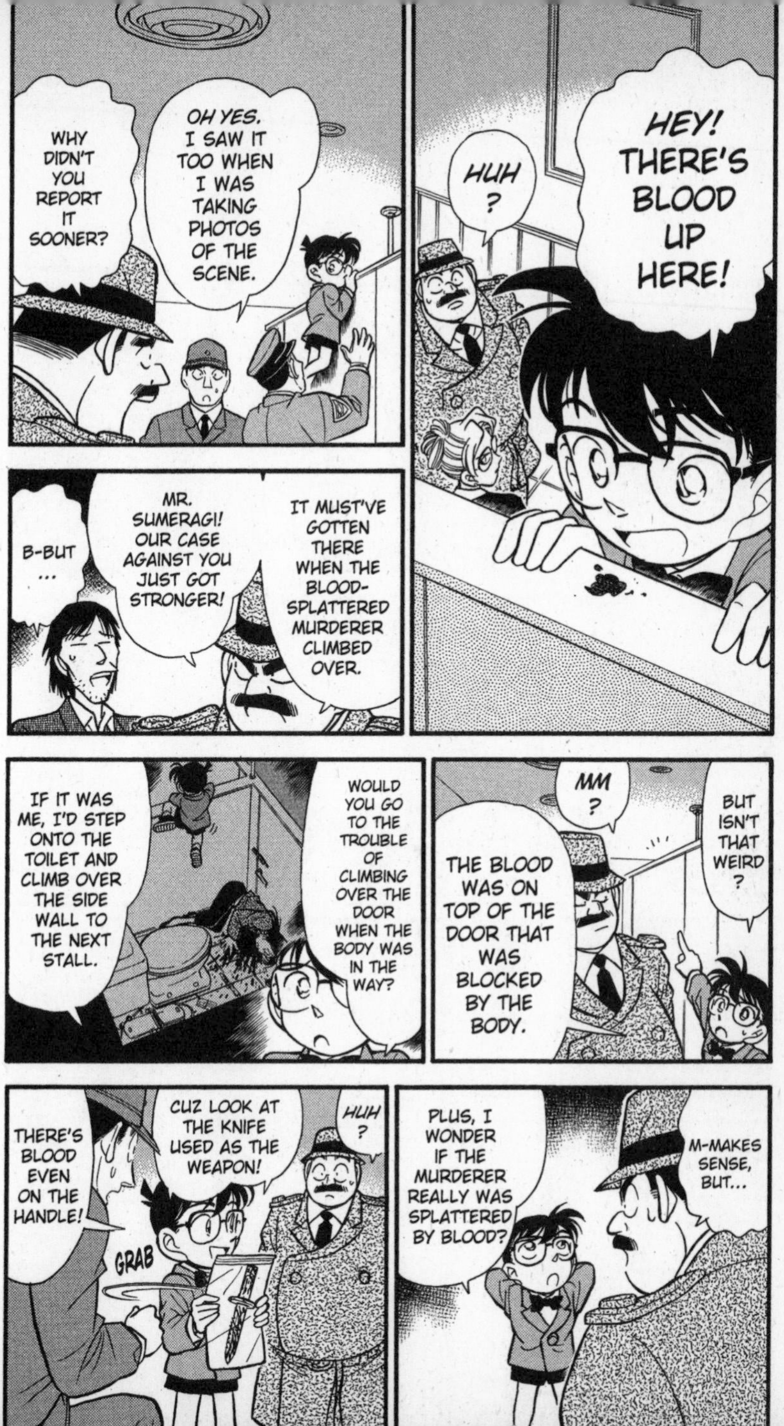
HEY! THERE'S BLOOD UP HERE!
HUH ?
OH YES. I SAW IT TOO WHEN I WAS TAKING PHOTOS OF THE SCENE.
WHY DIDN'T YOU REPORT IT SOONER?
IT MUST'VE GOTTEN THERE WHEN THE BLOOD-SPLATTERED MURDERER CLIMBED OVER.
MR. SUMERAGI! OUR CASE AGAINST YOU JUST GOT STRONGER!
B-BUT ...
BUT ISN'T THAT WEIRD ?
MM ?
THE BLOOD WAS ON TOP OF THE DOOR THAT WAS BLOCKED BY THE BODY.
WOULD YOU GO TO THE TROUBLE OF CLIMBING OVER THE DOOR WHEN THE BODY WAS IN THE WAY?
IF IT WAS ME, I'D STEP ONTO THE TOILET AND CLIMB OVER THE SIDE WALL TO THE NEXT STALL.
M-MAKES SENSE, BUT...
PLUS, I WONDER IF THE MURDERER REALLY WAS SPLATTERED BY BLOOD?
HUH ?
CUZ LOOK AT THE KNIFE USED AS THE WEAPON!
THERE'S BLOOD EVEN ON THE HANDLE!
GRAB

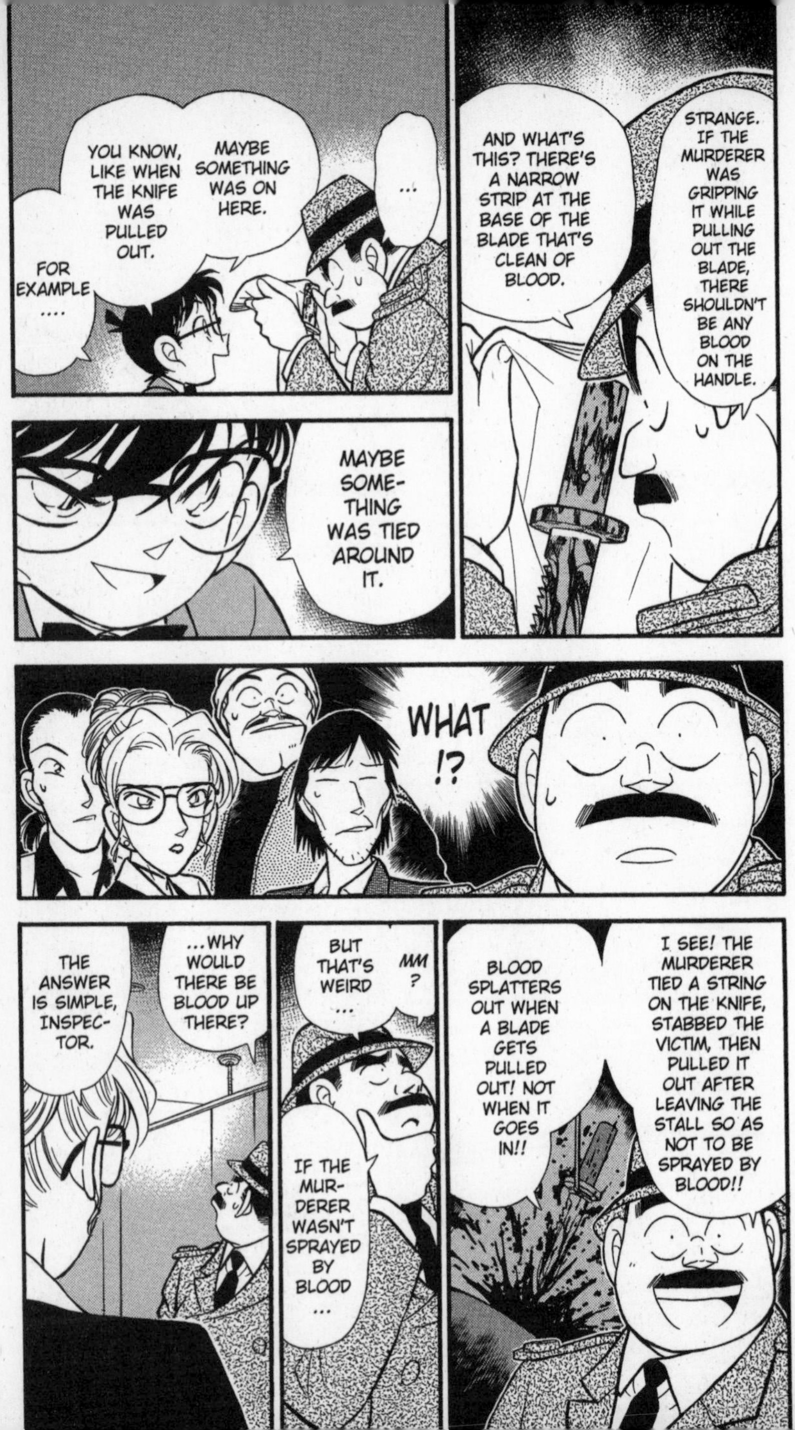
STRANGE. IF THE MURDERER WAS GRIPPING IT WHILE PULLING OUT THE BLADE, THERE SHOULDN'T BE ANY BLOOD ON THE HANDLE.
AND WHAT'S THIS? THERE'S A NARROW STRIP AT THE BASE OF THE BLADE THAT'S CLEAN OF BLOOD.
...
MAYBE SOMETHING WAS ON HERE.
YOU KNOW, LIKE WHEN THE KNIFE WAS PULLED OUT.
FOR EXAMPLE ....
MAYBE SOME-THING WAS TIED AROUND IT.
WHAT !?
I SEE! THE MURDERER TIED A STRING ON THE KNIFE, STABBED THE VICTIM, THEN PULLED IT OUT AFTER LEAVING THE STALL SO AS NOT TO BE SPRAYED BY BLOOD!!
BLOOD SPLATTERS OUT WHEN A BLADE GETS PULLED OUT! NOT WHEN IT GOES IN!!
MM ?
BUT THAT'S WEIRD ...
IF THE MUR-DERER WASN'T SPRAYED BY BLOOD ...
...WHY WOULD THERE BE BLOOD UP THERE?
THE ANSWER IS SIMPLE, INSPEC-TOR.

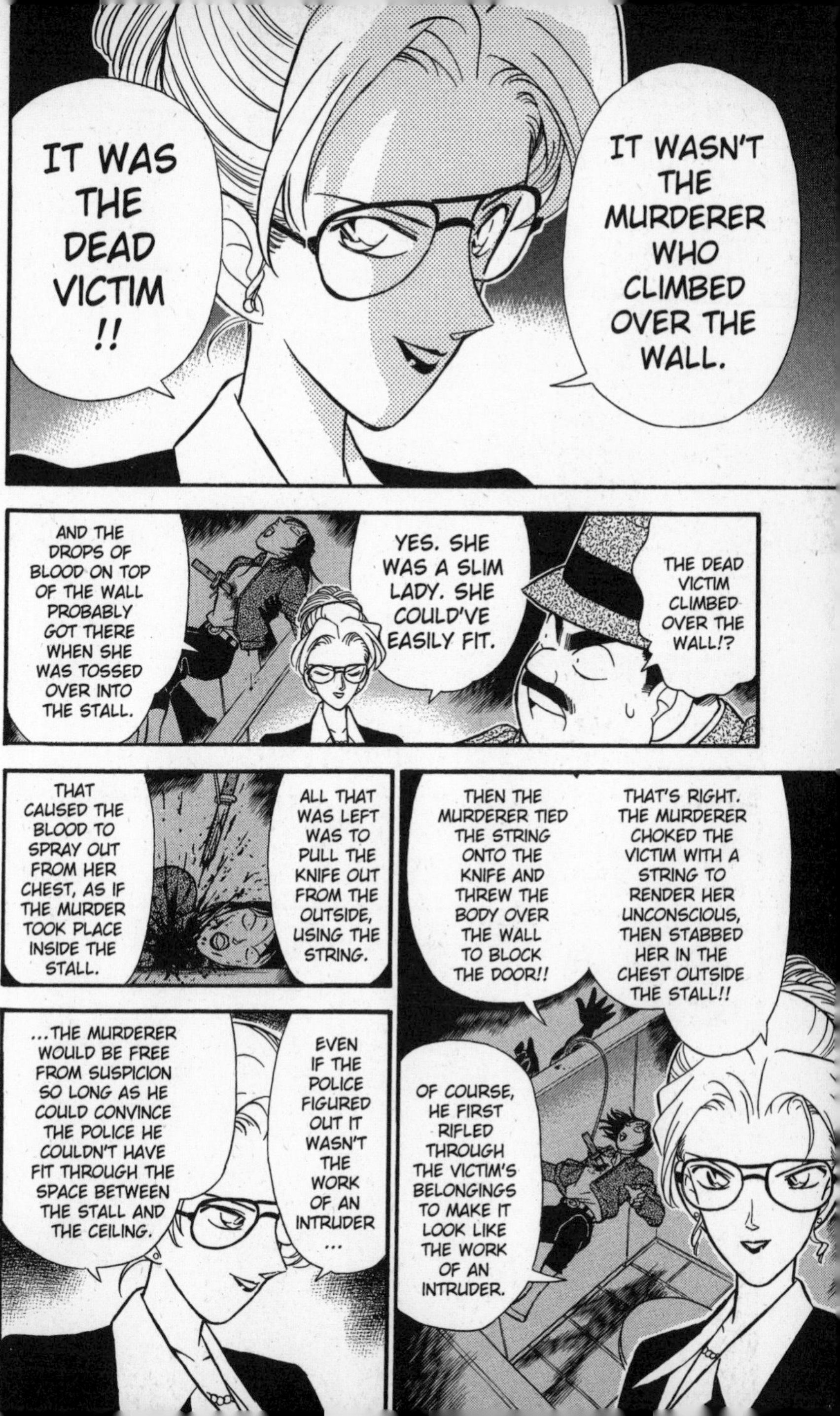
IT WASN'T THE MURDERER WHO CLIMBED OVER THE WALL.
IT WAS THE DEAD VICTIM!!
THE DEAD VICTIM CLIMBED OVER THE WALL!?
YES. SHE WAS A SLIM LADY. SHE COULD'VE EASILY FIT.
AND THE DROPS OF BLOOD ON TOP OF THE WALL PROBABLY GOT THERE WHEN SHE WAS TOSSED OVER INTO THE STALL.
THAT'S RIGHT. THE MURDERER CHOKED THE VICTIM WITH A STRING TO RENDER HER UNCONSCIOUS, THEN STABBED HER IN THE CHEST OUTSIDE THE STALL!!
THEN THE MURDERER TIED THE STRING ONTO THE KNIFE AND THREW THE BODY OVER THE WALL TO BLOCK THE DOOR!!
OF COURSE, HE FIRST RIFLED THROUGH THE VICTIM'S BELONGINGS TO MAKE IT LOOK LIKE THE WORK OF AN INTRUDER.
ALL THAT WAS LEFT WAS TO PULL THE KNIFE OUT FROM THE OUTSIDE, USING THE STRING.
THAT CAUSED THE BLOOD TO SPRAY OUT FROM HER CHEST, AS IF THE MURDER TOOK PLACE INSIDE THE STALL.
EVEN IF THE POLICE FIGURED OUT IT WASN'T THE WORK OF AN INTRUDER...
...THE MURDERER WOULD BE FREE FROM SUSPICION SO LONG AS HE COULD CONVINCE THE POLICE HE COULDN'T HAVE FIT THROUGH THE SPACE BETWEEN THE STALL AND THE CEILING.

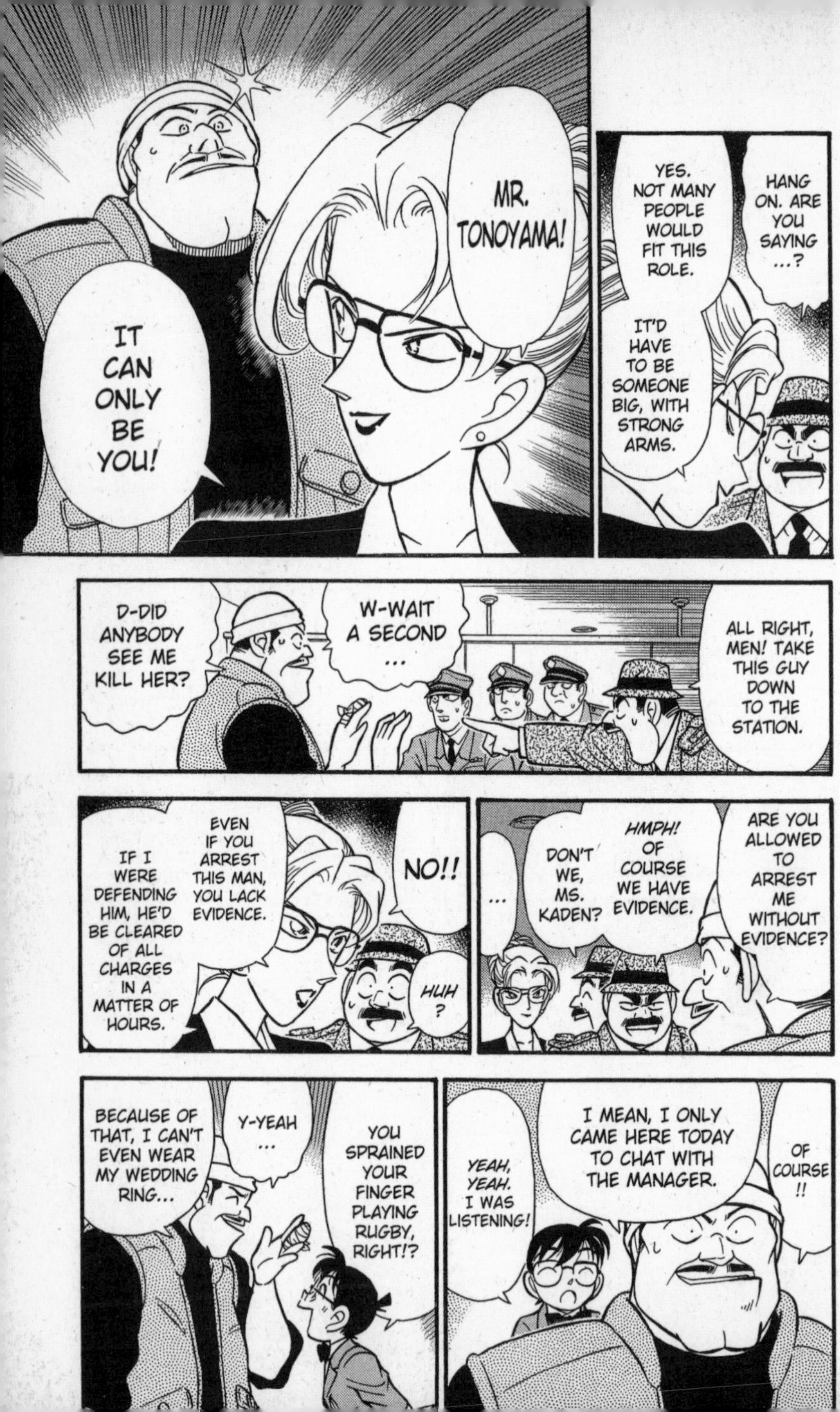
HANG ON. ARE YOU SAYING ...?
YES. NOT MANY PEOPLE WOULD FIT THIS ROLE.
IT'D HAVE TO BE SOMEONE BIG, WITH STRONG ARMS.
MR. TONOYAMA!
IT CAN ONLY BE YOU!
ALL RIGHT, MEN! TAKE THIS GUY DOWN TO THE STATION.
W-WAIT A SECOND ...
D-DID ANYBODY SEE ME KILL HER?
ARE YOU ALLOWED TO ARREST ME WITHOUT EVIDENCE?
HMPH! OF COURSE WE HAVE EVIDENCE.
DON'T WE, MS. KADEN?
...
NO!!
EVEN IF YOU ARREST THIS MAN, YOU LACK EVIDENCE.
IF I WERE DEFENDING HIM, HE'D BE CLEARED OF ALL CHARGES IN A MATTER OF HOURS.
HUH?
OF COURSE!!
I MEAN, I ONLY CAME HERE TODAY TO CHAT WITH THE MANAGER.
YEAH, YEAH. I WAS LISTENING!
YOU SPRAINED YOUR FINGER PLAYING RUGBY, RIGHT!?
Y-YEAH ...
BECAUSE OF THAT, I CAN'T EVEN WEAR MY WEDDING RING...

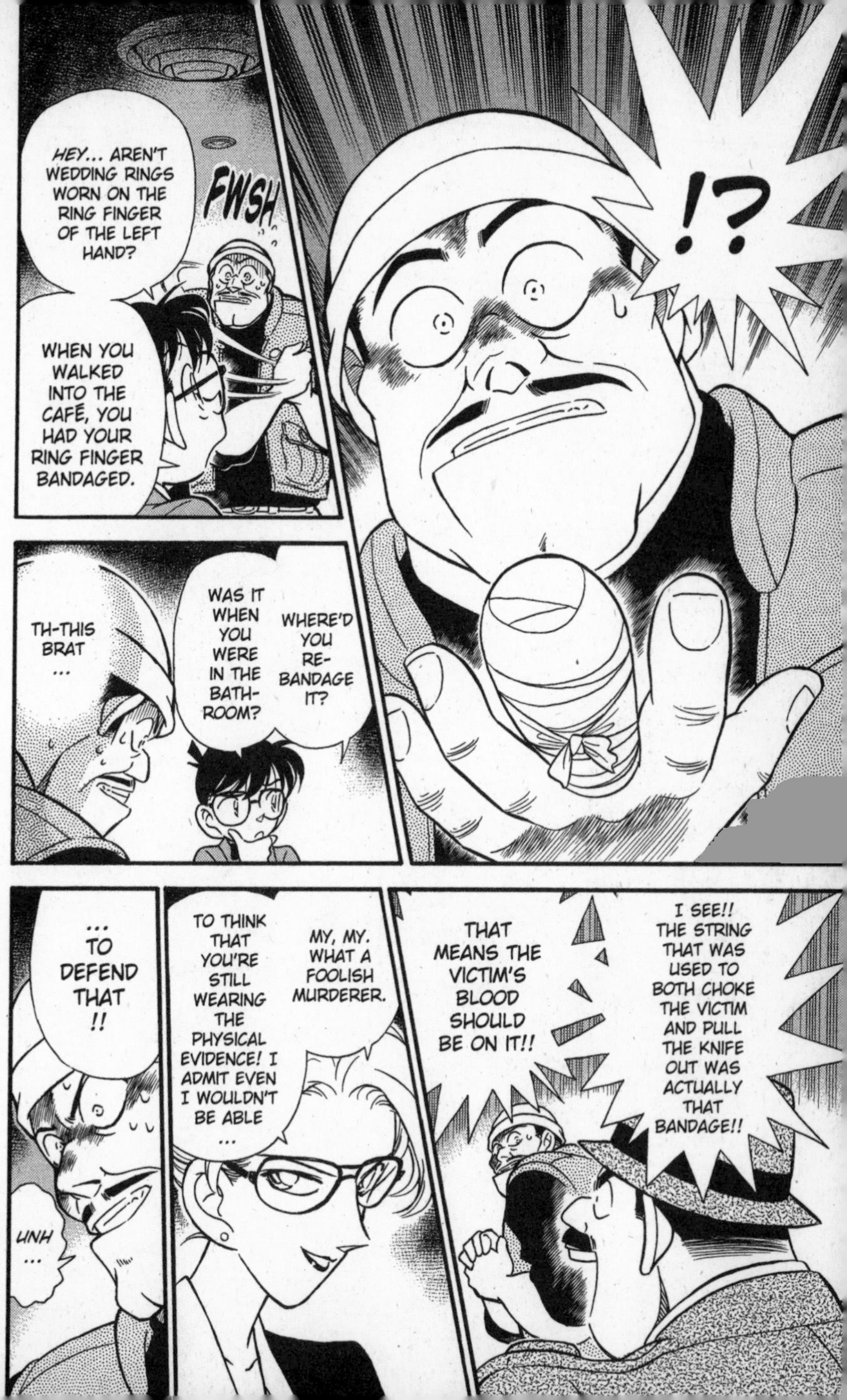
!?
HEY... AREN'T WEDDING RINGS WORN ON THE RING FINGER OF THE LEFT HAND?
FWSH
WHEN YOU WALKED INTO THE CAFÉ, YOU HAD YOUR RING FINGER BANDAGED.
WHERE'D YOU RE-BANDAGE IT?
WAS IT WHEN YOU WERE IN THE BATH-ROOM?
TH-THIS BRAT ...
I SEE!! THE STRING THAT WAS USED TO BOTH CHOKE THE VICTIM AND PULL THE KNIFE OUT WAS ACTUALLY THAT BANDAGE!!
THAT MEANS THE VICTIM'S BLOOD SHOULD BE ON IT!!
MY, MY. WHAT A FOOLISH MURDERER.
TO THINK THAT YOU'RE STILL WEARING THE PHYSICAL EVIDENCE! I ADMIT EVEN I WOULDN'T BE ABLE ...
... TO DEFEND THAT !!
UNH ...

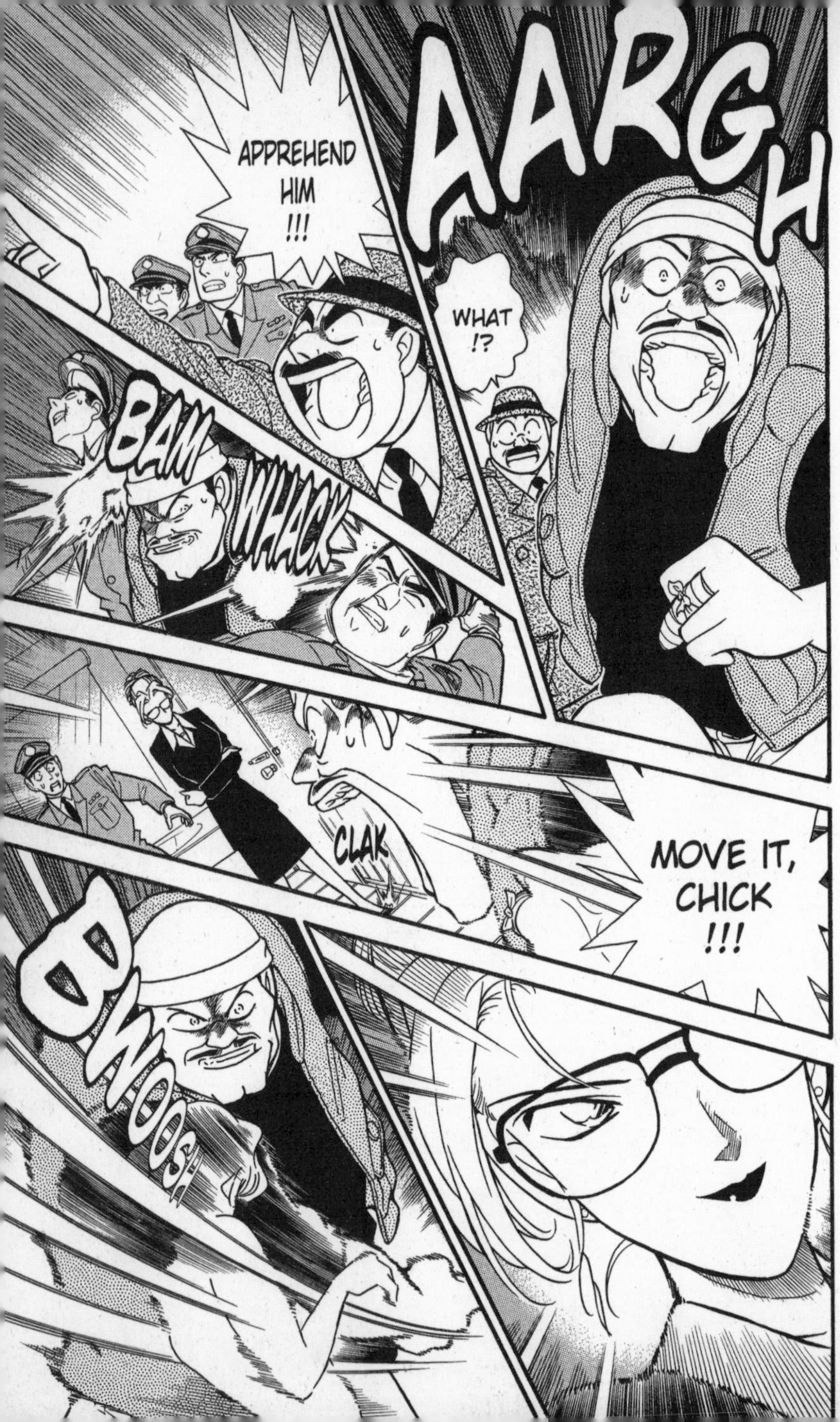
AARGH
WHAT !?
APPREHEND HIM !!!
BAM
WHACK
CLAK
MOVE IT, CHICK !!!
BWOOSH

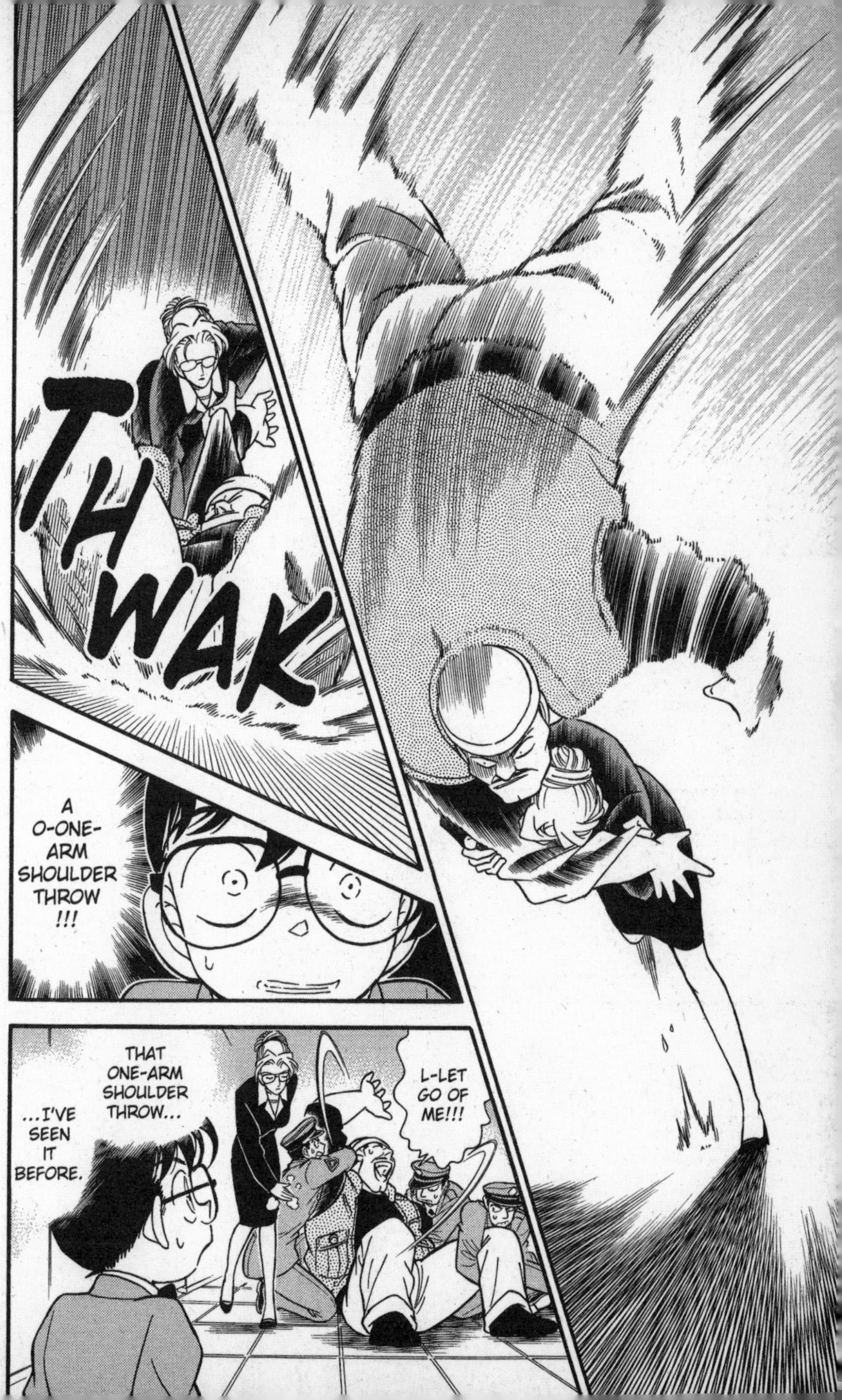
THWAK
A O-ONE-ARM SHOULDER THROW !!!
L-LET GO OF ME!!!
THAT ONE-ARM SHOULDER THROW...
...I'VE SEEN IT BEFORE.

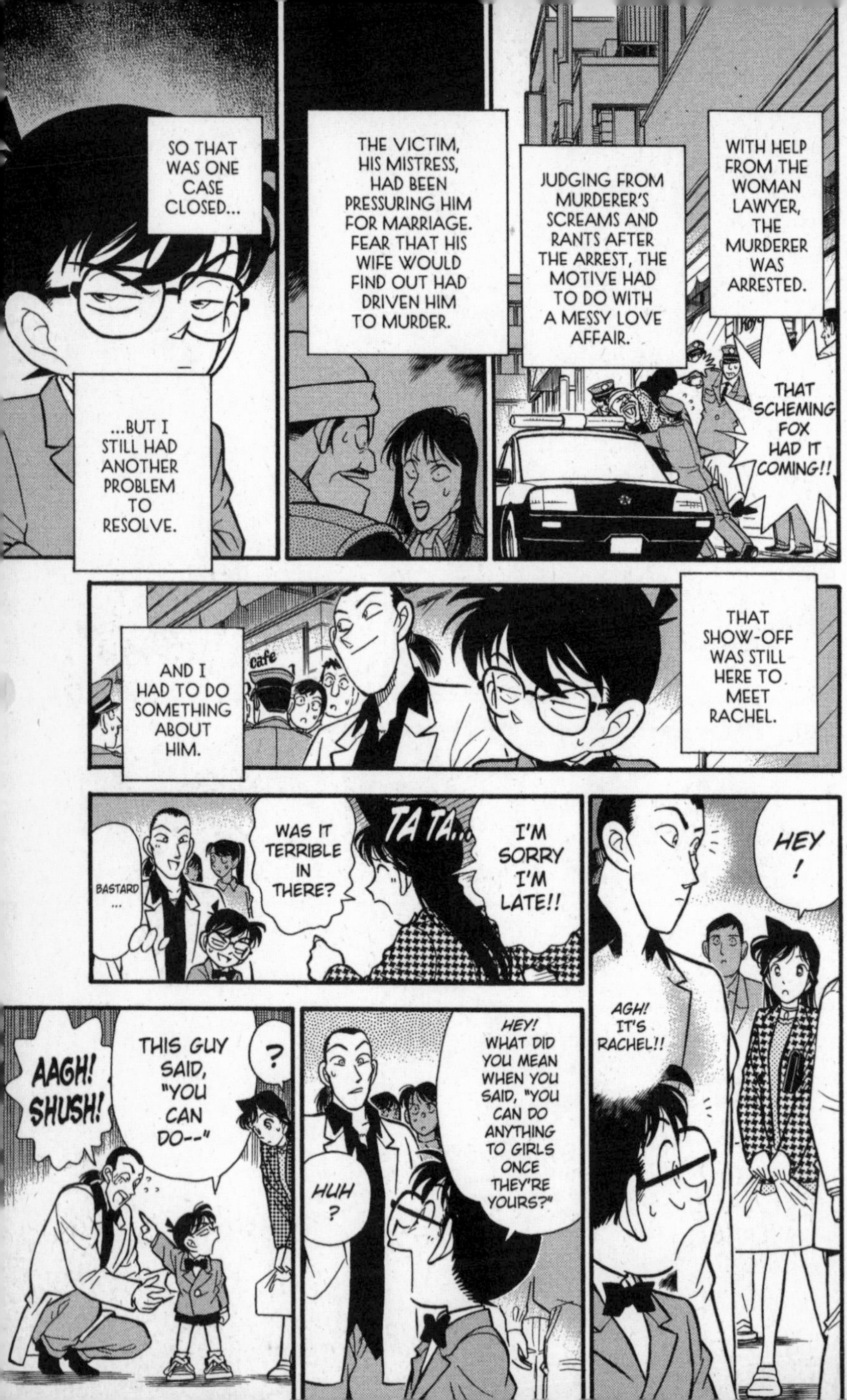
WITH HELP FROM THE WOMAN LAWYER, THE MURDERER WAS ARRESTED.
JUDGING FROM MURDERER'S SCREAMS AND RANTS AFTER THE ARREST, THE MOTIVE HAD TO DO WITH A MESSY LOVE AFFAIR.
THAT SCHEMING FOX HAD IT COMING!!
THE VICTIM, HIS MISTRESS, HAD BEEN PRESSURING HIM FOR MARRIAGE. FEAR THAT HIS WIFE WOULD FIND OUT HAD DRIVEN HIM TO MURDER.
SO THAT WAS ONE CASE CLOSED...
...BUT I STILL HAD ANOTHER PROBLEM TO RESOLVE.
THAT SHOW-OFF WAS STILL HERE TO MEET RACHEL.
AND I HAD TO DO SOMETHING ABOUT HIM.
HEY!
AGH! IT'S RACHEL!!
I'M SORRY I'M LATE!!
TA TA...
WAS IT TERRIBLE IN THERE?
BASTARD ...
HEY! WHAT DID YOU MEAN WHEN YOU SAID, "YOU CAN DO ANYTHING TO GIRLS ONCE THEY'RE YOURS?"
HUH?
?
THIS GUY SAID, "YOU CAN DO--"
AAGH! SHUSH!

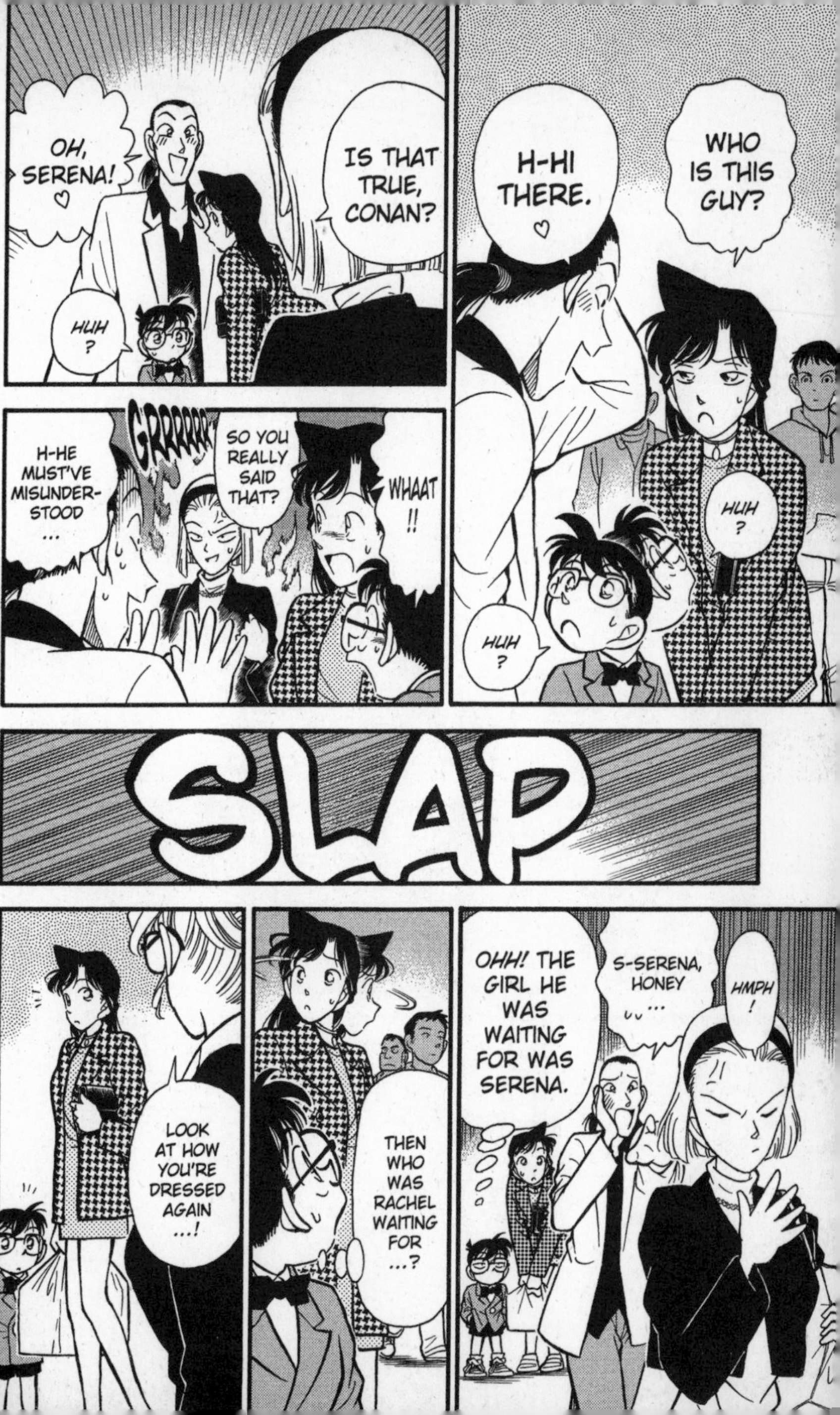
WHO IS THIS GUY?
H-HI THERE. ♡
HUH ?
HUH ?
IS THAT TRUE, CONAN?
OH, SERENA! ♡
HUH ?
WHAAT !!
SO YOU REALLY SAID THAT?
GRRRRRR
H-HE MUST'VE MISUNDERSTOOD ...
SLAP
HMPH !
S-SERENA, HONEY ...
OHH! THE GIRL HE WAS WAITING FOR WAS SERENA.
THEN WHO WAS RACHEL WAITING FOR ...?
LOOK AT HOW YOU'RE DRESSED AGAIN ...!

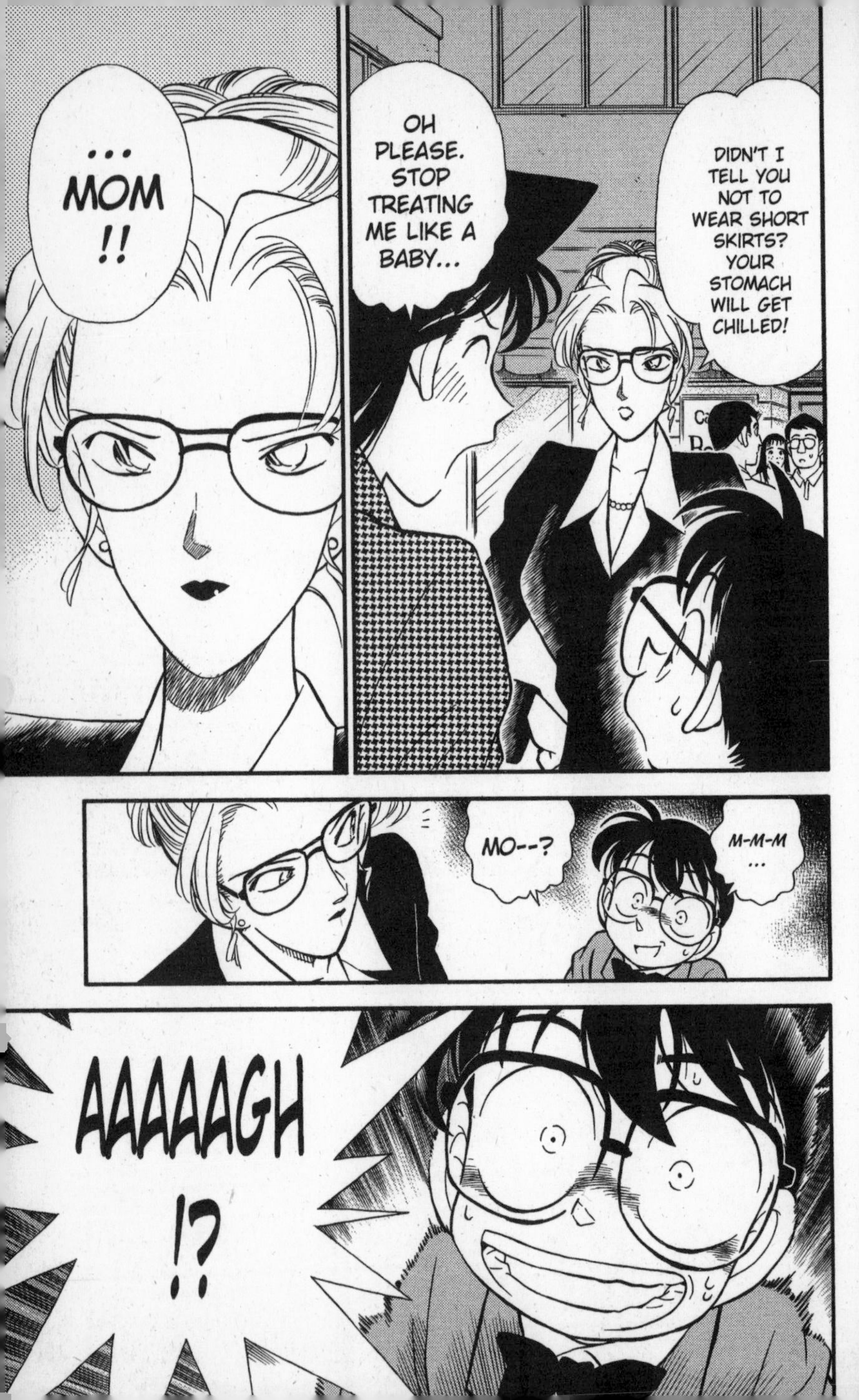
DIDN'T I TELL YOU NOT TO WEAR SHORT SKIRTS? YOUR STOMACH WILL GET CHILLED!
OH PLEASE. STOP TREATING ME LIKE A BABY...
...MOM!!
M-M-M...
MO--?
AAAAAGH!?

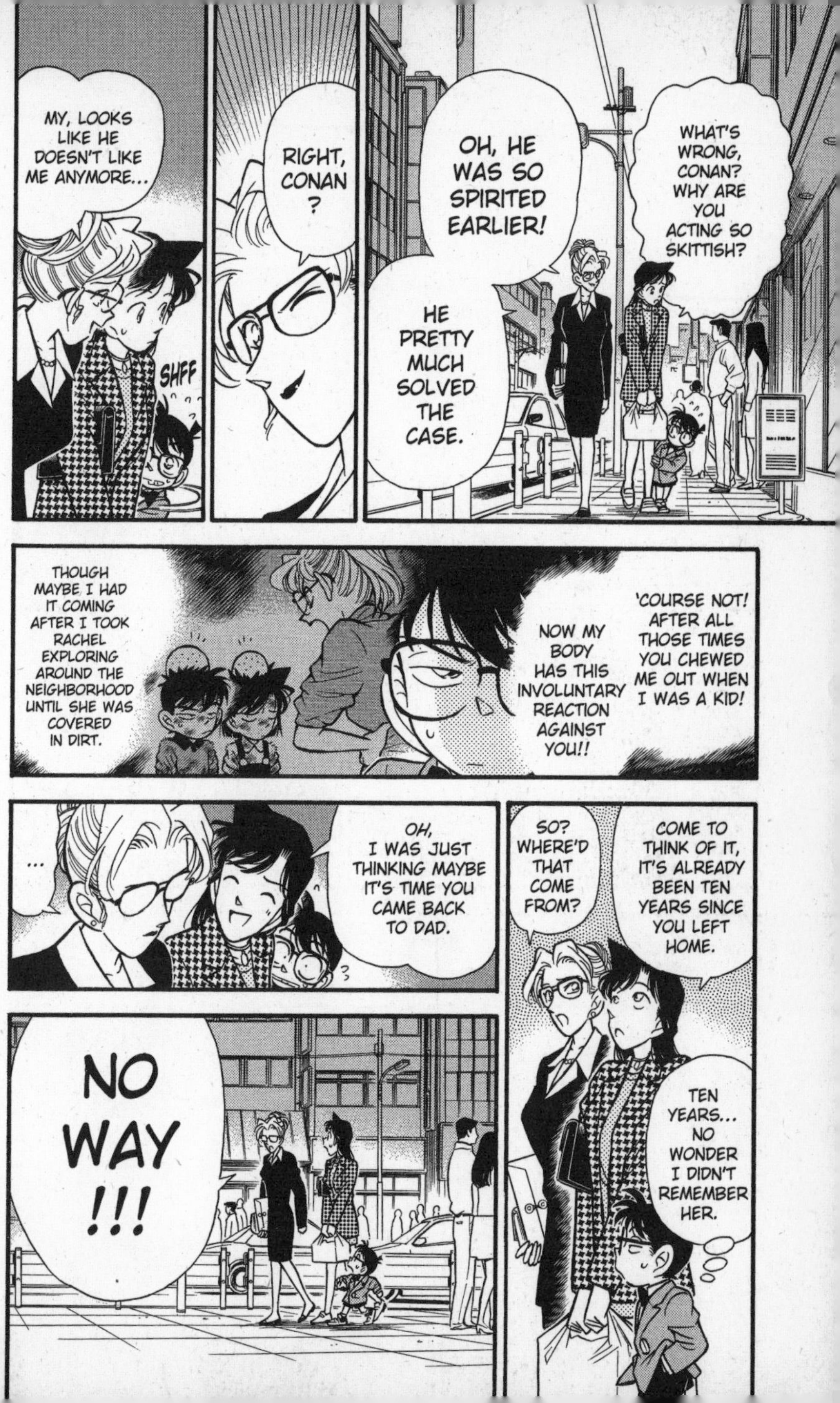
WHAT'S WRONG, CONAN? WHY ARE YOU ACTING SO SKITTISH?
OH, HE WAS SO SPIRITED EARLIER!
HE PRETTY MUCH SOLVED THE CASE.
RIGHT, CONAN?
MY, LOOKS LIKE HE DOESN'T LIKE ME ANYMORE...
SHFF
'COURSE NOT! AFTER ALL THOSE TIMES YOU CHEWED ME OUT WHEN I WAS A KID!
NOW MY BODY HAS THIS INVOLUNTARY REACTION AGAINST YOU!!
THOUGH MAYBE I HAD IT COMING AFTER I TOOK RACHEL EXPLORING AROUND THE NEIGHBORHOOD UNTIL SHE WAS COVERED IN DIRT.
COME TO THINK OF IT, IT'S ALREADY BEEN TEN YEARS SINCE YOU LEFT HOME.
SO? WHERE'D THAT COME FROM?
TEN YEARS... NO WONDER I DIDN'T REMEMBER HER.
OH, I WAS JUST THINKING MAYBE IT'S TIME YOU CAME BACK TO DAD.
...
NO WAY!!!

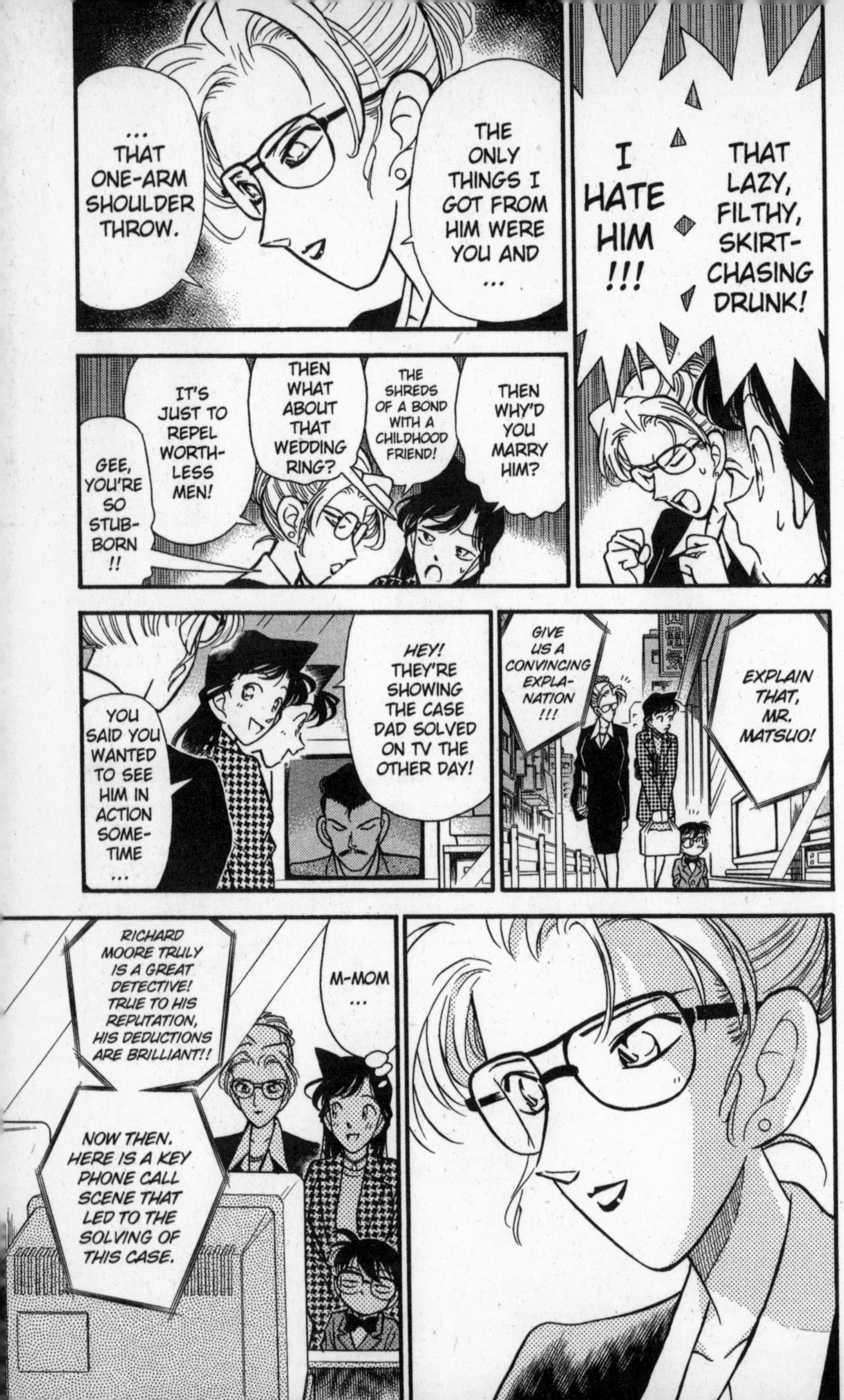
THAT LAZY, FILTHY, SKIRT-CHASING DRUNK!
I HATE HIM !!!
THE ONLY THINGS I GOT FROM HIM WERE YOU AND ...
... THAT ONE-ARM SHOULDER THROW.
THEN WHY'D YOU MARRY HIM?
THE SHREDS OF A BOND WITH A CHILDHOOD FRIEND!
THEN WHAT ABOUT THAT WEDDING RING?
IT'S JUST TO REPEL WORTHLESS MEN!
GEE, YOU'RE SO STUBBORN !!
EXPLAIN THAT, MR. MATSUO!
GIVE US A CONVINCING EXPLANATION !!!
HEY! THEY'RE SHOWING THE CASE DAD SOLVED ON TV THE OTHER DAY!
YOU SAID YOU WANTED TO SEE HIM IN ACTION SOMETIME ...
M-MOM ...
RICHARD MOORE TRULY IS A GREAT DETECTIVE! TRUE TO HIS REPUTATION, HIS DEDUCTIONS ARE BRILLIANT!!
NOW THEN. HERE IS A KEY PHONE CALL SCENE THAT LED TO THE SOLVING OF THIS CASE.

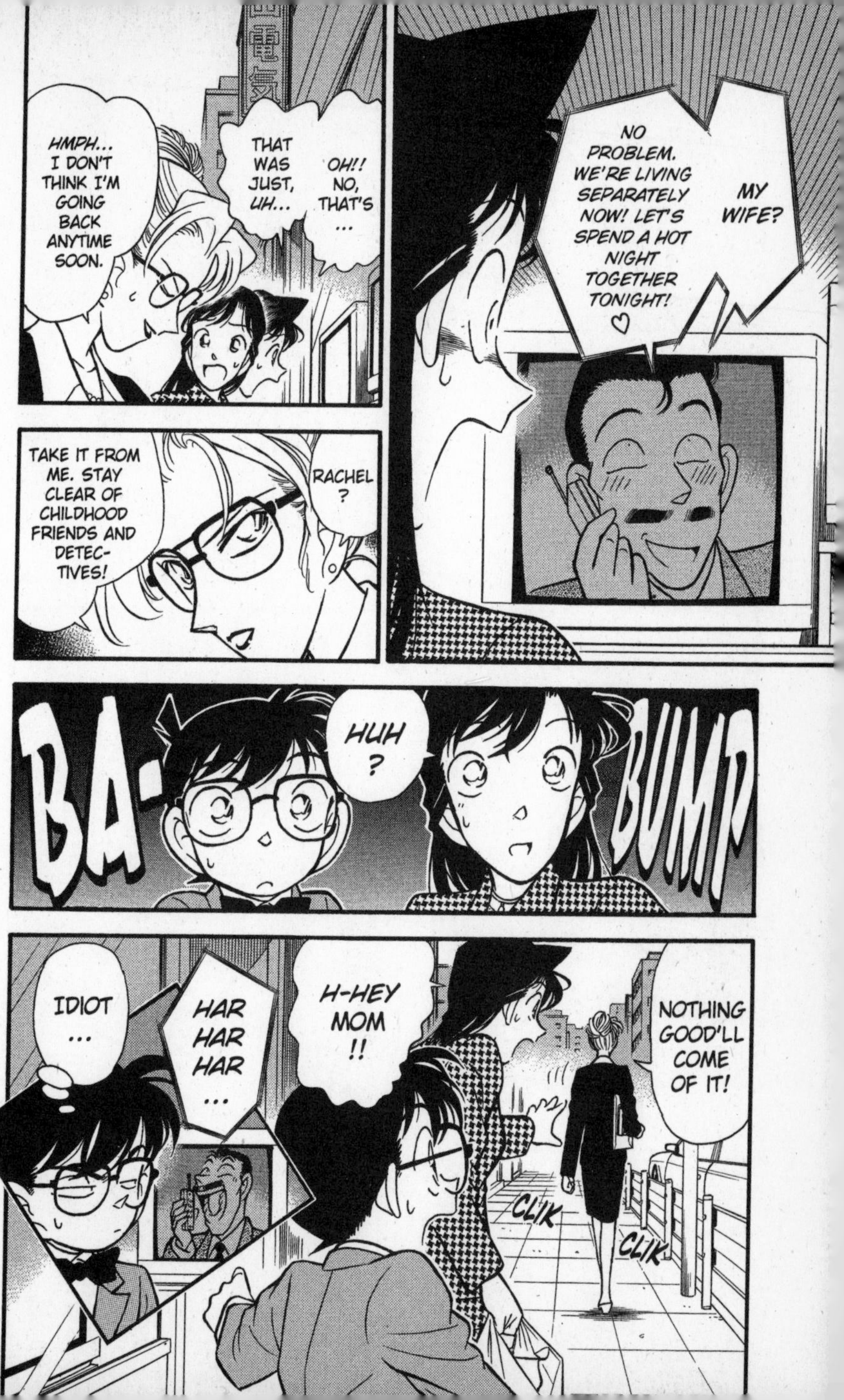
MY WIFE?
NO PROBLEM. WE'RE LIVING SEPARATELY NOW! LET'S SPEND A HOT NIGHT TOGETHER TONIGHT! ♡
OH!! NO, THAT'S ...
THAT WAS JUST, UH...
HMPH... I DON'T THINK I'M GOING BACK ANYTIME SOON.
RACHEL?
TAKE IT FROM ME. STAY CLEAR OF CHILDHOOD FRIENDS AND DETECTIVES!
BUMP
HUH?
BA-
NOTHING GOOD'LL COME OF IT!
CLIK
CLIK
H-HEY MOM!!
HAR HAR HAR ...
IDIOT ...

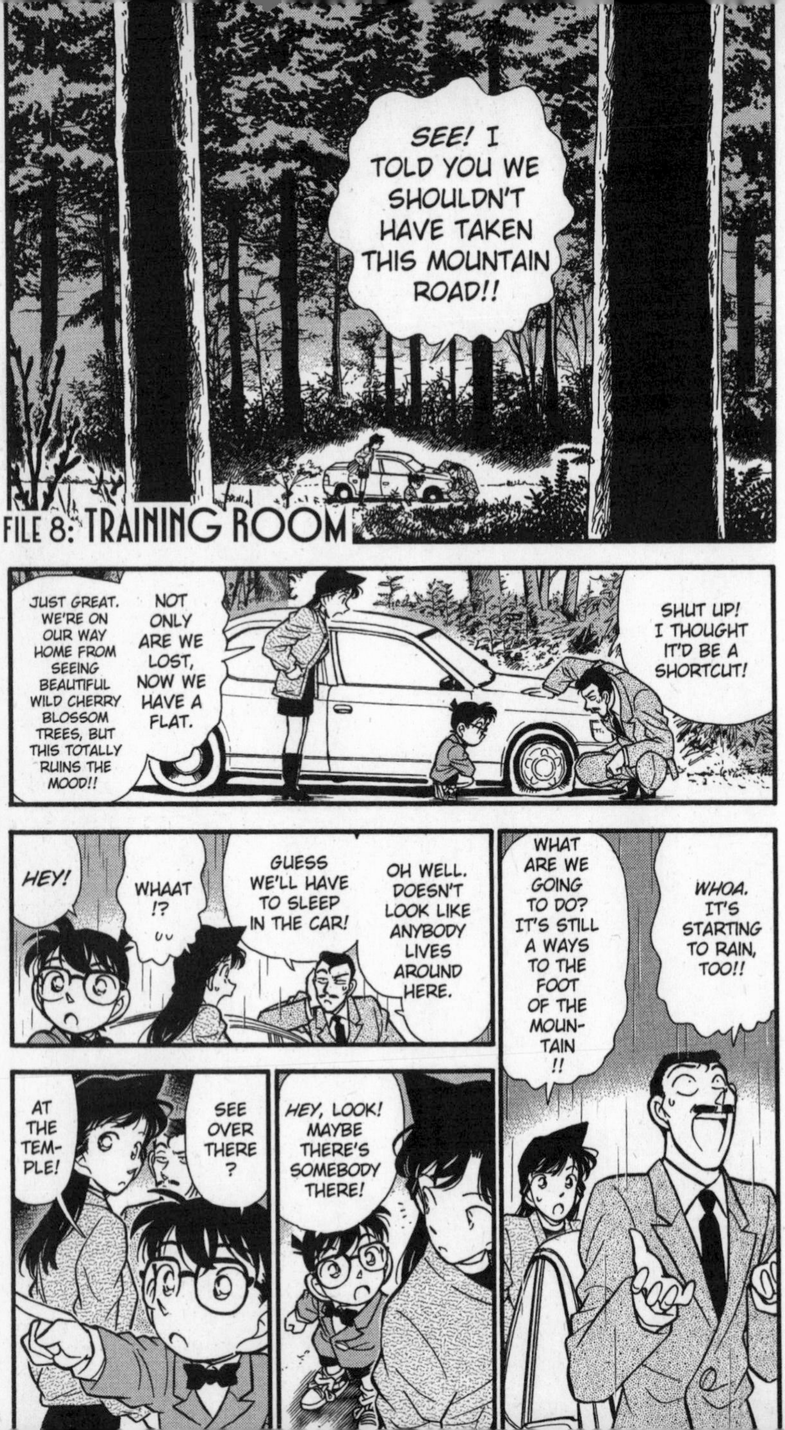
SEE! I TOLD YOU WE SHOULDN'T HAVE TAKEN THIS MOUNTAIN ROAD!!
FILE 8: TRAINING ROOM
SHUT UP! I THOUGHT IT'D BE A SHORTCUT!
NOT ONLY ARE WE LOST, NOW WE HAVE A FLAT.
JUST GREAT. WE'RE ON OUR WAY HOME FROM SEEING BEAUTIFUL WILD CHERRY BLOSSOM TREES, BUT THIS TOTALLY RUINS THE MOOD!!
WHOA. IT'S STARTING TO RAIN, TOO!!
WHAT ARE WE GOING TO DO? IT'S STILL A WAYS TO THE FOOT OF THE MOUN-TAIN!!
OH WELL. DOESN'T LOOK LIKE ANYBODY LIVES AROUND HERE.
GUESS WE'LL HAVE TO SLEEP IN THE CAR!
WHAAT!?
HEY!
HEY, LOOK! MAYBE THERE'S SOMEBODY THERE!
SEE OVER THERE?
AT THE TEMPLE!

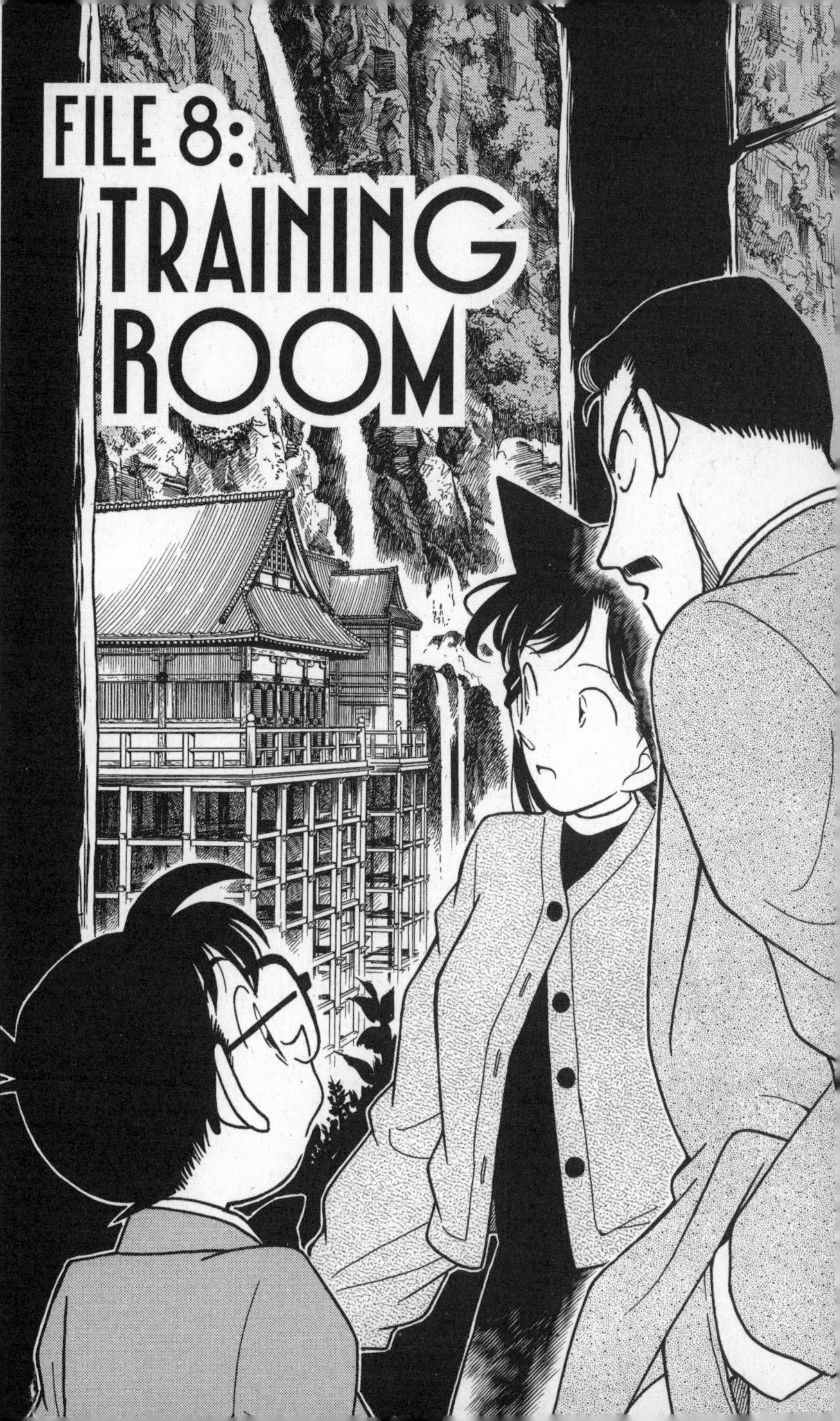
FILE 8:
TRAINING ROOM

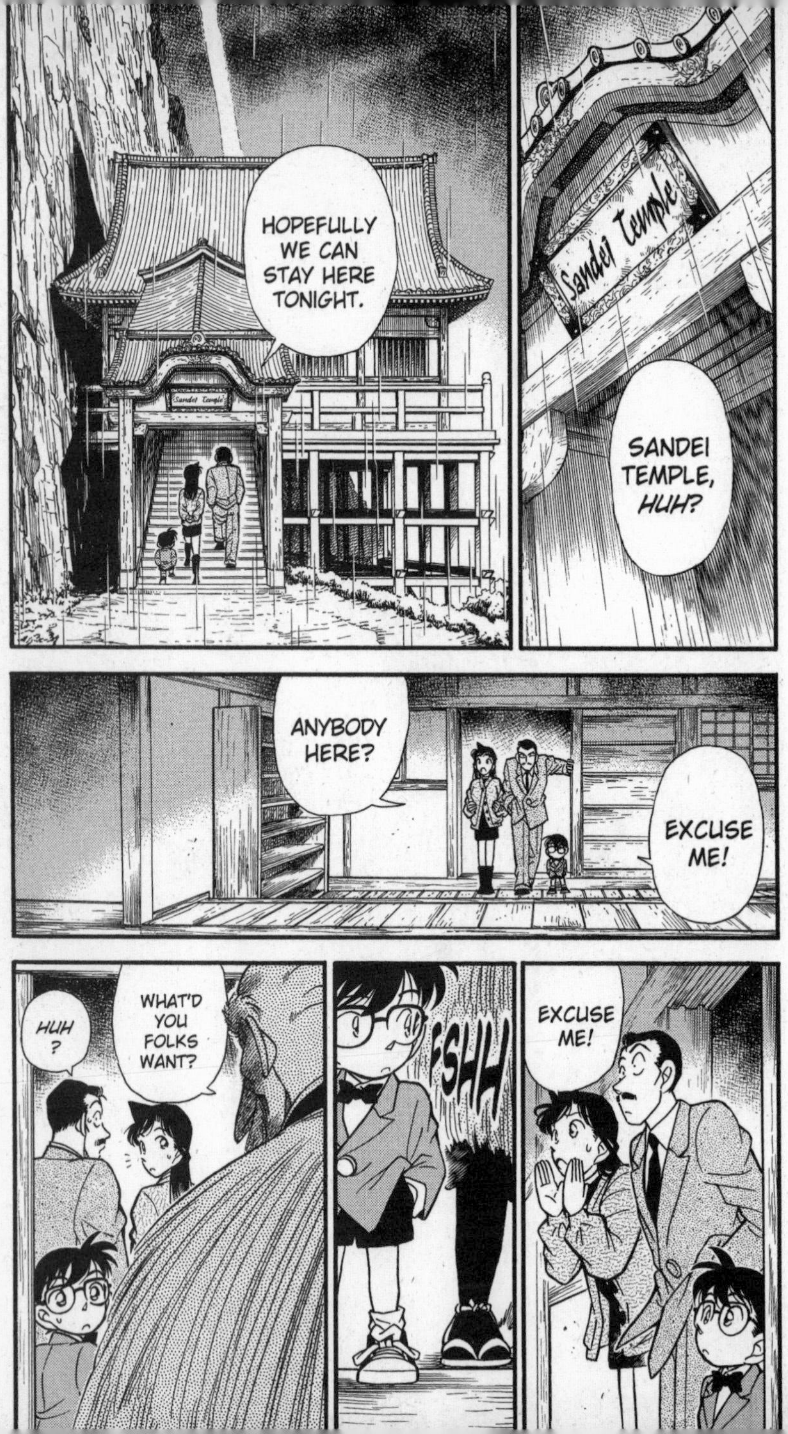
Sandei Temple
SANDEI TEMPLE, HUH?
HOPEFULLY WE CAN STAY HERE TONIGHT.
EXCUSE ME!
ANYBODY HERE?
EXCUSE ME!
FSHH
WHAT'D YOU FOLKS WANT?
HUH?

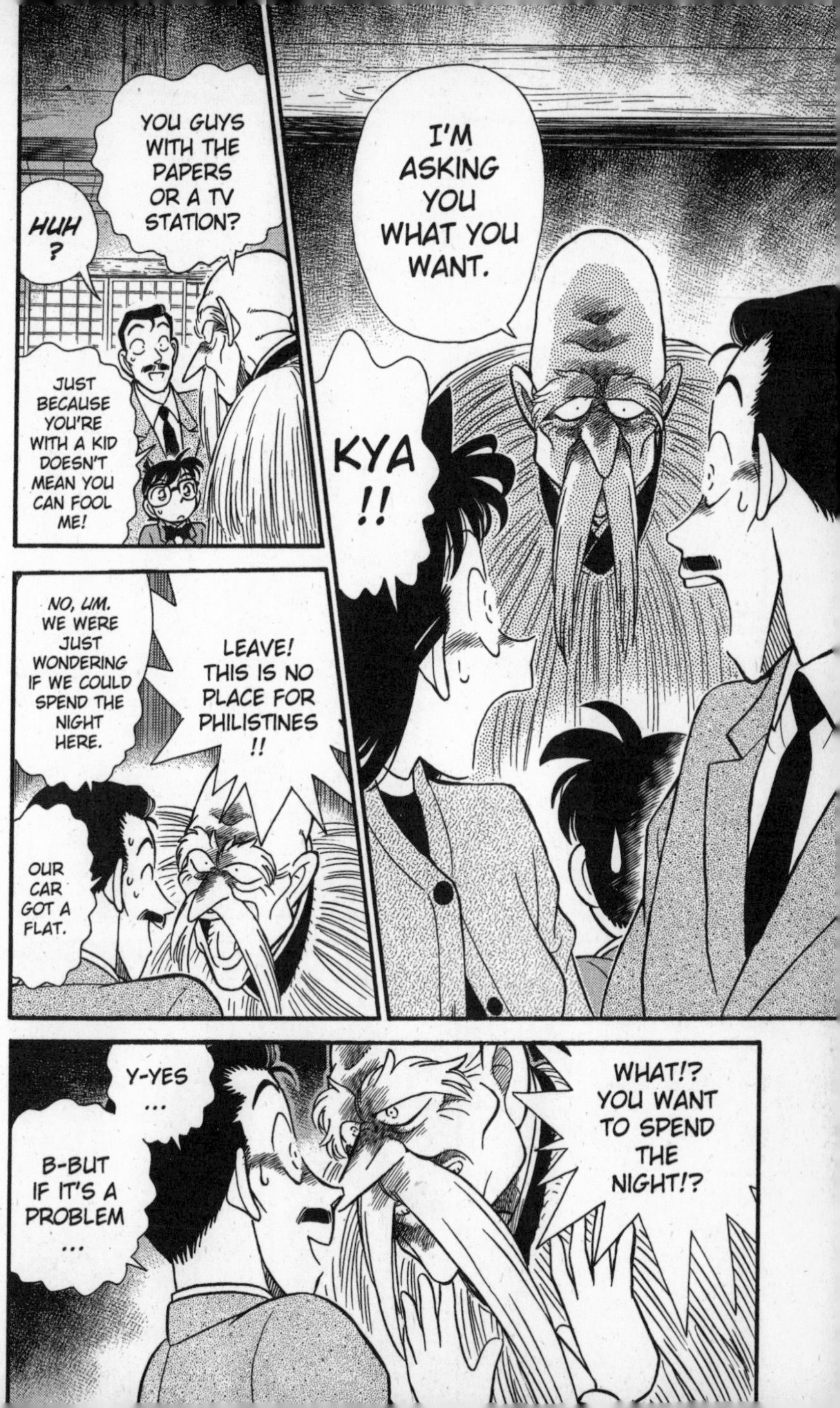
I'M ASKING YOU WHAT YOU WANT.
KYA !!
YOU GUYS WITH THE PAPERS OR A TV STATION?
HUH ?
JUST BECAUSE YOU'RE WITH A KID DOESN'T MEAN YOU CAN FOOL ME!
LEAVE! THIS IS NO PLACE FOR PHILISTINES !!
NO, UM. WE WERE JUST WONDERING IF WE COULD SPEND THE NIGHT HERE.
OUR CAR GOT A FLAT.
WHAT!? YOU WANT TO SPEND THE NIGHT!?
Y-YES ...
B-BUT IF IT'S A PROBLEM ...

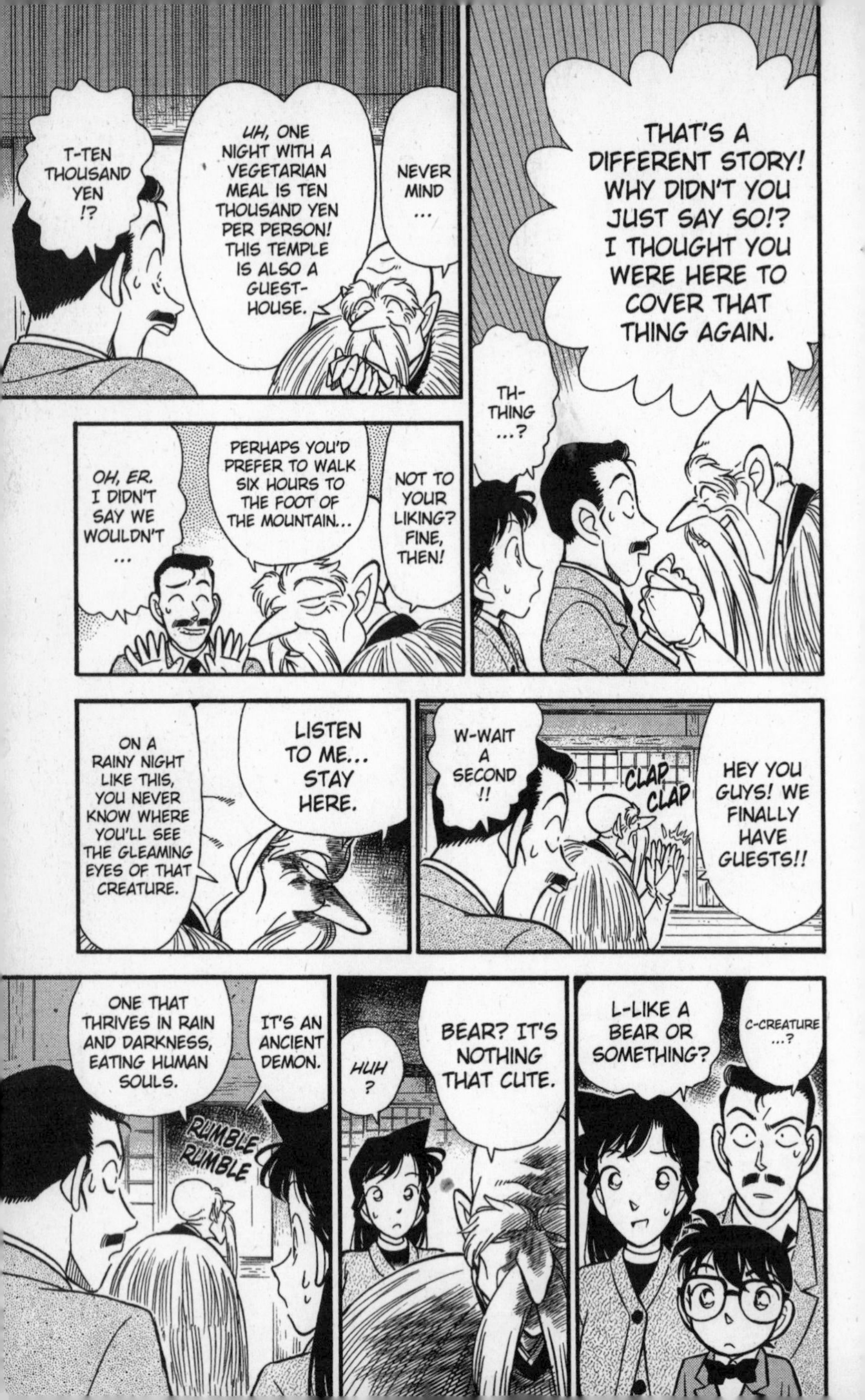
THAT'S A DIFFERENT STORY! WHY DIDN'T YOU JUST SAY SO!? I THOUGHT YOU WERE HERE TO COVER THAT THING AGAIN.
TH-THING ...?
NEVER MIND ...
UH, ONE NIGHT WITH A VEGETARIAN MEAL IS TEN THOUSAND YEN PER PERSON! THIS TEMPLE IS ALSO A GUEST-HOUSE.
T-TEN THOUSAND YEN !?
NOT TO YOUR LIKING? FINE, THEN!
PERHAPS YOU'D PREFER TO WALK SIX HOURS TO THE FOOT OF THE MOUNTAIN...
OH, ER. I DIDN'T SAY WE WOULDN'T ...
HEY YOU GUYS! WE FINALLY HAVE GUESTS!!
CLAP CLAP
W-WAIT A SECOND !!
LISTEN TO ME... STAY HERE.
ON A RAINY NIGHT LIKE THIS, YOU NEVER KNOW WHERE YOU'LL SEE THE GLEAMING EYES OF THAT CREATURE.
C-CREATURE ...?
L-LIKE A BEAR OR SOMETHING?
BEAR? IT'S NOTHING THAT CUTE.
HUH ?
IT'S AN ANCIENT DEMON.
ONE THAT THRIVES IN RAIN AND DARKNESS, EATING HUMAN SOULS.
RUMBLE RUMBLE

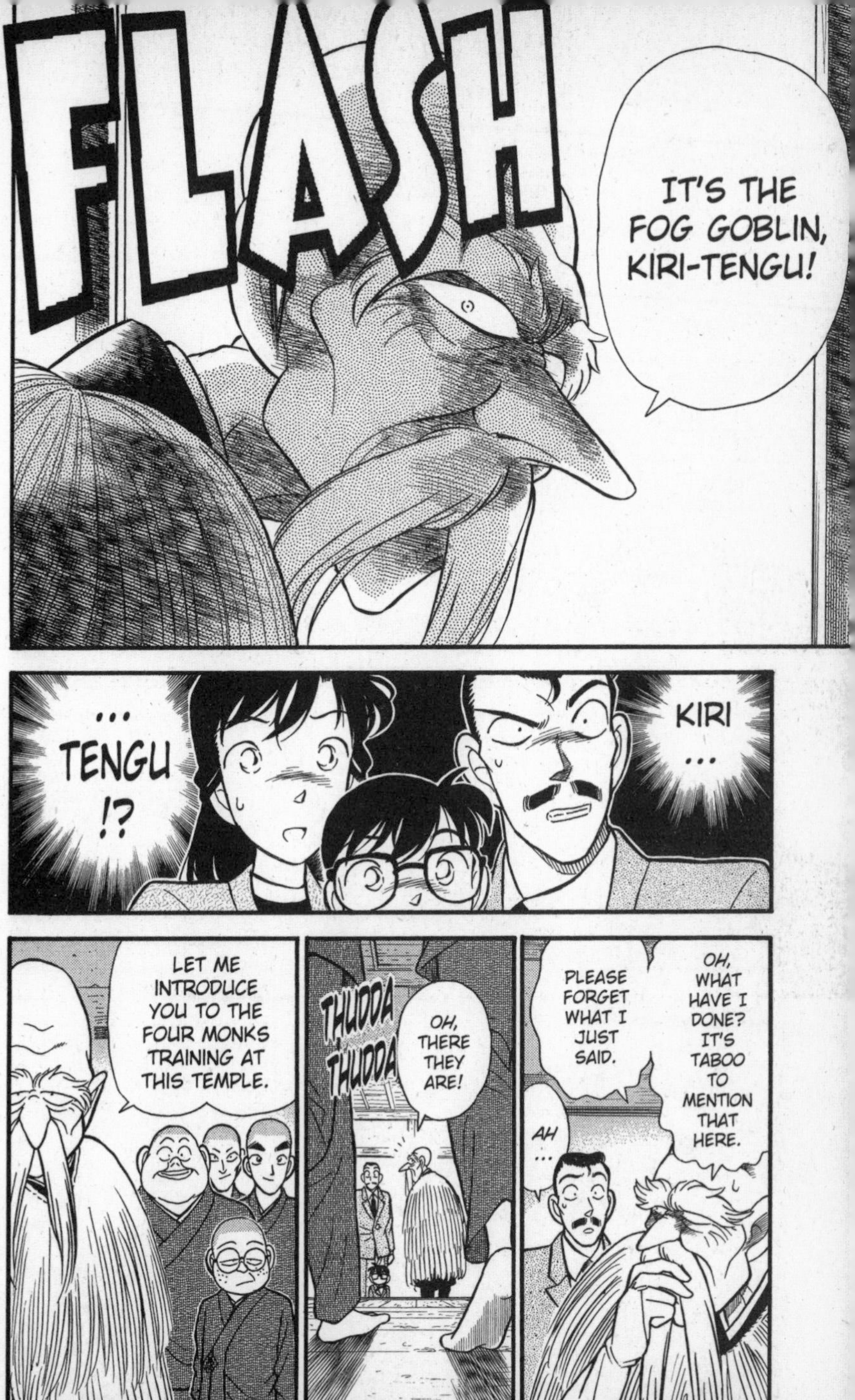
FLASH
IT'S THE FOG GOBLIN, KIRI-TENGU!
KIRI ...
... TENGU !?
OH, WHAT HAVE I DONE? IT'S TABOO TO MENTION THAT HERE.
PLEASE FORGET WHAT I JUST SAID.
AH ...
OH, THERE THEY ARE!
THUDDA THUDDA
LET ME INTRODUCE YOU TO THE FOUR MONKS TRAINING AT THIS TEMPLE.

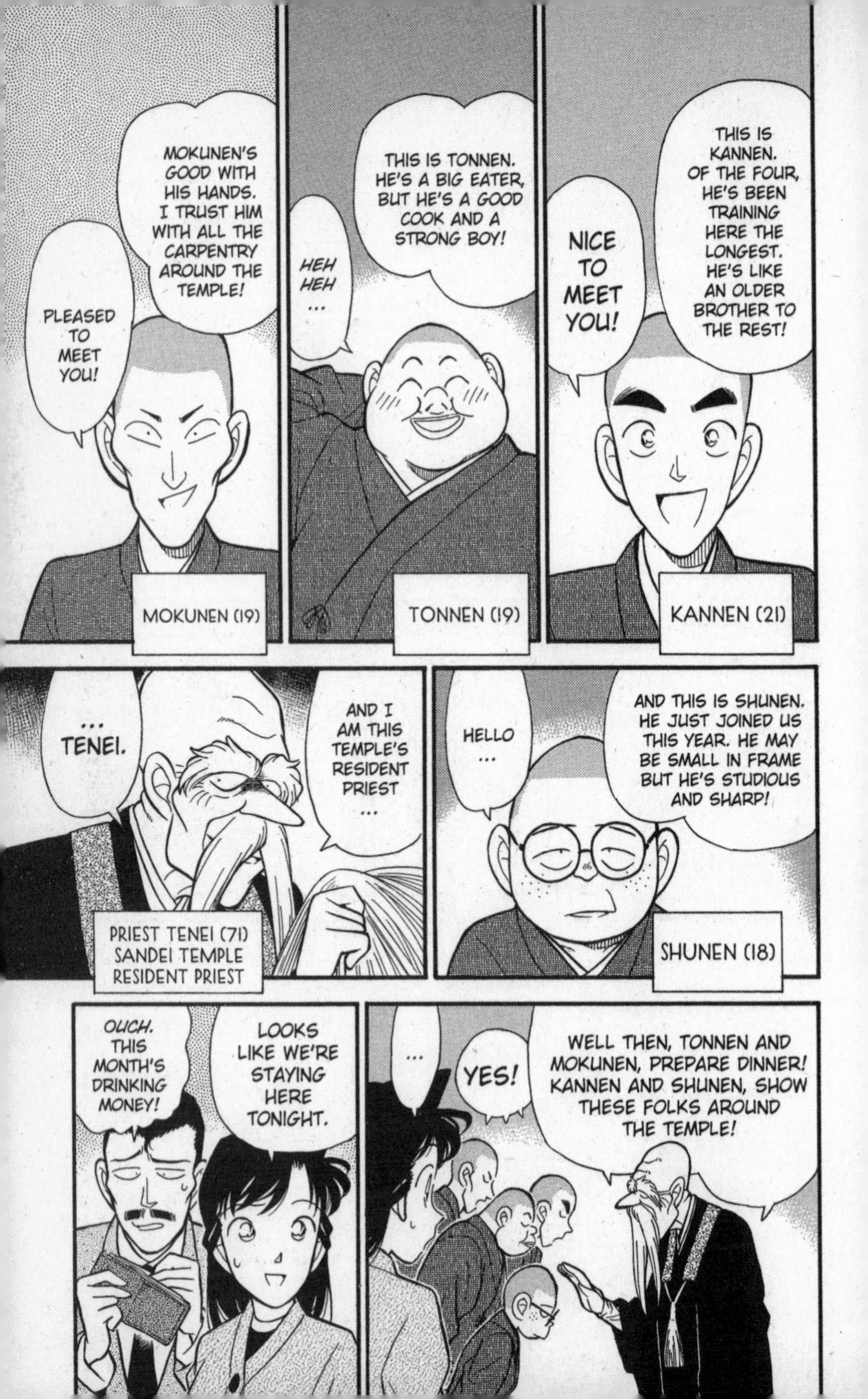

THIS IS KANNEN. OF THE FOUR, HE'S BEEN TRAINING HERE THE LONGEST. HE'S LIKE AN OLDER BROTHER TO THE REST!
NICE TO MEET YOU!
KANNEN (21)
THIS IS TONNEN. HE'S A BIG EATER, BUT HE'S A GOOD COOK AND A STRONG BOY!
HEH HEH ...
TONNEN (19)
MOKUNEN'S GOOD WITH HIS HANDS. I TRUST HIM WITH ALL THE CARPENTRY AROUND THE TEMPLE!
PLEASED TO MEET YOU!
MOKUNEN (19)
AND THIS IS SHUNEN. HE JUST JOINED US THIS YEAR. HE MAY BE SMALL IN FRAME BUT HE'S STUDIOUS AND SHARP!
HELLO ...
SHUNEN (18)
AND I AM THIS TEMPLE'S RESIDENT PRIEST ...
... TENEI.
PRIEST TENEI (71) SANDEI TEMPLE RESIDENT PRIEST
WELL THEN, TONNEN AND MOKUNEN, PREPARE DINNER! KANNEN AND SHUNEN, SHOW THESE FOLKS AROUND THE TEMPLE!
YES!
...
LOOKS LIKE WE'RE STAYING HERE TONIGHT.
OUCH. THIS MONTH'S DRINKING MONEY!

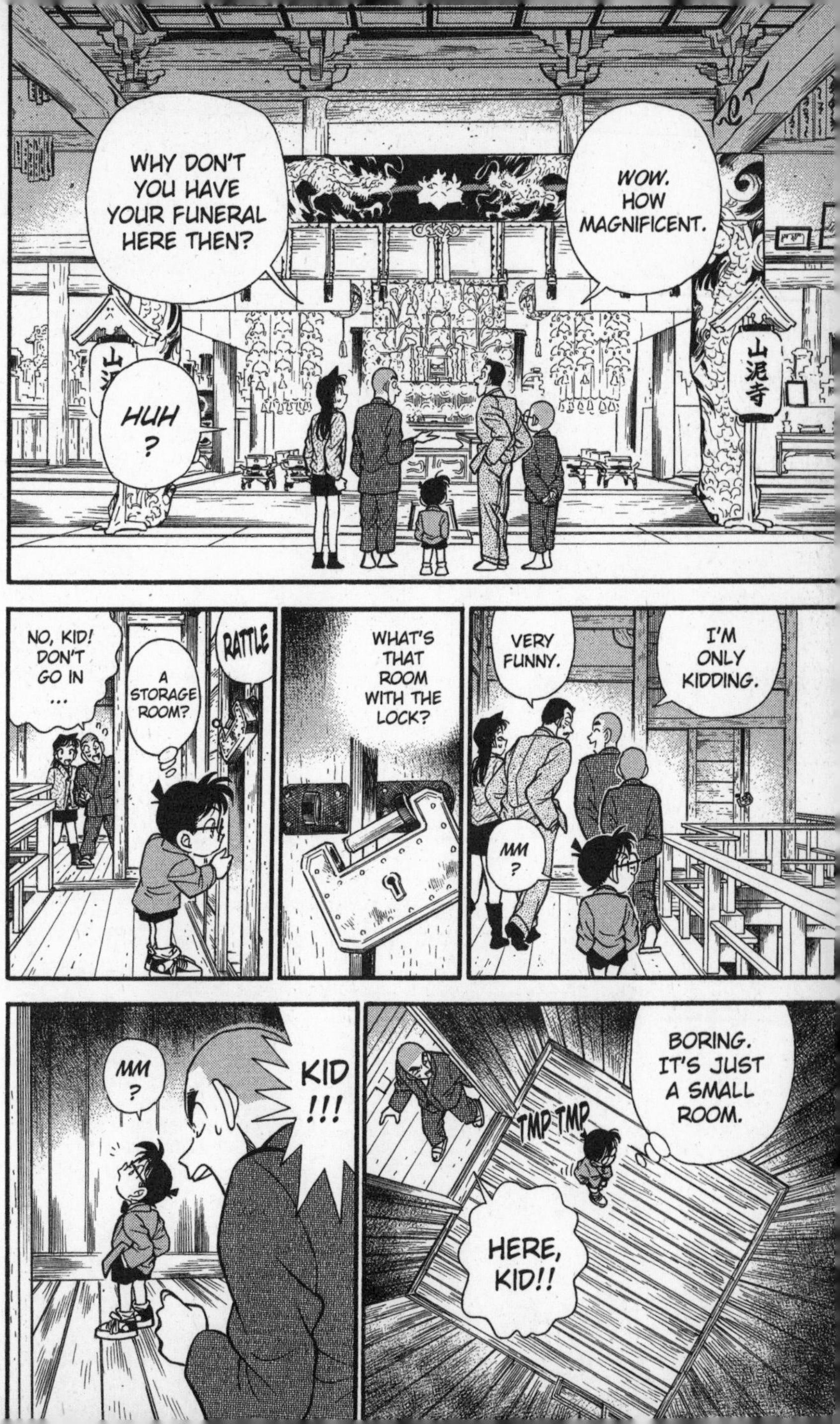
WOW. HOW MAGNIFICENT.
WHY DON'T YOU HAVE YOUR FUNERAL HERE THEN?
山泥寺
HUH ?
I'M ONLY KIDDING.
VERY FUNNY.
MM ?
WHAT'S THAT ROOM WITH THE LOCK?
RATTLE
A STORAGE ROOM?
NO, KID! DON'T GO IN ...
BORING. IT'S JUST A SMALL ROOM.
TMP TMP
HERE, KID!!
KID !!!
MM ?

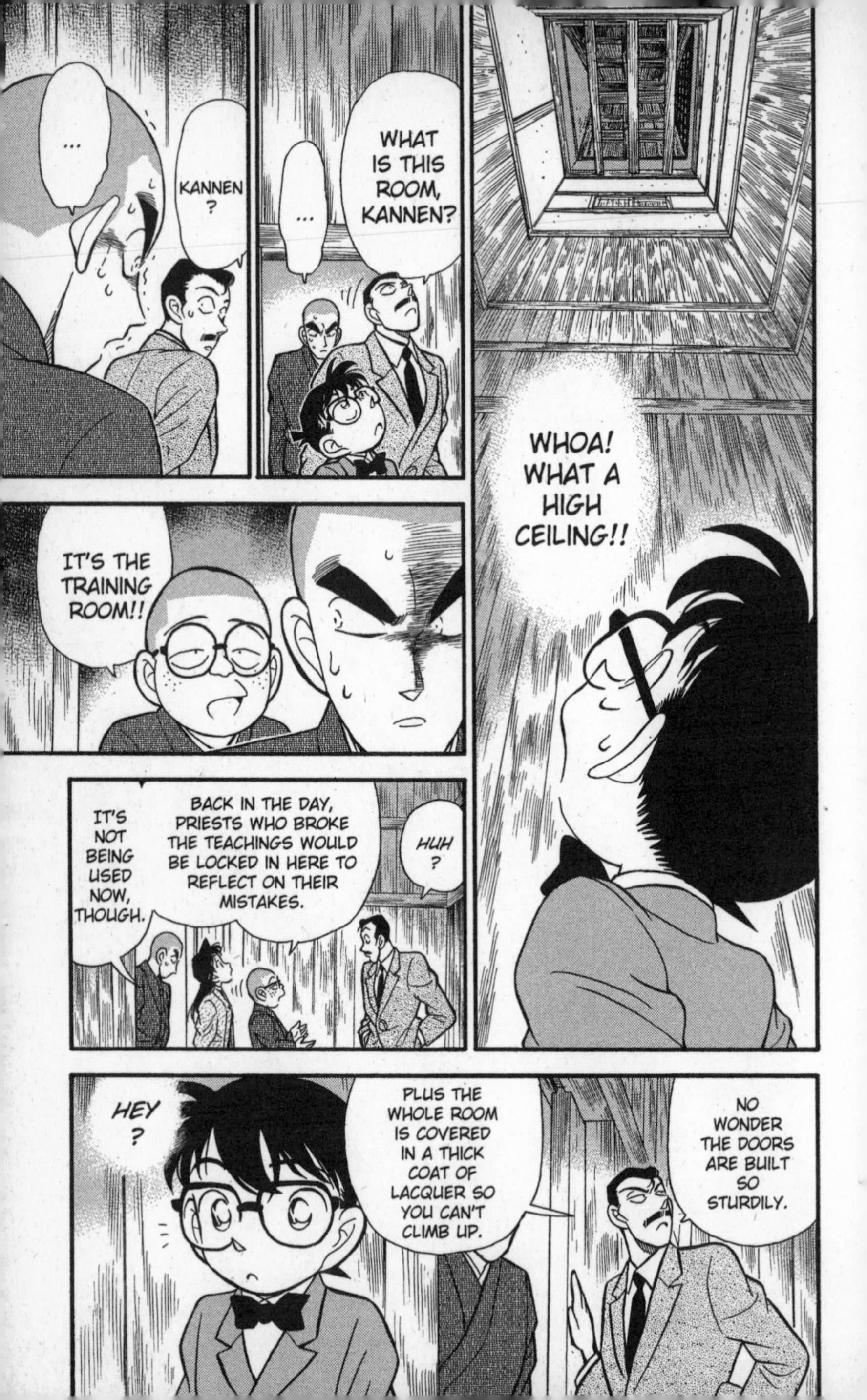
WHOA! WHAT A HIGH CEILING!!
WHAT IS THIS ROOM, KANNEN?
...
KANNEN ?
...
IT'S THE TRAINING ROOM!!
HUH ?
BACK IN THE DAY, PRIESTS WHO BROKE THE TEACHINGS WOULD BE LOCKED IN HERE TO REFLECT ON THEIR MISTAKES.
IT'S NOT BEING USED NOW, THOUGH.
NO WONDER THE DOORS ARE BUILT SO STURDILY.
PLUS THE WHOLE ROOM IS COVERED IN A THICK COAT OF LACQUER SO YOU CAN'T CLIMB UP.
HEY ?

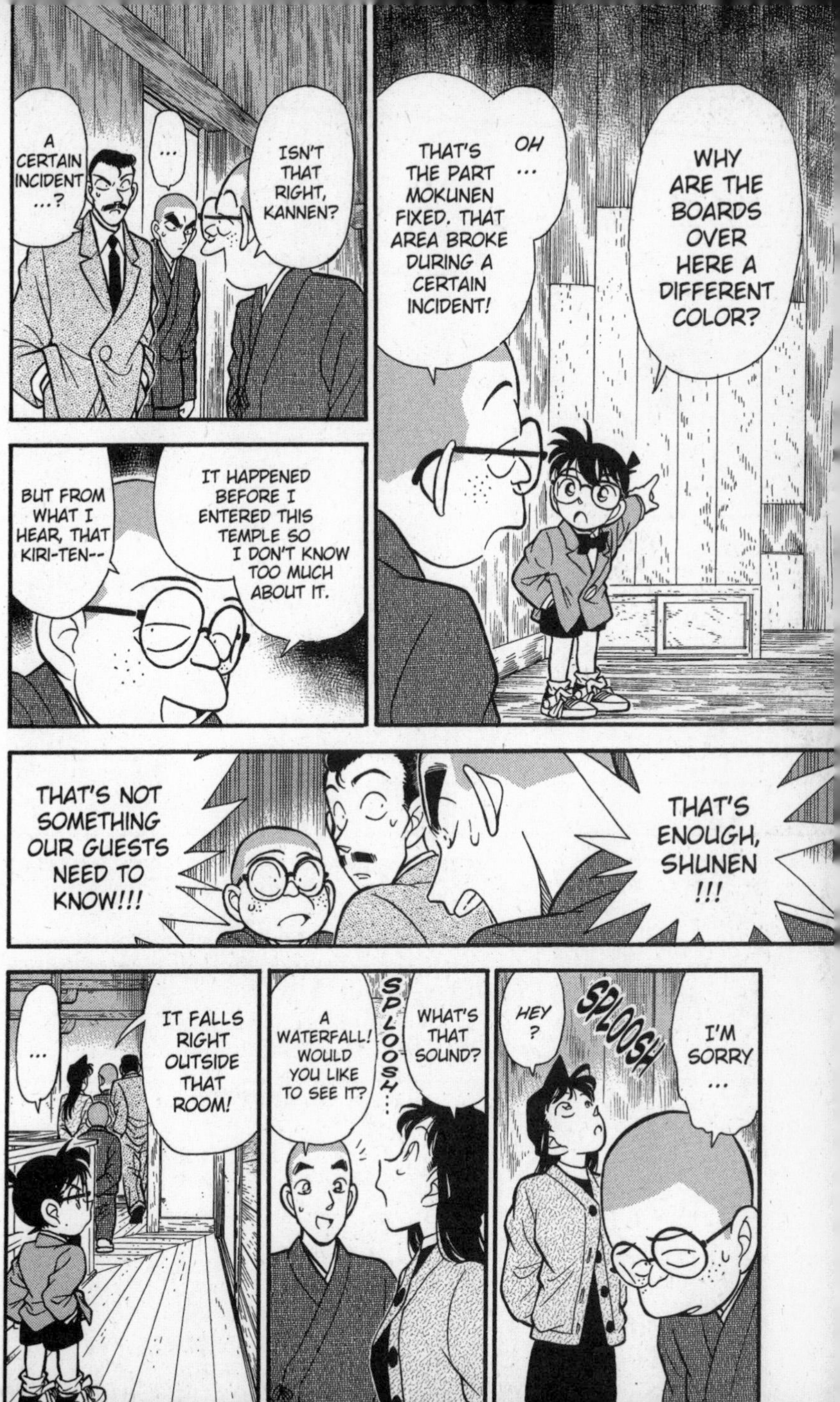

WHY ARE THE BOARDS OVER HERE A DIFFERENT COLOR?
OH ...
THAT'S THE PART MOKUNEN FIXED. THAT AREA BROKE DURING A CERTAIN INCIDENT!
ISN'T THAT RIGHT, KANNEN?
...
A CERTAIN INCIDENT ...?
IT HAPPENED BEFORE I ENTERED THIS TEMPLE SO I DON'T KNOW TOO MUCH ABOUT IT.
BUT FROM WHAT I HEAR, THAT KIRI-TEN--
THAT'S ENOUGH, SHUNEN !!!
THAT'S NOT SOMETHING OUR GUESTS NEED TO KNOW!!!
I'M SORRY ...
SPLOOSH
HEY ?
WHAT'S THAT SOUND?
SPLOOSH...
A WATERFALL! WOULD YOU LIKE TO SEE IT?
IT FALLS RIGHT OUTSIDE THAT ROOM!
...

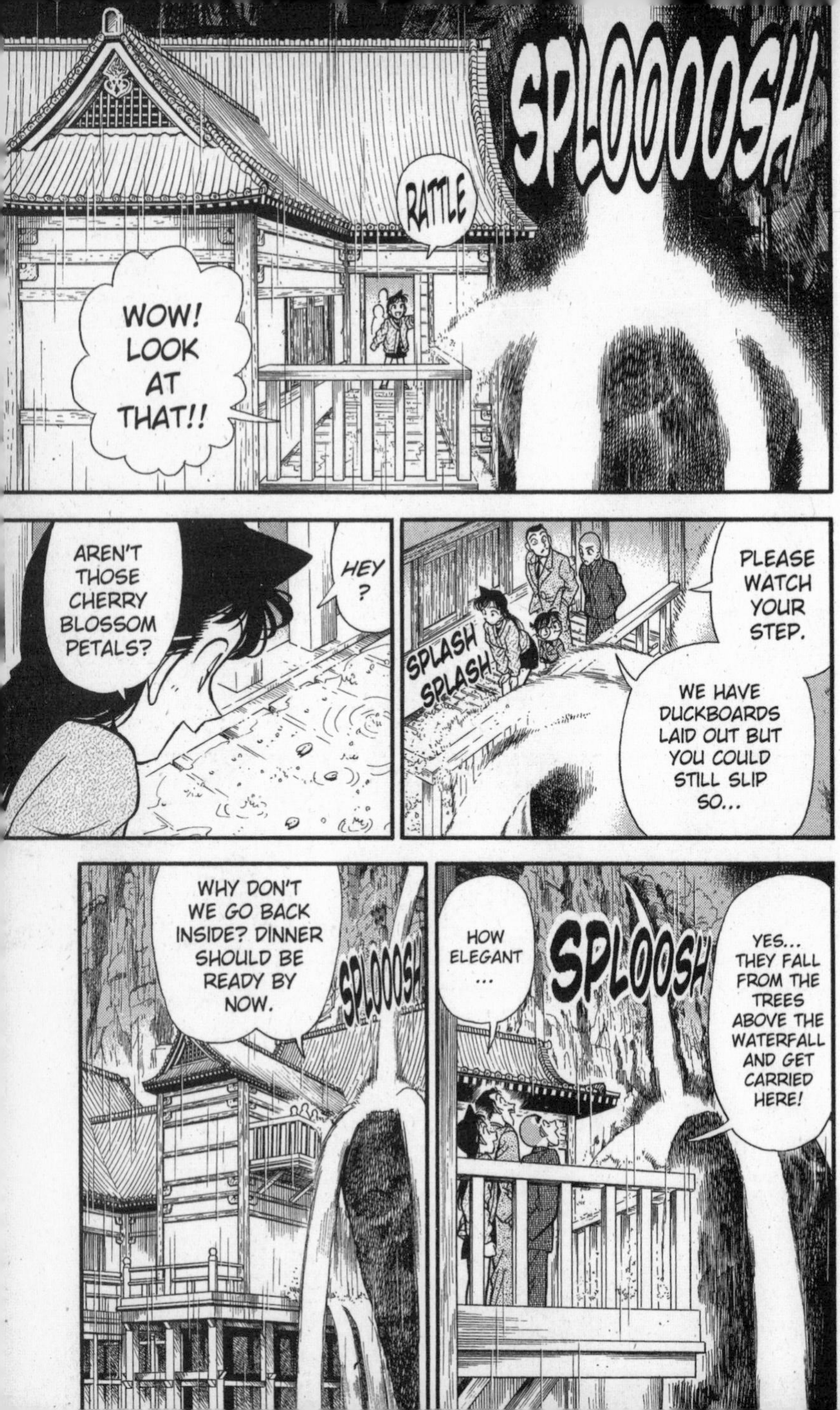
SPLOOOOSH
RATTLE
WOW! LOOK AT THAT!!
PLEASE WATCH YOUR STEP.
WE HAVE DUCKBOARDS LAID OUT BUT YOU COULD STILL SLIP SO...
SPLASH SPLASH
HEY ?
AREN'T THOSE CHERRY BLOSSOM PETALS?
YES... THEY FALL FROM THE TREES ABOVE THE WATERFALL AND GET CARRIED HERE!
SPLOOSH
HOW ELEGANT ...
SPLOOOSH
WHY DON'T WE GO BACK INSIDE? DINNER SHOULD BE READY BY NOW.

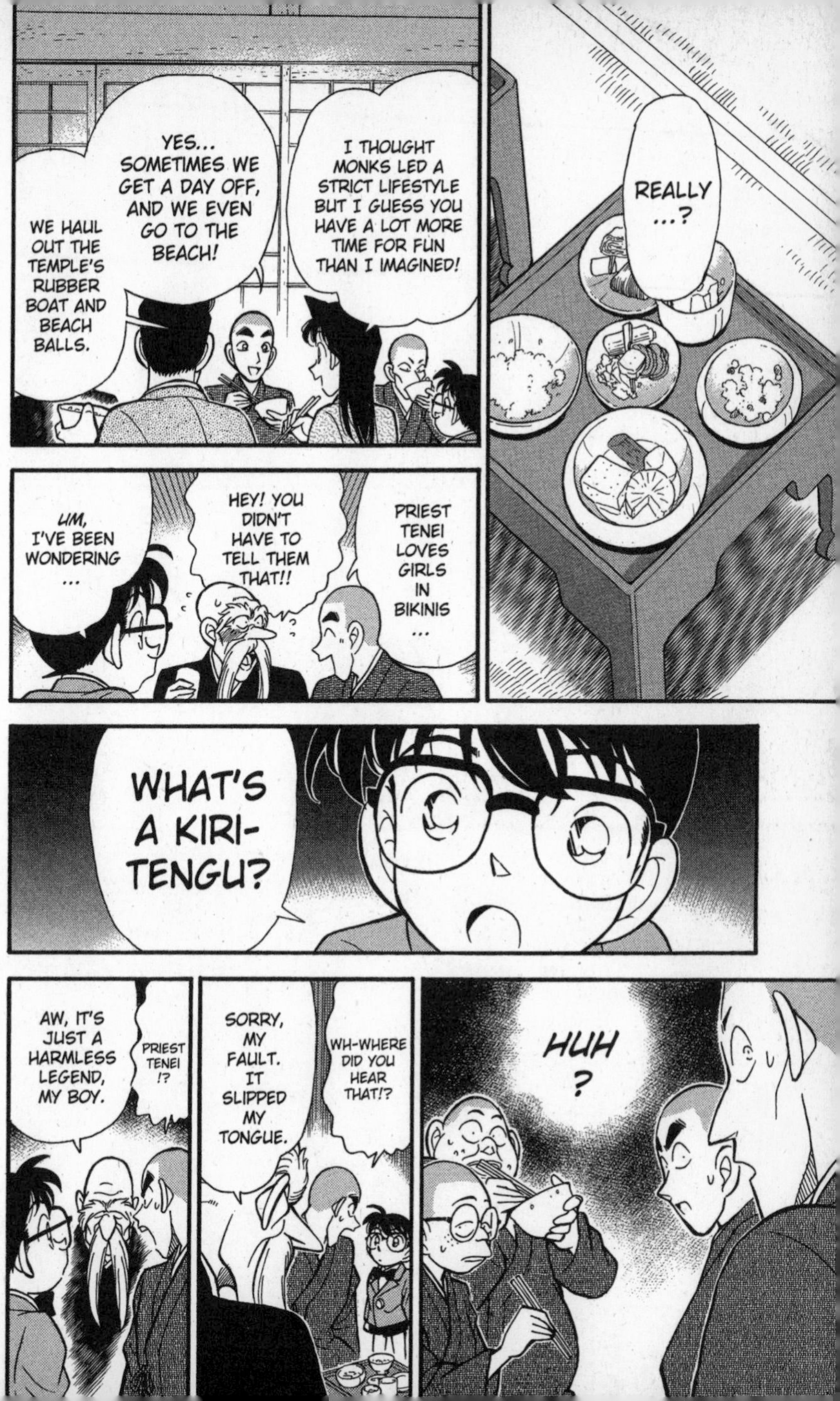
REALLY ...?
I THOUGHT MONKS LED A STRICT LIFESTYLE BUT I GUESS YOU HAVE A LOT MORE TIME FOR FUN THAN I IMAGINED!
YES... SOMETIMES WE GET A DAY OFF, AND WE EVEN GO TO THE BEACH!
WE HAUL OUT THE TEMPLE'S RUBBER BOAT AND BEACH BALLS.
PRIEST TENEI LOVES GIRLS IN BIKINIS ...
HEY! YOU DIDN'T HAVE TO TELL THEM THAT!!
UM, I'VE BEEN WONDERING ...
WHAT'S A KIRI-TENGU?
HUH ?
WH-WHERE DID YOU HEAR THAT!?
SORRY, MY FAULT. IT SLIPPED MY TONGUE.
PRIEST TENEI !?
AW, IT'S JUST A HARMLESS LEGEND, MY BOY.

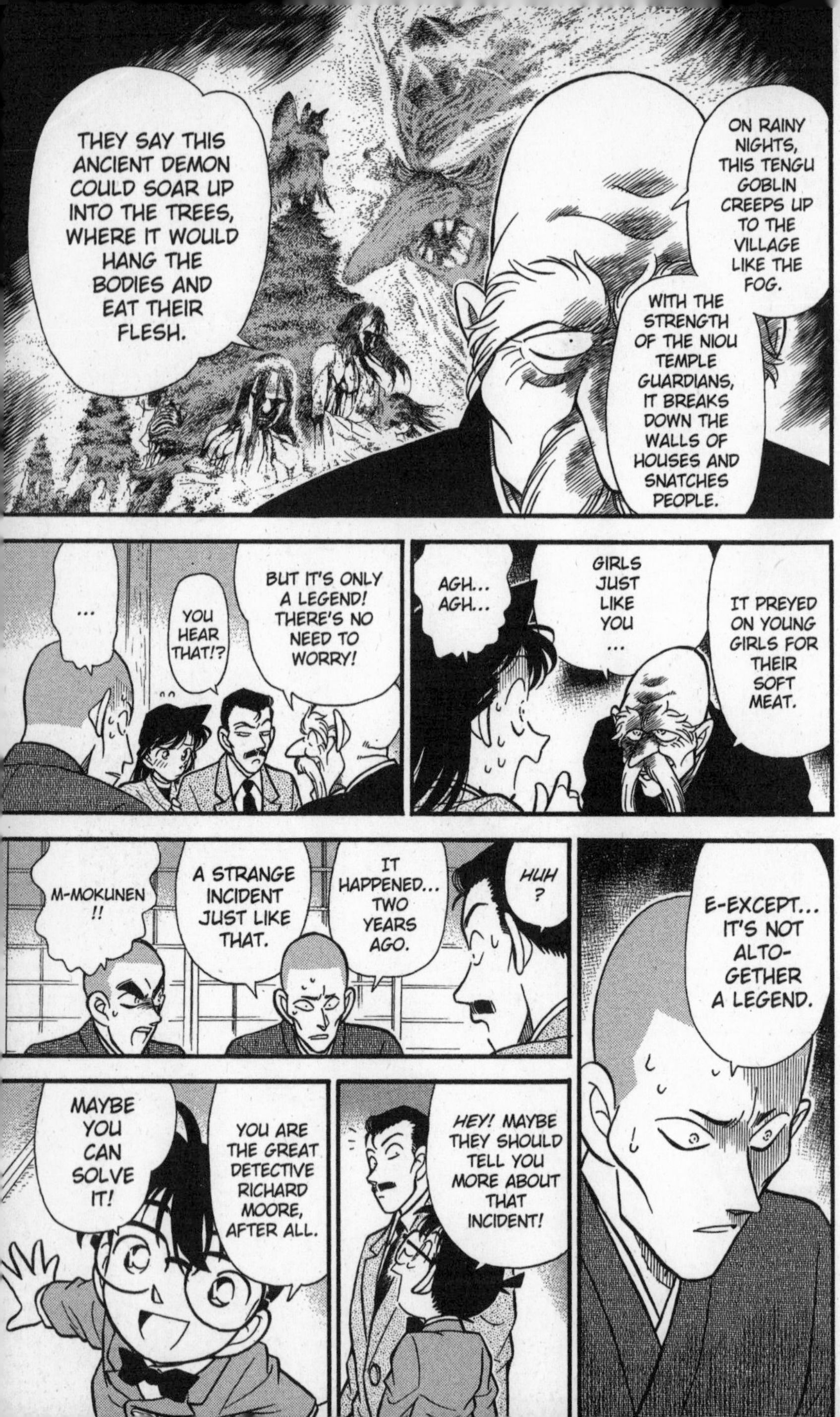
ON RAINY NIGHTS, THIS TENGU GOBLIN CREEPS UP TO THE VILLAGE LIKE THE FOG.
WITH THE STRENGTH OF THE NIOU TEMPLE GUARDIANS, IT BREAKS DOWN THE WALLS OF HOUSES AND SNATCHES PEOPLE.
THEY SAY THIS ANCIENT DEMON COULD SOAR UP INTO THE TREES, WHERE IT WOULD HANG THE BODIES AND EAT THEIR FLESH.
IT PREYED ON YOUNG GIRLS FOR THEIR SOFT MEAT.
GIRLS JUST LIKE YOU ...
AGH... AGH...
BUT IT'S ONLY A LEGEND! THERE'S NO NEED TO WORRY!
YOU HEAR THAT!?
...
E-EXCEPT... IT'S NOT ALTO-GETHER A LEGEND.
HUH?
IT HAPPENED... TWO YEARS AGO.
A STRANGE INCIDENT JUST LIKE THAT.
M-MOKUNEN!!
HEY! MAYBE THEY SHOULD TELL YOU MORE ABOUT THAT INCIDENT!
YOU ARE THE GREAT DETECTIVE RICHARD MOORE, AFTER ALL.
MAYBE YOU CAN SOLVE IT!

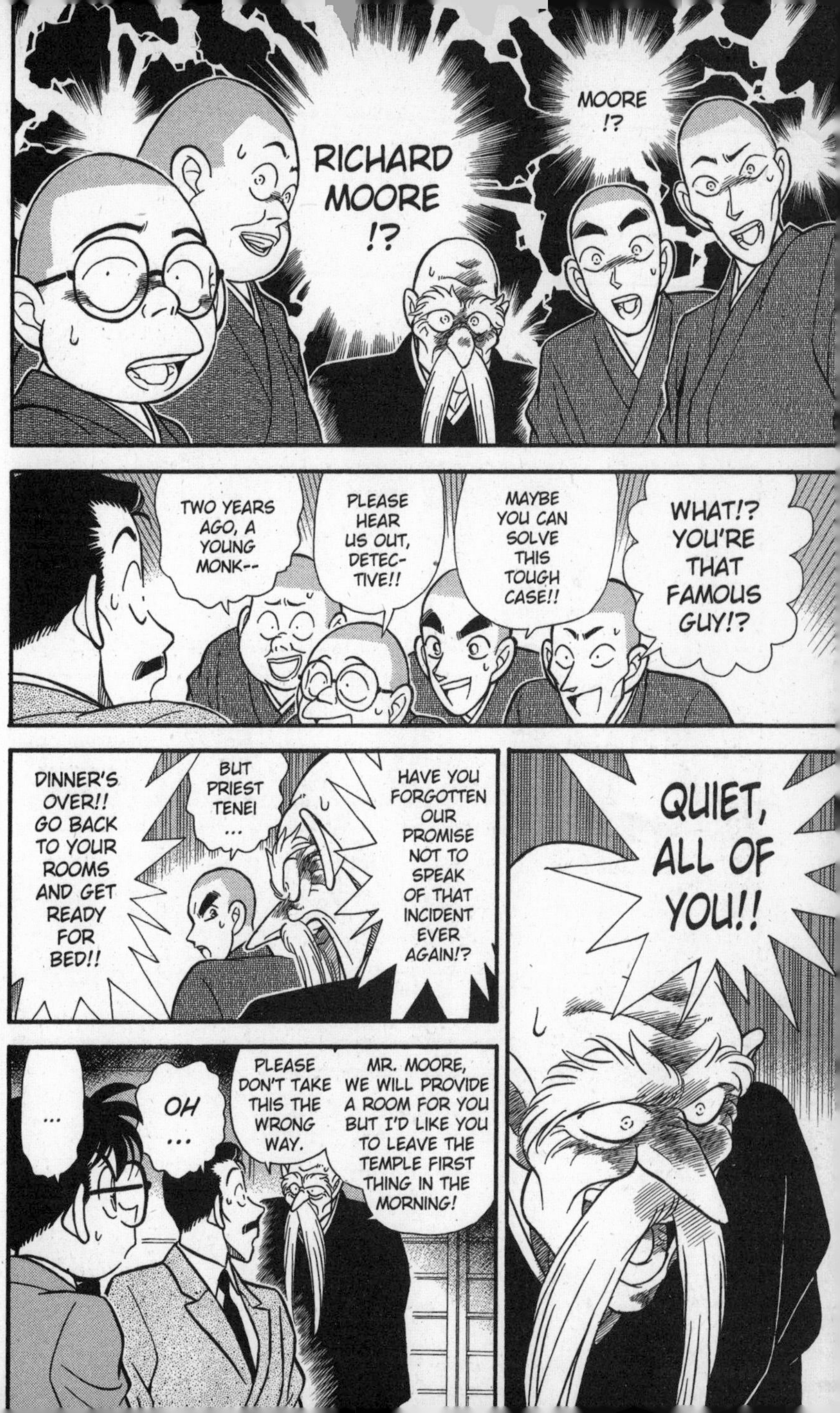
MOORE !?
RICHARD MOORE !?
WHAT!? YOU'RE THAT FAMOUS GUY!?
MAYBE YOU CAN SOLVE THIS TOUGH CASE!!
PLEASE HEAR US OUT, DETECTIVE!!
TWO YEARS AGO, A YOUNG MONK--
QUIET, ALL OF YOU!!
HAVE YOU FORGOTTEN OUR PROMISE NOT TO SPEAK OF THAT INCIDENT EVER AGAIN!?
BUT PRIEST TENEI ...
DINNER'S OVER!! GO BACK TO YOUR ROOMS AND GET READY FOR BED!!
MR. MOORE, WE WILL PROVIDE A ROOM FOR YOU BUT I'D LIKE YOU TO LEAVE THE TEMPLE FIRST THING IN THE MORNING!
PLEASE DON'T TAKE THIS THE WRONG WAY.
OH ...
...

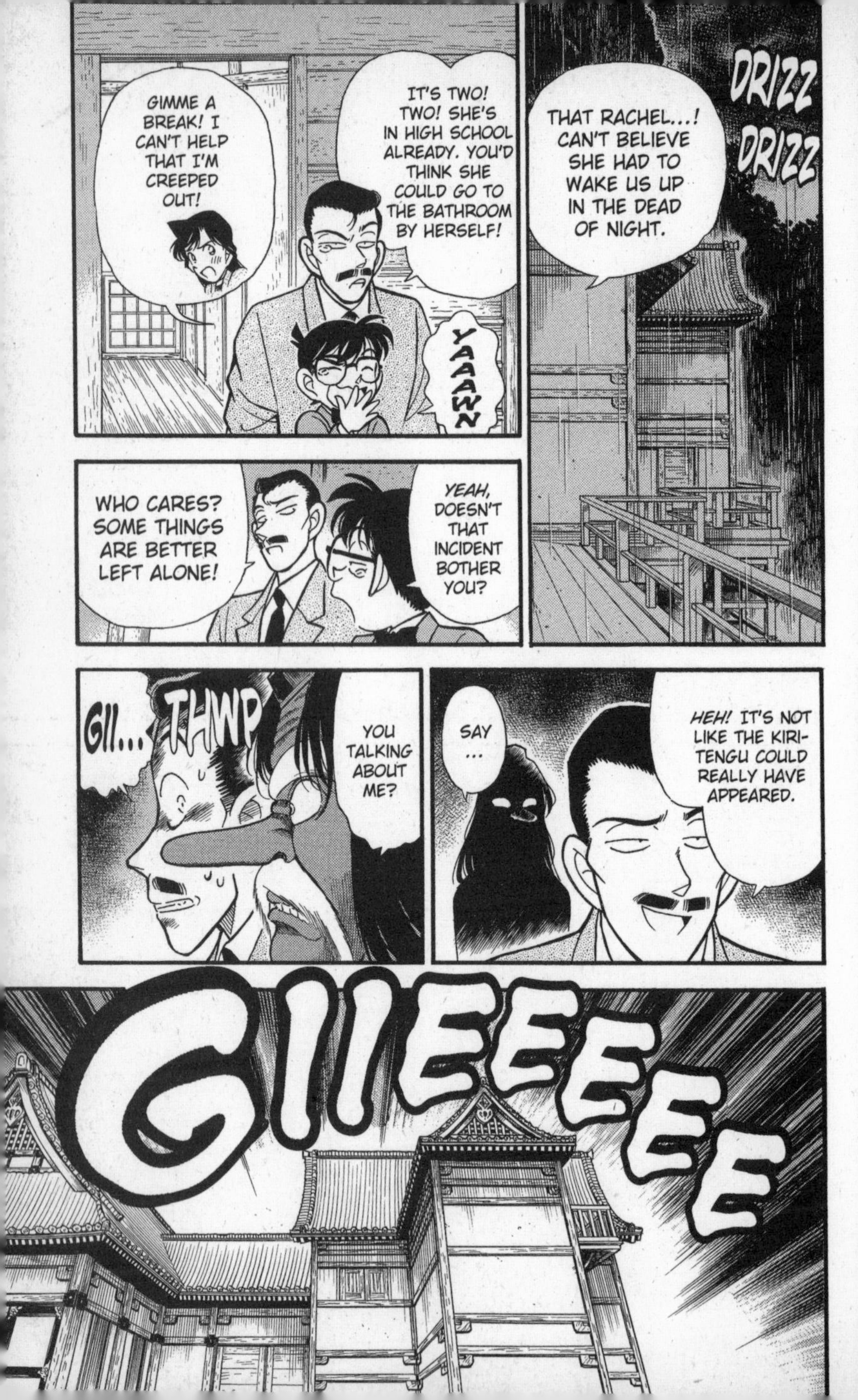
DRIZZ DRIZZ
THAT RACHEL...! CAN'T BELIEVE SHE HAD TO WAKE US UP IN THE DEAD OF NIGHT.
IT'S TWO! TWO! SHE'S IN HIGH SCHOOL ALREADY. YOU'D THINK SHE COULD GO TO THE BATHROOM BY HERSELF!
YAAAWN
GIMME A BREAK! I CAN'T HELP THAT I'M CREEPED OUT!
YEAH, DOESN'T THAT INCIDENT BOTHER YOU?
WHO CARES? SOME THINGS ARE BETTER LEFT ALONE!
HEH! IT'S NOT LIKE THE KIRI-TENGU COULD REALLY HAVE APPEARED.
SAY ...
YOU TALKING ABOUT ME?
GII...
THWP
GIIEEEEEE

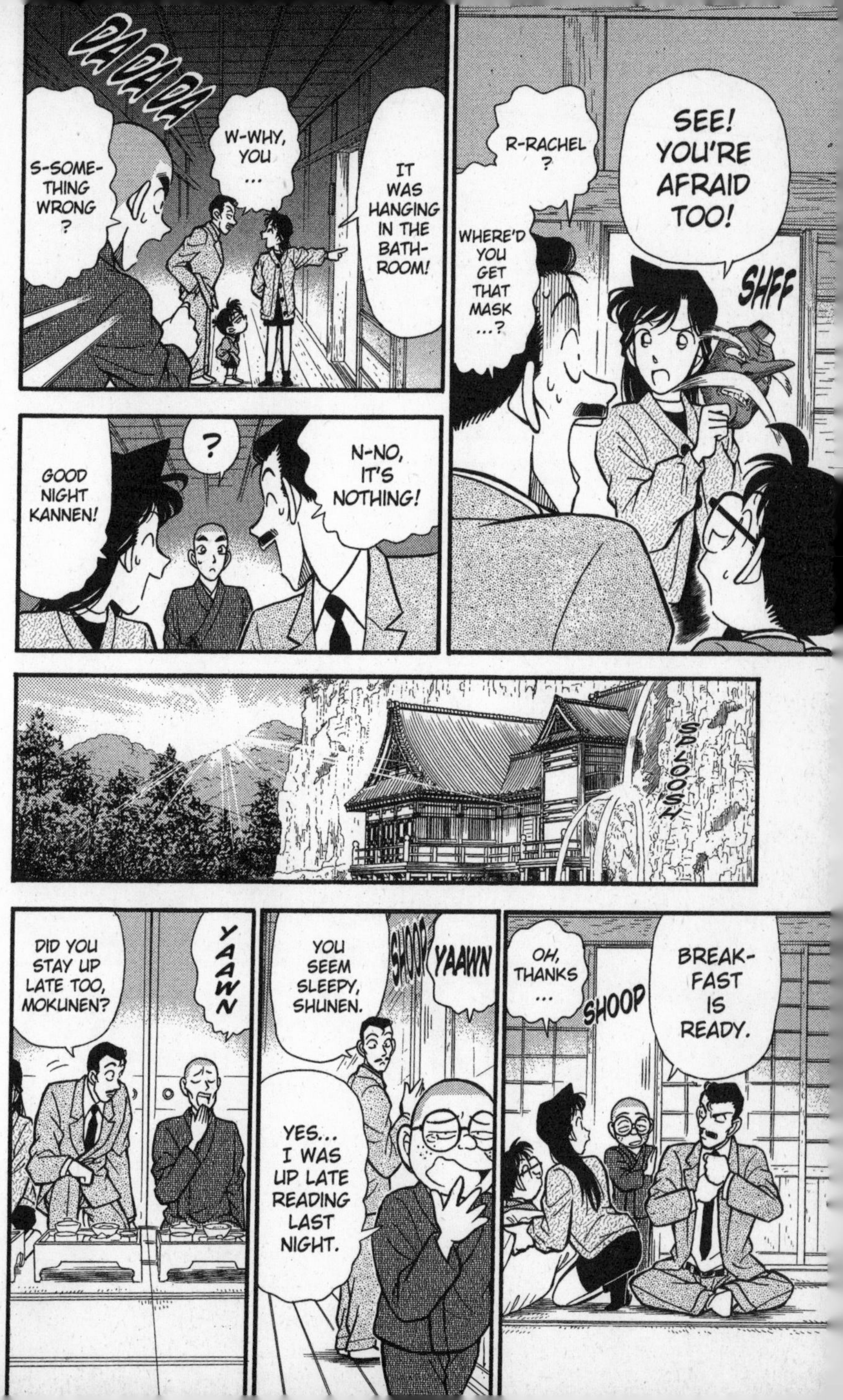
SEE! YOU'RE AFRAID TOO!
SHFF
R-RACHEL ?
WHERE'D YOU GET THAT MASK ...?
DA DA DA DA
IT WAS HANGING IN THE BATH-ROOM!
W-WHY, YOU ...
S-SOME-THING WRONG ?
N-NO, IT'S NOTHING!
?
GOOD NIGHT KANNEN!
SPLOOSH
BREAK-FAST IS READY.
SHOOP
OH, THANKS ...
YAAWN
SHOOP
YOU SEEM SLEEPY, SHUNEN.
YES... I WAS UP LATE READING LAST NIGHT.
YAAWN
DID YOU STAY UP LATE TOO, MOKUNEN?

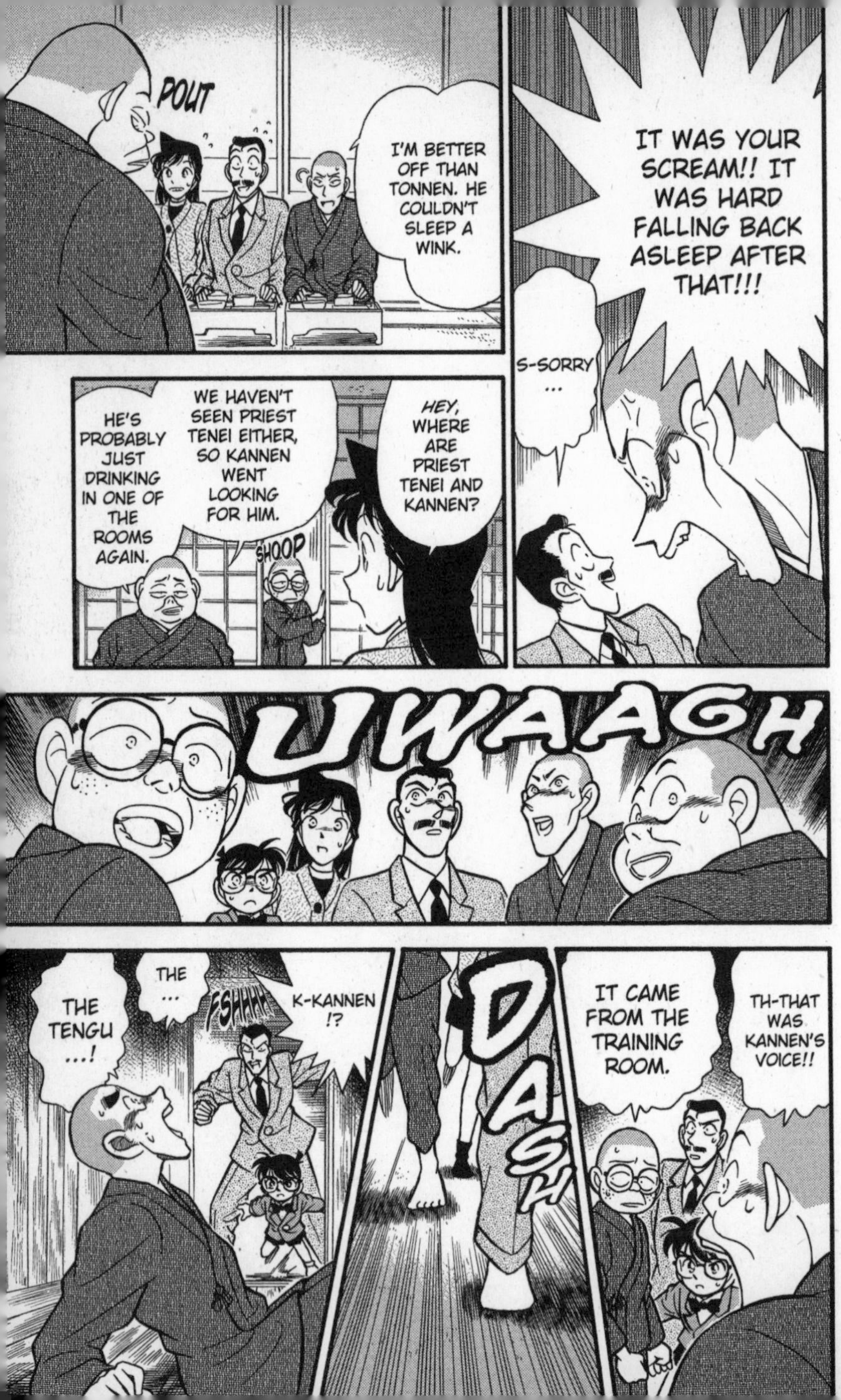
IT WAS YOUR SCREAM!! IT WAS HARD FALLING BACK ASLEEP AFTER THAT!!!
S-SORRY ...
I'M BETTER OFF THAN TONNEN. HE COULDN'T SLEEP A WINK.
POUT
HEY, WHERE ARE PRIEST TENEI AND KANNEN?
WE HAVEN'T SEEN PRIEST TENEI EITHER, SO KANNEN WENT LOOKING FOR HIM.
HE'S PROBABLY JUST DRINKING IN ONE OF THE ROOMS AGAIN.
SHOOP
UWAAAGH
TH-THAT WAS KANNEN'S VOICE!!
IT CAME FROM THE TRAINING ROOM.
DASH
K-KANNEN !?
FSHHH
THE ...
THE TENGU ...!

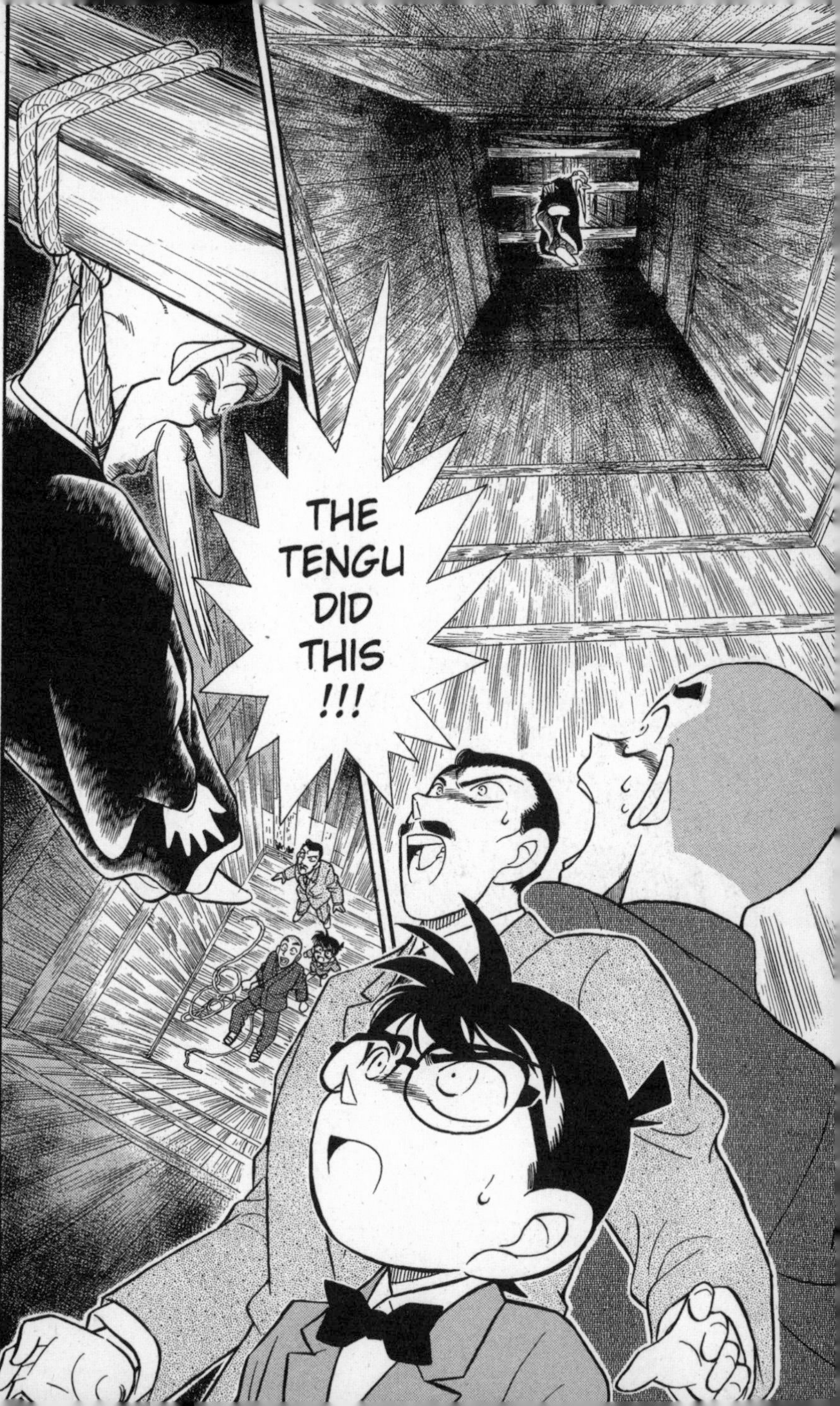
THE TENGU DID THIS !!!

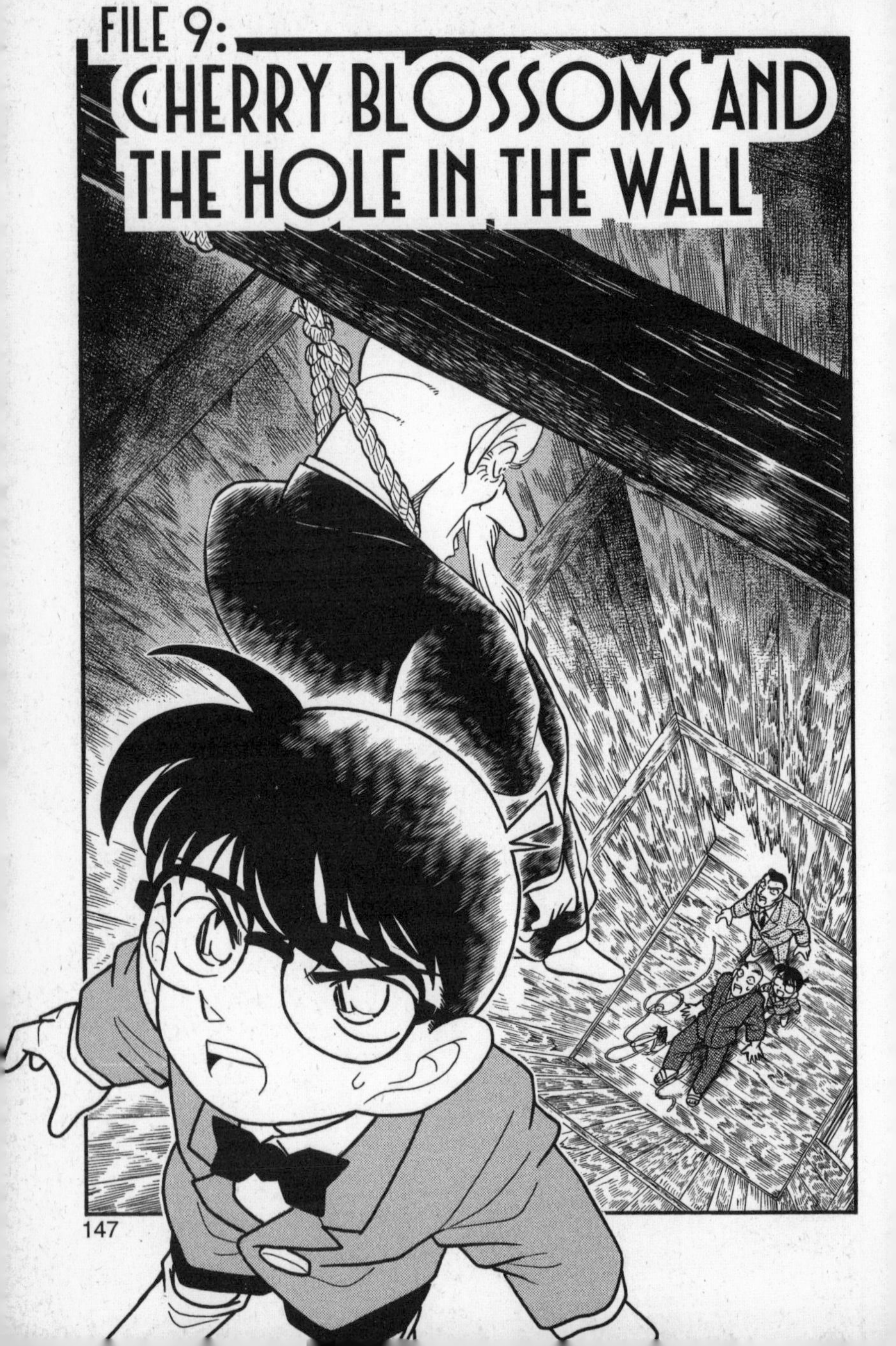
FILE 9:
CHERRY BLOSSOMS AND THE HOLE IN THE WALL

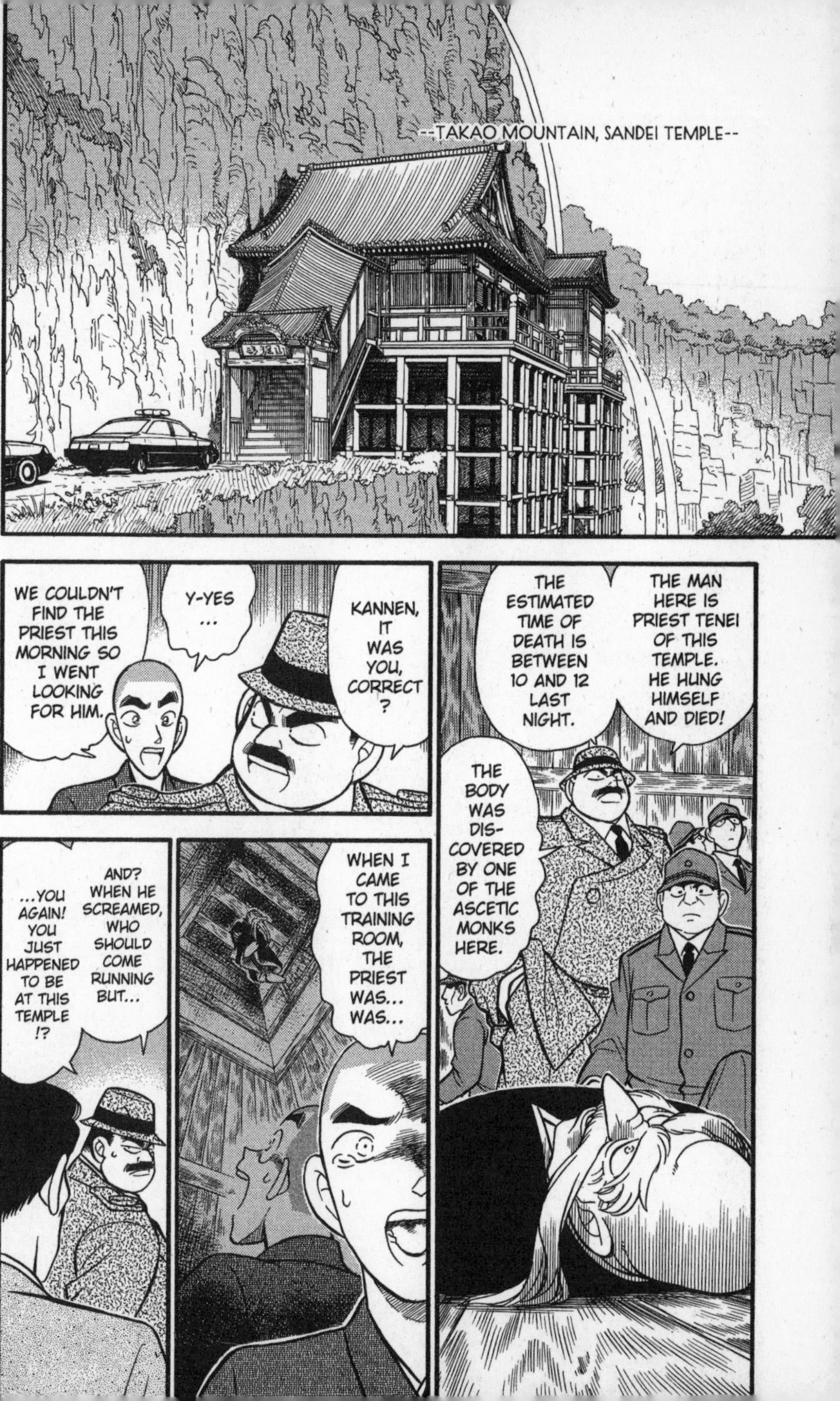
--TAKAO MOUNTAIN, SANDEI TEMPLE--
THE MAN HERE IS PRIEST TENEI OF THIS TEMPLE. HE HUNG HIMSELF AND DIED!
THE ESTIMATED TIME OF DEATH IS BETWEEN 10 AND 12 LAST NIGHT.
THE BODY WAS DIS-COVERED BY ONE OF THE ASCETIC MONKS HERE.
KANNEN, IT WAS YOU, CORRECT?
Y-YES...
WE COULDN'T FIND THE PRIEST THIS MORNING SO I WENT LOOKING FOR HIM.
WHEN I CAME TO THIS TRAINING ROOM, THE PRIEST WAS... WAS...
AND? WHEN HE SCREAMED, WHO SHOULD COME RUNNING BUT...
...YOU AGAIN! YOU JUST HAPPENED TO BE AT THIS TEMPLE!?

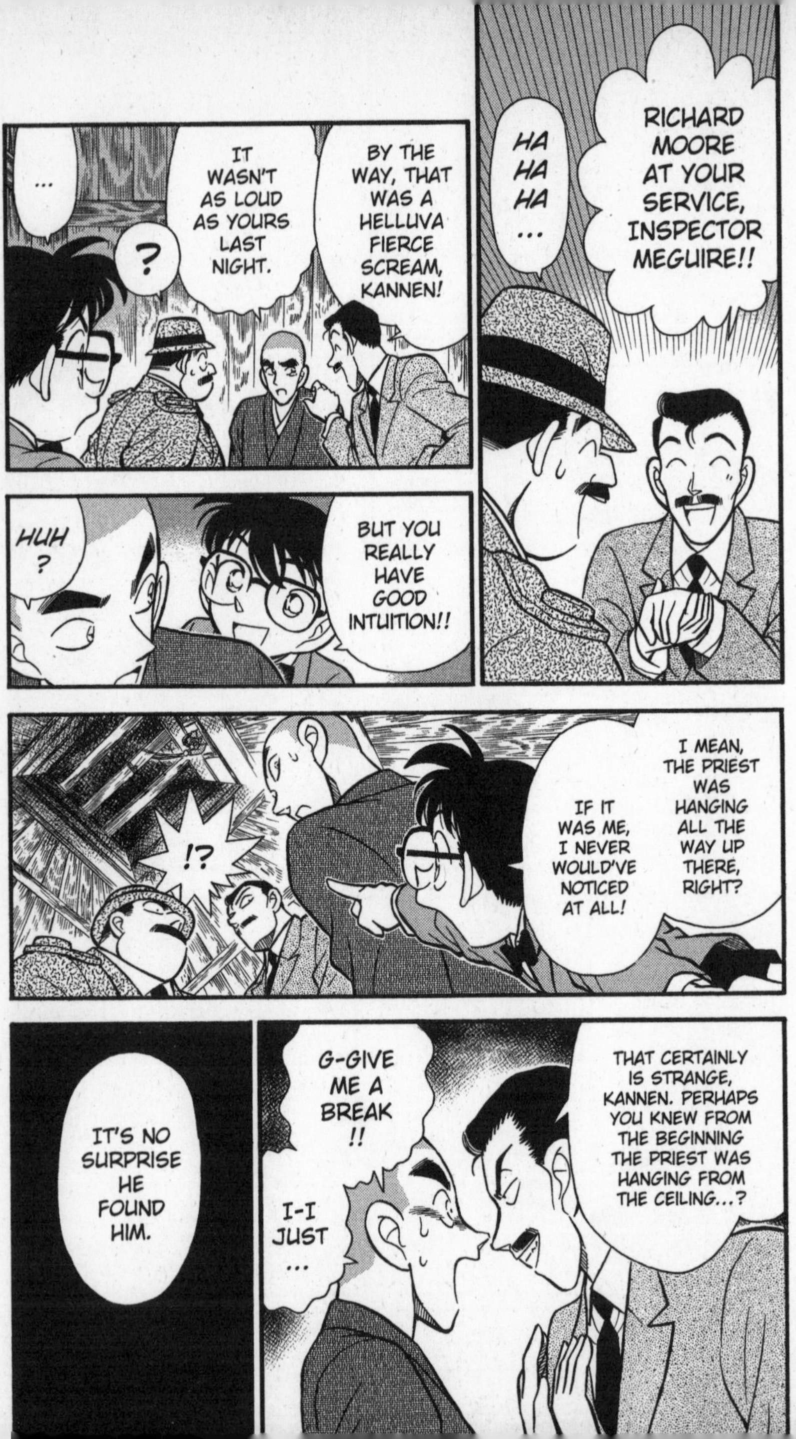
RICHARD MOORE AT YOUR SERVICE, INSPECTOR MEGUIRE!!
HA HA HA ...
BY THE WAY, THAT WAS A HELLUVA FIERCE SCREAM, KANNEN!
IT WASN'T AS LOUD AS YOURS LAST NIGHT.
?
...
BUT YOU REALLY HAVE GOOD INTUITION!!
HUH?
I MEAN, THE PRIEST WAS HANGING ALL THE WAY UP THERE, RIGHT?
IF IT WAS ME, I NEVER WOULD'VE NOTICED AT ALL!
!?
THAT CERTAINLY IS STRANGE, KANNEN. PERHAPS YOU KNEW FROM THE BEGINNING THE PRIEST WAS HANGING FROM THE CEILING...?
G-GIVE ME A BREAK!!
I-I JUST ...
IT'S NO SURPRISE HE FOUND HIM.

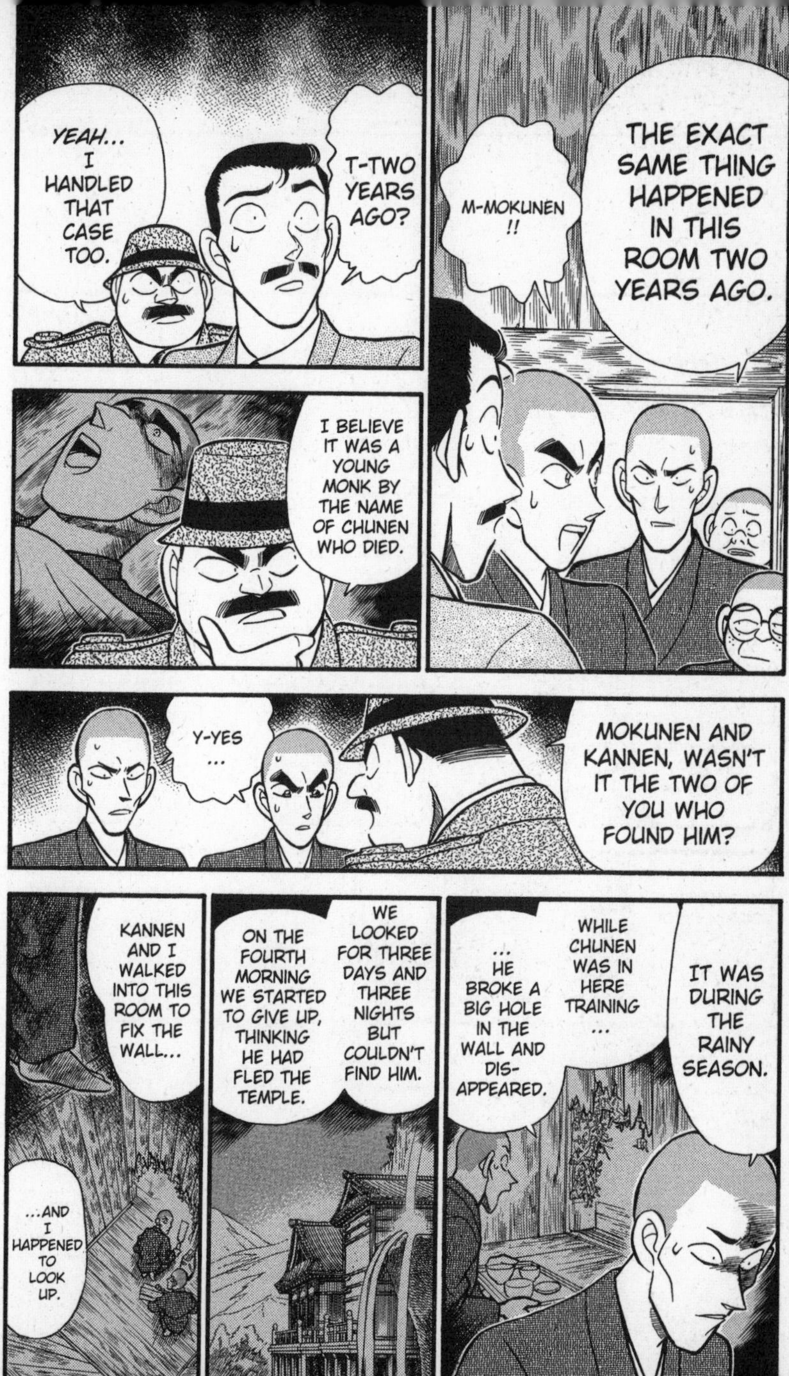
THE EXACT SAME THING HAPPENED IN THIS ROOM TWO YEARS AGO.
M-MOKUNEN !!
T-TWO YEARS AGO?
YEAH... I HANDLED THAT CASE TOO.
I BELIEVE IT WAS A YOUNG MONK BY THE NAME OF CHUNEN WHO DIED.
MOKUNEN AND KANNEN, WASN'T IT THE TWO OF YOU WHO FOUND HIM?
Y-YES ...
IT WAS DURING THE RAINY SEASON.
WHILE CHUNEN WAS IN HERE TRAINING ...
... HE BROKE A BIG HOLE IN THE WALL AND DIS-APPEARED.
WE LOOKED FOR THREE DAYS AND THREE NIGHTS BUT COULDN'T FIND HIM.
ON THE FOURTH MORNING WE STARTED TO GIVE UP, THINKING HE HAD FLED THE TEMPLE.
KANNEN AND I WALKED INTO THIS ROOM TO FIX THE WALL...
...AND I HAPPENED TO LOOK UP.

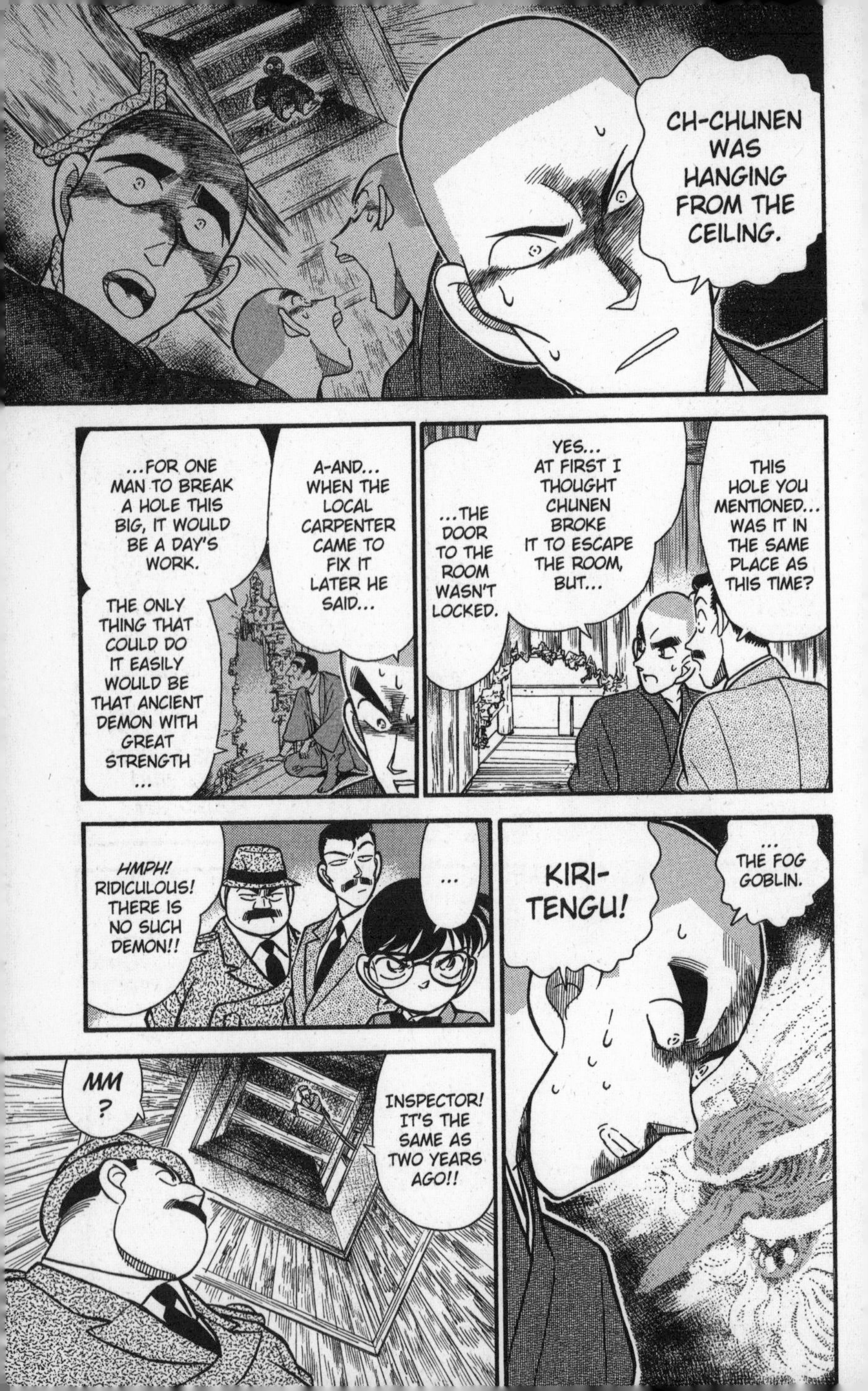
CH-CHUNEN WAS HANGING FROM THE CEILING.
THIS HOLE YOU MENTIONED... WAS IT IN THE SAME PLACE AS THIS TIME?
YES... AT FIRST I THOUGHT CHUNEN BROKE IT TO ESCAPE THE ROOM, BUT...
...THE DOOR TO THE ROOM WASN'T LOCKED.
A-AND... WHEN THE LOCAL CARPENTER CAME TO FIX IT LATER HE SAID...
...FOR ONE MAN TO BREAK A HOLE THIS BIG, IT WOULD BE A DAY'S WORK.
THE ONLY THING THAT COULD DO IT EASILY WOULD BE THAT ANCIENT DEMON WITH GREAT STRENGTH...
KIRI-TENGU!
... THE FOG GOBLIN.
...
HMPH! RIDICULOUS! THERE IS NO SUCH DEMON!!
INSPECTOR! IT'S THE SAME AS TWO YEARS AGO!!
MM ?

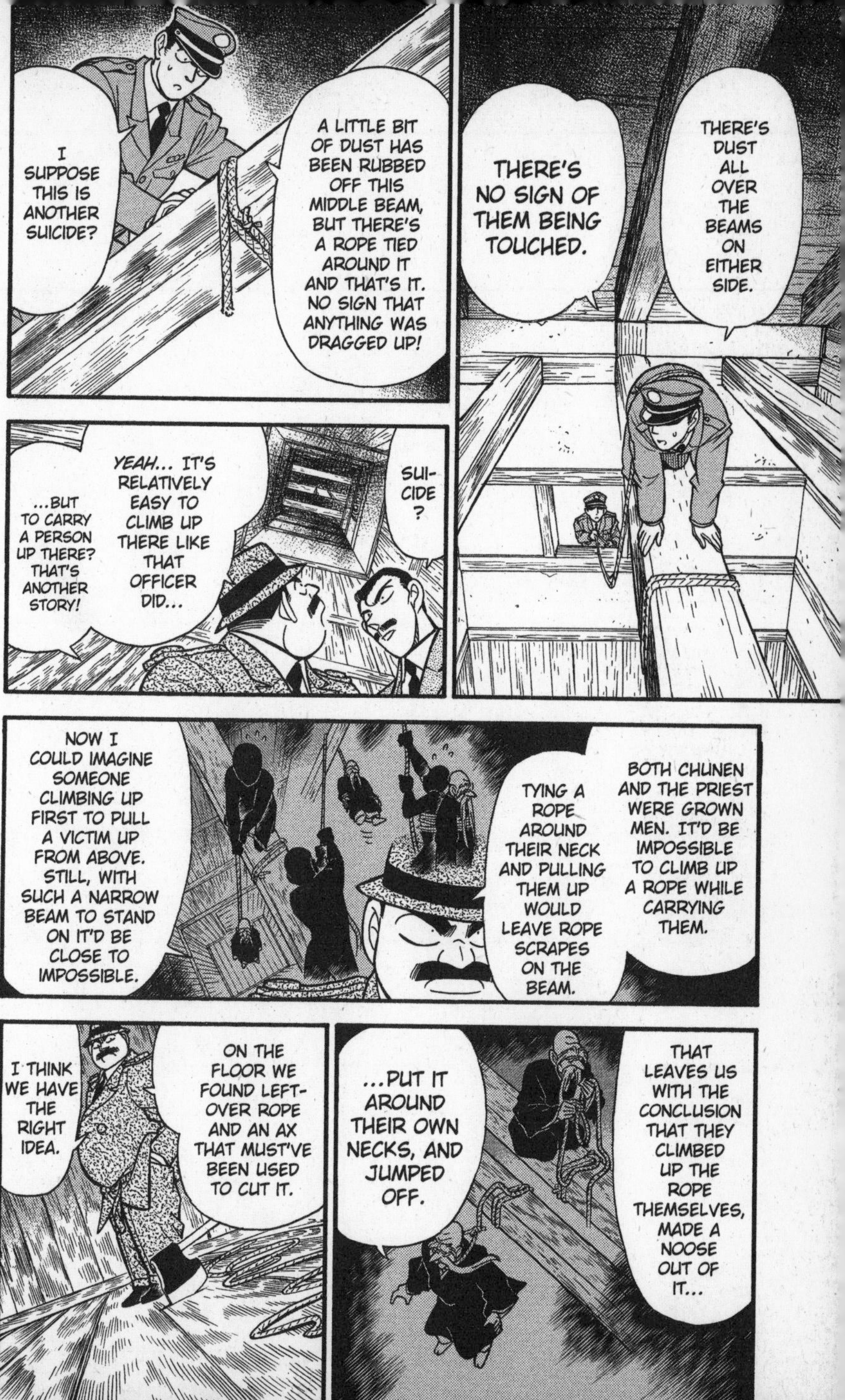
THERE'S DUST ALL OVER THE BEAMS ON EITHER SIDE.
THERE'S NO SIGN OF THEM BEING TOUCHED.
A LITTLE BIT OF DUST HAS BEEN RUBBED OFF THIS MIDDLE BEAM, BUT THERE'S A ROPE TIED AROUND IT AND THAT'S IT. NO SIGN THAT ANYTHING WAS DRAGGED UP!
I SUPPOSE THIS IS ANOTHER SUICIDE?
SUI-CIDE?
YEAH... IT'S RELATIVELY EASY TO CLIMB UP THERE LIKE THAT OFFICER DID...
...BUT TO CARRY A PERSON UP THERE? THAT'S ANOTHER STORY!
BOTH CHUNEN AND THE PRIEST WERE GROWN MEN. IT'D BE IMPOSSIBLE TO CLIMB UP A ROPE WHILE CARRYING THEM.
TYING A ROPE AROUND THEIR NECK AND PULLING THEM UP WOULD LEAVE ROPE SCRAPES ON THE BEAM.
NOW I COULD IMAGINE SOMEONE CLIMBING UP FIRST TO PULL A VICTIM UP FROM ABOVE. STILL, WITH SUCH A NARROW BEAM TO STAND ON IT'D BE CLOSE TO IMPOSSIBLE.
THAT LEAVES US WITH THE CONCLUSION THAT THEY CLIMBED UP THE ROPE THEMSELVES, MADE A NOOSE OUT OF IT...
...PUT IT AROUND THEIR OWN NECKS, AND JUMPED OFF.
ON THE FLOOR WE FOUND LEFT-OVER ROPE AND AN AX THAT MUST'VE BEEN USED TO CUT IT.
I THINK WE HAVE THE RIGHT IDEA.

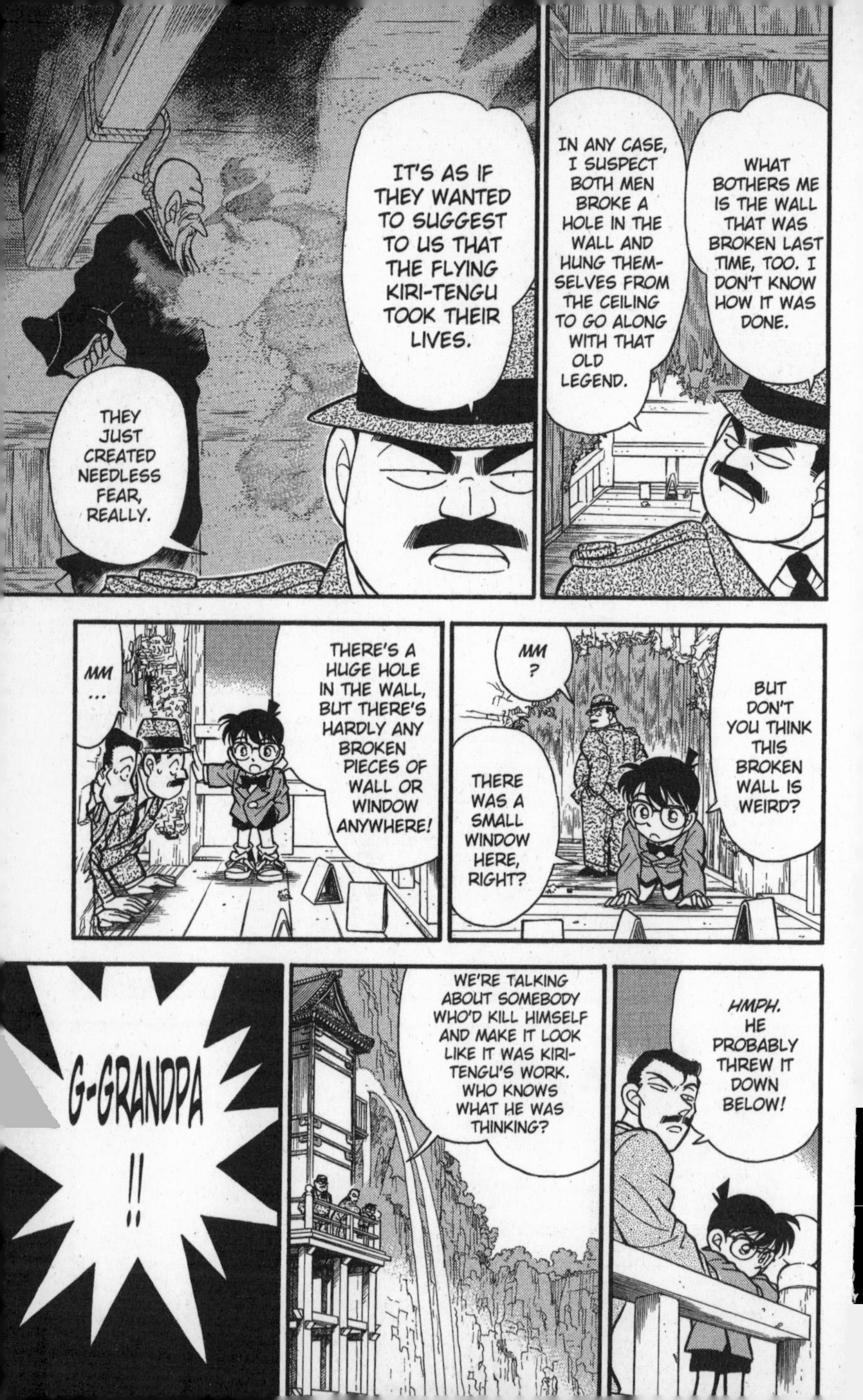

WHAT BOTHERS ME IS THE WALL THAT WAS BROKEN LAST TIME, TOO. I DON'T KNOW HOW IT WAS DONE.
IN ANY CASE, I SUSPECT BOTH MEN BROKE A HOLE IN THE WALL AND HUNG THEM-SELVES FROM THE CEILING TO GO ALONG WITH THAT OLD LEGEND.
IT'S AS IF THEY WANTED TO SUGGEST TO US THAT THE FLYING KIRI-TENGU TOOK THEIR LIVES.
THEY JUST CREATED NEEDLESS FEAR, REALLY.
BUT DON'T YOU THINK THIS BROKEN WALL IS WEIRD?
MM ?
THERE WAS A SMALL WINDOW HERE, RIGHT?
THERE'S A HUGE HOLE IN THE WALL, BUT THERE'S HARDLY ANY BROKEN PIECES OF WALL OR WINDOW ANYWHERE!
MM ...
HMPH. HE PROBABLY THREW IT DOWN BELOW!
WE'RE TALKING ABOUT SOMEBODY WHO'D KILL HIMSELF AND MAKE IT LOOK LIKE IT WAS KIRI-TENGU'S WORK. WHO KNOWS WHAT HE WAS THINKING?
G-GRANDPA !!

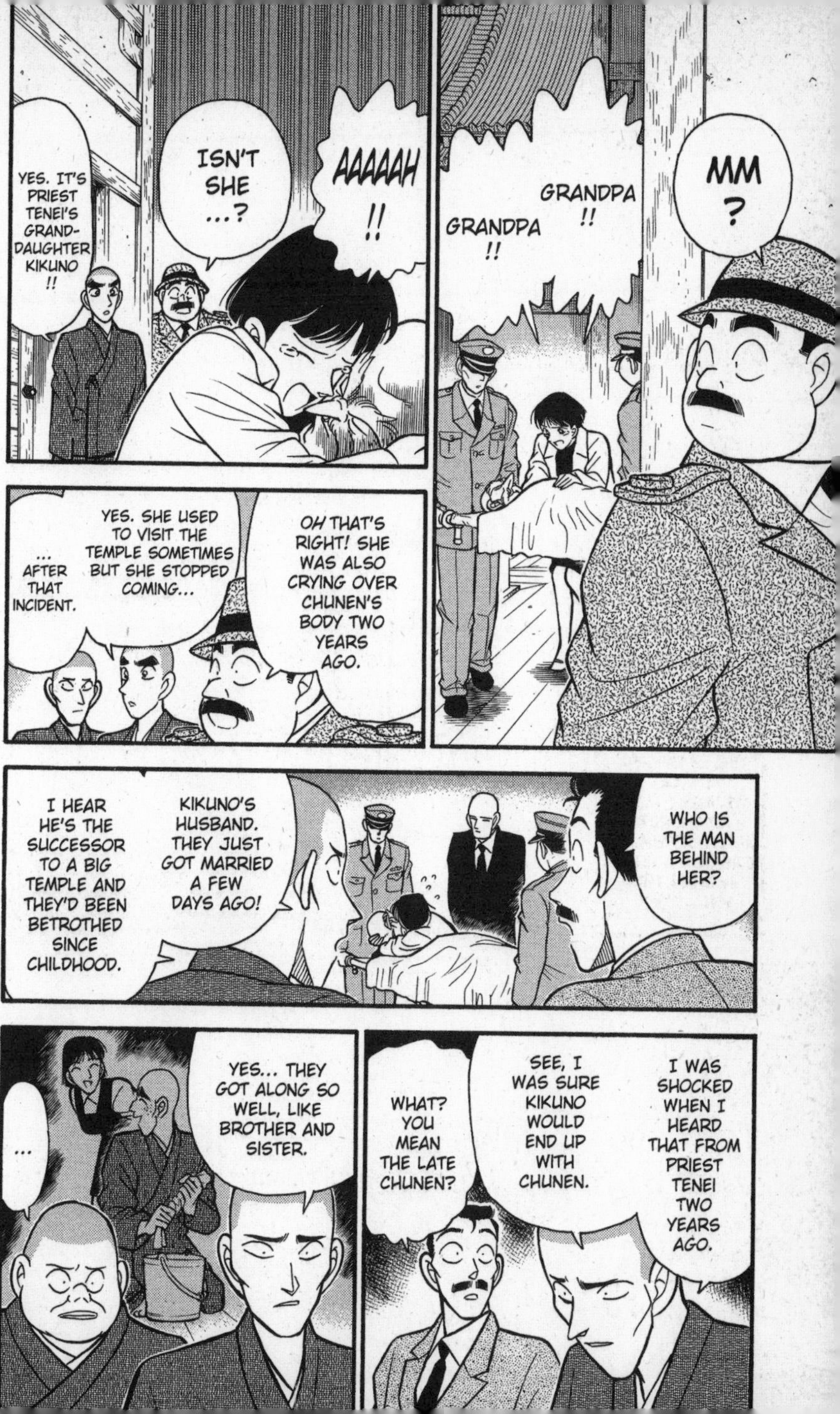
MM ?
GRANDPA !!
GRANDPA !!
AAAAAH !!
ISN'T SHE ...?
YES. IT'S PRIEST TENEI'S GRAND-DAUGHTER KIKUNO !!
OH THAT'S RIGHT! SHE WAS ALSO CRYING OVER CHUNEN'S BODY TWO YEARS AGO.
YES. SHE USED TO VISIT THE TEMPLE SOMETIMES BUT SHE STOPPED COMING...
... AFTER THAT INCIDENT.
WHO IS THE MAN BEHIND HER?
KIKUNO'S HUSBAND. THEY JUST GOT MARRIED A FEW DAYS AGO!
I HEAR HE'S THE SUCCESSOR TO A BIG TEMPLE AND THEY'D BEEN BETROTHED SINCE CHILDHOOD.
I WAS SHOCKED WHEN I HEARD THAT FROM PRIEST TENEI TWO YEARS AGO.
SEE, I WAS SURE KIKUNO WOULD END UP WITH CHUNEN.
WHAT? YOU MEAN THE LATE CHUNEN?
YES... THEY GOT ALONG SO WELL, LIKE BROTHER AND SISTER.
...

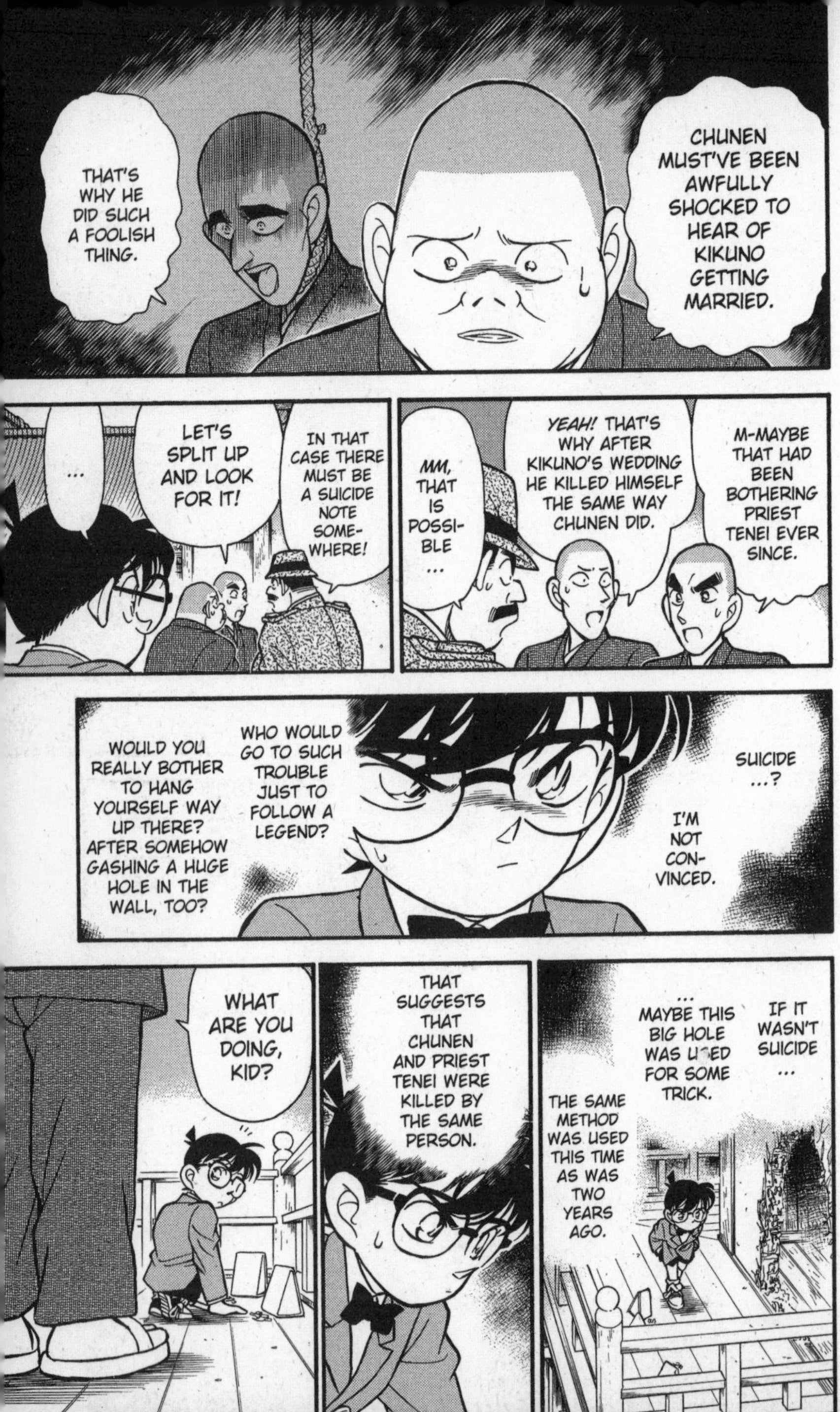
CHUNEN MUST'VE BEEN AWFULLY SHOCKED TO HEAR OF KIKUNO GETTING MARRIED.
THAT'S WHY HE DID SUCH A FOOLISH THING.
M-MAYBE THAT HAD BEEN BOTHERING PRIEST TENEI EVER SINCE.
YEAH! THAT'S WHY AFTER KIKUNO'S WEDDING HE KILLED HIMSELF THE SAME WAY CHUNEN DID.
MM, THAT IS POSSIBLE ...
IN THAT CASE THERE MUST BE A SUICIDE NOTE SOMEWHERE!
LET'S SPLIT UP AND LOOK FOR IT!
...
SUICIDE ...?
I'M NOT CONVINCED.
WHO WOULD GO TO SUCH TROUBLE JUST TO FOLLOW A LEGEND?
WOULD YOU REALLY BOTHER TO HANG YOURSELF WAY UP THERE? AFTER SOMEHOW GASHING A HUGE HOLE IN THE WALL, TOO?
IF IT WASN'T SUICIDE ...
... MAYBE THIS BIG HOLE WAS USED FOR SOME TRICK.
THE SAME METHOD WAS USED THIS TIME AS WAS TWO YEARS AGO.
THAT SUGGESTS THAT CHUNEN AND PRIEST TENEI WERE KILLED BY THE SAME PERSON.
WHAT ARE YOU DOING, KID?

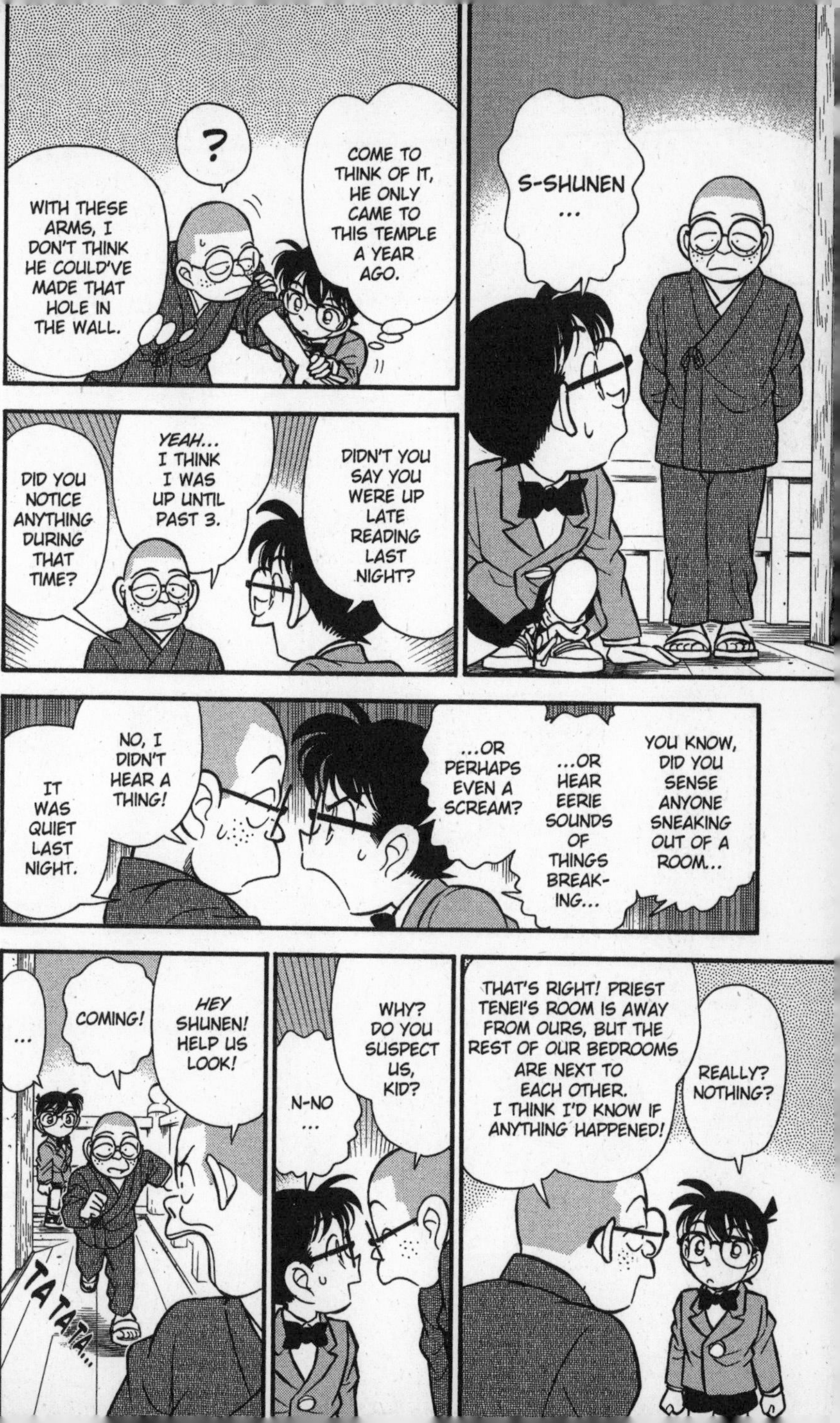
S-SHUNEN ...
COME TO THINK OF IT, HE ONLY CAME TO THIS TEMPLE A YEAR AGO.
?
WITH THESE ARMS, I DON'T THINK HE COULD'VE MADE THAT HOLE IN THE WALL.
DIDN'T YOU SAY YOU WERE UP LATE READING LAST NIGHT?
YEAH... I THINK I WAS UP UNTIL PAST 3.
DID YOU NOTICE ANYTHING DURING THAT TIME?
YOU KNOW, DID YOU SENSE ANYONE SNEAKING OUT OF A ROOM...
...OR HEAR EERIE SOUNDS OF THINGS BREAK-ING...
...OR PERHAPS EVEN A SCREAM?
NO, I DIDN'T HEAR A THING!
IT WAS QUIET LAST NIGHT.
REALLY? NOTHING?
THAT'S RIGHT! PRIEST TENEI'S ROOM IS AWAY FROM OURS, BUT THE REST OF OUR BEDROOMS ARE NEXT TO EACH OTHER. I THINK I'D KNOW IF ANYTHING HAPPENED!
WHY? DO YOU SUSPECT US, KID?
N-NO ...
HEY SHUNEN! HELP US LOOK!
COMING!
...
TATATA...

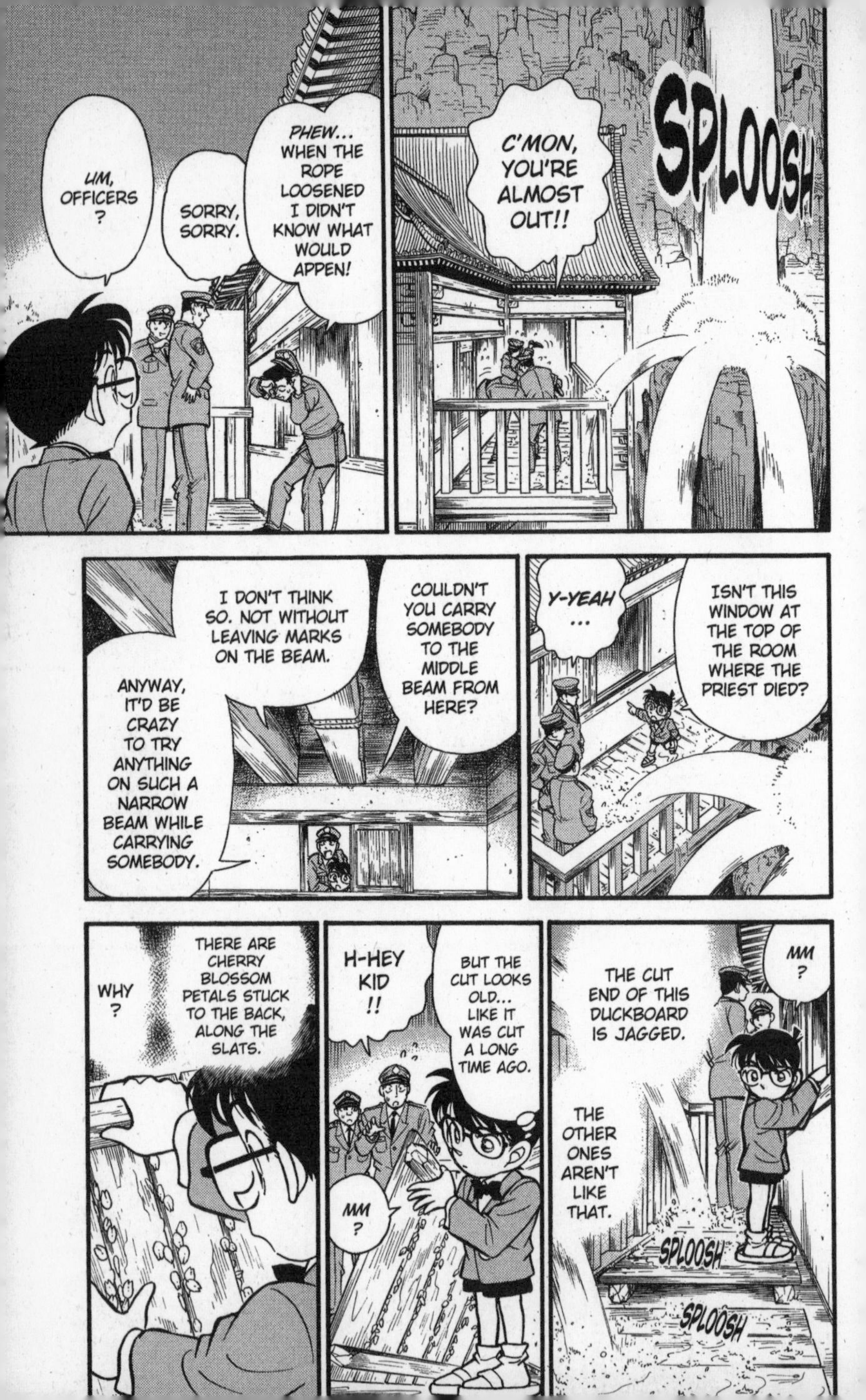
SPLOOSH
C'MON, YOU'RE ALMOST OUT!!
PHEW... WHEN THE ROPE LOOSENED I DIDN'T KNOW WHAT WOULD APPEN!
SORRY, SORRY.
UM, OFFICERS ?
ISN'T THIS WINDOW AT THE TOP OF THE ROOM WHERE THE PRIEST DIED?
Y-YEAH ...
COULDN'T YOU CARRY SOMEBODY TO THE MIDDLE BEAM FROM HERE?
I DON'T THINK SO. NOT WITHOUT LEAVING MARKS ON THE BEAM.
ANYWAY, IT'D BE CRAZY TO TRY ANYTHING ON SUCH A NARROW BEAM WHILE CARRYING SOMEBODY.
MM ?
THE CUT END OF THIS DUCKBOARD IS JAGGED.
THE OTHER ONES AREN'T LIKE THAT.
SPLOOSH
SPLOOSH
BUT THE CUT LOOKS OLD... LIKE IT WAS CUT A LONG TIME AGO.
H-HEY KID !!
MM ?
THERE ARE CHERRY BLOSSOM PETALS STUCK TO THE BACK, ALONG THE SLATS.
WHY ?

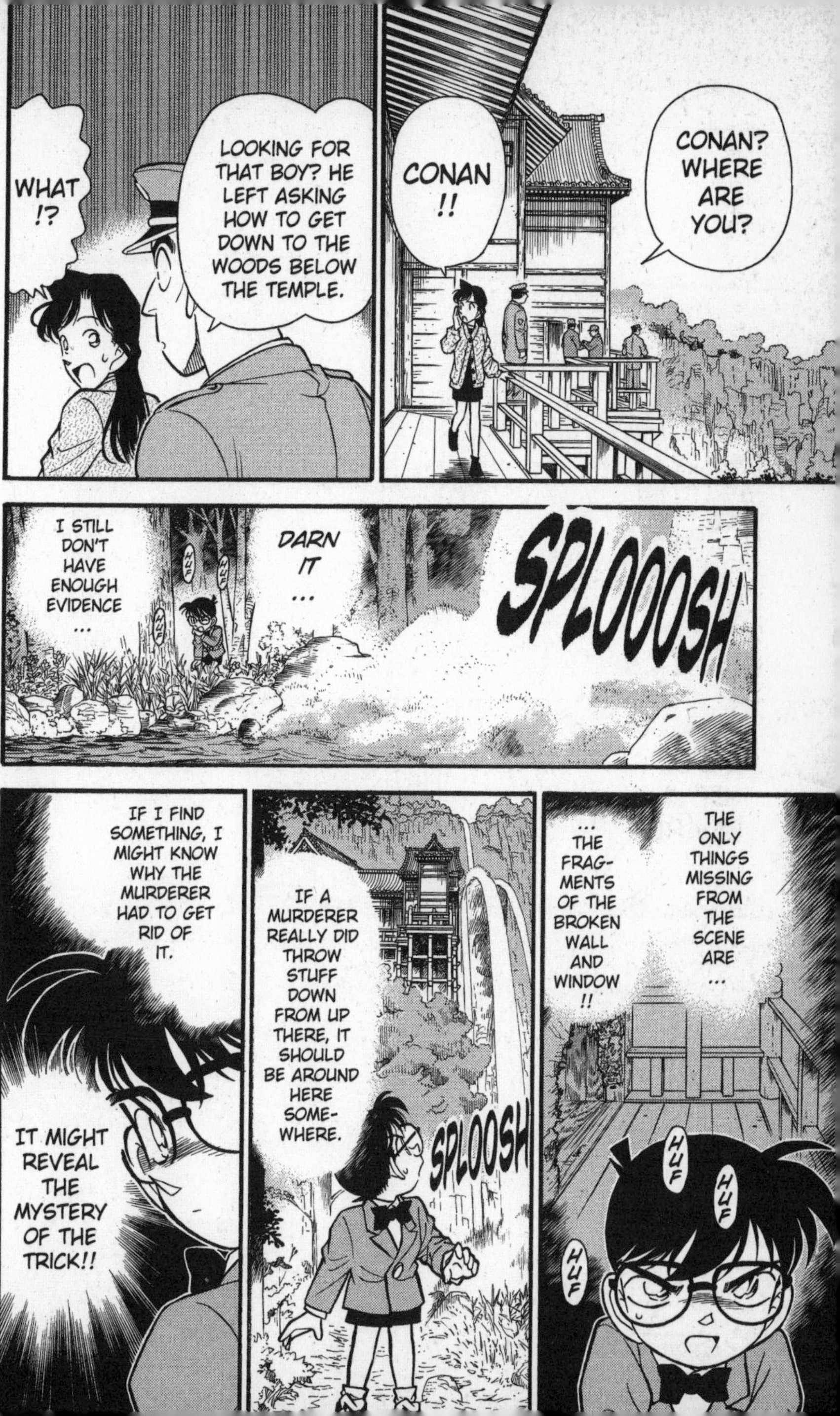
CONAN? WHERE ARE YOU?
CONAN !!
LOOKING FOR THAT BOY? HE LEFT ASKING HOW TO GET DOWN TO THE WOODS BELOW THE TEMPLE.
WHAT !?
SPLOOOSH
DARN IT ...
I STILL DON'T HAVE ENOUGH EVIDENCE ...
HUF
HUF
HUF
THE ONLY THINGS MISSING FROM THE SCENE ARE ...
... THE FRAG- MENTS OF THE BROKEN WALL AND WINDOW !!
HUF
HUF
HUF
IF A MURDERER REALLY DID THROW STUFF DOWN FROM UP THERE, IT SHOULD BE AROUND HERE SOME- WHERE.
SPLOOSH
IF I FIND SOMETHING, I MIGHT KNOW WHY THE MURDERER HAD TO GET RID OF IT.
IT MIGHT REVEAL THE MYSTERY OF THE TRICK!!

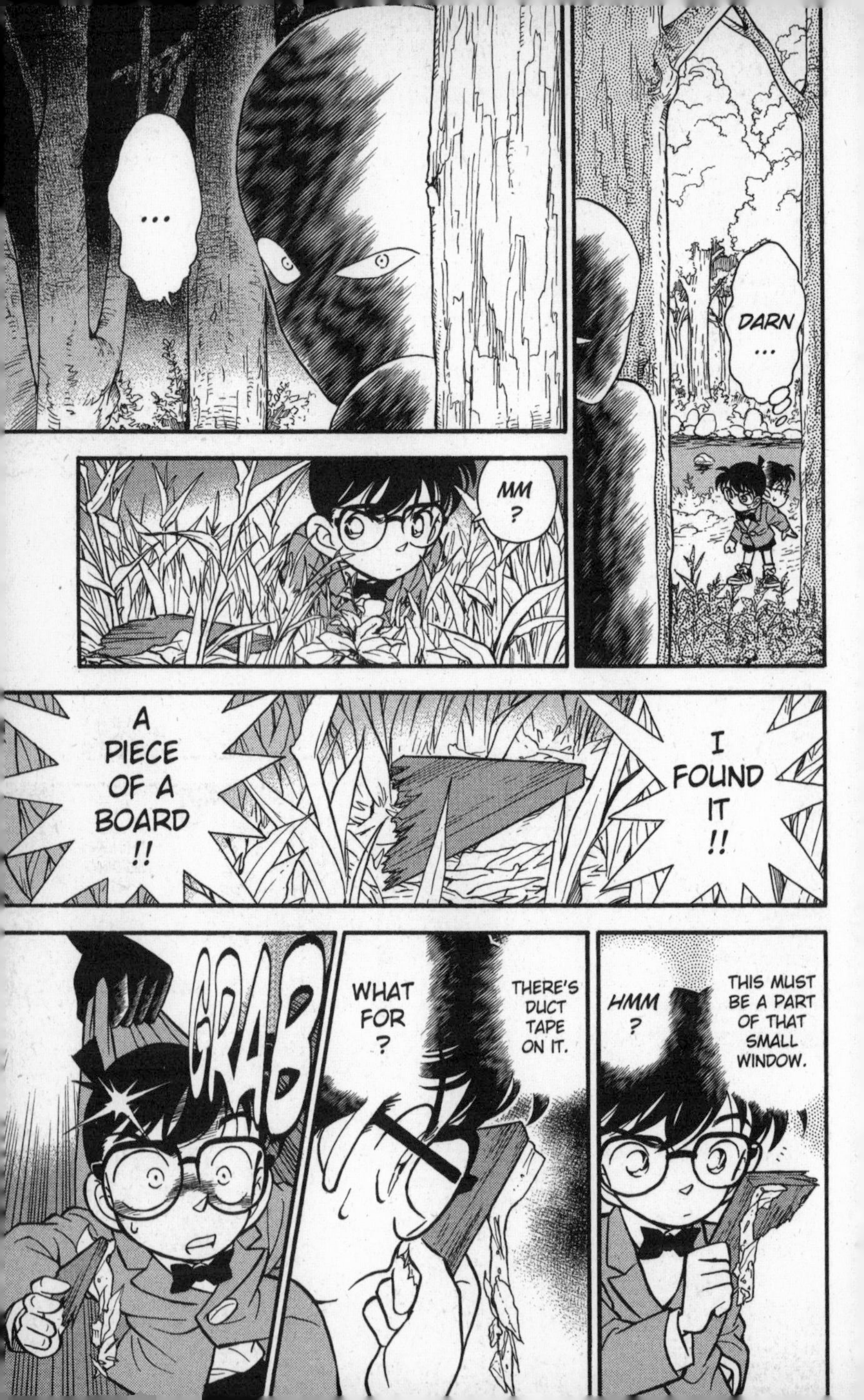
DARN ...
...
MM ?
I FOUND IT !!
A PIECE OF A BOARD !!
THIS MUST BE A PART OF THAT SMALL WINDOW.
HMM ?
THERE'S DUCT TAPE ON IT.
WHAT FOR ?
GRAB

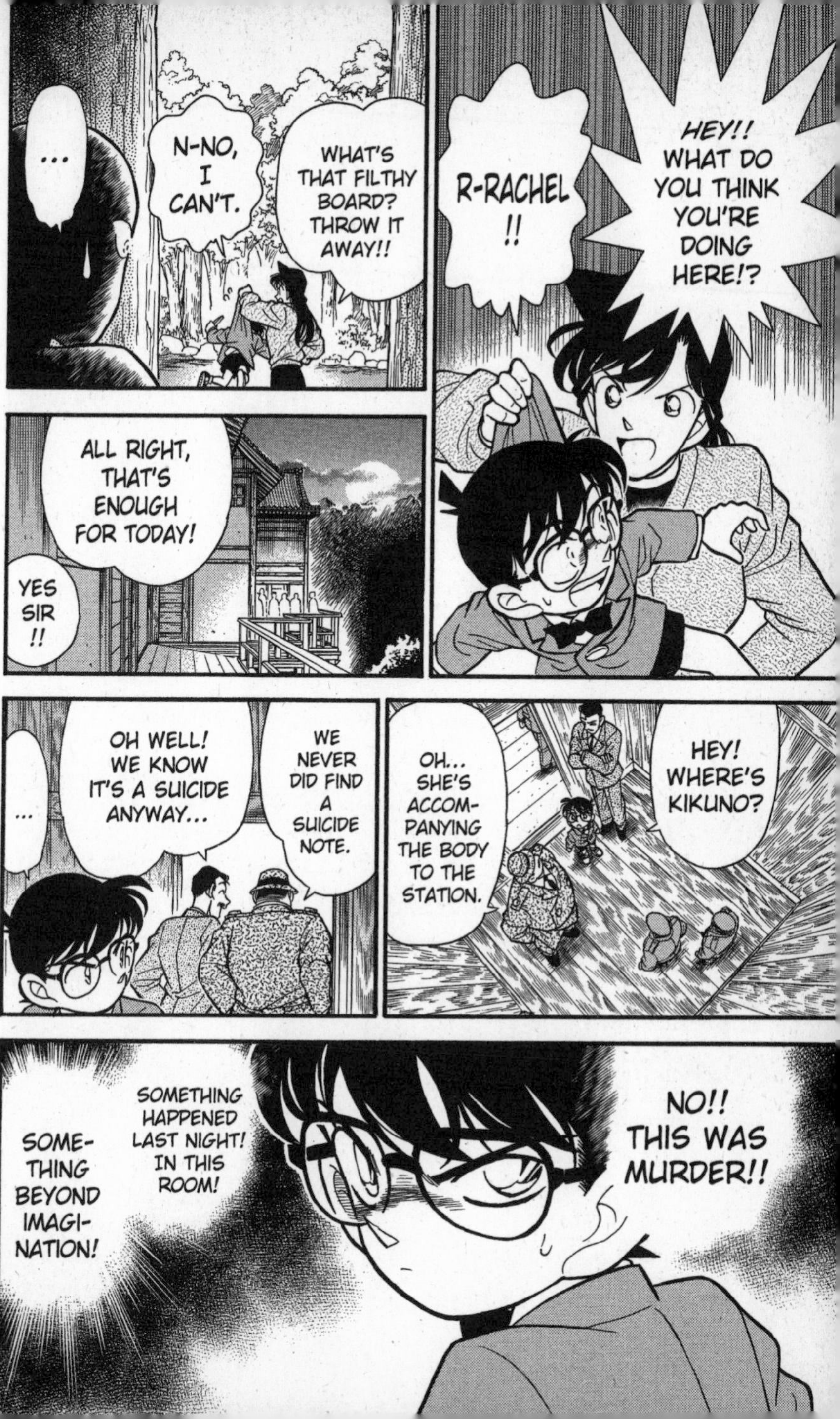
HEY!! WHAT DO YOU THINK YOU'RE DOING HERE!?
R-RACHEL !!
WHAT'S THAT FILTHY BOARD? THROW IT AWAY!!
N-NO, I CAN'T.
...
ALL RIGHT, THAT'S ENOUGH FOR TODAY!
YES SIR !!
HEY! WHERE'S KIKUNO?
OH... SHE'S ACCOMPANYING THE BODY TO THE STATION.
WE NEVER DID FIND A SUICIDE NOTE.
OH WELL! WE KNOW IT'S A SUICIDE ANYWAY...
...
NO!! THIS WAS MURDER!!
SOMETHING HAPPENED LAST NIGHT! IN THIS ROOM!
SOMETHING BEYOND IMAGINATION!

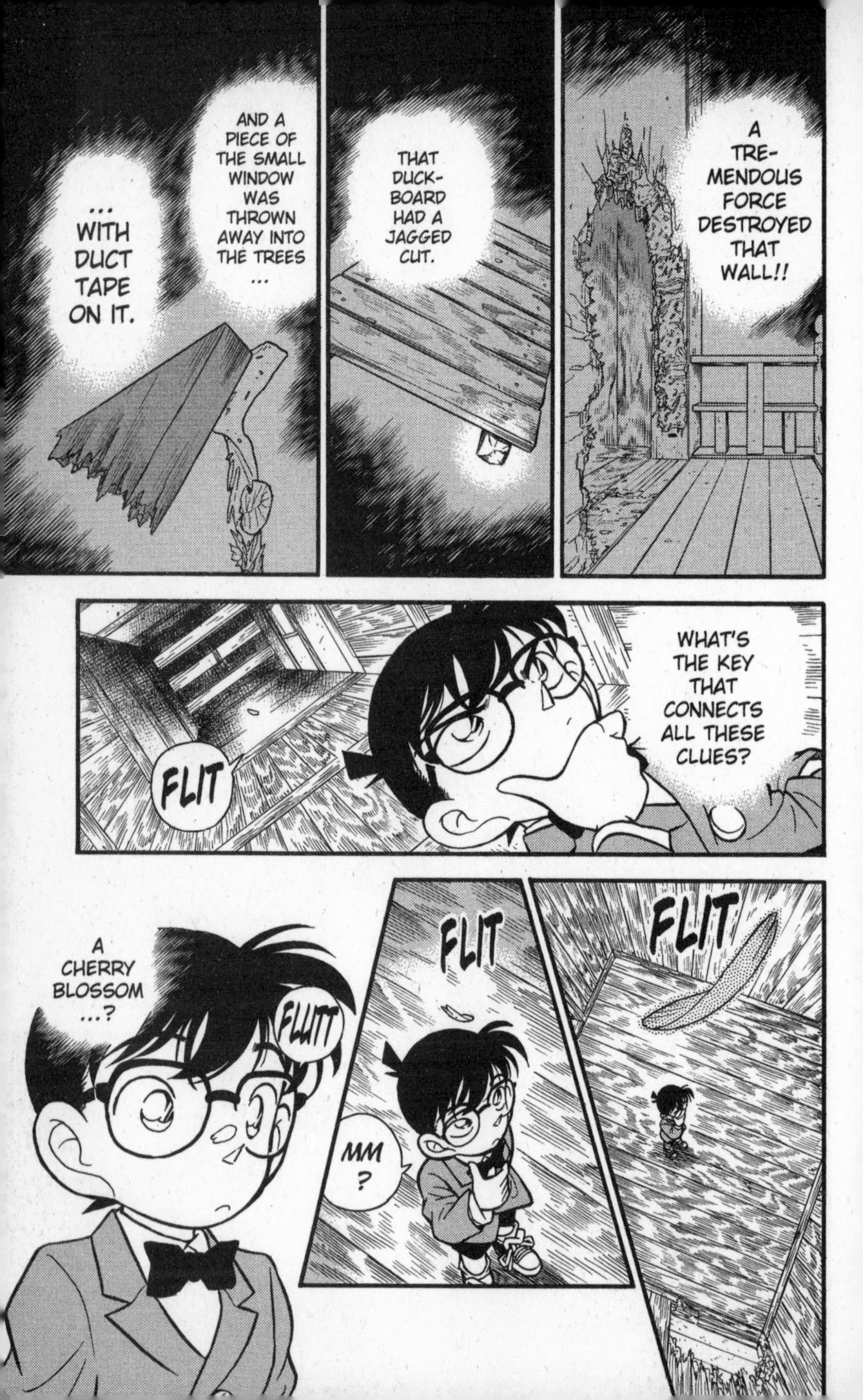
A TREMENDOUS FORCE DESTROYED THAT WALL!!
THAT DUCKBOARD HAD A JAGGED CUT.
AND A PIECE OF THE SMALL WINDOW WAS THROWN AWAY INTO THE TREES ...
...WITH DUCT TAPE ON IT.
WHAT'S THE KEY THAT CONNECTS ALL THESE CLUES?
FLIT
FLIT
FLIT
MM ?
FLUTT
A CHERRY BLOSSOM ...?

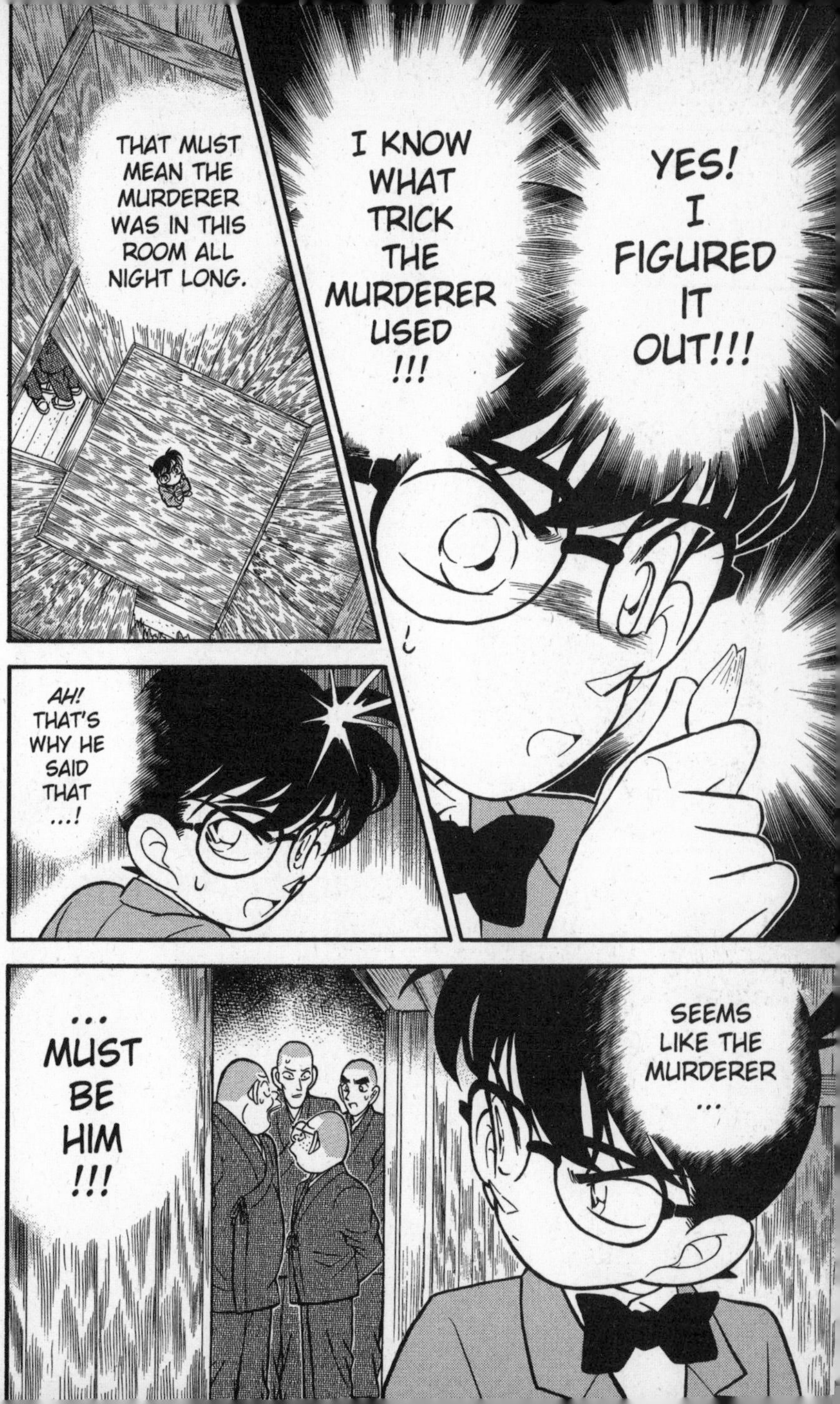
YES! I FIGURED IT OUT!!!
I KNOW WHAT TRICK THE MURDERER USED !!!
THAT MUST MEAN THE MURDERER WAS IN THIS ROOM ALL NIGHT LONG.
AH! THAT'S WHY HE SAID THAT ...!
SEEMS LIKE THE MURDERER ...
... MUST BE HIM !!!

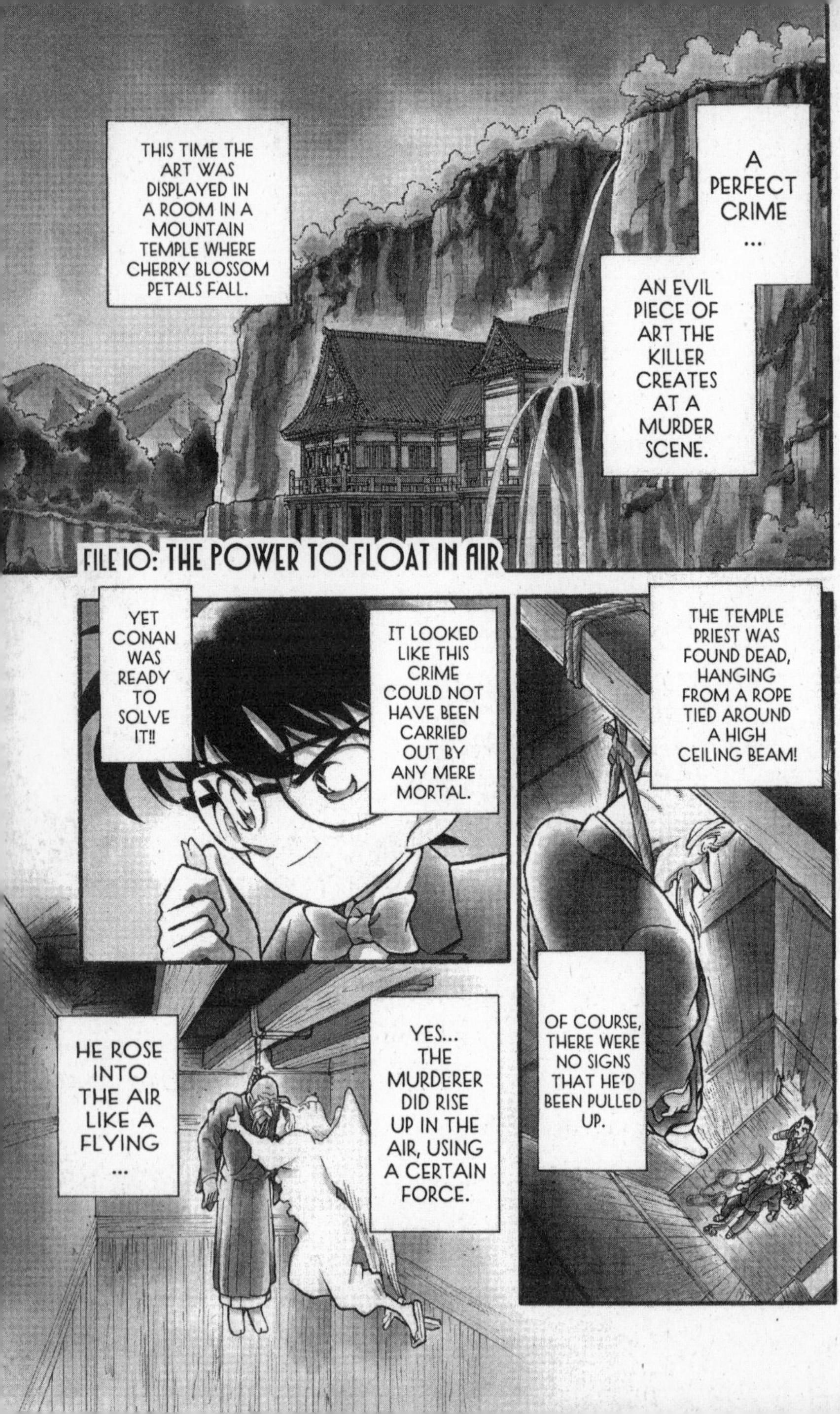
A PERFECT CRIME ...
AN EVIL PIECE OF ART THE KILLER CREATES AT A MURDER SCENE.
THIS TIME THE ART WAS DISPLAYED IN A ROOM IN A MOUNTAIN TEMPLE WHERE CHERRY BLOSSOM PETALS FALL.
FILE 10: THE POWER TO FLOAT IN AIR
THE TEMPLE PRIEST WAS FOUND DEAD, HANGING FROM A ROPE TIED AROUND A HIGH CEILING BEAM!
OF COURSE, THERE WERE NO SIGNS THAT HE'D BEEN PULLED UP.
IT LOOKED LIKE THIS CRIME COULD NOT HAVE BEEN CARRIED OUT BY ANY MERE MORTAL.
YET CONAN WAS READY TO SOLVE IT!!
YES... THE MURDERER DID RISE UP IN THE AIR, USING A CERTAIN FORCE.
HE ROSE INTO THE AIR LIKE A FLYING ...

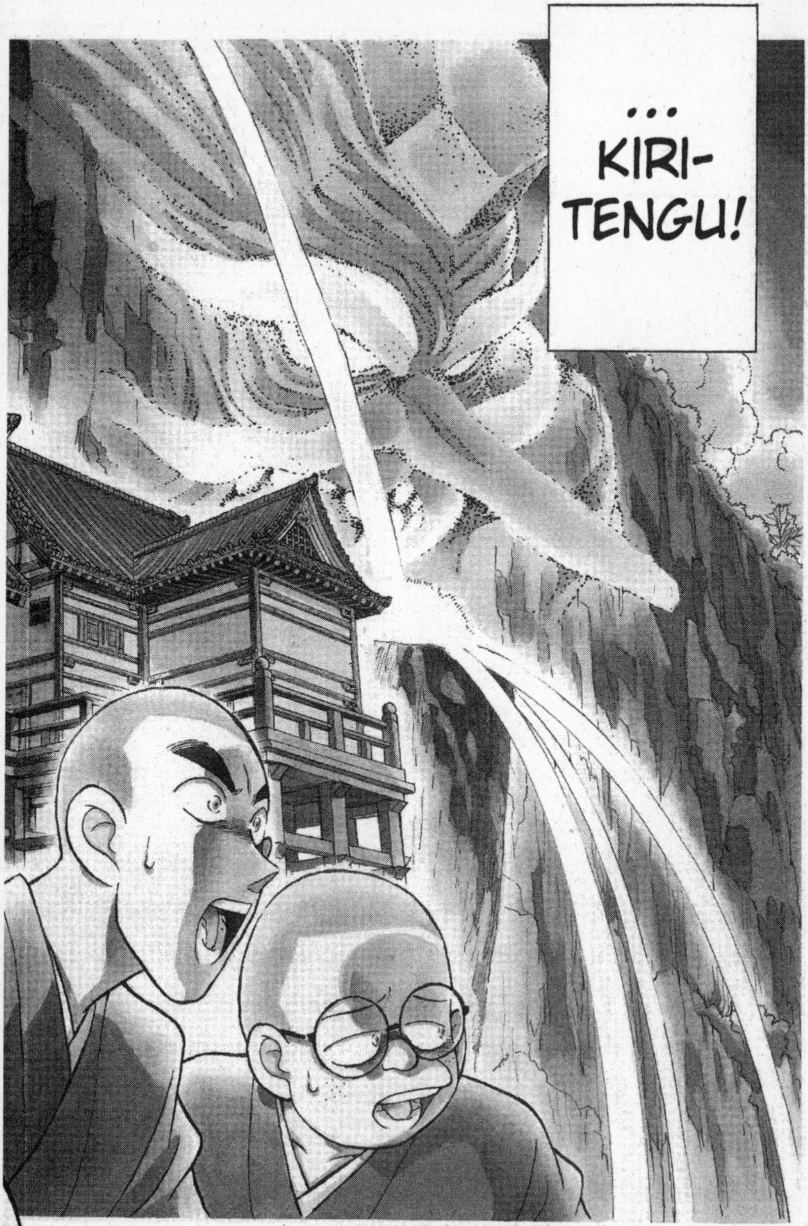
...KIRI-TENGU!

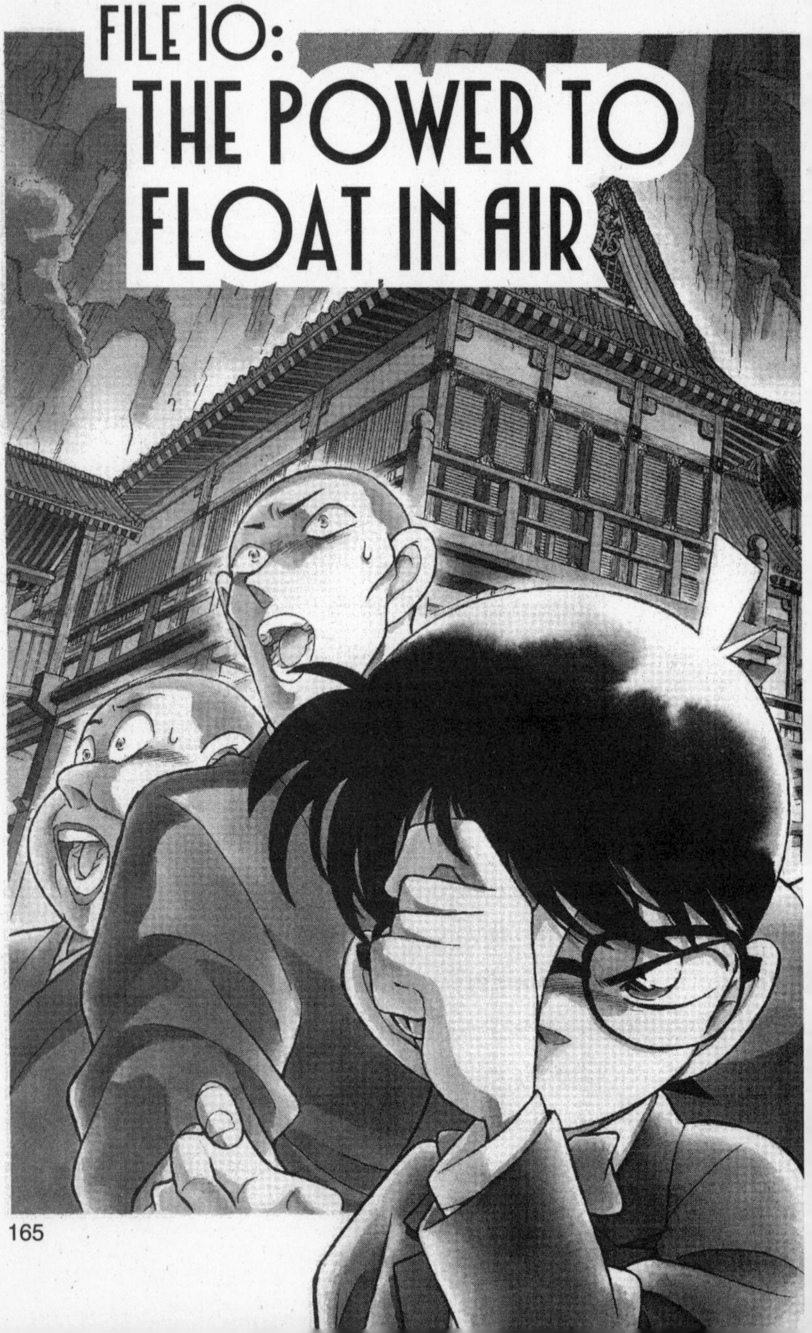
FILE 10:
THE POWER TO FLOAT IN AIR

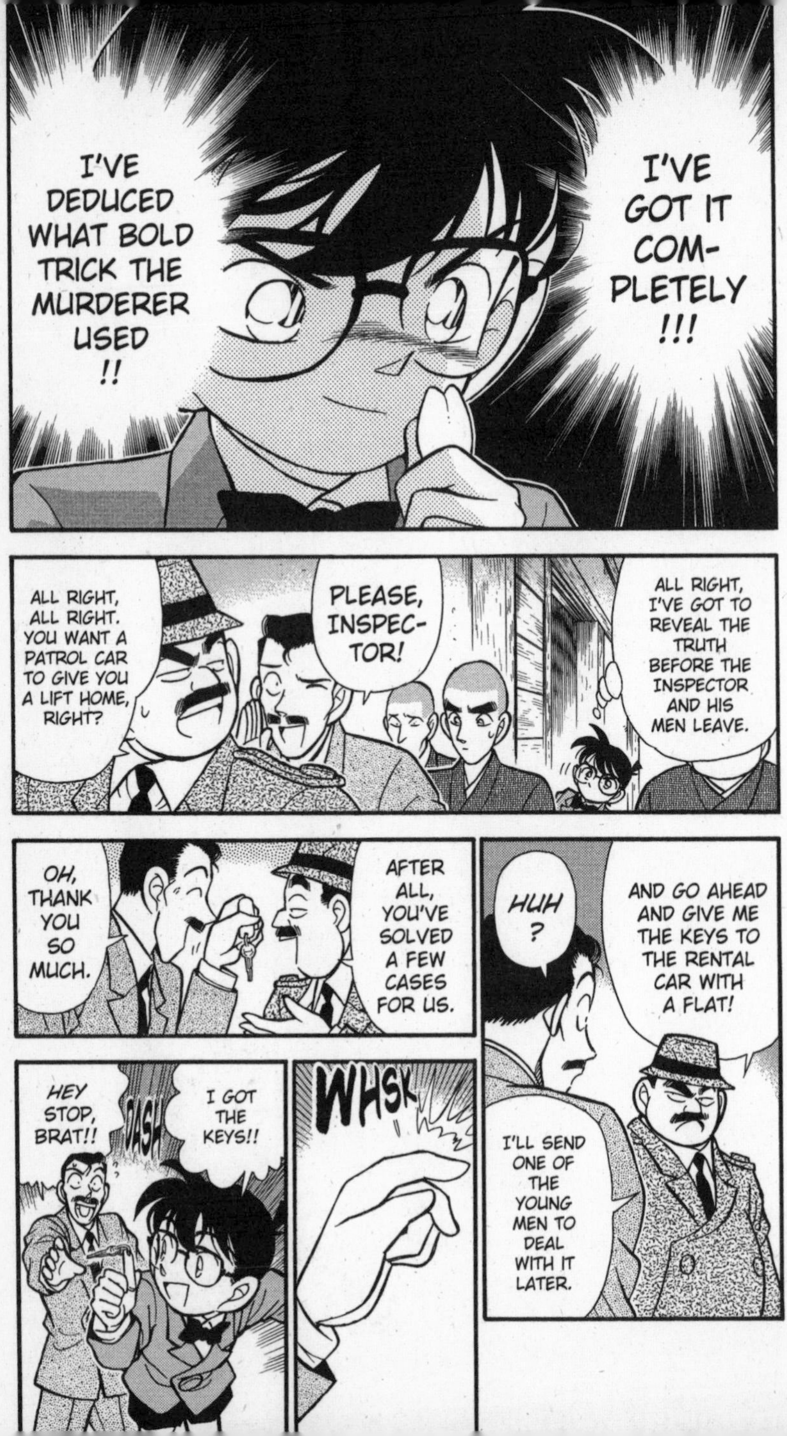
I'VE GOT IT COM-PLETELY!!!
I'VE DEDUCED WHAT BOLD TRICK THE MURDERER USED!!
ALL RIGHT, I'VE GOT TO REVEAL THE TRUTH BEFORE THE INSPECTOR AND HIS MEN LEAVE.
PLEASE, INSPEC-TOR!
ALL RIGHT, ALL RIGHT. YOU WANT A PATROL CAR TO GIVE YOU A LIFT HOME, RIGHT?
AND GO AHEAD AND GIVE ME THE KEYS TO THE RENTAL CAR WITH A FLAT!
HUH?
I'LL SEND ONE OF THE YOUNG MEN TO DEAL WITH IT LATER.
AFTER ALL, YOU'VE SOLVED A FEW CASES FOR US.
OH, THANK YOU SO MUCH.
WHSK
I GOT THE KEYS!!
DASH
HEY STOP, BRAT!!

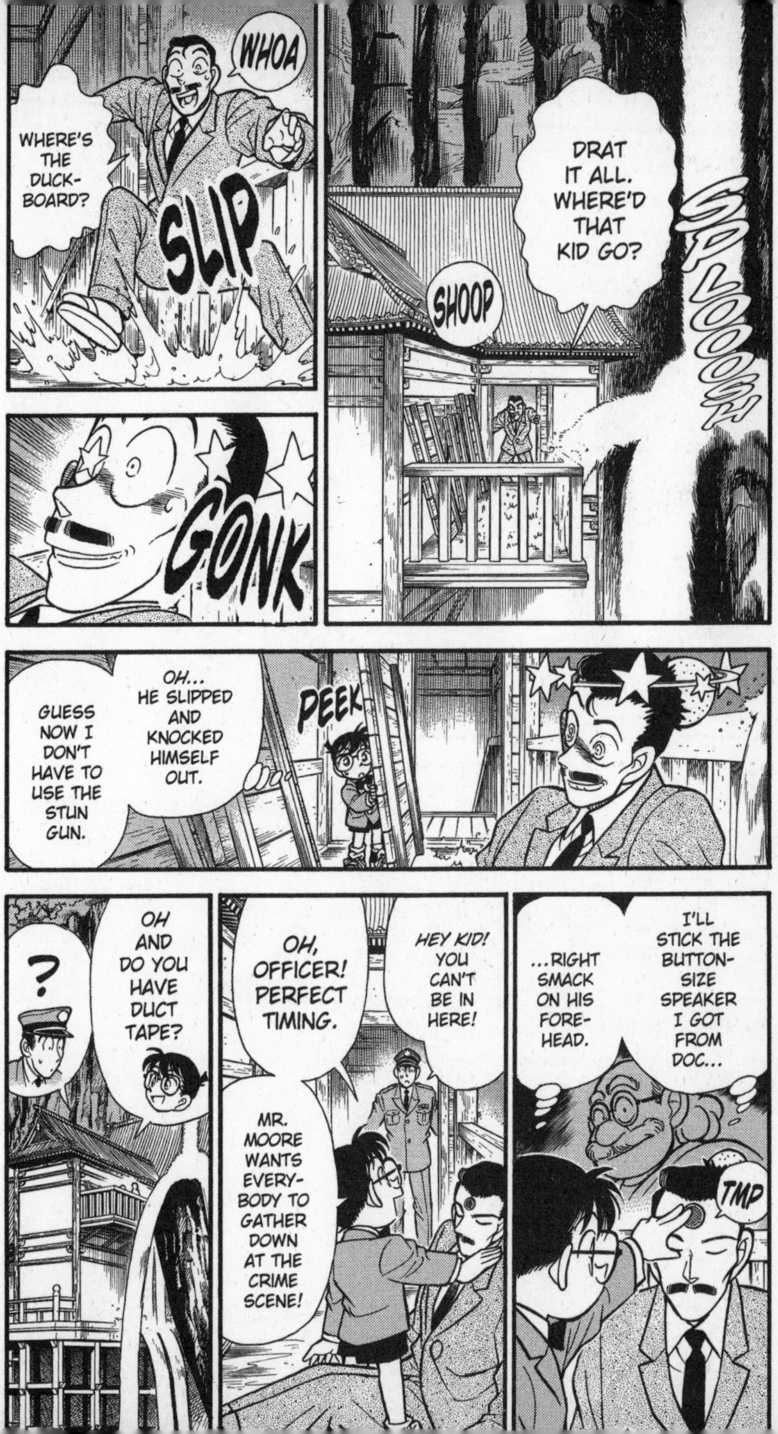
DRAT IT ALL. WHERE'D THAT KID GO?
SHOOP
WHOA
WHERE'S THE DUCK-BOARD?
SLIP
GONK
OH... HE SLIPPED AND KNOCKED HIMSELF OUT.
GUESS NOW I DON'T HAVE TO USE THE STUN GUN.
PEEK
I'LL STICK THE BUTTON-SIZE SPEAKER I GOT FROM DOC...
...RIGHT SMACK ON HIS FOREHEAD.
TMP
HEY KID! YOU CAN'T BE IN HERE!
OH, OFFICER! PERFECT TIMING.
MR. MOORE WANTS EVERYBODY TO GATHER DOWN AT THE CRIME SCENE!
OH AND DO YOU HAVE DUCT TAPE?
?

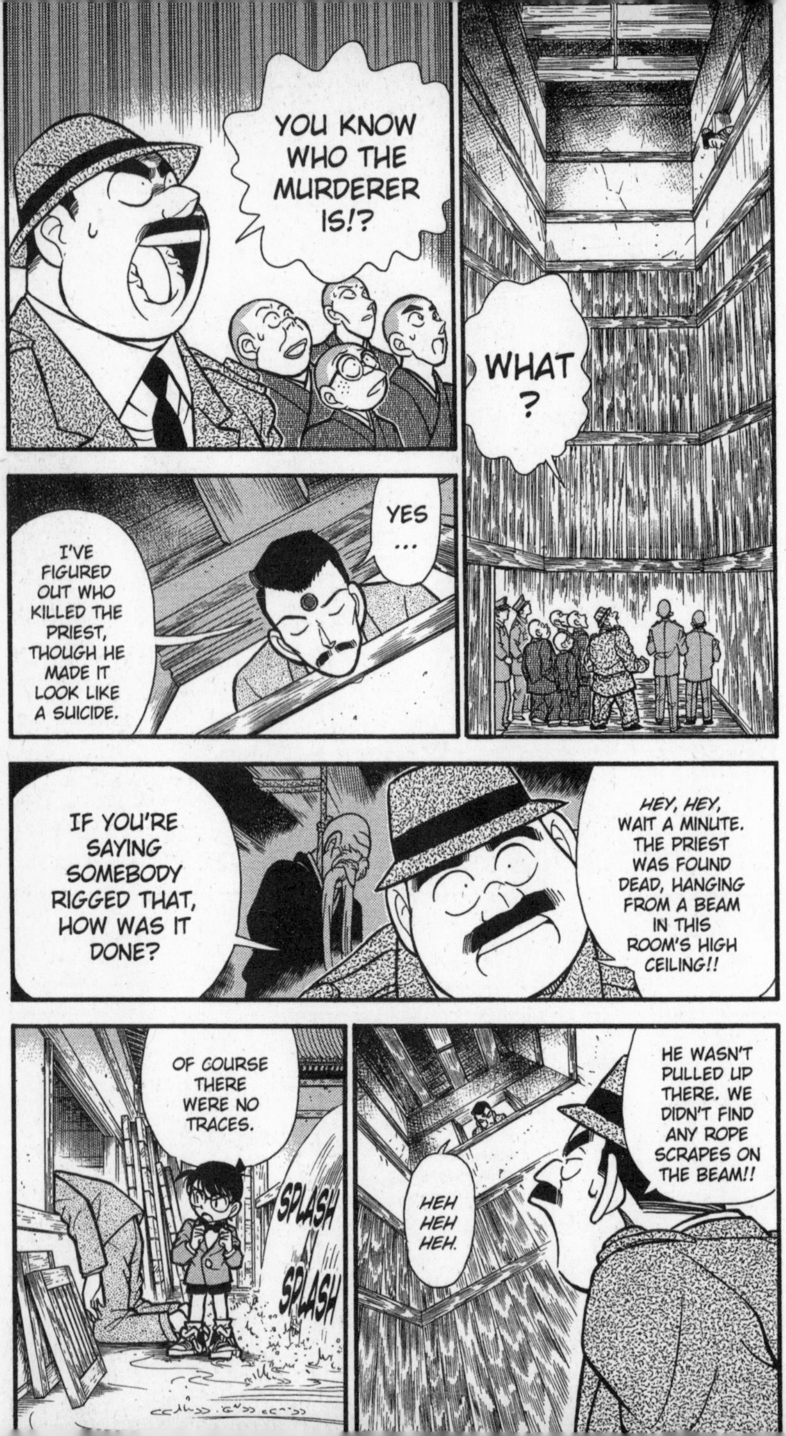
WHAT?
YOU KNOW WHO THE MURDERER IS!?
YES...
I'VE FIGURED OUT WHO KILLED THE PRIEST, THOUGH HE MADE IT LOOK LIKE A SUICIDE.
HEY, HEY, WAIT A MINUTE. THE PRIEST WAS FOUND DEAD, HANGING FROM A BEAM IN THIS ROOM'S HIGH CEILING!!
IF YOU'RE SAYING SOMEBODY RIGGED THAT, HOW WAS IT DONE?
HE WASN'T PULLED UP THERE. WE DIDN'T FIND ANY ROPE SCRAPES ON THE BEAM!!
HEH HEH HEH.
OF COURSE THERE WERE NO TRACES.
SPLASH
SPLASH

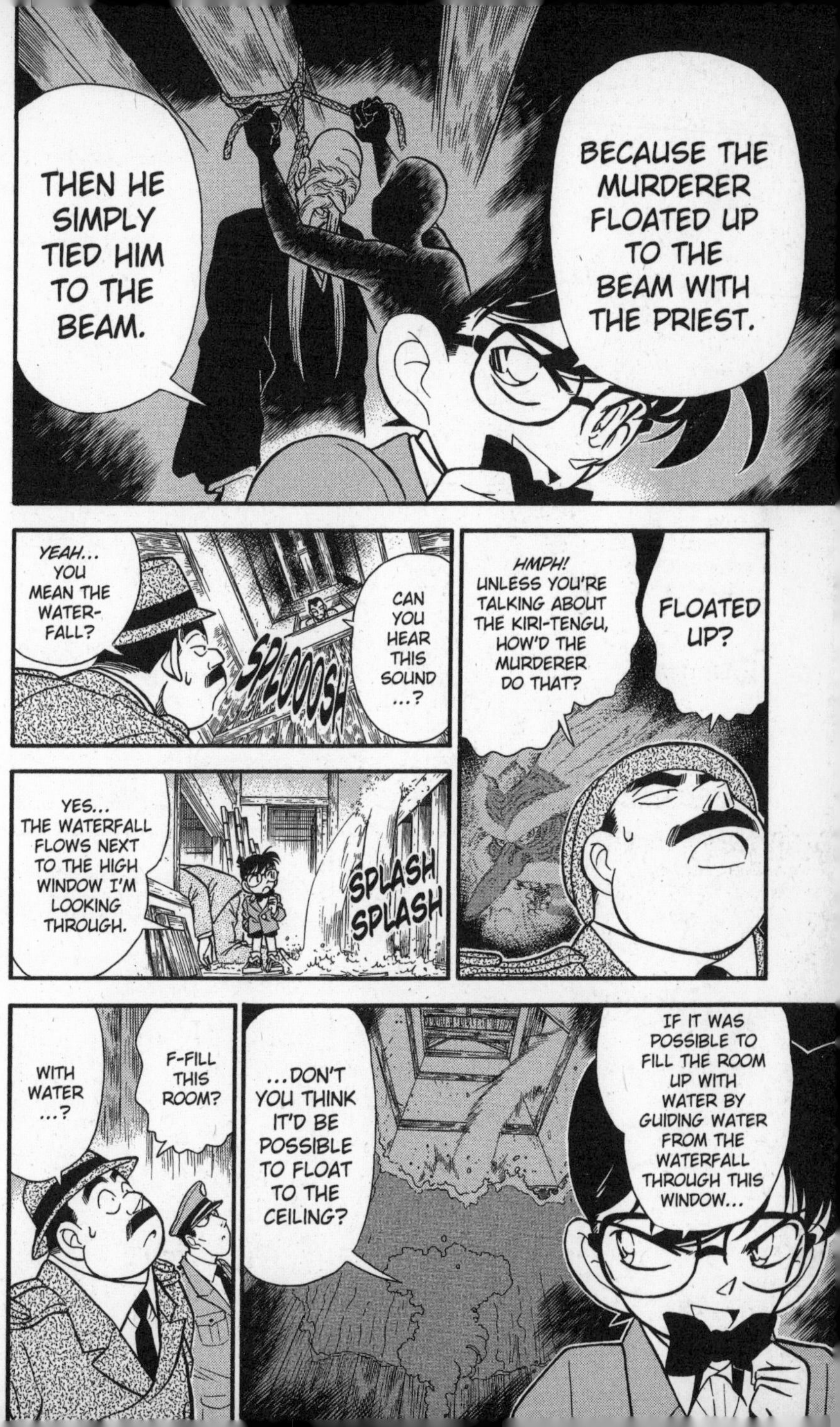
BECAUSE THE MURDERER FLOATED UP TO THE BEAM WITH THE PRIEST.
THEN HE SIMPLY TIED HIM TO THE BEAM.
FLOATED UP?
HMPH! UNLESS YOU'RE TALKING ABOUT THE KIRI-TENGU, HOW'D THE MURDERER DO THAT?
CAN YOU HEAR THIS SOUND ...?
SPLOOOSH
YEAH... YOU MEAN THE WATER-FALL?
SPLASH SPLASH
YES... THE WATERFALL FLOWS NEXT TO THE HIGH WINDOW I'M LOOKING THROUGH.
IF IT WAS POSSIBLE TO FILL THE ROOM UP WITH WATER BY GUIDING WATER FROM THE WATERFALL THROUGH THIS WINDOW...
...DON'T YOU THINK IT'D BE POSSIBLE TO FLOAT TO THE CEILING?
F-FILL THIS ROOM?
WITH WATER ...?

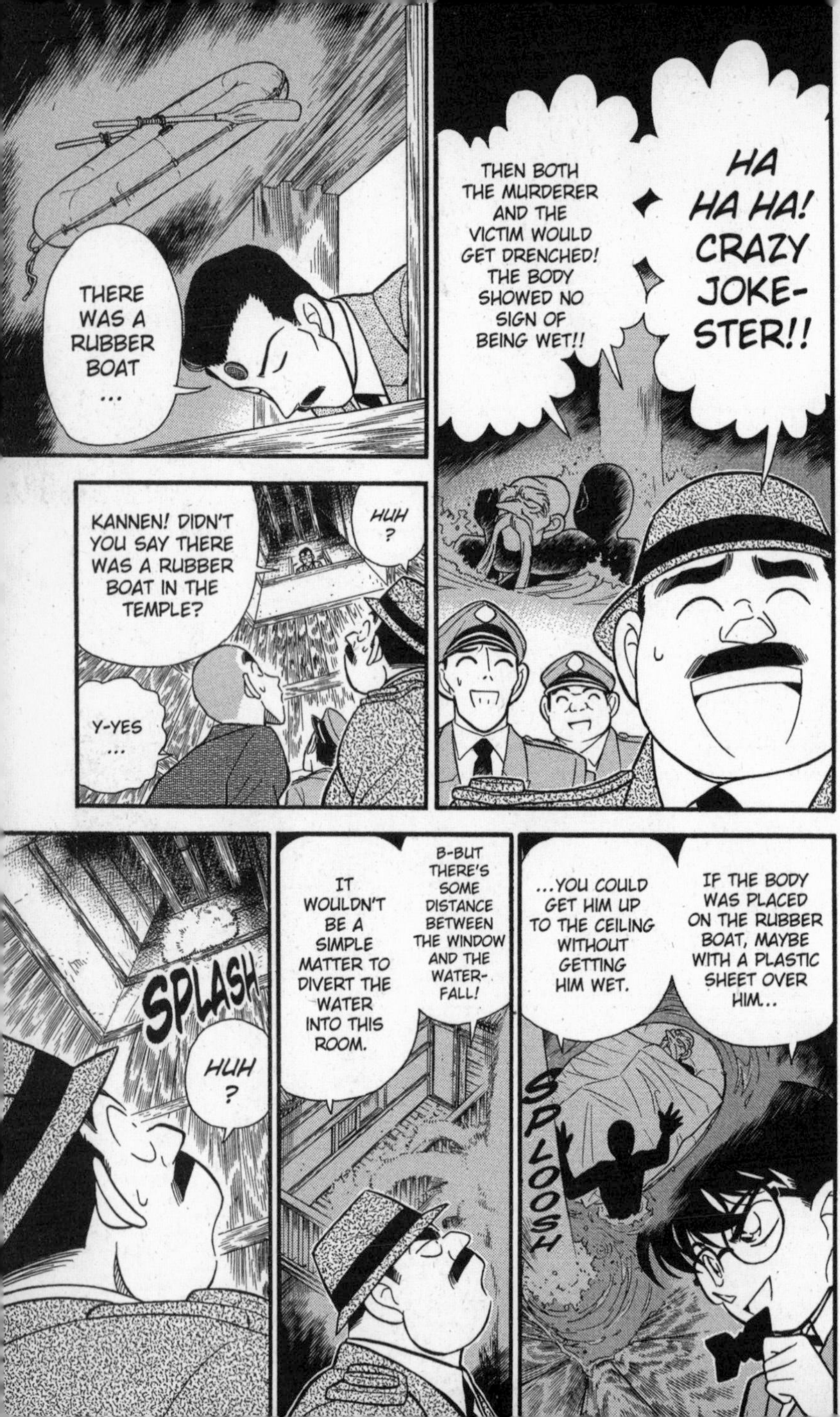
HA HA HA! CRAZY JOKE-STER!!
THEN BOTH THE MURDERER AND THE VICTIM WOULD GET DRENCHED! THE BODY SHOWED NO SIGN OF BEING WET!!
THERE WAS A RUBBER BOAT ...
HUH ?
KANNEN! DIDN'T YOU SAY THERE WAS A RUBBER BOAT IN THE TEMPLE?
Y-YES ...
IF THE BODY WAS PLACED ON THE RUBBER BOAT, MAYBE WITH A PLASTIC SHEET OVER HIM..
...YOU COULD GET HIM UP TO THE CEILING WITHOUT GETTING HIM WET.
SPLOOSH
B-BUT THERE'S SOME DISTANCE BETWEEN THE WINDOW AND THE WATER-FALL!
IT WOULDN'T BE A SIMPLE MATTER TO DIVERT THE WATER INTO THIS ROOM.
SPLASH
HUH ?

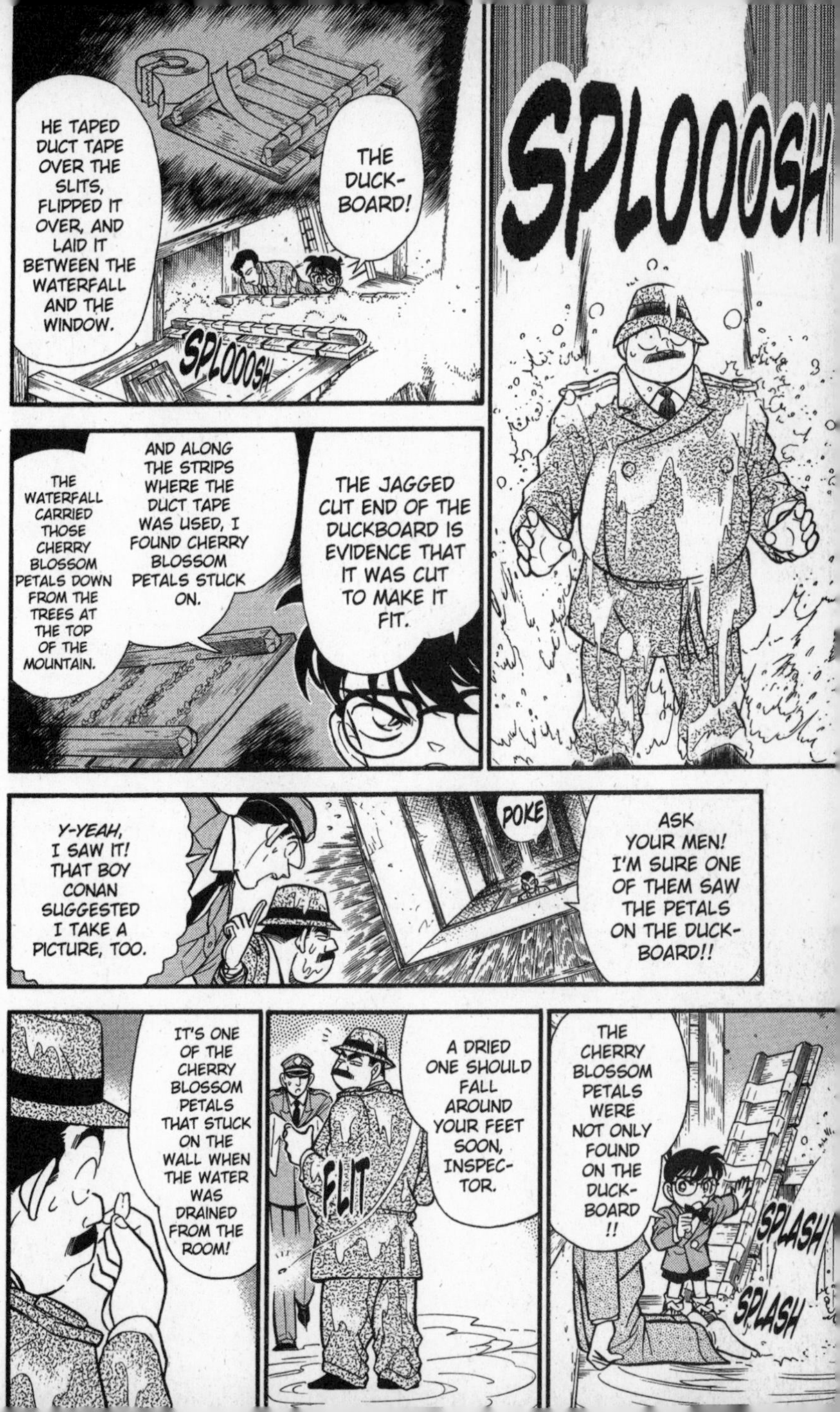
SPLOOOSH
THE DUCK-BOARD!
HE TAPED DUCT TAPE OVER THE SLITS, FLIPPED IT OVER, AND LAID IT BETWEEN THE WATERFALL AND THE WINDOW.
SPLOOOSH
THE JAGGED CUT END OF THE DUCKBOARD IS EVIDENCE THAT IT WAS CUT TO MAKE IT FIT.
AND ALONG THE STRIPS WHERE THE DUCT TAPE WAS USED, I FOUND CHERRY BLOSSOM PETALS STUCK ON.
THE WATERFALL CARRIED THOSE CHERRY BLOSSOM PETALS DOWN FROM THE TREES AT THE TOP OF THE MOUNTAIN.
ASK YOUR MEN! I'M SURE ONE OF THEM SAW THE PETALS ON THE DUCK-BOARD!!
POKE
Y-YEAH, I SAW IT! THAT BOY CONAN SUGGESTED I TAKE A PICTURE, TOO.
SPLASH
SPLASH
THE CHERRY BLOSSOM PETALS WERE NOT ONLY FOUND ON THE DUCK-BOARD !!
A DRIED ONE SHOULD FALL AROUND YOUR FEET SOON, INSPEC-TOR.
FLIT
IT'S ONE OF THE CHERRY BLOSSOM PETALS THAT STUCK ON THE WALL WHEN THE WATER WAS DRAINED FROM THE ROOM!

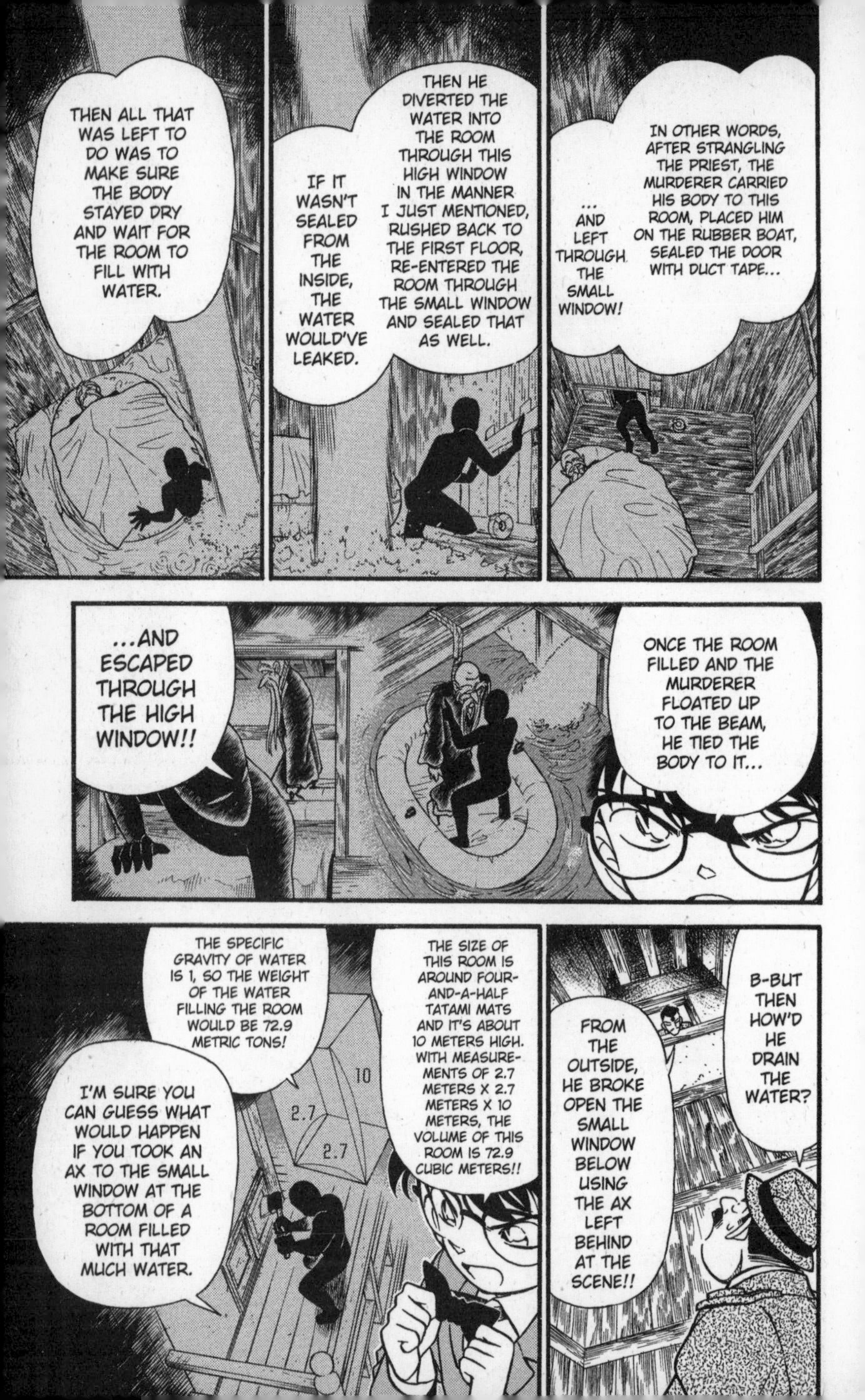
IN OTHER WORDS, AFTER STRANGLING THE PRIEST, THE MURDERER CARRIED HIS BODY TO THIS ROOM, PLACED HIM ON THE RUBBER BOAT, SEALED THE DOOR WITH DUCT TAPE...
... AND LEFT THROUGH THE SMALL WINDOW!
THEN HE DIVERTED THE WATER INTO THE ROOM THROUGH THIS HIGH WINDOW IN THE MANNER I JUST MENTIONED, RUSHED BACK TO THE FIRST FLOOR, RE-ENTERED THE ROOM THROUGH THE SMALL WINDOW AND SEALED THAT AS WELL.
IF IT WASN'T SEALED FROM THE INSIDE, THE WATER WOULD'VE LEAKED.
THEN ALL THAT WAS LEFT TO DO WAS TO MAKE SURE THE BODY STAYED DRY AND WAIT FOR THE ROOM TO FILL WITH WATER.
ONCE THE ROOM FILLED AND THE MURDERER FLOATED UP TO THE BEAM, HE TIED THE BODY TO IT...
...AND ESCAPED THROUGH THE HIGH WINDOW!!
B-BUT THEN HOW'D HE DRAIN THE WATER?
FROM THE OUTSIDE, HE BROKE OPEN THE SMALL WINDOW BELOW USING THE AX LEFT BEHIND AT THE SCENE!!
THE SIZE OF THIS ROOM IS AROUND FOUR-AND-A-HALF TATAMI MATS AND IT'S ABOUT 10 METERS HIGH. WITH MEASUREMENTS OF 2.7 METERS X 2.7 METERS X 10 METERS, THE VOLUME OF THIS ROOM IS 72.9 CUBIC METERS!!
10
2.7
2.7
THE SPECIFIC GRAVITY OF WATER IS 1, SO THE WEIGHT OF THE WATER FILLING THE ROOM WOULD BE 72.9 METRIC TONS!
I'M SURE YOU CAN GUESS WHAT WOULD HAPPEN IF YOU TOOK AN AX TO THE SMALL WINDOW AT THE BOTTOM OF A ROOM FILLED WITH THAT MUCH WATER.

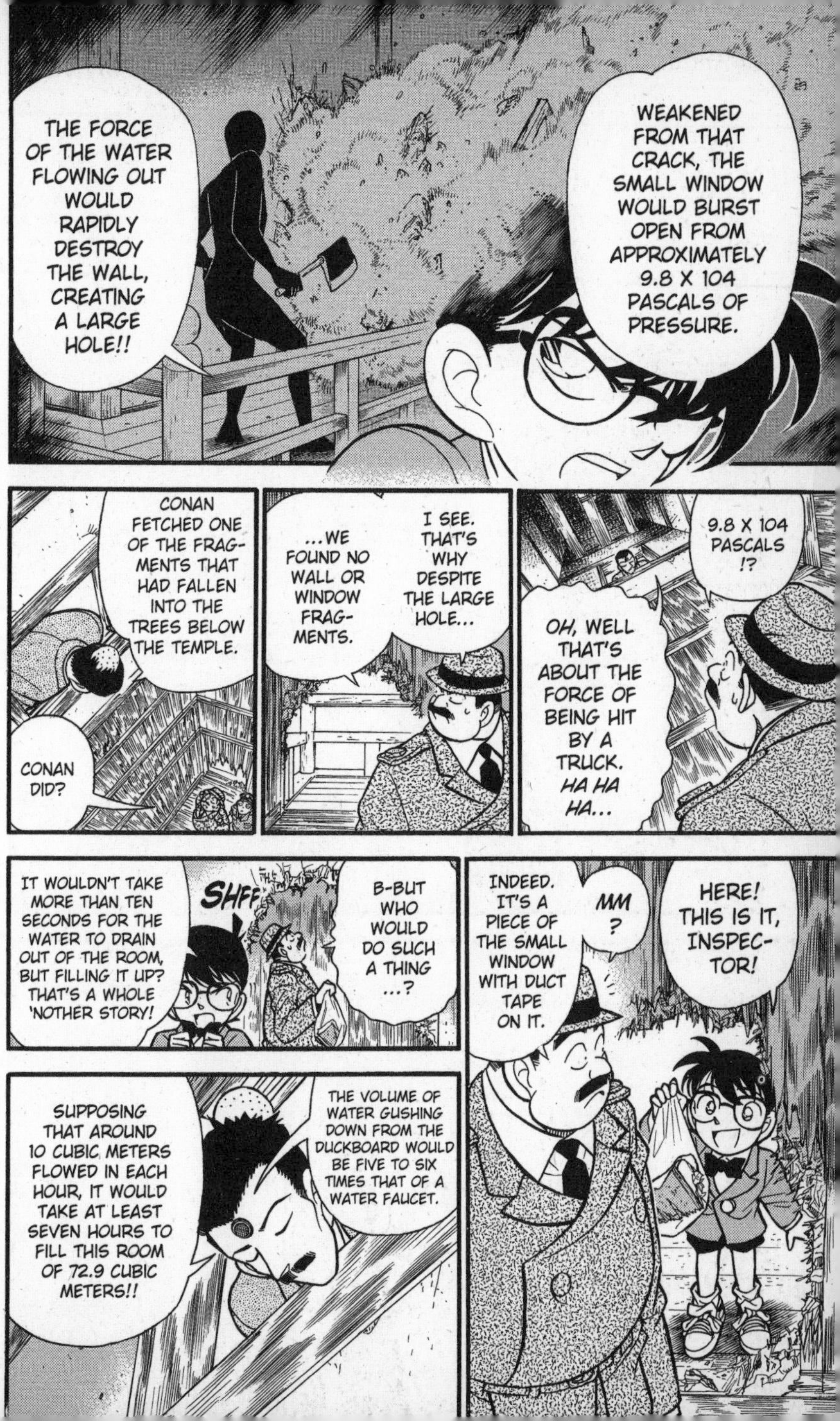

WEAKENED FROM THAT CRACK, THE SMALL WINDOW WOULD BURST OPEN FROM APPROXIMATELY 9.8 X 104 PASCALS OF PRESSURE.
THE FORCE OF THE WATER FLOWING OUT WOULD RAPIDLY DESTROY THE WALL, CREATING A LARGE HOLE!!
9.8 X 104 PASCALS !?
OH, WELL THAT'S ABOUT THE FORCE OF BEING HIT BY A TRUCK. HA HA HA...
I SEE. THAT'S WHY DESPITE THE LARGE HOLE...
...WE FOUND NO WALL OR WINDOW FRAGMENTS.
CONAN FETCHED ONE OF THE FRAGMENTS THAT HAD FALLEN INTO THE TREES BELOW THE TEMPLE.
CONAN DID?
HERE! THIS IS IT, INSPECTOR!
MM ?
INDEED. IT'S A PIECE OF THE SMALL WINDOW WITH DUCT TAPE ON IT.
B-BUT WHO WOULD DO SUCH A THING ...?
SHFF
IT WOULDN'T TAKE MORE THAN TEN SECONDS FOR THE WATER TO DRAIN OUT OF THE ROOM, BUT FILLING IT UP? THAT'S A WHOLE 'NOTHER STORY!
THE VOLUME OF WATER GUSHING DOWN FROM THE DUCKBOARD WOULD BE FIVE TO SIX TIMES THAT OF A WATER FAUCET.
SUPPOSING THAT AROUND 10 CUBIC METERS FLOWED IN EACH HOUR, IT WOULD TAKE AT LEAST SEVEN HOURS TO FILL THIS ROOM OF 72.9 CUBIC METERS!!

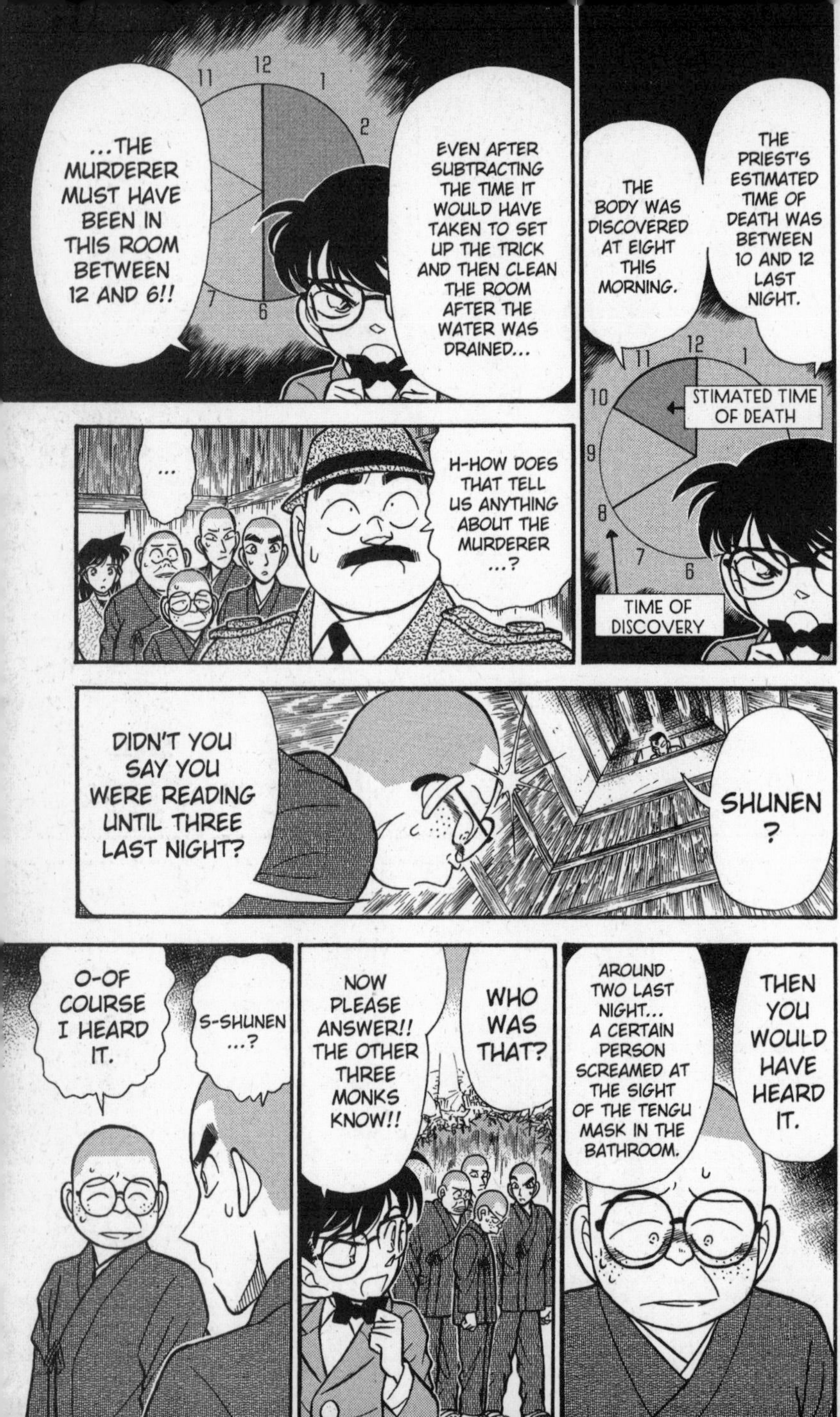
THE PRIEST'S ESTIMATED TIME OF DEATH WAS BETWEEN 10 AND 12 LAST NIGHT.
THE BODY WAS DISCOVERED AT EIGHT THIS MORNING.
STIMATED TIME OF DEATH
TIME OF DISCOVERY
EVEN AFTER SUBTRACTING THE TIME IT WOULD HAVE TAKEN TO SET UP THE TRICK AND THEN CLEAN THE ROOM AFTER THE WATER WAS DRAINED...
...THE MURDERER MUST HAVE BEEN IN THIS ROOM BETWEEN 12 AND 6!!
H-HOW DOES THAT TELL US ANYTHING ABOUT THE MURDERER ...?
...
SHUNEN ?
DIDN'T YOU SAY YOU WERE READING UNTIL THREE LAST NIGHT?
THEN YOU WOULD HAVE HEARD IT.
AROUND TWO LAST NIGHT... A CERTAIN PERSON SCREAMED AT THE SIGHT OF THE TENGU MASK IN THE BATHROOM.
WHO WAS THAT?
NOW PLEASE ANSWER!! THE OTHER THREE MONKS KNOW!!
S-SHUNEN ...?
O-OF COURSE I HEARD IT.

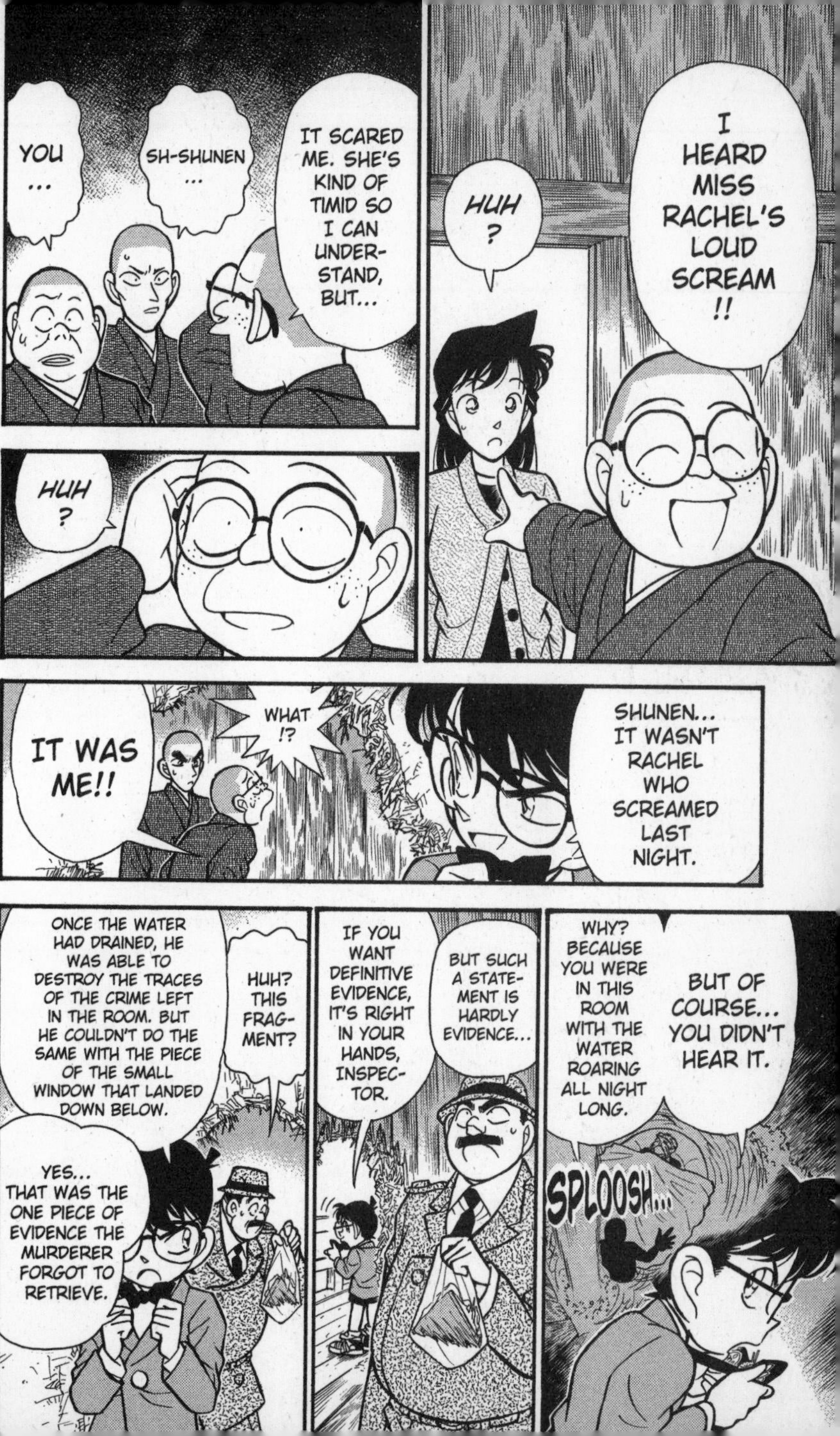
I HEARD MISS RACHEL'S LOUD SCREAM !!
HUH ?
IT SCARED ME. SHE'S KIND OF TIMID SO I CAN UNDER-STAND, BUT...
SH-SHUNEN ...
YOU ...
HUH ?
SHUNEN... IT WASN'T RACHEL WHO SCREAMED LAST NIGHT.
WHAT !?
IT WAS ME!!
BUT OF COURSE... YOU DIDN'T HEAR IT.
WHY? BECAUSE YOU WERE IN THIS ROOM WITH THE WATER ROARING ALL NIGHT LONG.
SPLOOSH...
BUT SUCH A STATE-MENT IS HARDLY EVIDENCE...
IF YOU WANT DEFINITIVE EVIDENCE, IT'S RIGHT IN YOUR HANDS, INSPEC-TOR.
HUH? THIS FRAG-MENT?
ONCE THE WATER HAD DRAINED, HE WAS ABLE TO DESTROY THE TRACES OF THE CRIME LEFT IN THE ROOM. BUT HE COULDN'T DO THE SAME WITH THE PIECE OF THE SMALL WINDOW THAT LANDED DOWN BELOW.
YES... THAT WAS THE ONE PIECE OF EVIDENCE THE MURDERER FORGOT TO RETRIEVE.

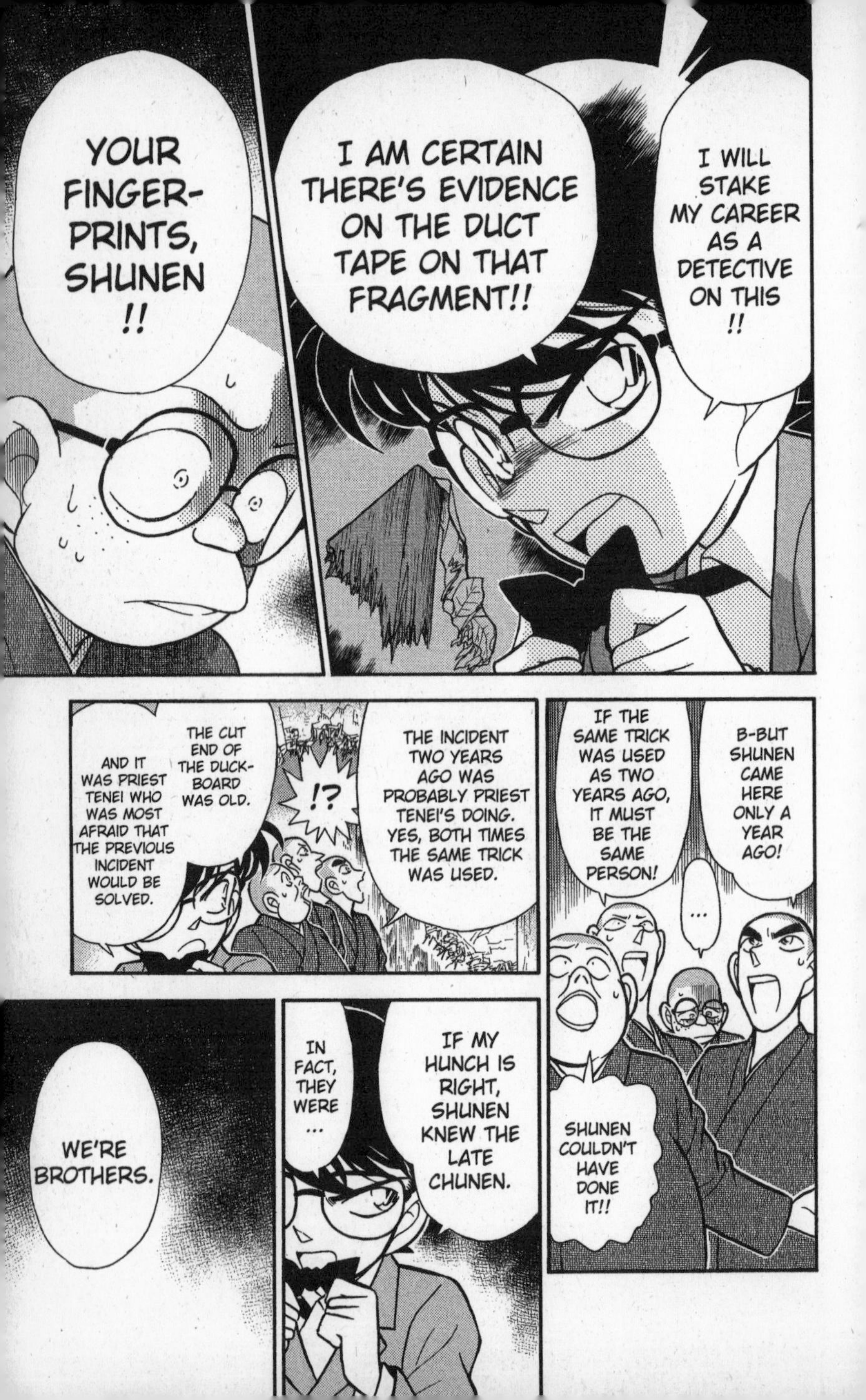
I WILL STAKE MY CAREER AS A DETECTIVE ON THIS!!
I AM CERTAIN THERE'S EVIDENCE ON THE DUCT TAPE ON THAT FRAGMENT!!
YOUR FINGER-PRINTS, SHUNEN!!
B-BUT SHUNEN CAME HERE ONLY A YEAR AGO!
IF THE SAME TRICK WAS USED AS TWO YEARS AGO, IT MUST BE THE SAME PERSON!
...
SHUNEN COULDN'T HAVE DONE IT!!
THE INCIDENT TWO YEARS AGO WAS PROBABLY PRIEST TENEI'S DOING. YES, BOTH TIMES THE SAME TRICK WAS USED.
!?
THE CUT END OF THE DUCK-BOARD WAS OLD.
AND IT WAS PRIEST TENEI WHO WAS MOST AFRAID THAT THE PREVIOUS INCIDENT WOULD BE SOLVED.
IF MY HUNCH IS RIGHT, SHUNEN KNEW THE LATE CHUNEN.
IN FACT, THEY WERE...
WE'RE BROTHERS.

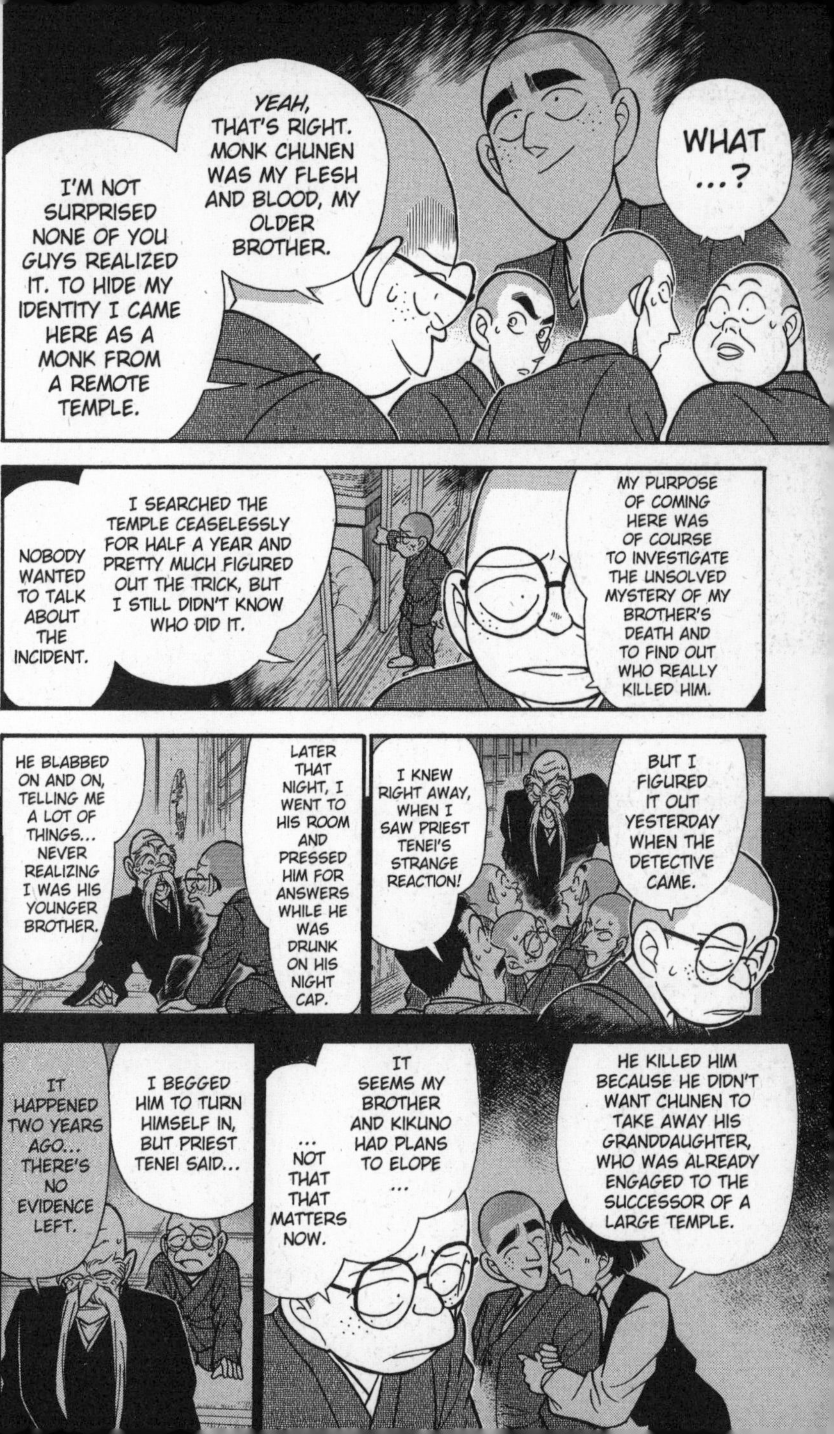
WHAT ...?
YEAH, THAT'S RIGHT. MONK CHUNEN WAS MY FLESH AND BLOOD, MY OLDER BROTHER.
I'M NOT SURPRISED NONE OF YOU GUYS REALIZED IT. TO HIDE MY IDENTITY I CAME HERE AS A MONK FROM A REMOTE TEMPLE.
MY PURPOSE OF COMING HERE WAS OF COURSE TO INVESTIGATE THE UNSOLVED MYSTERY OF MY BROTHER'S DEATH AND TO FIND OUT WHO REALLY KILLED HIM.
I SEARCHED THE TEMPLE CEASELESSLY FOR HALF A YEAR AND PRETTY MUCH FIGURED OUT THE TRICK, BUT I STILL DIDN'T KNOW WHO DID IT.
NOBODY WANTED TO TALK ABOUT THE INCIDENT.
BUT I FIGURED IT OUT YESTERDAY WHEN THE DETECTIVE CAME.
I KNEW RIGHT AWAY, WHEN I SAW PRIEST TENEI'S STRANGE REACTION!
LATER THAT NIGHT, I WENT TO HIS ROOM AND PRESSED HIM FOR ANSWERS WHILE HE WAS DRUNK ON HIS NIGHT CAP.
HE BLABBED ON AND ON, TELLING ME A LOT OF THINGS... NEVER REALIZING I WAS HIS YOUNGER BROTHER.
HE KILLED HIM BECAUSE HE DIDN'T WANT CHUNEN TO TAKE AWAY HIS GRANDDAUGHTER, WHO WAS ALREADY ENGAGED TO THE SUCCESSOR OF A LARGE TEMPLE.
IT SEEMS MY BROTHER AND KIKUNO HAD PLANS TO ELOPE ...
... NOT THAT THAT MATTERS NOW.
I BEGGED HIM TO TURN HIMSELF IN, BUT PRIEST TENEI SAID...
IT HAPPENED TWO YEARS AGO... THERE'S NO EVIDENCE LEFT.

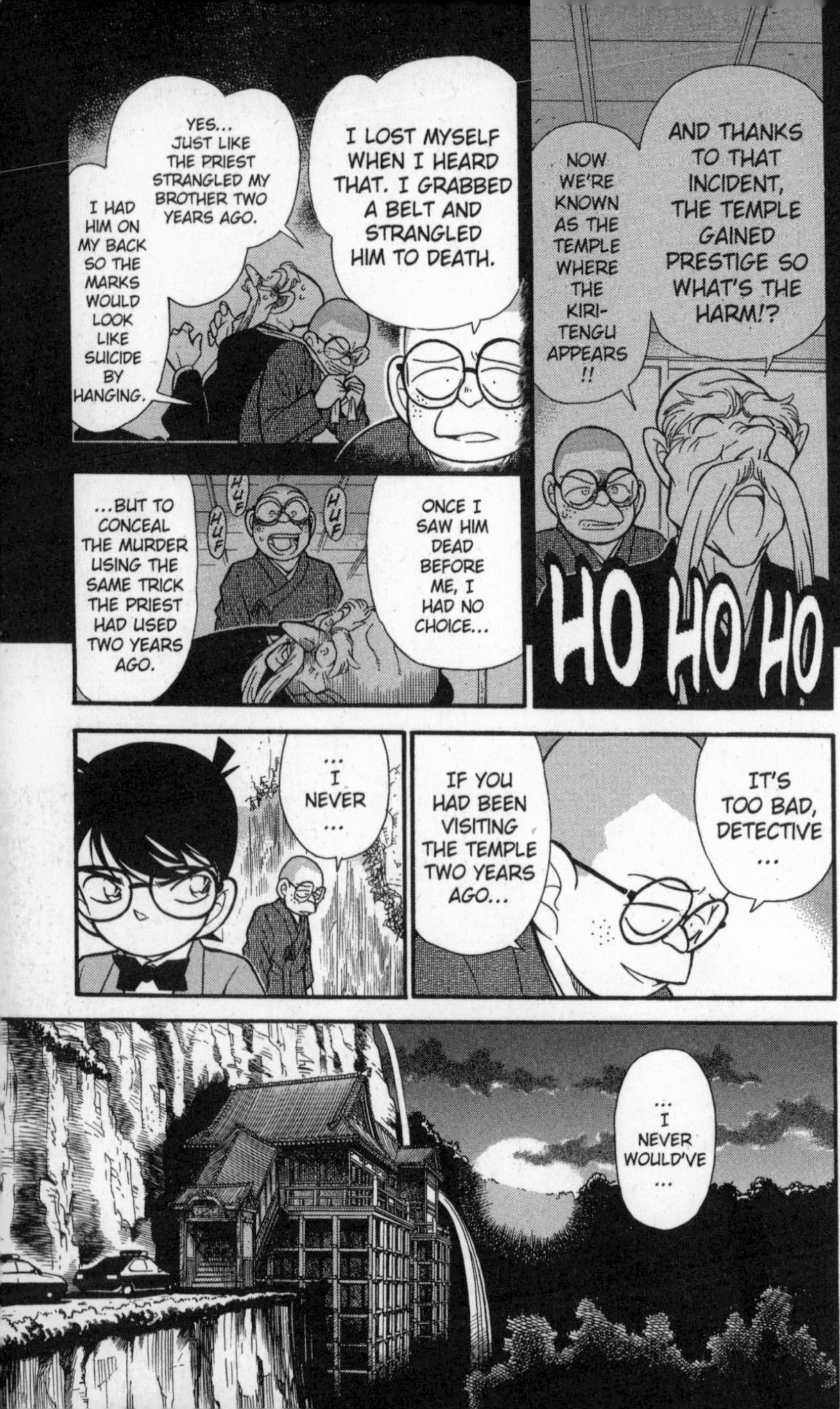
AND THANKS TO THAT INCIDENT, THE TEMPLE GAINED PRESTIGE SO WHAT'S THE HARM!?
NOW WE'RE KNOWN AS THE TEMPLE WHERE THE KIRI-TENGU APPEARS!!
HO HO HO
I LOST MYSELF WHEN I HEARD THAT. I GRABBED A BELT AND STRANGLED HIM TO DEATH.
YES... JUST LIKE THE PRIEST STRANGLED MY BROTHER TWO YEARS AGO.
I HAD HIM ON MY BACK SO THE MARKS WOULD LOOK LIKE SUICIDE BY HANGING.
ONCE I SAW HIM DEAD BEFORE ME, I HAD NO CHOICE...
HUF HUF HUF
...BUT TO CONCEAL THE MURDER USING THE SAME TRICK THE PRIEST HAD USED TWO YEARS AGO.
IT'S TOO BAD, DETECTIVE...
IF YOU HAD BEEN VISITING THE TEMPLE TWO YEARS AGO...
...I NEVER...
...I NEVER WOULD'VE...

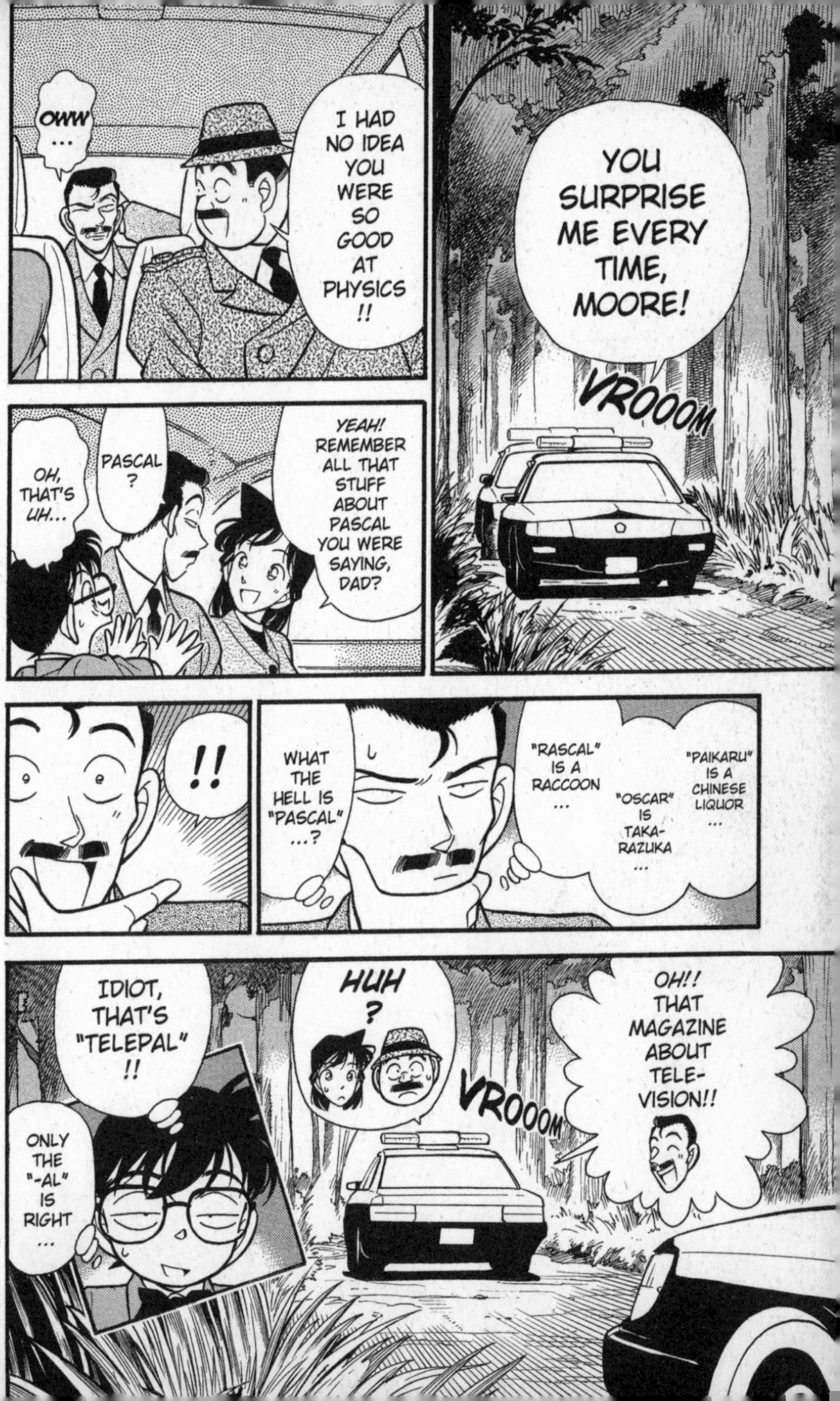
YOU SURPRISE ME EVERY TIME, MOORE!
VROOOM
I HAD NO IDEA YOU WERE SO GOOD AT PHYSICS!!
OWW...
YEAH! REMEMBER ALL THAT STUFF ABOUT PASCAL YOU WERE SAYING, DAD?
PASCAL?
OH, THAT'S UH...
WHAT THE HELL IS "PASCAL"...?
"RASCAL" IS A RACCOON...
"OSCAR" IS TAKARAZUKA...
"PAIKARU" IS A CHINESE LIQUOR...
!!
OH!! THAT MAGAZINE ABOUT TELEVISION!!
VROOOM
HUH?
IDIOT, THAT'S "TELEPAL"!!
ONLY THE "-AL" IS RIGHT...

Hello, Aoyama here.

People often ask me...since I have characters named after mystery authors such as Conan Doyle, Agatha Christie, and Maurice Leblanc, why not Ellery Queen? Ha hah! Actually, I've been saving that name for a special character. She finally makes an appearance in this volume. You know! It's *her*, Rachel's...On second thought, you'll just have to read to find out. ♥

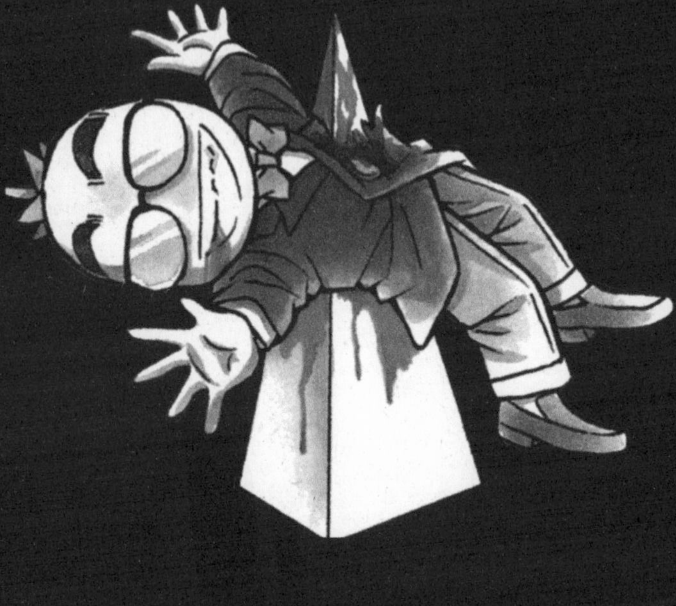

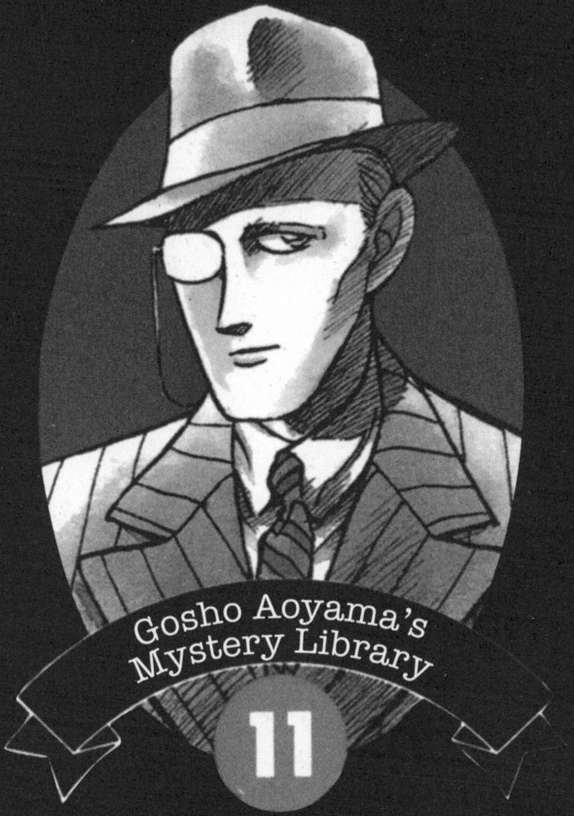
Gosho Aoyama's
Mystery Library
11

ELLERY QUEEN

When New York Police Department Inspector Richard Queen is faced with a difficult case, he consults his son Ellery, who steps onto the scene and solves the case with his brilliant theories!! He stands over 180cm in height and wears a rimless monocle. An avid collector of old books, he has a weakness for rare books. He bases his deductions purely on logic and doesn't reveal his findings until he is certain. Although he can sound pretentious and irritate those around him, his father Richard's trust is unshakeable because in the end Ellery always solves the case. By the way, within each story Ellery himself relates his cases to the public. In reality, "Ellery Queen" is the pen name of two writers, Frederic Dannay and Manfred Lee, who came up with the name as they began their mystery writing careers. (I recommend *The Egyptian Cross Mystery*.)

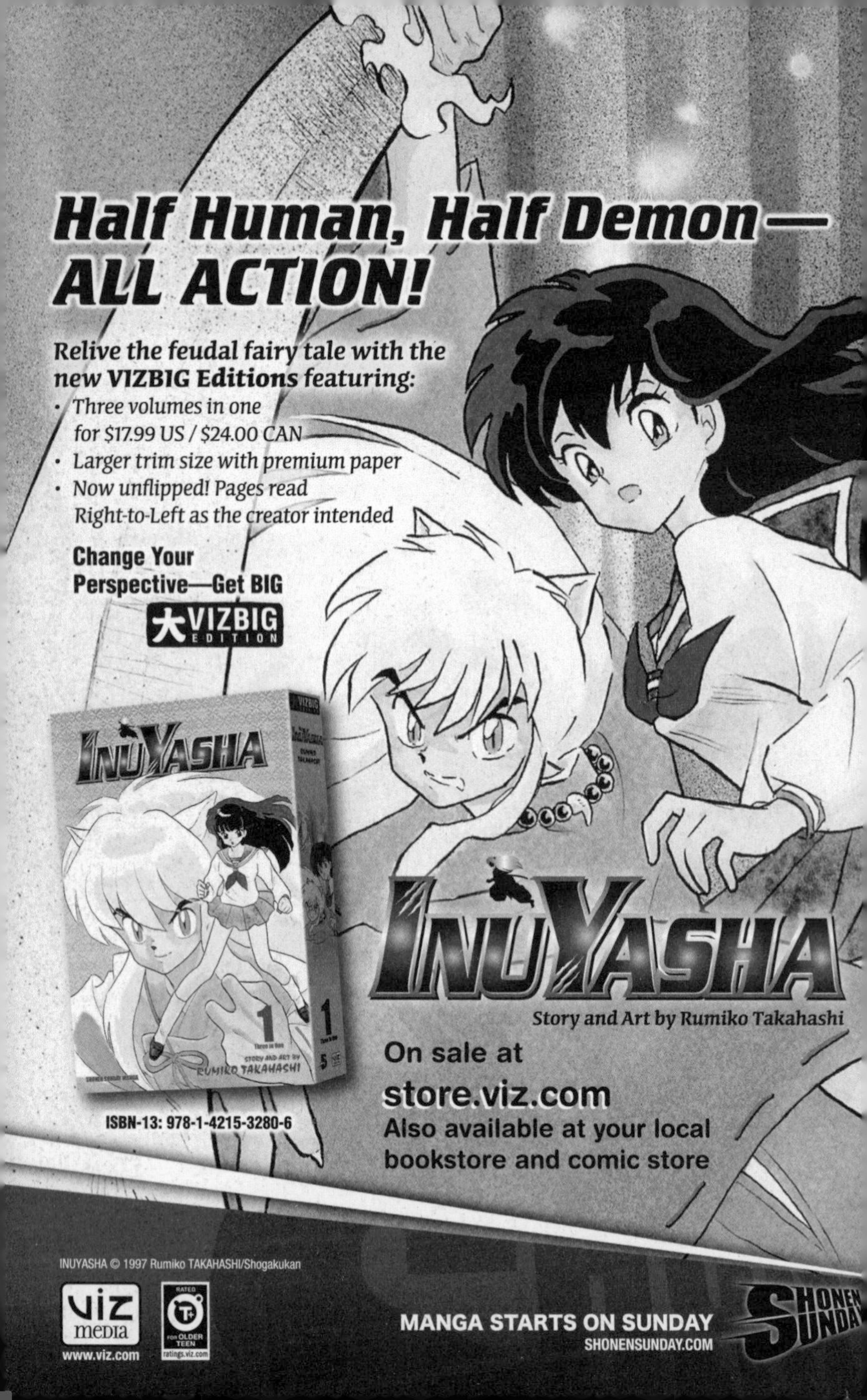
Half Human, Half Demon—
ALL ACTION!
Relive the feudal fairy tale with the new VIZBIG Editions featuring:
• Three volumes in one for $17.99 US / $24.00 CAN
• Larger trim size with premium paper
• Now unflipped! Pages read Right-to-Left as the creator intended
Change Your Perspective—Get BIG
大 VIZBIG EDITION
INUYASHA
RUMIKO TAKAHASHI
ISBN-13: 978-1-4215-3280-6
INUYASHA
Story and Art by Rumiko Takahashi
On sale at
store.viz.com
Also available at your local bookstore and comic store
INUYASHA © 1997 Rumiko TAKAHASHI/Shogakukan
viz media
www.viz.com
RATED T+ FOR OLDER TEEN
ratings.viz.com
MANGA STARTS ON SUNDAY
SHONENSUNDAY.COM
SHONEN SUNDAY

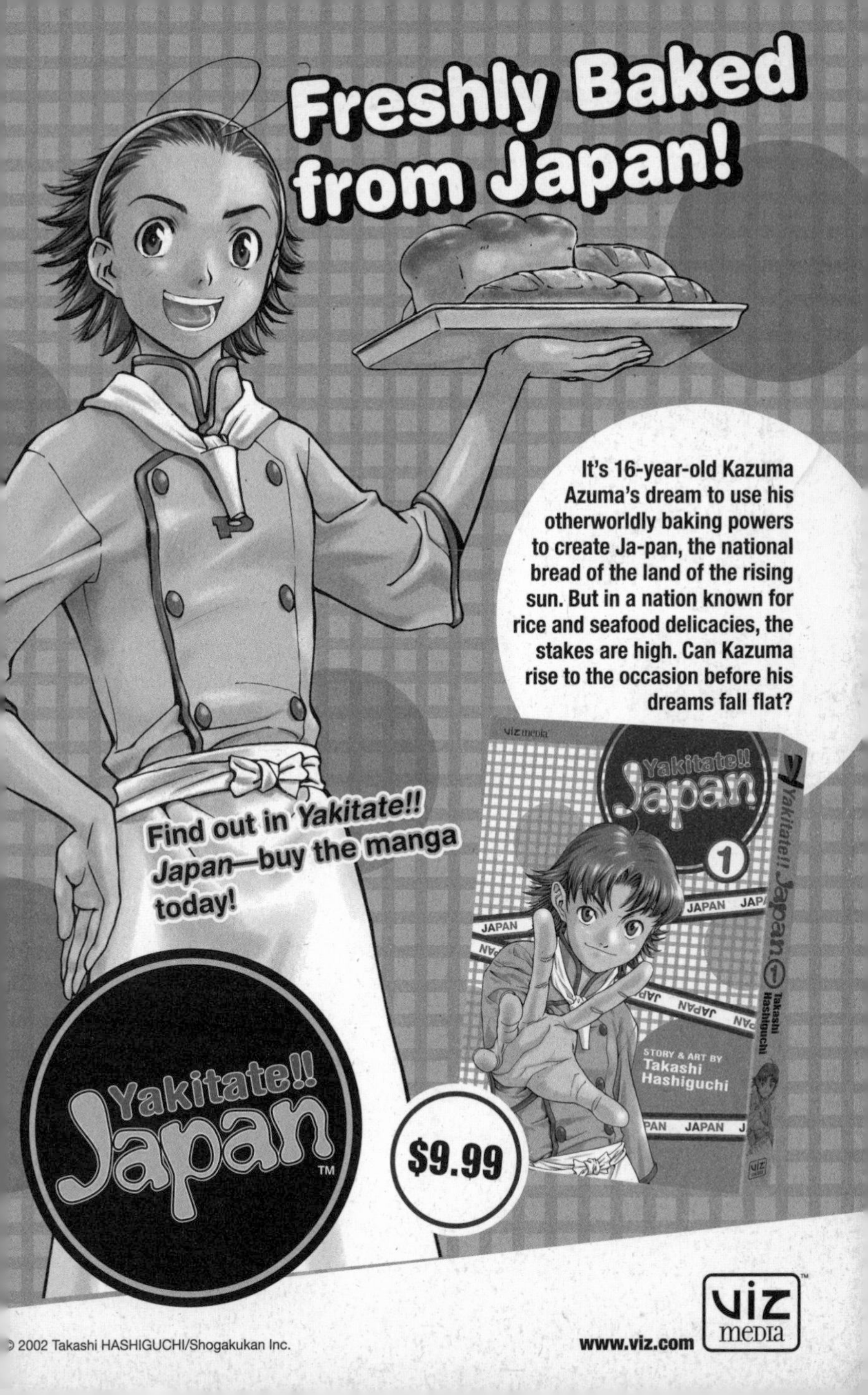
Freshly Baked from Japan!
It's 16-year-old Kazuma Azuma's dream to use his otherworldly baking powers to create Ja-pan, the national bread of the land of the rising sun. But in a nation known for rice and seafood delicacies, the stakes are high. Can Kazuma rise to the occasion before his dreams fall flat?
Find out in Yakitate!! Japan—buy the manga today!
viz media
Yakitate!! Japan
1
JAPAN
STORY & ART BY
Takashi Hashiguchi
Yakitate!! Japan™
$9.99
© 2002 Takashi HASHIGUCHI/Shogakukan Inc.
www.viz.com
viz media™

At Your Indentured Service

Hayate's parents are bad with money, so they sell his organs to pay their debts. Hayate doesn't like this plan, so he comes up with a new one—kidnap and ransom a girl from a wealthy family. Solid plan… so how did he end up as her butler?

Find out in *Hayate the Combat Butler*— buy the manga at store.viz.com!

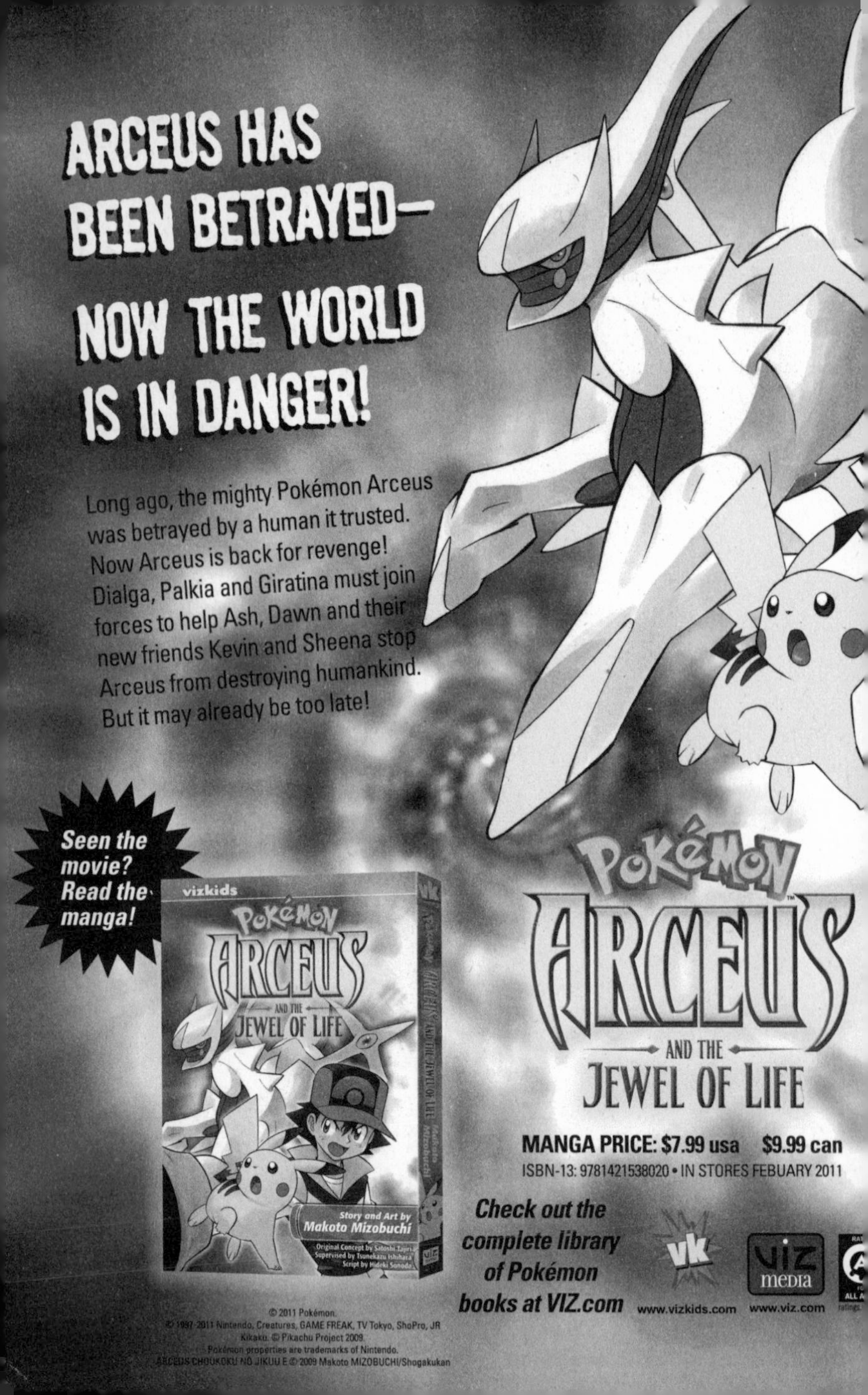
ARCEUS HAS BEEN BETRAYED—
NOW THE WORLD IS IN DANGER!
Long ago, the mighty Pokémon Arceus was betrayed by a human it trusted. Now Arceus is back for revenge! Dialga, Palkia and Giratina must join forces to help Ash, Dawn and their new friends Kevin and Sheena stop Arceus from destroying humankind. But it may already be too late!
Seen the movie? Read the manga!
vizkids
Pokémon
ARCEUS
AND THE
JEWEL OF LIFE
Story and Art by
Makoto Mizobuchi
Original Concept by Satoshi Tajiri
Supervised by Tsunekazu Ishihara
Script by Hideki Sonoda
Pokémon
ARCEUS
AND THE
JEWEL OF LIFE
MANGA PRICE: $7.99 usa $9.99 can
ISBN-13: 9781421538020 • IN STORES FEBUARY 2011
Check out the complete library of Pokémon books at VIZ.com
www.vizkids.com
VIZ media
www.viz.com
© 2011 Pokémon.
© 1997-2011 Nintendo, Creatures, GAME FREAK, TV Tokyo, ShoPro, JR Kikaku. © Pikachu Project 2009.
Pokémon properties are trademarks of Nintendo.
ARCEUS CHOUKOKU NO JIKUU E © 2009 Makoto MIZOBUCHI/Shogakukan

11